COMPETITION LAW AND INTELLECTUAL PROPERTY IN CHINA

COMPETITION LAW AND INTELLECTUAL PROPERTY IN CHINA

Edited by

IOANNIS KOKKORIS

Chair in Law and Economics at the Centre for Commercial Law Studies,
Queen Mary University of London

SPYROS MANIATIS

Professor of Intellectual Property and Director of the Centre for Commercial Law
Studies at Queen Mary University of London

XIAOYE WANG

Professor of Law at the Chinese Academy of Social Sciences

Associate Editor

CRISTINA VOLPIN

Associate Lecturer in Competition Law, Centre for Commercial Law Studies,
Queen Mary University of London

OXFORD
UNIVERSITY PRESS

OXFORD
UNIVERSITY PRESS

Great Clarendon Street, Oxford, OX2 6DP,
United Kingdom

Oxford University Press is a department of the University of Oxford.
It furthers the University's objective of excellence in research, scholarship,
and education by publishing worldwide. Oxford is a registered trade mark of
Oxford University Press in the UK and in certain other countries

First Edition published in 2019

Impression: 1

Published in the United States of America by Oxford University Press
198 Madison Avenue, New York, NY 10016, United States of America

British Library Cataloguing in Publication Data
Data available

Library of Congress Control Number: 2018957185

ISBN 978–0–19–879352–6

Printed and bound by
CPI Group (UK) Ltd, Croydon, CR0 4YY

TABLE OF CONTENTS

TABLE OF CASES

CHINA

EUROPEAN COURT OF JUSTICE

GERMANY

UNITED STATES

TABLE OF LEGISLATION

xix

TABLE OF TREATIES AND INTERNATIONAL INSTRUMENTS

---

[1] https://www.wipo.int/wipolex/en/other_treaties/details.jsp?group_id=22&treaty_id=231

NOTES ON EDITORS AND CONTRIBUTORS

Editors

Ioannis Kokkoris

Professor Ioannis Kokkoris holds a Chair in Law and Economics at the Centre for Commercial Law Studies, Queen Mary University of London, UK. He is an expert on competition law and economics. His main research interests are in the area of law and economics, comparative competition law/economics, and policy focusing on EU, China, and ASEAN, as well as intellectual property. Professor Kokkoris has formerly served as Principal Case Officer/Economic Advisor in the Mergers branch at the Office of Fair Trading, UK where he dealt with leading cases such as NASDAQ/LSE, NYSE/Euronext, Global/GCap, and was a member of the drafting team of the UK Merger Guidelines. He has also worked on abuse of dominance cases as well as cartels and other anticompetitive agreements cases. He has previously served as an Economist in the Merger Task Force at the DG Competition-European Commission.

He is the Co-Founder and Executive Director of the Institute for Global Law, Economics and Finance as well as the Sino UK Centre for Commercial Law, Economics and Business, established by Queen Mary University of London, UK Tsinghua University China, and Renmin University, China and has worked as a Consultant at the Federal Trade Commission, USA. Professor Kokkoris has led and worked on funded projects by the European Bank for Reconstruction and Development, World Bank, the European Commission, the Organization for Security and Cooperation in Europe, and other international institutions. He is a special advisor to a number of competition authorities and frequently advises companies on competition enforcement issues in a number of jurisdictions, and delivers training programmes for companies, competition authorities, and courts. He has authored and co-authored more than seventeen books, more than sixty articles, and twenty chapters. He is on the editorial board of various international journals.

Spyros Maniatis

Spyros Maniatis is Professor of Intellectual Property and Director of the Centre for Commercial Law Studies at Queen Mary University of London. He is co-author of *Trade Marks, Trade Names, and Unfair Competition World Law and Practice* and *Trade Marks in Europe: A Practical Jurisprudence*. Professor Maniatis is a lawyer, academic, and IP specialist who works closely with IP practitioners and whose primary area of expertise is international and European trade mark law. He has been teaching trade mark law since 1995 at a postgraduate level (e.g. at the LLM in International and Comparative Law of Trade Marks, Designs and Unfair Competition at Queen Mary along with David Llewellyn, a solicitor and editor of *Kerly's Law of Trade Marks and Trade Names*). He has published many articles and has contributed parts or chapters to several works on IP law.

Xiaoye Wang

Xiaoye Wang holds a Doctor Juris from University Hamburg in 1993, and is Professor of Law at the Chinese Academy of Social Sciences, and Distinguished Professor at Hunan University. She serves as Vice President of the Chinese Society of Economic Law, Consultant Expert for the Anti-Monopoly Commission under the State Council, and was advisor for the Drafting Committee of the China's AML under the State Council and the National People's Congress (NPC), and the Head of the Consultant Committee for WTO Trade and Competition Policy under MOFCOM. She has published over 300 papers in Chinese, German, and English, and is the author and editor of twenty books including *Monopole und Wettbewerb in der chinesischen Wirtschaft* (J.C.B. Mohr, 1993), *Competition Law in China* (Kluwer Law International and *The Evolution of China's Antimonopoly Law* (Edward Elgar, 2014), and lectured twice on antitrust law for the Standing Committee of NPC. She visited Max-Planck Institutes for Private Law, and for Innovation & Competition many times, and as Fulbright scholar spent one year at Chicago-Kent College of Law. She was a founding member of ACF, and Advisor to CUTS C-CIER and to the American Antitrust Institute.

Associate Editor

Cristina Volpin

Dr Volpin works as a Competition Expert at the OECD, Directorate for Financial and Enterprise Affairs. She was previously an associate lecturer and research fellow in competition law at the Centre for Commercial Law Studies, Queen Mary University of London. She has over five years' experience as a lawyer gained at two top-tier Italian law firms (Gianni Origoni Grippo Cappelli & Partners, and Chiomenti). She contributed to various international projects, including the study on the review of the European Merger Regulation regarding minority shareholdings. She is guest editor of the *Antitrust Bulletin* and has published in the *Common Market Law Review* and other leading journals. Her book on the rules of evidence in EU competition law is forthcoming, along with other publications on the interaction between IP and competition law and on innovation and competition law. She was a Visiting Research student at University College London, where she is a Fellow at the Centre for Law, Economics and Society. She graduated in Law from the University of Padua and holds a PhD in EU Competition Law from the same University.

Contributors

Ken Dai

Ken Dai is a partner at Denton's Law Offices in Shanghai. As one of the earliest private practitioners focusing on the practice area of antitrust, Ken Dai has advised numerous companies and enterprises (in particular multinationals) on the various aspects of China's Anti-Monopoly Law, including merger filing, pricing policies, antitrust review of distribution agreements, abuse of market dominance, antitrust and intellectual property rights, and private antitrust litigations. He has presented clients in merger filing cases as State Administration for Market Regulation (previously, Ministry of Commerce); provided clients with anti-monopoly compliance service for business strategies and commercial agreements; and represented clients in the negotiation and lawsuit of monopoly disputes.

Yajie Gao

Yajie Gao is a PhD candidate, at the Centre for Commercial Law Studies, Queen Mary, University of London UK. Yajie is doing research into anti-monopoly review of concentrations in the digital economy from a comparative perspective. Her supervisors are Professor Ioannis Kokkoris and Dr Maria Ioannidou. She has participated in research projects organized by the Ministry of Commerce under direction of Dr Wei Han, has co-authored the Chapter 7 for this volume with Professor Xiaoye Wang. Yajie has finished preliminary translation draft (from English to Chinese) of I. Kokkoris and H. Shelanski, *EU Merger Control—A Legal and Economic Analysis*, (OUP). She received her LLB and a BA in Economics (Finance) degrees from East China University of Political Science and Law, China ('ECUPL') in 2013, and her LLM from Ghent University, Belgium in 2015, and ECUPL in 2016 respectively.

Fabio Giacopello

Fabio has been a 'Recommended lawyer' by Legal500, 'Notable practitioner' by Chamber and Partners, 'IP Star' by Managing Intellectual Property, and is a member of the INTA Anti-Counterfeiting Committee (China Sub-Committee), an arbitrator at the Shanghai International Arbitration Center (SHIAC), and a partner at HFG Law & Intellectual Property, since 2010.

Xi Liao

Xi Liao is a Managing Associate based in Linklaters Beijing office. He has represented multinational companies as well as Chinese SOEs and domestic firms on various aspects of competition and antitrust law, including the PRC and multi-jurisdictional merger filings, investigation and compliance, and behavioural counselling. His practice spans multiple sectors, including, among others, automotive, manufacturing, healthcare, consumer goods, energy, chemical, and financial services.

Xi has extensive experience in handling antitrust issues relating to the automotive sector. He regularly assists companies active in the automotive sector relating to various compliance initiatives, including carrying out internal audits, providing compliance training, updating agreements and business policies, and restructuring business models. Xi was listed by Who's Who Legal in the survey of *Future Leaders (Non-Partner)—Competition 2017*. He also won the Best Antitrust Writing Awards in 2016 by Concurrence. He was shortlisted for '*Rising Star—competition law*' in 2015–2016 by China Law & Practice. Xi received his LLM in both China and the US. Xi is active in the PRC and in New York State. He is a native Chinese speaker and fluent in English.

Duncan Matthews

Professor Duncan Matthews is a member of the Centre for Commercial Law Studies. He has held academic positions as a lecturer in law at the University of Warwick and as a research fellow at the ESRC Centre for the Study of Globalisation and Regionalisation, also at the University of Warwick. He has worked as a researcher at a policy think-tank (the National Institute for Economic and Social Research, London) and as an EU lobbyist. He has acted as an advisor to the Directorate General Trade of the European Commission; the ECAP II EC-ASEAN Intellectual Property Rights Co-operation Programme; the American Association for the Advancement of Science (AAAS); the United Nations Development Programme (UNDP); the European Parliament Committee on International Trade; the European Patent Office (EPO); the UK Strategic Advisory Board for Intellectual Property Policy (SABIP); and the UK Intellectual Property Office (IPO) Expert Advisory Group on Trade and Development. Professor Matthews is a member of the Chartered Institute of Patent Attorneys (CIPA) Education Committee and also worked with the Centre for the Management of Intellectual Property in Health Research and Development (MIHR) on an *IP Handbook of Best Practices*. He is co-founder and coordinator of the European Intellectual Property Teachers' Network (EIPTN).

Anna Mitchell

Anna is a Managing Associate in Linklaters Competition/Antitrust practice in Hong Kong. She specializes in advising global clients on a range of Asian antitrust issues and Asian clients on global antitrust issues. Since moving to Hong Kong in January 2013, Anna has advised a number of Hong Kong companies in relation to compliance with the new Hong Kong competition legislation. She has also developed a strong regional expertise and has been involved in merger control filings and investigations in a number of Asia-Pacific jurisdictions including China, Korea, Japan, Indonesia, and India. Prior to moving to Hong Kong, Anna was based in Linklaters' London office, where she specialized in EU and UK competition matters. Her work included cartel investigations, merger control filings, market investigations, implementation of compliance programmes, and state aid advice. In 2012,

Anna completed a nine-month secondment to the in-house competition team at the Royal Bank of Scotland plc. Anna has experience of advising clients across a broad range of sectors, in particular the retail, pharmaceutical, financial services, commodities, and mining sectors.

Burton Ong

Dr Burton Ong, LLB (NUS); LLM (Harv); BCL/DPhil (Oxon) is an Associate Professor at the Faculty of Law, National University of Singapore (NUS), where he teaches and researches in the fields of competition law, intellectual property, and contract law. He is an Advocate and Solicitor of the Supreme Court of Singapore, as well as an Attorney and Counsellor-at-Law in New York State. He has served as a consultant on competition policy matters in Singapore and the ASEAN region in both the public and private sectors. He is the editor of *The Regionalisation of Competition Law and Policy Within the ASEAN Economic Community* (Cambridge University Press, 2018) and is a Director (Competition Law) at the EW Barker Centre for Law and Business at the National University of Singapore.

Charles Pommiès

Charles is a counsel in Allen & Overy's Brussels office specializing in competition law. Charles has witnessed the rapid developments of Chinese competition law during his tenure in Allen & Overy's Beijing office between 2014 and 2018. His practice covers a broad variety of matters, including assisting leading US, European, and Asian companies in antitrust investigations (cartels and abuses of dominant position) and complex merger control reviews in the EU and China. Charles' clients are active in a wide range of industries, including pharmaceuticals, consumer electronics, chemicals, transportation, automotive, and financial institutions.

A graduate of the Sorbonne University and *Sciences-Po* in Paris and the New York University School of Law, Charles is admitted to the Bar in both France and Belgium. Charles has previously practised antitrust law in Washington DC and Paris.

François Renard

François an EU antitrust specialist, has managed and spearheaded Allen & Overy's Greater China Antitrust Practice since November 2008. He has extensive experience of advising Western and Asian clients on APAC (including China), EU, and other national competition laws. In China, Francois secured MOFCOM's conditional clearances including for the acquisition of AZ Electronics by Merck KGaA (which won the *GCR's Merger Control Matter of the Year—Asia-Pacific, Middle East and Africa in 2015*), the acquisition of Samsung's hard disk business by Seagate (which won *the GCR's Matter of the Year in 2012*) and the acquisition of Alcon by Novartis (the first PRC conditional clearance under the PRC 2010 remedy rules). Francois has also been the leading lawyer acting as supervisory trustee in several proceedings. He has also been the chief representative of leading companies on their responses to the antitrust investigation launched by NDRC in the infant milk, financial, pharmaceutical, medical devices, and hotel sectors.

In Hong Kong, Francois has actively cooperated with and commented on the Guidelines prepared by the Competition Commission. He is the Vice President of the HK Competition Association, (http://www.hkcompetitionassociation.org). He also assists companies to respond to the HK Competition Commission investigations and to prepare for and to comply with the HK Competition Ordinance. On outbound and pan-APAC matters, Francois has assisted several Asian companies in managing their APAC or global antitrust matters. Francois was co-chairman of the antitrust group at the EU Chamber of Commerce of Beijing between June 2009 and 2011. He has been one of the few EU experts invited to speak to and train officials from each of the three Chinese antitrust authorities. Francois is listed as a leading lawyer in PLC's antitrust cross-border category in China, International Who's Who of Competition Lawyers, Global Competition Review (GCR), Chambers APAC and IFLR 1000, respectively. He was also the winner of the ILO Client Choice Award 2015 for the Competition and Antitrust category in China.

Francois is a lecturer at the Institute of European Studies (Brussels) and was invited as a visiting professor to one of the major Beijing universities (CUPSL) in 2014. Francois speaks English, French, Italian, and Dutch. Francois obtained his law degree from the Free University of Brussels, and obtained an LLM in European Law from the Institute of European Studies in Brussels, and another LLM from Duke University in the United States. He regularly speaks and writes on the subject of antitrust. Francois is admitted to the Belgian Bar and in Hong Kong, and is a junior lecturer at the Institute of European Studies (Brussels).

Guan H. Tang

Guan is Senior Lecturer in Commercial Law Asia and PhD supervisor in comparative commercial law at Queen Mary University of London. She was Senior Lecturer in Law at Northumbria University (2015) and Associate Professor of Law at Shanghai University of Finance and Economics (2009–2015).

Graduated from Shenzhen University, Guan's academic journey started when she was awarded a governmental scholarship in 1998 , undertaking her Masters at Queen's University Belfast, where she researched information technology and the law with a focus on IPRs in China. She later read law with Professor Hector MacQueen and received her PhD at the University of Edinburgh Law School. Benefiting from a dual academic experience, Guan appreciates the legislative and cultural diversity, and sits on several advisory boards in China and Europe. Guan's research consists of a strong theme of comparative IP law and the public interest, with an insight about the developments of the rule of law in China from a commercial law perspective and their relevance to the rest of the world. Her works include *Copyright and the Public Interest in China* (Edward Elgar Publishing, 2011).

Tao Tao

Tao Tao, LLB (Hons) (NUS) is an Associate at Rajah & Tann Singapore LLP. He is an Advocate and Solicitor of the Supreme Court of Singapore, and specializes in civil and commercial disputes resolution. He is the co-author of the chapter 'Monopoly Agreements, Trade Associations and Competition Culture in China' in *Cartels in Asia: Law & Practice* (Wolters Kluwer Hong Kong Limited, 2015).

Mark Williams

Mark Williams is Professor of Law in University of Melbourne Law School and teaches competition law, Hong Kong company/commercial law, corporate social responsibility, and People's Republic of China (PRC) economic law. He has published in various leading law journals, including the *Journal of Business Law*, the *Competition Review*, and the *Antitrust Bulletin and the Competition Policy International*. He has also contributed to books and studies on competition-related topics and has undertaken consultancy work in the competition law field for the Japanese and Chinese governments as well as leading law firms. He is a regular speaker at various business groups' seminars and conferences. His books include *Competition Policy and Law in China, Hong Kong and Taiwan* (Cambridge University Press, 2005), he co-authored *Secured Finance Law in China and Hong Kong* (Cambridge University Press, 2010), and edited *Political Economy of Competition Law* (Cambridge University Press, 2013). Mark is Professor of Law and teaches competition law with an interest in Asian competition generally and that of China and Hong Kong more particularly. He also teaches company and commercial law, corporate governance, corporate social responsibility, again with a particular interest in Asian jurisdictions, and the economic law of the People's Republic of China. He has taught for twenty-five years in the UK, Hong Kong, China, and now Australia at both undergraduate and postgraduate levels. He has acted as a doctoral examiner for several leading law schools.

Paul has undertaken consultancy assignments in the competition law field for the Japanese and Chinese governments, APEC and ASEAN as well as for leading international law firms. He is a regular speaker at various international academic conferences and professional and business groups' seminars. He has been a regular contributor to international competition events hosted by the United Nations, ASEAN, and APEC. He was also the founder of the Asian Competition Forum and has been its Executive Director since 2005. He was appointed in July 2013 to be a member of the Telecommunications (Competition Provisions) Appeal Board in Hong Kong.

Xiuqin Lin

Dr Xiuqin Lin, born in 1965, graduated from Southwest University of Political Science & Law in 1985, and obtained an LLB. She graduated from Xiamen University in 1988, majoring in Civil Law, and obtained her LLM. She became a visiting scholar in London University between 1998 and 1999 and then a post-graduate student at Oxford University, where she obtained a MSt in Legal Research in 2002. She graduated from Xiamen University in 2003 with a PhD degree on international law. Currently she is the Vice Dean of the Law School at Xiamen University and also a PhD Supervisor at the Law School and Intellectual Property Research Institute of Xiamen University. She is an arbitrator of Xiamen Arbitration Committee and a lawyer of Fujian Xiamen Fidelity Law Firm. Her research interests include patent law, trademark law, competition law, and copyright law.

Under her leadership, more than five key research projects at state, ministerial, and provincial levels have been achieved, including *Legal System Study for Promoting Technology Innovation of Self-governing Intellectual Property Rights*. She has published an academic work entitled *Patent Compulsory Licensing under the TRIPs Agreement*, which won third prize for Excellent Social Science Achievement in Fujian Province. In addition, she has more than ten theses published in *Chinese Journal of Law, Modern Law Science, Journal of Xiamen University & Social Sciences, Intellectual Prop*erty, and *Electronic Intellectual Property.* Some of them are listed as follows: 'An Examination on the Concept of Self-governing Intellectual Property Rights'; 'An Economic Analysis of Joint Innovation and Relevant Regulation against Monopoly'; 'The Improvement of Patent Compulsory License Systems in China'; 'An Approach of the Economics of Law to the Advantages and Disadvantages of the Patent System—While Coping with the Necessary Amendments to China's Patent Law'; and 'Legal Reflections of the Requirements of Local Working of Patents'.

Alan Xu

Alan XU is a PRC licensed lawyer of LUSHENG Law Firm and has practiced IP laws for over 11 years. He has vast experience in representing and advising international clients on matters covering all varieties of patent, trademark, copyright, trade secret, trade name, domain name and unfair competition issues. Alan XU has handled landmark cases in China, which received awards from courts and industrial organisations. Example includes representing Italian door and window manufacturer against local infringer (awarded as one of the Top 10 IP Cases in Zhejiang Province of 2016).

Fay Zhou

Fay is a partner and head of the China competition practice based in Linklaters LLP Beijing Representative Office. Her practice includes advising multinational and Chinese clients concerning competition/antitrust law and other regulatory issues, including making notifications and obtaining clearance for proposed mergers and acquisitions. Fay's experience includes advising clients on high profile and complex merger notifications in sectors involving healthcare, commodities, chemicals, home appliance, and TMT, including 20% of the conditional approvals MOFCOM has made so far. Her recent cases include Linde/Praxair, AB InBev/SABMiller (remedy case), China Merchants/Sinotrans, Novartis/GSK, CNR/CSR, Glencore/Xstrata (remedy case), Gambro/Baxter (remedy case), BP/Sinopec. Fay also has extensive experience in assisting clients in handling government investigations on cartel activities and abuse of dominance, and counselling clients on competition law compliance.

Fay has also been invited (as the only lawyer from an international law firm) to attend the task force to draft the antitrust guidelines by Chinese enforcement authorities. Fay previously served in the Chinese Ministry of Commerce for eight years and has acquired a thorough understanding of the dynamic regulatory environment in China. After receiving her LLM from Harvard Law School, she practiced with international law firms for ten years. She is qualified to practice law in China and New York State.

Dong Zhu, is Assistant Professor **in** Xiamen University, and Intellectual Property Research Institute of Xiamen University, China.

1

INTRODUCTION TO IP AND ANTI-MONOPOLY LEGISLATION AND PRACTICE IN CHINA

Ioannis Kokkoris, *Spyros Maniatis,** and Yajie Gao****

1. Intellectual Property Law

1.1 Development history of China's intellectual property legal system

Intellectual property ('**IP**') is result of commodity economy and science and technology development. Different from developed Western countries who began their IP legislation in the seventeenth to eighteenth centuries, the People's Republic of China ('**China**') experienced a process from 'being forced to get involved in' to 'actively making use of' IP only 200–300 years later. The century evolution of IP in China could be divided into four stages.[1] The first stage: Passive Acceptance. China's IP protection system is generally considered to originate from the end of the Qing Dynasty. It is a product of reform policy implemented by the Qing Government with the aim of learning from the West. For the first time, the *Regulation on Rewarding Creation and Invention to Rejuvenate the Industry* enacted by Guangxu Emperor introduced a patent system to China. Nevertheless, the regulation was annulled with the failure of his 'Hundred Days of Reform'.

* Kokkoris Ioannis is Chair in Law and Economics at the Centre for Commercial Law Studies, Queen Mary, University of London, UK.
** Spyros Maniatis is Professor of Intellectual Property and Director of the Centre for Commercial Law Studies at Queen Mary University of London.
*** Yajie Gao is PhD candidate from the Centre for Commercial Law Studies, Queen Mary, University of London, UK.
1 Handong Wu, 'Policy and Science Research into China's Intellectual Property Policy' (2006) 7 China Intellectual Property News, 2–3.

The second stage: Selective Arrangement. Ever since the establishment of the People's Republic of China in 1949, several administrative rules were released to protect IP, which were not, strictly speaking, laws. From the 1970s to the early 1990s, relevant legislative work was enhanced, with the enactment of the *Trademark Law of the People's Republic of China* ('**Trademark Law**'), *Patent Law of the People's Republic of China* ('**Patent Law**'), and *Copyright Law of the People's Republic of China* ('**Copyright Law**') in 1982, 1984, and 1990 respectively. China's IP legal system thus began to be established, and the legislation in this period was based on selective institutional arrangements.

The third stage: Adjustment Period. From the 1990s to the early twenty-first century, China's IP regime entered an important stage for development and improvement. In preparation for becoming an official member of the World Trade Organization, Chinese legislators overhauled the Trademark Law (in 1993 and 2001), Patent Law (in 1992 and 2000), and Copyright Law (in 2001), and enacted *Regulations of China on the Protection of New Varieties of Plants* in 1997, *Regulations on the Protection of Layout-designs of Integrated Circuits* in 2001, and other regulations. In a nutshell, China managed to transform from low-level to high-level IP law and transit from localization to internationalization within just ten years. At international level, the *Memorandum of Understanding on Intellectual Property Rights* between the Governments of China and the United States of America ('**US**') expedited the internationalization of China's IP policy. Domestically, acting as a newly industrialized country, China greatly needed to promote the development of science and technology through strengthening IP protection. A number of legislative amendments basically helped to achieve modernization of institutional innovation.

The fourth stage: The New Era of Strategic Initiative. Establishment of National IP Protection Working Group and the National IP Strategy Formulation Leading Group in 2004 and 2005 signified that China's IP regime had entered a new strategic stage. Until now, an IP legal system with rational coordination between specific IP laws (such as the Patent Law, Copyright Law, and Trademark Law amended in 2008, 2010, and 2013 respectively) and *Anti-Unfair Competition Law of China* ('**AUCL**') has been established in China, having the *Constitution Law of China* as its foundation and *General Principles of the Civil Law* as its support. Nevertheless, a degree of systematization still needs to be upgraded. For example, there is no business secret protection law, and relevant provisions are scattered in *Contract Law*, AUCL, and *Criminal Law*.

Major international conventions and treaties on IP protection already entered into by China include but are not limited to *Convention Establishing the World Intellectual Property Organization* (in 1980), *Paris Convention for the Protection of Industrial Property* (in 1984), *Madrid Agreement Concerning the International Registration of Marks* (in 1990), *Intellectual Property Treaties of Integrated Circuits* (in 1989), *Berne Convention for the Protection of Literary and Artistic Works* (in 1992), *Universal Copyright Convention* (in 1992), *Patent Cooperation Treaty* (in 1994), *International Convention for the Protection of New Varieties of Plants* (in 1999), *Agreement on Trade-Related Aspects of Intellectual Property Rights* (in 2001), *World Intellectual Property Organization Copyright Treaty* (in 2007), and *WIPO Performances and Phonograms Treaty* (in 2007).

1.2 'Dual-track approach' to regulate IP in China

1.2.1 Administrative management

China runs a 'dual-track' approach to regulating IP, namely administrative management and judicial protection. As for administrative management, Chinese administrative agencies are in charge of registration, authorization, settling IP-related disputes, as well as investigating and punishing violations against IP. Various bureaus, departments, and ministries from both central and local levels are entitled to enforce different branches of IP laws in China. More specifically, the central government directs and coordinates agencies at province or city levels to carry out specific law enforcement work. An efficient and rational IP customs protection mechanism has also been set up, having Patent Law, Trademark Law, Copyright Law, *Foreign Trade Law of China* ('**Foreign Trade Law**'), and *Customs Law of China* as the basic principles, and *Regulations of China on Customs Protection of Intellectual Property Rights* and *Measures of the General Administration of Customs of China on the Implementation of the Regulations of China on Customs Protection of Intellectual Property Rights* as specific instructions, which corresponds with the 'Border Measures' required by the *Agreement on Trade-Related Aspects of Intellectual Property Rights*.[2] Before approval of the State Council's Institutional Reform Program ('**Program**') by the 1st Session of the 13th National People's Congress on 17 March 2018,[3] there were eleven central agencies each managing a specific branch of IP in China. For more details, please find Figure 1.1 below.

---

[2] ANNEX 1C, AGREEMENT ON TRADE-RELATED ASPECTS OF INTELLECTUAL PROPERTY RIGHTS, PART III ENFORCEMENT OF INTELLECTUAL PROPERTY RIGHTS, SECTION 4: SPECIAL REQUIREMENTS RELATED TO BORDER MEASURES, available at <https://www.wto.org/english/docs_e/legal_e/27-trips.pdf> accessed 8 May 2018.

[3] The 1st Session of the 13th National People's Congress's Decision on the State Council's Institutional Reform Program [2018], available at <http://www.gov.cn/xinwen/2018-03/17/content_5275072.htm> accessed 8 May 2018.

	Administrative Agency	Type of IP
1	State Intellectual Property Office (**'SIPO'**)	Patent and Integrated Circuit Layout Design Right
2	Trademark Office of the State Administration for Industry and Commerce (**'SAIC'**)	Trademark
3	National Copyright Administration	Copyright
4	Anti-Monopoly and Anti-Unfair Competition Enforcement Bureau of the SAIC	Prevention of Unfair Competition
5	General Administration of Quality Supervision, Inspection and Quarantine (**'GAQSIQ'**)	Geographical Indications of Origin
6	Ministry of Agriculture	Agricultural Plant Variety Right
7	State Forestry Administration	Forestry Plant Variety Right
8	Ministry of Commerce (**'MOFCOM'**)	IP in Relation to International Trade
9	Ministry of Science and Technology	IP in Relation to Science and Technology
10	General Administration of Customs	IP in Relation to Import and Export Goods
11	Ministry of Industry and Information Technology	Internet Domain Name

Figure 1.1

The State Administration for Market Regulation ('**SAMR**') was established and directly affiliated with the State Council, integrating the competence of the State Administration for Industry and Commerce ('**SAIC**'), the Price Supervision and Anti-Monopoly Bureau under the National Development and Reform Commission ('**NDRC**'), the Anti-Monopoly Bureau under the Ministry of Commerce ('**MOFCOM**'), and the Anti-Monopoly Commission under the State Council and others.[4] The SAMR has ended the era of three Chinese administrative departments taking charge of anti-monopoly enforcement. One of the main responsibilities of the SAMR is to enforce the anti-monopoly laws and regulations. SAMR shall promote and guide the implementation of competition policy and fair competition review system; review concentration of business operators; govern monopolistic agreement, abuse of dominant market position, and abuse of administrative power; guide Chinese undertakings to respond to relevant overseas anti-monopoly investigations/suits; as well as be in charge of the daily work of the Anti-Monopoly Commission affiliated with the State Council.[5]

---

[4] 2(1) Establishing the State Administration for Market Regulation, Statement on the State Council's Institutional Reform Program [2018], available at <http://www.gov.cn/guowuyuan/2018-03/14/content_5273856.htm> accessed 8 May 2018.

[5] Provisions on Function Configuration, Internal Organization and Staff of the State Administration for Market Regulation, Article 3(4) In Charge of the Unified Anti-Monopoly Enforcement, 10 September 2018, available at <http://www.gov.cn/zhengce/2018-09/10/content_5320813.htm> accessed 13 September 2018.

The SIPO 1.0 was restructured and the new state intellectual property office—National Intellectual Property Administration, PRC ('**CNIPA**')[6] absorbs competence of SIPO 1.0, SAIC (trademark), and GAQSIQ (Geographical Indications of Origin). CNIPA will be managed by the SAMR. Main responsibilities of CNIPA include, but are not limited to, formulating and implementing IP policies to protect trademark, patent, geographical indication of origin, and integrated circuit layout design; enacting department regulations; guiding law enforcement pertaining to trademark and patent, as well as local IP dispute resolution/settlement and rights protection assistance.[7] Law enforcement responsibilities of trademark and patent shall be borne by the comprehensive law enforcement team of market supervision.[8]

1.2.2 Judicial protection

On 24 April 2017, the Supreme People's Court of China ('**SPC**') released the *Outline of the Juridical Protection of Intellectual Property in China (2016–2020)* ('**Outline**').[9] It is the first time the SPC has published a protection outline specifically targeted at a special judicial field. The Outline gives clear guiding ideology, basic principles, major objectives, and key measures with respect to IP judicial protection work. In accordance with the Outline, an IP judicial protection mechanism has been established with judicial protection acting as the guiding role, having civil trial as the foundation and the parallel development of administrative trial and criminal trial. Ever since the first IP case was accepted in February 1985, the Chinese People's Courts have dealt with a dramatic increase in the number of cases, covering unfair competition disputes and all the IP prescribed by the *Agreement on Trade Related Aspects of Intellectual Property Rights*.

The Chinese IP trial mechanism has also been gradually optimized. The SPC set up the IP trial division in October 1995. Since November 2014, IP Courts have been successively set up in Beijing, Guangzhou, and Shanghai. In early 2017, IP Courts were established successively in Nanjing, Suzhou, Chengdu, and Wuhan. Co-trial of IP civil, administrative, and criminal cases was practised all over China

---

[6] As of 30 August 2018 the official website of the National Intellectual Property Administration, PRC ('**CNIPA**') has become <http://www.cnipa.gov.cn/>while the abbreviation of the state intellectual property office (SIPO) has been exchanged with the CNIPA since 28 August 2018.

[7] Provisions on Function Configuration, Internal Organization and Staff of the National Intellectual Property Administration, Article 3(2) In Charge of the Protection of Intellectual Property Rights, 11 September 2018, available at <http://www.scopsr.gov.cn/bbyw/qwfb/201809/t20180911_308252.html> accessed 13 September 2018.

[8] 2(9) Re-Structuring the State Intellectual Property Office, Statement on the State Council's Institutional Reform Program [2018], available at <http://www.gov.cn/guowuyuan/2018-03/14/content_5273856.htm> accessed 8 May 2018.

[9] The Supreme People's Court of China, 'Outline of the Juridical Protection of IP Released by the Supreme People's Court for the First Time, Together with the White Paper of IP Protection and Ten of the Most Typical IP Cases' [2017], available at <http://www.court.gov.cn/zixun-xiangqing-41872.html> accessed 8 May 2018.

since July 2016. By the end of 2016, 224 intermediate people's courts have been designated by the SPC or are empowered by relevant laws to have special jurisdiction over civil disputes in relation to patent, plant variety right, integrated circuit layout design, monopoly, and recognition of well-known trademarks. Moreover, 167 grass-root people's courts have been approved by the SPC to hear general IP civil cases. Furthermore, thirty-four IP judicial interpretations and more than forty judicial policy documents enacted by the SPC from 1985 to 2016 so enabling IP judicial protection play the leading role.[10]

2. Anti-Monopoly Law

After almost two decades of discussion, *Anti-Monopoly Law of the People's Republic of China* ('**AML**') came into effect on 1 August 2008. AML was enacted to prevent and restrain monopolistic conducts, protect fair market competition, enhance economic efficiency, safeguard the interests of Chinese consumers and society as a whole, and promote the healthy development of its socialist market economy.[11] It also applies to monopolistic conducts outside the territory of China but serves to eliminate or restrict competition in the domestic market of China.[12] In terms of substantive provisions, it mainly transplants from those of the European Union ('**EU**') and the US, while also keeping Chinese characteristics. Until now, a supporting system consisting of administrative regulations, guidelines, and provisions enacted by the State Council and the SAMR[13] has been established.

AML also regulates administrative dominance (Article 8 and Chapter 5). The AML itself only covers civil and administrative liabilities, without criminal liability, provision of the civil liability being very vague (Article 50) and the administrative liability being capped with punishment of CNY 500,000 (Article 48). Only bidders and bid-inventors acting in collusion with each other might be sentenced.[14]

---

[10] Part I Status of Development, Outline of the Juridical Protection of Intellectual Property in China (2016–2020) [2017].

[11] Article 1 of the *Anti-Monopoly Law of the People's Republic of China* ('AML').

[12] Article 2 of the AML.

[13] In fact, the administrative institutes enacting relevant regulations, guidelines, and provisions were the State Council, the Anti-Monopoly Commission, the MOFCOM, the NDRC, and the SAIC. On 28 September 2018, *Decision of the State Council on Revising Certain Administrative Regulations* (Order No. 703 of the State Council) was promulgated. Article 7 of the Order amended Articles 3 and 4 of the *Provisions of the State Council on the Thresholds for Notifying Concentration of Business Operators*, exchanging 'the department in charge of commerce of the State Council' with 'the agency in charge of anti-monopoly enforcement of the State Council'. Available at <http://www.gov.cn/zhengce/content/2018-09/28/content_5326316.htm> accessed 30 September 2018. On 29 September 2018, the SAMR released seven guidelines pertaining to anti-monopoly notification of concentration of business operators. The main amendment is to exchange 'Anti-Monopoly Bureau of the MOFCOM' with 'the Anti-Monopoly Bureau of the SAMR'. Available at <http://samr.saic.gov.cn/xw/yw/wjfb/> accessed 30 September 2018. Please be noted that the SAIC has been absorbed by the SAMR and ceased to exist.

[14] Article 223 of the *Criminal Law of the People's Republic of China*.

Furthermore, senior executives are not liable for anti-monopoly infringement of business operators.

From the perspective of subject and procedure, the implementation of Chinese anti-monopoly laws and regulations could be divided into public enforcement and private enforcement.[15] Public enforcement refers to administrative actions taken by Chinese competition authorities to investigate and punish monopolistic conducts, while private enforcement is civil litigation initiated by undertakings or consumers against monopolistic conducts for civil liabilities. Equipped with professional enforcers, statutory authority, and national coerce force, public enforcement plays the leading role. One of the most important reasons why plaintiffs have lost a large number of civil monopolistic litigations is the huge burden of proof they have to bear. In order to provide clearer answers to the series of questions put forward during anti-monopolistic civil litigation and to ease burden of plaintiffs, *Provisions of the Supreme People's Court on Certain Issues Relating to the Application of Law in Hearing Cases Involving Civil Disputes Arising out of Monopolistic Acts* were promulgated on 3 May 2012 and came into effect on 1 June 2012.[16]

Another arrangement which separates the Chinese anti-monopoly legal system from the others is the enforcement agencies. Under direction of the Anti-Monopoly Commission, being in charge of organizing, coordinating, and guiding anti-monopoly work,[17] it used to be the Price Supervision and Anti-Monopoly Bureau ('**PSAMB**') under the NDRC, the Anti-Monopoly and Anti-Unfair Competition Enforcement Bureau ('**AMAUCEB**') under the SAIC, and the Anti-Monopoly Bureau ('**AMB**') under the MOFCOM who enforced anti-monopoly rules in practice, while branches of relevant authorities from levels of province, autonomous region, or municipality could also be empowered to enforce anti-monopoly or anti-unfair competition laws and regulations.[18] The Program approved by the 1st Session of the 13th National People's Congress has changed this triumvirate. The SAMR, directly under the State Council, was established on the basis of the SAIC, the GAQSIQ, and the China Food and Drug Administration, absorbing competence of the PSAMB under the NDRC, the AMB under the MOFCOM, and the Anti-Monopoly Commission. The SAIC is no longer reserved.[19]

---

[15] Xianlin Wang, 'Economic Reform Driven by the Market and Emergence & Development of China's Anti-Monopoly Law' (Vol. 1, 2015) Competition Law and Policy Review, 8–10.

[16] Available at <http://www.court.gov.cn/fabu-xiangqing-3989.html> accessed 8 May 2018.

[17] Article 9 of the AML.

[18] Article 10 of the AML.

[19] 2(1) Establishing the State Administration for Market Regulation, Statement on the State Council's Institutional Reform Program [2018], available at <http://www.gov.cn/guowuyuan/2018-03/14/content_5273856.htm> accessed 8 May 2018.

3. Anti-Unfair Competition Law

Over a long period of time ever since the founding of PRC, China ran a planned economy in which competition was recognized as the special fruit of a capitalistic economy and was not given enough attention by the then government. China's competition policy and legislation entered an important era from 1992, in which the aim of establishing a market economy with Chinese characteristics was put forward by the 14th Congress of Communist Party of China.[20] In order to ensure the healthy development of the socialist market economy, encourage and protect fair competition, prevent acts of unfair competition, and safeguard legitimate rights and interests of business operators and consumers,[21] the Anti-Unfair Competition Law was promulgated in 1993 ('**1993 AUCL**'). There was a dispute with respect to what legislation model should be applied in China's competition legal system ever since the legislative initiation in 1987. Finally, there was consensus that China lacked a mature practice foundation for the promulgation of a systematic anti-monopoly law, while certain monopolistic conducts had already brought side effects to the market which shall be regulated by law. This explains why the 1993 AUCL not only regulates unfair competitive conducts, but also cover certain monopolistic acts—unfair competitive conducts taken by public utilities, administrative monopoly, price dumping, tie-in, and bid-rigging.[22]

With the transformation from a planned economy to a market economy, the gradual establishment of a market self-regulatory mechanism, fiercer competition in the market, more prominent conducts which could destroy order of a market economy, infringe legitimate rights and interests of consumers, and damage public interests, promulgation of AML only came fourteen years later in 2007. The 1993 AUCL was amended in 2017 and came into effect on 1 January 2018 ('**2018 AUCL**'). Since then, China's competition system clearly consists of anti-unfair competition law and anti-monopoly law, between which no intersection exists any more in theory.

In general, the 2018 AUCL introduces provisions in relation to internet and e-commerce (Articles 6 and 12). What's worth mentioning is that 'consumer rights and interests' were introduced in Article 2(2), which means that the status of consumers is estimated to be upgraded in the future competition enforcement. The 2018 AUCL continues to pay high attention to and fully implement the notion of

---

[20] Ex-President Zemin Jiang, 'Speed up Reform and Opening up to the Outside World and Modernization Construction, and Achieve the Great Success of Socialist Cause with Chinese Characteristics' [1992], available at <http://cpc.people.com.cn/GB/64162/134902/8092276.html> accessed 8 May 2018.
[21] Article 1 of the *Anti-unfair Competition Law of the People's Republic of China* ('**1993 AUCL**').
[22] Articles 6, 7, 11, 12, and 15 of the 1993 AUCL.

limited intervention and market efficiency, chiefly with regard to counterfeiting, misleading propaganda, business discredit, commercial bribes, business secrets, and improper prize-giving sales. Besides the AML and 2018 AUCL, certain anti-monopoly and anti-unfair competition provisions could also be found in Product Quality Law, Law on the Protection of Consumer Rights and Interests, Advertising Law, Foreign Trade Law, Price Law, Tender Law, and other administrative regulations, such as Telecommunications Regulations.

4. Relationship between the Anti-Monopoly Law and IP Law

In June 2008, the *State Intellectual Property Strategic Outline* ('**Strategic Outline**') was released by the State Council. The Strategic Outline requires the legislator to promulgate relevant laws and regulations to define boundaries of IP rationally, prevent abuse of IP, and maintain the fair and competitive market order and legitimate rights and interests of the public.[23] As early as March 2009, the SAIC had started to work on drafting *Anti-Monopoly Enforcement Guidelines Regarding Intellectual Property*. However, considering that it was less than one year since promulgation of AML, and the authorities only had limited experience in enforcing anti-monopoly law in IP areas, it was premature to enact all-round and complete anti-monopoly guidelines against abuse of IP which conform to Chinese practice. After years of research, the SAIC released *Provisions on Prohibiting the Abuse of Intellectual Property Rights to Eliminate, Restrict Competition* ('**Provisions**') on 7 April 2015,[24] which came into effect on 1 August 2015.[25] Nevertheless, the Provisions cannot replace anti-monopoly guidelines against abuse of IP, since the Provisions belong to department regulation promulgated by only one of the then three Chinese competition agencies, relevant application scope only covers anti-monopoly enforcement activities undertaken by the SAIC, and excludes those of the NDRC and the MOFCOM.

On the basis of Article 55 of AML ('AML is not applicable to undertakings who exercise their intellectual property rights in accordance with the laws and administrative

---

[23] The State Council, Part I Preface, 'State Intellectual Property Strategic Outline' [2008], available at <http://www.gov.cn/zwgk/2008-06/10/content_1012269.htm> accessed 8 May 2018.

[24] Order of the State Administration for Industry and Commerce No. 74 [2015], available at <http://old.saic.gov.cn/fldyfbzdjz/zcfg/zcfg/201507/t20150724_159428.html> accessed 8 May 2018.

[25] The State Administration for Industry and Commerce ('**SAIC**'), 'Promote Competition and Innovation, Create a Sound Market Environment—To Understand the Provisions on Prohibiting the Abuse of Intellectual Property Rights to Eliminate, Restrict Competition' [2015], available at <http://old.saic.gov.cn/fldyfbzdjz/zcfg/zcfg/201508/t20150803_159661.html> accessed 8 May 2018.

regulations on intellectual property rights; however, AML shall be applicable to the undertakings who eliminate or restrict market competition by abusing their intellectual property rights') and Article 9 of AML ('The State Council shall establish an anti-monopoly commission to be in charge of organizing, coordinating and guiding anti-monopoly work and to perform the following duties: ... (3) formulating and releasing anti-monopoly guidelines; ...'), the Anti-Monopoly Commission initiated drafting work of the *Anti-Monopoly Guidelines Against Abuse of Intellectual Property Rights* ('**Guidelines**') in the first half of 2015. The NDCR, SAIC, and MOFCOM drafted certain part of the Guidelines in accordance with their respective competence (SAIC—non-price related anti-competitive agreement, non-price related abuse of dominant market position, and administrative dominance; NDRC—price related anti-competitive agreement and price related abuse of dominant market position; MOFCOM—concentration which has or probably will have the ability to eliminate or restrict competition), after which it would be the Anti-Monopoly Commission who shall compile, amend different drafts, and release the final official version. Moreover, the SIPO 1.0 also provided its own draft.

Mr. Handong Zhang, the Director General of the then PSAMB under the NDRC commented that it is just the time to strengthen IP protection, while anti-monopoly enforcement against IP abuse shall also be adhered to.[26]

Intellectual property was the subject of early anti-unfair competition law. Even if the modern anti-unfair competition law is far from being limited to IP, protection of IP is still one of the basic tasks. Anti-unfair competition law shall apply where there is no explicit IP provisions. Under influence of the *Paris Convention for the Protection of Industrial Property*, Chinese anti-unfair competition law is included in IP enforcement. The most popular IP textbooks and comprehensive monographs regard AUCL as a component; while competition law textbooks also include AUCL. In practice, anti-unfair competition cases are categorized under IP cases in Chinese courts. Most of the judges applied AUCL in accordance with thinking and method of IP protection.[27] The 2018 AUCL amended the previous IP-related provisions. To name Article 6 as an example, the scope of confusion has been expanded, including unauthorized use of influential domain names, website names, and web pages of others. Furthermore, Article 12 also prohibits business operators from forcing redirection, forcing uninstalling and malicious incompatibility when engaging in production and business activities through the internet.

---

[26] Yiming Liu, 'The SIPO Introduces Situation of IP Protection, while Relevant Experts Believe that Abuse of IP will Become the New Target of Anti-Monopoly Enforcement' [2018] *Legal Daily*, available at <http://www.legaldaily.com.cn/index/content/2018-04/26/content_7530538.htm?node=20908> accessed 8 May 2018.

[27] Xiangjun Kong, 'Competition Law Orientation of Anti-Unfair Competition Law' (2017) 5 Law Review, 24.

5. Case Analysis

This section presents some typical cases concerning the intersection of anti-monopoly and IP already dealt with by previous Chinese competition authorities and judged by the Chinese people's court. SAIC used to be the main body which enforced AUCL among the three Chinese competition authorities. In practice, the SAIC preferred the AUCL to the AML. Compared with the SAIC, the NDRC seemed to be more powerful and its decisions have also attracted wider international attention, such as the Qualcomm Case. The MOFCOM is much more active in reviewing concentrations concerning IP, and at least fourteen conditionally cleared decisions in this respect have been released. As for the judgment made by the Guangdong High People's Court in the *Huawei Technology Co. Ltd. v. InterDigital Technology Corp.* case ('*Huawei v. IDC*'), it reflects Chinese people's court's attitude towards abuse of IP which could constitute a monopoly, responding to the most heatedly discussed questions in standard-essential patent ('**SEP**') licence, such as how to define the relevant market, how to determine the FRAND royalties, and whether an injunction sought by the licensor is with goodwill or not.

5.1 NDRC

In November 2013, the NDRC initiated an anti-monopoly investigation into Qualcomm Incorporated ('**Qualcomm**') in response to a complaint. After collecting evidence, analysing conduct, and listening to Qualcomm's statement and defence opinions, the NDRC concluded that Qualcomm had abused its dominant market position in CDMA, WCDMA, and LTE wireless communications, SEP licence market, and baseband chipset market through: (1) charging unfairly high royalties; (2) tying in wireless communication non-SEP licence; and (3) attaching unreasonable conditions in baseband chipset sales. Taking into consideration the seriousness, scope, and duration of Qualcomm's abuse, the NDRC ordered Qualcomm to cease illegal conducts, and punished Qualcomm with fines of 8 per cent of its turnover obtained in China in 2013, amounting to CNY 6.088 billion.[28] What is worth noting is that the NDRC is not the only competition authority who has taken action: the Korea Fair Trade Commission,[29] and the EU

---

[28] The National Development and Reform Commission ('**NDRC**'), 'The NDRC Ordered Qualcomm with Rectification and Fine of CNY 6 Billion for Abuse of Dominant Market Position' [2013], available at <http://www.ndrc.gov.cn/xwzx/xwfb/201502/t20150210_663822.html> accessed 8 May 2018.

[29] Korea Fair Trade Commission, 'KFTC Imposes Sanctions against Qualcomm's Abuse of SEPs of Mobile Communications' [2016], available at <http://www.ftc.go.kr/solution/skin/doc.html?fn=50ba93a6149acc5be3cae03dc2f4de97e254681689def7a42b2e4ae6eaaf1924&rs=/fileupload/data/result/BBSMSTR_000000002402/> accessed 8 May 2018.

Commission[30] fined Qualcomm 1.03 trillion won and EUR 997 million in December 2016 and January 2018 respectively for abuse of its dominant market position.

Since conducts of Qualcomm had restricted competition, obstructed and inhibited technological innovation and development, and harmed consumer rights and interests, the NDRC concluded that Article 17 of AML (selling commodities at unfairly high prices; conducting tie-in sale of commodities without justifiable reasons, and adding other unreasonable trading conditions to transactions) had been breached. During the investigation, Qualcomm cooperated and proactively put forward a package of remedies, namely: (1) to provide a list of patents when licensing wireless communications SEPs and not charge for expired patents; (2) not to require the licensee to grant back its non-SEPs against its will and not to compel the licensee to grant back relevant patents without paying reasonable royalties; (3) as for wireless communications terminals sold and used in China, not to charge SEP royalties on the basis of wholesale retail price of the terminal, when sticking to relatively high licence rate; (4) not to tie in non-SEP when licensing SEPs to the Chinese licensees; and (5) not to set accepting and paying for expired patents, granting back for free, tying in non-wireless-communications-SEPs, not challenging the licence agreement as pre-conditions for supply of baseband chipsets.[31]

The Qualcomm case set a record high with respect to the amount of fines since the AML came into effect on 1 August 2008. It not only attracted international attention, but also had an effect on both legislation and practice. The Guidelines (Article 14—Charge Excessive High Royalties for IP License, Article 15—Refuse to License IP, Article 16—Tie in Concerning IP, and Article 17—Unreasonable Trading Conditions Concerning IP) respond to lessons learnt from the Qualcomm case. After the punishment decision, Qualcomm declared to have gradually signed new 3G and 4G Chinese patent licence agreements with more than 100 companies, including the largest Chinese mobile device suppliers, in accordance with the rectification plan submitted to and approved by the NDRC,[32] among which ten of the top ten largest Chinese original equipment manufacturers had accepted the new licence agreements until 26 December 2016.[33] Even if having to go through

---

[30] EU Commission, 'Antitrust: Commission Fines Qualcomm €997 Million for Abuse of Dominant Market Position' [2018], available at <http://europa.eu/rapid/press-release_IP-18-421_en.htm> accessed 8 May 2018.

[31] Part III Legal Basis of the Administrative Penalty and the Decision, NDRC Administrative Penalty Decision [2015] No. 1, available at <http://jjs.ndrc.gov.cn/fjgld/201503/t20150302_666170.html> accessed 8 May 2018.

[32] Qualcomm, 'Qualcomm builds momentum in China with Oppo licensing agreement' [2016], available at <https://www.qualcomm.com/news/onq/2016/07/31/qualcomm-builds-momentum-china-oppo-licensing-agreement> accessed 8 May 2018.

[33] Qualcomm, 'Qualcomm Signs 3G/4G China Patent License Agreement with Gionee—10 of the top 10 largest Chinese OEMs have accepted NDRC terms' [2016], available at <https://www.

patent infringement litigations, invalidity proceedings, and other related litigations in China, Germany, France, and the US, Qualcomm and Meizu still settled in the end, reaching a patent licence agreement whereby Qualcomm would grant Meizu a worldwide royalty-bearing patent licence, which is consistent with remedies submitted by Qualcomm to the NDRC.[34]

5.2 MOFCOM

Ever since implementation of the AML in August 2008, the MOFCOM has conditionally cleared thirty-six concentrations, fourteen among which involved IP.[35] Remedies in relation to IP can be classified into four categories: (1) requiring undertakings concerned to stick to fair, reasonable, and non-discriminatory ('**FRAND**') commitments already made to the standard setting organization ('**SSO**'); (2) ordering the licensor not to apply for SEP injunctions against potential licensee with goodwill; (3) prohibiting SEP licensor from making acceptance of non-SEP by the licensee as the pre-condition; and (4) requiring the SEP assignee to continue to abide by commitments already made by the SEP assignor to SSOs and the MOFCOM, or else transfer of SEP shall not be undertaken.[36] Below, four typical concentrations in this regard would be further analysed.

5.2.1 Conditional clearance of Bayer's acquisition of Monsanto

On 5 December 2016, MOFCOM received notification from Bayer Aktiengesellschaft Kwa Investment Co. ('**Bayer**') of its acquisition of Monsanto Company ('**Monsanto**').[37] MOFCOM defined non-selective herbicide, vegetable seed, corn seed sterilization coating agent, corn seed insecticide coating agent, hybrid corn seed, trait of different crops, and digital agriculture as relevant product markets. As for non-selective herbicides, vegetable seed, corn seed sterilization coating agent, corn seed insecticide coating agent, and hybrid corn seed, the relevant

---

qualcomm.com/news/releases/2016/12/26/qualcomm-signs-3g4g-china-patent-license-agreement-gionee> accessed 8 May 2018.

[34] Qualcomm, 'Qualcomm and Meizu Sign 3G/4G Global Patent License Agreement - Agreement Resolves All Patent Disputes Between the Companies' [2016], available at <https://www.qualcomm.com/news/releases/2016/12/30/qualcomm-and-meizu-sign-3g4g-global-patent-license-agreement> accessed 8 May 2018.

[35] Anti-Monopoly Bureau under the MOFCOM, 'Notice and Announcement', available at <http://fldj.mofcom.gov.cn/article/ztxx/> accessed 8 May 2018.

[36] Speech delivered by ex-Director General, Mr. Ming Shang, of the Anti-Monopoly Bureau under the MOFCOM during the 4th 'China Competition Policy Forum' and the International Symposium on Intellectual Property and Anti-Trust in October 2015.

[37] MOFCOM Announcement No. 31 of 2018 on Anti-Monopoly Review Decision concerning the Conditional Approval of Concentration of Undertakings in the Case of Acquisition of Equity Interests of Monsanto Company by Bayer Aktiengesellschaft Kwa Investment Co. ('**MOFCOM Announcement No. 31 of 2018**'), available at <http://fldj.mofcom.gov.cn/article/ztxx/201803/20180302719123.shtml> accessed 8 May 2018.

geographical market is China, while the relevant geographical market for trait of different crops and digital agriculture is the global market.[38] MOFCOM found that the concentration would eliminate or restrict competition in the Chinese non-selective herbicide market, Chinese long-day onion seed market, Chinese carrot seed sales market after cutting and machining, Chinese fruit tomato seed market, international corn, soybean, cotton, and rape trait market, and international digital agriculture market.[39]

In the end, MOFCOM required Bayer, Monsanto, and the new undertaking to be established ('**New Undertaking**') to perform the following obligations:[40]

(a) To divest Bayer's vegetable seed business on a global scale, including relevant facilities, personnel, IP (patent, know-how and trademark), and other tangible and intangible assets;
(b) To divest Bayer's non-selective herbicide business (glufosinate-ammonium business) on a global scale, including relevant facilities, personnel, IP (patent, know-how and trademark), and other tangible and intangible assets;
(c) To divest Bayer's corn, soybean, cotton, and rape's trait business on a global scale, including relevant facilities, personnel, IP (patent, know-how, and trademark), and other tangible and intangible assets; and
(d) Within five years ever since Bayer, Monsanto, and the New Undertaking's commercialized digital agricultural products enter the Chinese market, to permit digital agricultural software applications developed by all the Chinese digital agricultural software application developers to connect to Bayer, Monsanto and the New Undertaking's digital agricultural platforms applied in China in accordance with FRAND provisions, and to permit all the Chinese users to register so as to make use of Bayer, Monsanto, and the New Undertaking's digital agricultural products or applications.

5.2.2 *Conditional clearance of Nokia's acquisition of Alcatel Lucent*

On 21 April 2015, Nokia Oyj ('**Nokia**') notified to MOFCOM for its acquisition of Alcatel Lucent with EUR 15.6 billion.[41] On 15 April 2015, both parties entered into a memorandum of understanding ('**MOU**'). In accordance with the MOU, the transaction would be completed through public offer in both French and American stock exchanges. After the transaction, Nokia would hold 100 per cent of shares in Alcatel Lucent, while previous shareholders of Alcatel Lucent

[38] Part III Relevant Markets, MOFCOM Announcement No. 31 of 2018.
[39] Part IV Competitive Analysis, MOFCOM Announcement No. 31 of 2018.
[40] Part VI Decisions, MOFCOM Announcement No. 31 of 2018.
[41] MOFCOM Announcement No. 44 of 2015 on Anti-Monopoly Review Decision concerning the Conditional Approval of Concentration of Undertakings in the Case of Acquisition of Alcatel Lucent by Nokia Oyj ('**MOFCOM Announcement No. 44 of 2015**'), available at <http://fldj.mofcom.gov.cn/article/ztxx/201510/20151001139743.shtml> accessed 8 May 2018.

would hold 33.5 per cent of shares in the new undertaking to be established.[42] The investigation showed that Nokia and Alcatel Lucent had horizontal overlap in wireless communications network equipment and services markets. Wireless communications network equipment could further be divided into radio access network ('**RAN**') and core network systems ('**CNS**').[43] After investigation and analysis, the MOFCOM found that the acquisition would eliminate or restrict competition in the Chinese wireless communications SEP licence market.[44]

The MOFCOM accepted commitments proposed by Nokia and required Nokia to abide by the commitments under its supervision. To be more specific, as for 2G, 3G, and 4G cellular communications SEPs already obtained by Nokia on the closing day of the acquisition, including Alcatel Lucent's 2G, 3G, and 4G cellular communications SEPs:[45]

(a) Nokia confirms to support the following principle: on condition of equality, Nokia shall not apply for SEPs injunction to prohibit implementation of FRAND standards, unless the licensor has already offered FRAND license conditions, while potential licensees do not have the good will to sign and observe the FRAND license provisions. In determining whether the licensor or the licensee is with good will or not, one element is advised to be taken into account: without undue delay, one party is willing to initiate the dispute in relation to whether license conditions put forward by Nokia is consistent with the FRAND commitment to an independent adjudicator reasonably accepted by both parties, to be bound by the decision made by the adjudicator, sign FRAND license agreement in accordance with the decision and pay for compensations and FRAND license fees which might be required by the decision and agreement.

(b) When transferring SEPs to third parties in the future, Nokia shall keep Chinese licensees and other Chinese companies who are during active negotiation for the license informed of conditions of the transfer in time, especially detailed information of name and address of the assignee, effective date of the transfer and specific rights which will be transferred. For transfer of certain SPEs to third parties which would significantly affect value of Nokia's SEPs package to be licensed by Nokia to potential Chinese licensees, any Chinese licensee already existed before the transfer is entitled to negotiate for a new royalty rate before the previous (license) agreement would expire. Similarly, for the potential Chinese licensees who will be in negotiation with Nokia during Nokia's transferring certain SEPs to third parties, if the transfer would significantly

---

[42] Part II General Information of the Case, MOFCOM Announcement No. 44 of 2015.
[43] Part III 1 Relevant Product Markets, MOFCOM Announcement No. 44 of 2015.
[44] Part IV Competitive Analysis, MOFCOM Announcement No. 44 of 2015.
[45] Part VI Decisions, MOFCOM Announcement No. 44 of 2015.

affect value of Nokia's SPEs package, Nokia agrees to consider license fees. In order to avoid ambiguity, besides certain SEPs potentially to be transferred, the re-negotiation or new license fees shall also take into account new SEPs to be included in Nokia's SEPs package.

(c) When transferring certain SEPs to new assignees in the future, the new assignees shall continue to abide FRAND commitments already made by Nokia to SSOs. In another word, FRAND obligations shall also be transferred together with certain SEPs to the assignee.

(d) The MOFCOM is entitled to supervise whether Nokia will obey the commitments mentioned above. Nokia shall report to the MOFCOM the performance circumstances of obligations above within forty-five days upon end of each Chinese financial year. The report obligation shall be borne by Nokia from effective date of the decision (19 October 2015) to 18 October 2020.

5.2.3 *Conditional clearance of acquisition by Microsoft of Nokia's devices and services business*

On 13 September 2013, MOFCOM received notification of the acquisition. In accordance with the stock and asset purchase agreement signed between Microsoft International Holdings B.V. ('**Microsoft**') and Nokia Corporation ('**Nokia**') on 2 September 2013,[46] Microsoft would buy out Nokia's devices and services business for EUR 5.44 billion, while Nokia would keep all the patents in relation to communications and smartphones. The target business included all the entities and assets of Nokia's devices and services business department, including mobile phone, intelligent device business, a design team, and sales of Nokia's devices and services production facility, equipment and services, marketing and relevant supporting operation. Devices and services department of Nokia had manufacturing plants of mobile phones and smart phones in China, Korea, Vietnam, Finland, Brazil, Mexico, and other countries. After the transaction, all the manufacturing plants would be transferred to Microsoft, which meant that Nokia would no longer manufacture mobile phones or smart phones by itself.[47]

Microsoft and Nokia are vertically related in many relevant product markets. To be more specific, Microsoft manufactures and supplies the Surface series laptop PC; develops and licences mobile intelligent terminal operating systems, including smart phone operating systems (Windows Phone) and laptop PC operating systems (Windows RT and Windows 8); and develops and licences technology

---

[46] MOFCOM Announcement No. 24 of 2014 on Anti-Monopoly Review Decision concerning the Conditional Approval of Concentration of Undertakings in the Case of Acquisition of Nokia Corporation's Devices & Services Business by Microsoft Corporation ('**MOFCOM Announcement No. 24 of 2014**'), available at <http://fldj.mofcom.gov.cn/article/ztxx/201404/20140400542415.shtml> accessed 8 May 2018.

[47] Part II General Information of the Case, MOFCOM Announcement No. 24 of 2014.

patents in relation to mobile smart terminals. As for Nokia, it not only manufactures and sells functional phones and smart phones, but also obtains huge amount of 2G, 3G, and 4G communications technology patents. In accordance with businesses which were covered by the transaction, the MOFCOM mainly analysed markets of smart phone, mobile intelligent terminal operating system, and patent licence in relation to mobile intelligent terminal. The MOFCOM defined relevant geographical market as China.[48]

MOFCOM found that the vertical relationship between Microsoft's mobile intelligent terminal operating system and Nokia's smart phone would not eliminate or restrict competition. Nevertheless, Microsoft might abuse its dominant market position in Android operating system licence to eliminate or restrict China's smart phone market. Furthermore, the transaction could also trigger Nokia to abuse its communications SEPs.[49] In the end, MOFCOM concluded that the concentration might eliminate or restrict competition in China's smart phone market, and required undertakings concerned with adherence to the following commitments:[50]

Microsoft's commitments:

(a) As for Microsoft's SEPs applied in smart phones, which are essential for industrial standards and would be licensed on FRAND conditions as already committed to SSOs by Microsoft, as of the closing date of this transaction, Microsoft shall continue to obey the principles below:
  i. To continue to abide by commitments already made to the SSOs and license its SEPs under FRAND conditions;
  ii. Not to apply for injunctions or exclusion order against smart phones manufactured by undertakings located in China pertaining to the SEPs mentioned above;
  iii. Not to require the licensee to license its patents back to Microsoft when licensing the SEPs above, unless the licensee possesses patents essential for the same industry; and
  iv. To only transfer SEPs above to the new assignee when the latter agrees to continue to follow the principles above.
  The four principles mentioned above (i–iv) shall be bound by reciprocity principle. That is to say, for a potential licensee, to whom the commitments mentioned above are applicable, if it possesses SEPs which not only have connection with Microsoft's products (such as Windows smart phone) but are also bound by FRAND commitments, it shall also abide by the same principles with respect to the SEPs.
(b) As for 'project patents' (patents licensed by Microsoft under the Android, EAS, RDP and exFAT patent projects, including but not limited to patents listed in Annex 1 and corresponding Chinese patents, '**non-SEPs**'), as of closing date of the concentration, Microsoft shall:

---

[48] Part III Relevant Markets, MOFCOM Announcement No. 24 of 2014.
[49] Part IV Competitive Analysis, MOFCOM Announcement No. 24 of 2014.
[50] Part VI Decisions, MOFCOM Announcement No. 24 of 2014.

    i. Continue to non-exclusively licence the non-SEPs above to smart phone manufacturers located in China under its current Android, EAS, RDP and exFAT project licence, covering smart phones manufactured, used or sold in China;

    ii. When continue to license the non-SEPs above,
- patent royalty rate shall neither be higher than the royalty rate charged by Microsoft before the concentration, nor higher than the royalty rate stipulated by current agreement for current licensees;
- other non-price provisions and conditions shall keep essentially the same after the transaction; within the scope of (b) ii., Microsoft could consider providing more favorable treatment to new or existing licensees because of specific circumstances and market environment.

    iii. Within the five years since effective date of the decision (8 April 2014) to 8 April 2019, not transfer any non-SEPs listed in Annex 1 or Annex 2 to any new assignee. After the five years, Microsoft will transfer its non-SEPs to a new assignee only if the latter agrees with all the licence commitments already made by Microsoft before.

    iv. After the closing day, shall only apply for the non-SEPs injunctions after having confirmed that the potential licensees will have not negotiated with good will. Nevertheless, actions to be taken shall be in line with existing business practice.

(c) Unless otherwise explicitly required by the commitments above, this commitment shall not be understood as requiring Microsoft to licence its patents in a way not consistent with the business practice before Microsoft's acquisition of Nokia's Devices and Services business. To avoid ambiguity, any expression in this paragraph shall not impair or change the validity of the whole commitments.

(d) Except for certain conditions, the commitments mentioned above will be effective for eight years until 8 April 2022.

(e) The MOFCOM is entitled to supervise whether Microsoft will obey the commitments mentioned above.

Nokia's commitments:

(a) Nokia confirms to continue implementing commitments already made to the SSOs, and to license SEPs in accordance with FRAND principles which are in line with the SSOs' IP policy.

(b) Nokia confirms to abide by the following principle: with pre-condition of equity, not to prohibit implementation of the standards with FRAND commitments through applying for injunctions against SEPs, unless the licensor has already provided licence conditions in line with FRAND principle, while the potential licensee does not sign and abide by the FRAND licence provisions with good will.

(c) When deciding whether a licensor or licensee is with goodwill or not, with pre-condition of equity, in line with SSOs' IP policies and constant development of relevant judicial interpretation, one of the elements to be considered could be: without undue delay, one party is willing to initiate the dispute in relation to whether licence conditions put forward by Nokia is consistent with its FRAND commitment to an independent adjudicator reasonably accepted by both parties, to be bound by decisions made by the adjudicator, to sign FRAND licence agreement in accordance with the decision and to pay for compensations and FRAND licence fees which might be required by the decision and agreement.

(d) Under equal condition, Nokia shall continue to abide by FRAND commitments already made to SSOs, licence SEPs in accordance with the SSOs' IP policies, without compelling the licensees to accept Nokia's licence of patents which do not have to abide by FRAND commitments.

(e) Nokia shall transfer SEPs to the new assignee only when the latter agrees to continue to follow the FRAND commitments already made by Nokia to SSOs (reiterated hereby), so as to transfer the FRAND commitments to the new assignee at the same time.

(f) When valuing each FRAND licence, Nokia shall take into consideration of all the elements concerned, including but not limited to patent licence or patent package, licence period, licenced product, business model of selling or distributing these products, standards concerned, adoption scope by the market of the standardization function, agreement structure, any reverse license or other non-currency compensation value, arrangement for fees payment and application scope under any circumstances. After completion of this concentration, unless it is reasonable to make a change due to alteration of the elements above, under equal condition, Nokia shall not deviate from the current FRAND royalty rate of various cellular communications SEPs packages.

(g) The commitments above shall not be understood as would
  i. affect rights and obligations of Nokia beyond the scope of the current FRAND obligations in relation to SEPs;
  ii. restrict Nokia's legitimate rights and interests to license or transfer any of its patents;
  iii. lead to any amendment to agreement between Nokia and any third parties; or
  iv. require Nokia to obtain licence of any technology which is not needed.

(h) (f) is not applicable to any company who claims any patents for mobile communications products or services manufactured, sold, or provided by Nokia, even if Nokia has already made commitments above.
  (i) The MOFCOM is entitled to supervise whether Nokia will obey the commitments mentioned above.

5.2.4 *Conditional clearance of Google's acquisition of Motorola Mobility*

On 30 September 2011, the MOFCOM received notification from Google Inc. ('**Google**') for its acquisition of Motorola Mobility, Inc. ('**Motorola Mobility**').[51] MOFCOM paid much of its attention to the Chinese market, and concluded that the concentration would eliminate or restrict competition in relevant market and required Google to bear the following obligations:[52]

(a) It is in line with the current business practice for Google to license the Android platform on the basis of open-source for free. Nevertheless, this should not

---

[51] MOFCOM Announcement No. 25 of 2012 on Anti-Monopoly Review Decision concerning the Conditional Approval of Concentration of Undertakings in the Case of Acquisition of Motorola Mobility, Inc. by Google Inc. ('**MOFCOM Announcement No. 25 of 2012**'), available at <http://fldj.mofcom.gov.cn/article/ztxx/201205/20120508134324.shtml> accessed 8 May 2018.
[52] Part IV Decisions, MOFCOM Announcement No. 25 of 2012.

affect Google's right to keep close-source or close the source of software (including but not limited to applications offered by the Android platform) in relation to Android platform. This obligation shall neither affect Google's ability to charge for products or services in relation to the Android platform.

(b) Google shall treat all the original device manufacturers non-discriminatorily with respect to the Android platform, which is only applicable to original device manufacturers who have already agreed not to differentiate or derive the Android platform. This obligation is neither applicable to the way for Google to provide, license, or distribute Android platform related products and services (including but not limited to applications offered by the Android platform).

(c) Google shall continue to bear the FRAND commitments already made by Motorola Mobility for its patents.

5.3 Chinese People's Courts

On 6 December 2011, Huawei Technology Co. Ltd. ('**Huawei**') initiated a suit against InterDigital Technology Corporation, InterDigital Communications, Inc., and InterDigital Inc. ('**IDC**') to Shenzhen Intermediate People's Court for abusing its dominant market position in the 3G wireless communications SEPs licence market. To be more specific, compared with royalties of SEPs charged to Apple, Samsung, and other companies,[53] IDC discriminately charged excessively high licence fees to Huawei. Moreover, IDC required Huawei to license its global wide patents to IDC for free, which constituted attaching unreasonable trade conditions. Huawei held that a licence package, consisting of both SEPs and non-SEPs, as well as 2G, 3G, and 4G SEPs, constituted tie-in. During the negotiation, IDC suddenly initiated suits against Huawei in a US federal court and the US International Trade Commission.[54] It could be regarded as refusal to deal. Accordingly, Huawei requested the court to order IDC to cease the excessive high pricing, discriminate pricing, tie-in, attaching unreasonable trading conditions and refusing to deal. In addition, compensation of CNY 20 million was also claimed.

Shenzhen Intermediate People's Court concluded that IDC had abused its dominant market position in each 3G wireless communications SEP licence market, required IDC to stop charging excessive high royalties, and compensate Huawei with CNY 20 million for commercial losses.[55] Nevertheless, the court of first instance did not support the tie-in claim put forward by Huawei with respect to licensing

---

[53] Part VI General Information of the License Agreements between IDC and Apple, Samsung, and the Others, (2013) YUE GAO FA MIN SAN ZHONG ZI No. 305, 8–9.

[54] Part V General Information of License Negotiation between Huawei and IDC, (2013) YUE GAO FA MIN SAN ZHONG ZI No. 305, 5–8.

[55] (2011) SHEN ZHONG FA ZHI MIN CHU ZI No. 857 and (2011) SHEN ZHONG FA ZHI MIN CHU ZI No. 858.

the 2G, 3G, and 4G SEPs, as well as international patents together as a package, but sustained the tie-in of non-SEPs to SEPs. Both Huawei and IDC appealed the judgments of first instance to Guangdong High People's Court, who made the final binding judgments in October 2013, dismissing the appeal and upholding judgments of the court of first instance.[56] The more detailed analysis below is based on the judgments made by the Guangdong High People's Court.

Relevant geographical markets are the US and China. Each SEP licence market under Chinese and American 3G communications technology standards (WCDMA, CDMA2000, and TD-SCDMA) constitutes a separate relevant product market.[57] Taking into consideration the uniqueness and irreplaceability of each SEP within the 3G standard, IDC enjoys 100 per cent of shares in each SEP licence market, so as to have the ability to hinder or affect other business operators from entering the relevant market. The court agrees with Huawei's proposition that IDC has a dominant market position in relevant market.[58] During negotiations of SEP licence, the patentee shall sign and perform the contract in accordance with FRAND principles,[59] since it is the patentee who controls almost all the information in relation to SEP licence while the counterparty knows little in this regard. Irrespective of the terms of a lump sum royalty or patent licence royalty rate, royalties required by IDC to Huawei were excessively higher than those required of Apple, Samsung, and other companies. It constituted both excessive high and discriminative pricing. Since Huawei was always with good will during the negotiation, the reason why IDC initiated lawsuits in the US could be explained by compelling Huawei to accept the excessive high royalties.[60]

Huawei v. IDC is not only the first anti-monopoly civil case almost totally won by the plaintiff, but also the first anti-monopoly lawsuit triggered by SEPs licence. It concerned the most cutting-edge and complicated legal issues and has attracted attention both home and abroad. It is also one of the ten most discussed cases in 2013 among all the cases dealt with by people's courts all across China. Chinese people's courts tried to find a reasonable balance between patent protection and anti-monopoly and explored complicated issues. Even if certain issues remain to be discussed, the judgments made by the Chinese people's courts set up their own trial standards, which is of great significance.

---

[56] (2013) YUE GAO FA MIN SAN ZHONG ZI No. 306 and (2013) YUE GAO FA MIN SAN ZHONG ZI No. 305.

[57] Part II Definition of Relevant Markets, Observations of the Court, (2013) YUE GAO FA MIN SAN ZHONG ZI No. 306, 18–20.

[58] Part III Whether IDC Has Dominant Position in Relevant Markets, Observations of the Court, (2013) YUE GAO FA MIN SAN ZHONG ZI No. 306, 20.

[59] Part IV Whether IDC shall License SEPs to Huawei in Accordance with the FRAND Commitment, (2013) YUE GAO FA MIN SAN ZHONG ZI No. 305, 16.

[60] Part IV Whether IDC Has Abused Its Dominant Market Position, Observations of the Court, (2013) YUE GAO FA MIN SAN ZHONG ZI No. 306, 20–21.

China has gathered certain experience in regulating abuse of IP which might constitute monopoly both in legislation and practice. Some of the cases have also triggered heated discussion all over the world, such as the *Qualcomm* case and the *Huawei v. IDC* case, which corresponds not only with the historical trend that China has become one of the three most influential anti-monopoly jurisdictions all over the world, but also with the increasingly important role played by the Chinese economy.

6. Way Forward

In the last few years we have seen an intense enforcement record of the People's Republic of China Anti-Monopoly Law by the Chinese competition authorities— the Ministry of Commerce, the State Administration for Industry & Commerce, and the National Development and Reform Commission. They actively enforced the AML through voluminous investigations and the courts have issued several thorough and intriguing judgments with respect to AML disputes.

In relation to IP enforcement, all of China's IP laws are being transformed—patent, trademark, and copyright laws—as well as numerous other IP-related regulations, including standards measures; service invention regulations; and regulations related to criminal enforcement. In addition, other more general laws have been amended or are under reform with important implications for global IP enforcement. The civil procedure law was recently amended, with potentially important repercussions for IP rights holders, particularly in terms of provisional measures for trade secrets.

Some of the cases have triggered heated debate all over the world, such as the *Qualcomm* case and the *Huawei v. IDC* case. With the State Council institutional reform, the new State Administration for Market Regulation will be the only competition authority at central level in China, which means that the vagueness in the competence allocation between the previous three competition authorities and other problems brought by institutional arrangement should be solved. Furthermore, since law enforcement responsibilities of trademark and patent shall also be borne by the comprehensive law enforcement team of the State Administration for Market Regulation, we believe that it will be much easier and more efficient for IP-related anti-monopoly and competition-related legislation and enforcement to go hand-in-hand in the future.

2

PATENT TYPE REQUIREMENTS AND PROCEDURE FROM FILING TO GRANTING

Fabio Giacopello

1. Introduction

1.1 Patent Law and related regulations: Historical background

The Patent Law of the People's Republic of China (hereinafter referred to as 'Patent Law') was first adopted at the 4th Meeting of the Standing Committee of the Sixth National People's Congress on 12 March 1984 and came into force on 1 April 1985.

The Patent Law was amended for the first time in accordance with the Decision of the Standing Committee of the Seventh National People's Congress on Amending the Patent Law of the People's Republic of China at its 27th Meeting on 4 September 1992 and took effect on 1 January 1993.

The second amendment came in accordance with the Decision of the Standing Committee of the Ninth National People's Congress on Amending the Patent Law of the People's Republic of China adopted on 25 August 2000 which took effect on 1 July 2001.

The current Patent Law is the result of the third amendment from its first version adopted with the Decision of the Standing Committee of the Eleventh National People's Congress on Amending the Patent Law of the People's Republic of China at its 6th Meeting on 27 December 2008. The newly revised Patent Law came into force on 1 October 2009.[1]

---

[1] According to a notice on SIPO website, available at http://english.sipo.gov.cn/laws/lawsregulations/201012/t20101210_553631.html, the Main Points of Revision to the Patent Law and Its Implementing Regulations are the following: 'The main points of the revision to the patent law include the following: enhance the threshold of patentability; provide regulations on the

The Implementing Regulations to the Patent Law supplement the provisions of the Patent Law and were issued for the first time with the second amendment of the Patent Law in 2001. Recently the Implementing Regulations were amended in 2010 as a consequence of the modifications to the Patent Law.[2]

In addition to the Patent Law and its Implementing Regulations, the patent system is complemented by the Guidelines for Examination of Patents issues by SIPO, which were modified recently in accordance with the amendment to the Patent Law.

1.2 The State Intellectual Property Office and the local Intellectual Property Offices

The intellectual property system in China was developed as a result of the policy of reform and opening-up. With the approval of the State Council, the Patent Office of the People's Republic of China (CPO) was founded in 1980. In 1998, with the restructuring of the government agencies, CPO was renamed State Intellectual Property Office (hereinafter also referred to as 'SIPO') and became a government institution directly under the State Council.

The State Intellectual Property Office consisted of two main bodies: (i) the Patent Administration Department which is in charge of patent examination and granting and (ii) the Board of Review that take care of re-examination and invalidation procedures.

---

protection of genetic resources; improve industrial design system; improve the confidentiality examination system for applications to a foreign country; invalidate the designation of foreign-related patent agencies; increase SIPO's responsibility for the distribution of patent information; endow the rights holders of industrial design the right of offering to sell, introduce a pre-litigation preservation measures, and include the cost of the rights holder incurred for stopping the infringement act to the calculation of damage compensation; codify prior art defense; allow parallel import; provide exceptions of drug and medical apparatus experimentation; improve the compulsory license system, and so on. The main points of revision to the implementing regulations include the following: provide supplementary requirements and detailed specifications for drafting patent application materials; specify the confidentiality examination system for applications to foreign countries; identify the definition of genetic resources, and prescribe on ways of disclosing the origin of genetic resources; enlarge the scope of preliminary examination for patent application; specify the patent right evaluation report system; improve compulsory license system; prescribe in detail the meaning and scope of the act of patent passing off; eliminate the maintenance fee for patent application, fees for requesting suspension of procedures, and some other items of charge; improve the reward and remuneration system for service invention-creations, and introduce the proscription of prioritizing the contracts between entity and the inventor or creator; adjust regulations on international applications entering Chinese national phase'.

[2] The Implementing Regulations to the Patent Law were promulgated by Decree No. 306 of the State Council of the People's Republic of China on 15 June 2001, amended for the first time on 28 December 2002, amended for the second time on 9 January 2010, and effective as of 1 February 2010.

The State Council General Office approved the Regulations of the Main Duties, Internal Structures, and Staff of the State Intellectual Property Office (SIPO) on 11 July 2008. From 28 August 2018, the English name abbreviation of National Intellectual Property Administration, PRC changed from SIPO to CNIPA. Since August 30 2018, the new domain name <english.cnipa.gov.cn> has been officially launched on the government website of the National Intellectual Property Administration, PRC. According to the above-mentioned responsibilities, the State Intellectual Property Office has established seven internal organizations (vice-departmental and ministerial level): (1) Office Department; (2) Treaty and Law Department; (3) Protection Coordination Department; (4) Department of International Cooperation (Hong Kong, Macao, and Taiwan office); (5) Patent Management Department; (6) Plan Development Department; (7) Personnel Department.

As required by the Patent Law,[3] local Intellectual Property Offices (also known as 'Local IPOs') have been set up in thirty-one provinces. Their main responsibility is to resolve in that local area patent disputes in cases of infringement or other malpractice. The local IP administrative authorities have the power of administrative enforcement, and are engaged in disseminating intellectual property information and promoting public awareness, but are not involved in patent examination.

1.3 Accession to international treaties in relation to Patents

The international conventions and treaties acceded by China with respect to those intellectual property rights administered by the SIPO are the following:

- Convention Establishing the World Intellectual Property Organization (3 June 1980)
- Paris Convention for the Protection of Industrial Property (19 March 1985)
- Patent Cooperation Treaty (1 January 1994)
- Budapest Treaty on the International Recognition of the Deposit of Microorganisms for the Purpose of Patent Procedure (1 July 1995)
- Locarno Agreement Establishing an International Classification for Industrial Designs (19 September 1996)
- Strasbourg Agreement Concerning the International Patent Classification (19 June 1997)
- Agreement on Trade-Related Aspects of Intellectual Property Rights (10 December 2001)

---

[3] Available at < http://english.sipo.gov.cn/news/index.htm >.

1.4 Statistics

SIPO received 1,102,000 invention patent applications in 2015, up by 18.7 per cent compared to the previous year, among which the number of domestic invention patent applications was 968,000 accounting for 87.8 per cent of the total, up by 20.9 per cent to the previous year. The number of applications from overseas entities reached 134,000, accounting for 12.2 per cent of the total; an increase of 5.2 per cent compared with the previous year. The number of invention patent applications kept a stable growth rate and the number of annual invention patent applications was greater than one million for the first time.

In 2015, SIPO received 1,128,000 utility model applications, increasing by 29.8 per cent from the previous year; and 569,000 applications for industrial design, up by 0.8 per cent from the previous year.

In 2015, SIPO granted 359,000 invention patents, up by 54.1 per cent from the previous year, among which 263,000 were granted to domestic applicants, accounting for 73.3 per cent of the total, and 96,000 were granted to foreign applicants, accounting for 26.7 per cent.

By the end of 2015, a total of 1,472,000 invention patents granted by SIPO have remained valid, up by 23.1 per cent year on year. Among which, 922,000 were domestic, which accounted for 62.6 per cent, up by 30.1 per cent, while 550,000 were from abroad, which accounted for 37.4 per cent, up by 12.9 per cent.[4]

1.5 Jurisdiction

China's Standing Committee on 31 August 2014 passed the decision which established specialized Intellectual Property ('IP') Courts in Beijing, Shanghai, and Guangzhou. The three cities were selected for a three year trial period, after which the IP Courts might be extended to other cities.

The Supreme People's Court gave implementation to the decision issuing Regulations on Jurisdiction of the IP Courts. By the end of 2014 all three IP courts were established and had started accepting cases.

The IP Courts have jurisdiction over the following cases:

• Civil and administrative judicial cases involving complex technology (e.g. patents, technical trade secrets, computer software, and semiconductor designs);

---

[4] Available at <http://english.sipo.gov.cn/laws/annualreports/2015/201606/P020160603402726016621.pdf>.

- Administrative review judicial cases against decisions regarding copyright, trademarks, and unfair competition made by government agencies of above the county level; and
- Civil judicial cases involving the recognition of well-known marks.

The IP Courts then have jurisdiction over patent litigation and other technology-related IP cases, any IP-related administrative review cases, and the appeal of an IP-infringement decision by a local IPO.

2. Definition and Requirements for Granting Patent

2.1 Invention, utility model, and design

The Chinese Patent Law regulates three types of 'invention-creations':[5] inventions, utility models, and designs. Layout of semiconductors[6] and plant varieties[7] are not included in Patent Law, however they receive protection according to separate legislation.

According to Article 2 of the Patent Law, 'Inventions mean new technical solutions proposed for a product, a process or the improvement thereof. Utility models mean new technical solutions proposed for the shape and structure of a product, or the combination thereof, which are fit for practical use.' Utility model patents may be granted in China—similarly to other legislations—for technical solutions that relate to shapes or structures, but not in relation to the process or methods.

Article 2 of the Patent Law further explains that 'design' in China is 'with respect to a product, new designs of the shape, pattern, or the combination thereof, or the combination of the color with shape and pattern, which are rich in an aesthetic appeal and are fit for industrial application'.

Chinese Patent Law provides for some exclusion from patentability, and particularly under Article 25, for (1) scientific discoveries; (2) rules and methods for intellectual activities; (3) methods for the diagnosis or treatment of diseases; (4) animal or plant varieties; (5) substances obtained by means of nuclear transformation; and

---

[5] The definition 'invention-creations' is provided directly in the Patent Law in Article 2.

[6] The 'Regulations on the Protection of Layout Design of Integrated Circuits' went into effect in China on 1 October 2001.

[7] On 20 March 1997, the State Council promulgated officially the 'Regulations of the People's Republic of China on the Protection of New Varieties of Plants'. The Regulations of plant varieties protection (PVP) conforms to the 1978 Act of the UPOV convention in principal. Thereafter China deposited its instrument officially for accession to the UPOV and became its 39th member state on 23 April 1999. There are two examining and approving authorities for plant variety rights in China, of which one is the Ministry of Agriculture (MOA) and the other, the State Forestry Administration (SFA). MOA and SFA are responsible for examining and granting new variety rights of agricultural plants and forest plants respectively according to the job responsibility.

(6) designs that are mainly used for marking the pattern, colour, or the combination of the two of prints.

In addition Article 5 excludes from patentability invention-creations that violate the social order or harm the public interest, and inventions that are accomplished by relying on genetic resources if these are used in violation of other provisions of law or administrative regulations.

2.2 Duration

According to Article 42 of the Patent Law the duration of the invention patent right is a maximum of twenty years commencing from the date of application. Utility model patent and design patent rights can have maximum duration of ten years from the date of application.

2.3 Conditions for granting invention and utility model patents

In line with international practice Article 22 of the Patent Law provides that inventions and utility models, in order to be granted a valid patent, shall possess novelty, creativity, and practical use.

Novelty 'means that the invention or utility model concerned is not an existing technology; no patent application is filed by unit or an individual for any identical invention with the Patent Administration Department under State Council before the date of the application for patent right and no identical invention or utility model is recorded in the patent application documents or the patent documentations which are published or announced after the date of the application'.

'Existing technologies' mean the technologies known to the public both domestically and abroad before the date of application. The current Patent Law adopts the 'absolute novelty standard' by requiring that the invention must by no means be disclosed or used anywhere in the world, by the same applicant or by others, before the filing date in China, except for certain foreign applications to which the Chinese application claims priority.[8]

In relation to utility models the requirement of the novelty is identical to invention patents in China. In particular, novelty means that, before the date of filing, no identical invention or utility model has been publicly disclosed in publications or has been publicly used or made known to the public anywhere in the world. Furthermore, there should be no other earlier-filed Chinese applications which

---

[8] Differently, under the previous Patent Law (2001), novelty was not destroyed if an invention had already been used in foreign countries, as long as it had not been used in China or published anywhere in the world before its filing in China.

describe the identical invention or utility model, even if the publication date thereof is after the date of filing of the present case.

Article 22 of the PRC Patent Law defines inventiveness in invention patents as prominent substantive features that represent 'notable progress' as compared to technology existing before the date of filing. Inventiveness means that, compared with the existing technologies, the invention possesses prominent substantive features and indicates remarkable advancements.

The requirement for inventive step in Utility Model in China is lower than that of invention patent. For utility models, only substantive features that represent 'progress' are required for inventive step.

Practical use means that the said invention or utility model can be used for production or be utilized in production.

2.4 Conditions for granting a design patent

In contrast with other countries, protection of new ornamental shapes is regulated within the framework of Patent Law and administered by the State Intellectual Property Office. According to Article 23 of the Patent Law, a design for which the patent right is granted is not an existing design, and no application is filed by any unit or individual for any identical design with the patent administration department under the State Council before the date of application for patent right, and no identical design is recorded in the patent documentations announced after the date of application. Designs for which the patent right is to be granted shall be ones which are distinctly different from the existing designs or the combinations of the features of existing designs. Designs for which a patent right is granted shall be ones which are not in conflict with the lawful rights acquired by others prior to the date of application. For the purposes of this Law, existing designs mean designs that are known to the public both domestically and abroad before the date of application.

2.5 Coexistence between utility model patent and application for invention patent

Despite the general rule fixed in Article 9 of the Patent Law that 'only one patent can be granted for the same invention', the same applicant can apply for a utility model patent and an invention patent with regard to the same invention on the same day. In this case, the utility model will probably be granted first and in order to avoid double patenting the applicant shall renounce the utility model so that the invention patent may be granted.

Based on this exception it is possible to first obtain protection with a utility model and later with an invention patent, waiving the utility model at the moment the invention patent is granted.

2.6 Co-ownership of the invention

Article 8 of the Chinese Patent Law regulates two main circumstances. Firstly where two entities, companies, or individual organizations achieve an invention through working together and secondly, where one entity achieves an invention-creation by entrustment of another entity. In the first circumstance, the right to apply for the patent shall be vested in all the entities that collaborated to reach the invention-creation, while in the second case the right to apply for the patent belongs to the entrusted entity. In both cases an agreement between the parties can modify the general rule.

Co-owned patents can be exploited by each of the co-owners separately, directly, or via ordinary licence agreement. In such cases the royalties shall be shared with the other co-owners. Nevertheless it is possible to regulate the exploitation in a different way by contract and if the contract exists, it prevails.

In case of lack of contractual regulation between co-owners, except from the above mentioned cases of direct exploitation by the co-owner and ordinary licence exercise, the exercise of the patent rights shall be subject to the consent of all the co-owners.

2.7 Employees' inventions

Employment invention-creations belong to the employer that has the right to apply for the patent and will be the owner of the patent once it is granted (Article 6 of the Patent Law). Employment invention-creations are those achieved in the course of performing the duties of an employee and those obtained mainly by using the material and technical conditions of an employer. However, for a non-employment invention-creation, the employee has the right to apply for the patent and once granted, the employee will be the patentee. Nevertheless, the parties can reach a different agreement regulating the ownership of the invention and eventually the patent.

The Implementing Regulations allow employer and employee to agree upon the standard for the reward. Alternatively, the employer may set forth the rules for such a reward in its internal regulations and policies. If employer and employee have not derogated via a private agreement or via the acceptance of the company policy, the default rule applies, according to which, the employer must (i) reward the employee at least RMB 3,000 for each invention patent, and at least RMB 1,000 for each utility model patent or design patent; (ii) remunerate annually the employee no less than 2 per cent of its business profits derived from the exploitation of the patent for an invention patent or a utility model patent, or no less than 0.2 per cent for a design patent; and (iii) pay no less than 10 per cent of the royalty to the employee when the employer licenses the patent to a third party.

2.8 Right to be named inventor

According to Article 17 of the Patent Law, an inventor has the right to be named as inventor or designer in the patent documents. Such a right cannot be waived with a contract.

2.9 Transfer, licence, and pledge

In order to transfer a granted patent or patent application, a written contract shall be concluded and such contract shall be recorded with the SIPO (Article 10 of the Patent Law). The transfer became effective from the date of recordation with SIPO.

After the granting, whoever wants to exploit a patent shall obtain authorization from the patent owner and sign a contract (Article 12 of the Patent Law). The licensee can be required to pay royalties for the exploitation of the patented invention-creation. According to Rule 14 of the Implementing Regulation to the Patent Law, the licence contract shall be recorded with SIPO within three months from the date in which it becomes effective.

Similarly, still in compliance with Rule 14 of the Implementing Regulation to the Patent Law, in case of pledge the pledger and pledgee shall undergo the recordation procedure with SIPO.

2.10 Compulsory licence

The Chinese Patent Law provides for several circumstances in which the SIPO can decide to grant a compulsory licence in relation to a granted patent. In particular Chapter VI of the Patent Law regulates 5 different cases.

Insufficient exploitation. Art. 48.1 of the Patent Law provides that after three years the patent is granted and four years after the patent is filed, a compulsory licence can be granted if the patentee fails to have the patent exploited without legitimate reasons. Rule 73 of the Implementing Regulations to Patent Law clarifies that 'insufficient exploitation' happens when the patentee fails to meet the demand for the domestic market.

Monopoly. Art. 48.2 provides that a compulsory license can be granted when the exercise of the patent is confirmed as monopoly and its negative impact on competition needs to be reduced or eliminated.

National Emergency. According to Art. 49 of the Patent Law, where a national emergency or any extraordinary state of affairs or public interest so requires, SIPO can grant a compulsory license for the exploitation of patent for invention, utility model, or design.

Public Health. According to Art. 50—for the benefit of public health—SIPO can grant a compulsory license for the manufacture and the export of a drug to countries or regions to conform to provisions of relevant international treaties to which China has acceded.

Dependent patent. Under Art. 51 of the Patent Law, when an invention or utility model, for which a patent has been obtained, represents a *major technical advancement* and the exploitation of the former implies the exploitation of the latter, the SIPO can grant a compulsory license.

In addition to the cases above, according to Article 14 of the Patent Law, a patent for invention owned by a State Owned Enterprise which is of great significance to public interest, can be widely applied and licensed to designated entities. In such cases the state-owned company will receive royalties from the designated entities.

2.11 Foreign applicant filing patent in China

There are several ways for a foreign applicant to obtain patent protection in China. According to Article 18 of the Patent Law, when a foreign applicant files a patent application for registration in China it shall be treated in accordance with the international treaties or agreements to which both China and the country of origin of the applicant have agreed or in accordance with the principle of reciprocity.

When a foreign entity, individual, or company wishes to apply for a patent in China it shall entrust a local patent agency to handle the patent matters. According to Article 20 of the Patent Law, among other obligations, the patent agency shall keep confidential the content of the inventions, unless the patent applications were published or announced.

From a procedural perspective, the foreign applicant can choose to file a patent firstly in China or to extend to China a patent already filed abroad. In the latter case the foreign applicant can enjoy the one year priority right under the Paris Convention or can obtain protection in China via a Patent Cooperation Treaty application which allows the applicant a thirty-month delay (or thirty-two-month delay with the payment of additional fees) in entering into the national phase.

2.12 Chinese applicant filing patent abroad—National security scrutiny

A Chinese individual, entity, or company may file for patent in foreign countries in accordance with the international treaties to which China has acceded (Article 20 of the Patent Law). SIPO will handle international patent applications in accordance with the relevant international treaties to which China has acceded and the relevant provisions of this law and regulations of the State Council.

In case the applicant wants to first file abroad and not in China for an invention or utility model created in China, it must submit the matter to SIPO in advance for confidentiality examination. In case the applicant violates Article 20, SIPO may subsequently—if and when the patent will be filed in China—not grant the patent or obtain its invalidation.

As far as the procedure for obtaining clearance, the Implementing Regulations clarify that the SIPO must decide as soon as possible after receipt of the application for confidentiality examination, whether national security issues or other significant national interests are involved and whether a further examination is necessary. If the applicant does not receive any notice from the SIPO regarding further examination within four months after filing the application for the confidentiality examination, the applicant is free to proceed to foreign patent filing.

If further examination is deemed necessary by the SIPO, a notification to the applicant shall be promptly sent. If the applicant does not receive a denial notice from the SIPO within six months after filing the application for the confidentiality examination, it is also free to carry out patent filings in foreign countries.

Where the patent is filed in China first, the request for confidentiality examination shall be filed at the same time of filing the application. If an applicant for a patent in China later files a PCT application—using SIPO as National Office—the national security scrutiny is performed automatically.

2.13 Scope of protection

Article 11 of the Patent Law provides that in relation to inventions and utility models, the owner can—from the moment in which the patent is granted—prohibit the exploitation of the patent and namely nobody can 'for production or business purposes, manufacture, use, offer to sell, sell, or import the patented products, use the patented method, or use, offer to sell, sell or import the products that are developed directly through the use of the patented method'.

In relation to a design patent right—once it is granted–the owner can prohibit anyone from exploiting the patent, 'i.e., it or he may not, for production or business purposes, manufacture, offer to sell, sell or import the design patent products'.

In addition to what is mentioned above, Article 13 provides that—after the patent is published—the applicant may require the unit or individual to pay an appropriate amount of royalties for exploitation of the patent, but cannot refrain others from using the patent until it is granted for protection.

3. Procedure from Filing to Granting Patent

3.1 Patent application: invention and utility model

In accordance with Article 26 of the Patent Law, the application for obtaining a patent for invention or utility model shall be made in writing and consist of a request, description, abstract, and claim. An application for an invention patent or utility model patent shall be limited to one invention or utility model.

An application for a design patent shall be limited to one design (Article 31 of the Patent Law). Notwithstanding such a general rule, multiple similar designs of the same product, no more than ten, may be used in one application for design patent.

Two or more designs of 'products of the same kind that are sold or used in sets,' as referred to in Article 31, paragraph 2 of the Patent Law, may also be used within one application. Products in sets often belong in the same general class, with the design of each product having the same design concept.

Rule 17 of the Implementing Regulations further clarifies the requirements of the request for patent application. Such request shall contain the following items:

- The title;
- Exact identification of the applicant via indication of the name, address, organization, post code, ID number, nationality;
- Name of the inventor or designer;
- The patent agency name, code, licence number and contact telephone number of the patent attorney appointed by the patent agency;
- Where the priority of an earlier application is claimed, the date and number of application of the prior application, as well as the name of the competent authority with which the application was filed;
- The signature or seal of the applicant or the patent agency;
- A list of application documents;
- A list of the documents appending to the application; and
- Any other relevant items which need to be indicated as per specific regulations.

The description of an application for an invention patent or utility model shall state the title and include the following items: technical field; background art, contents of the invention, description of figures, mode of carrying out the invention, or utility model.

Where an application for an invention patent contains disclosure of one or more nucleotide and/or amino acid sequences, the description shall contain a sequence listing in compliance with the standard prescribed by SIPO.

The description of the utility model for which a patent is applied for, shall contain drawings indicating the shape, structure, or their combination of the product for which protection is sought.

According to Rule 18 of the Implementing Regulations, the drawings of the invention or utility model shall be numbered and reference signs shall be used consistently throughout the application document. Reference signs not mentioned in the description shall not appear in the drawings and—vice versa—reference signs not mentioned in the drawings shall not appear in the description. In addition, the drawings shall not contain explanatory notes, except if indispensable.

Rule 19 of the Implementing Regulations clarifies that claims shall state the technical features of the invention or utility model. The patent application may contain independent claim or claims and also contain dependent claims (Article 20 of the Implementing Regulations). The dependent claim shall, by additional technical features, further define the claim which it refers to.

Claims shall be numbered consecutively and might contain chemical or mathematical formulae but no drawings. The technical terminology used in the claims shall be consistent with that used in the description and, in order to facilitate, make reference to the corresponding reference signs in the drawings of the description. Such reference signs shall not be construed as limiting the claims.

According to the most common practice Rule 21 of the Implementing Regulations provides that an independent claim of an invention or utility model shall contain a preamble portion and a characterizing portion. Those features, in combination with the features stated in the preamble portion, serve to define the scope of protection of the invention or utility model. Nevertheless such drafting methods can be waived where they are inappropriate due to the nature of the invention or utility model.

The abstract shall consist of a summary of the disclosure as contained in the application for the invention patent or utility model. The summary shall indicate the title of the invention or utility model, and the technical field to which the invention or utility model pertains, and shall be drafted in a way which allows for a clear understanding of the technical problem, the gist of the technical solution of that problem, and the principal use or uses of the invention or utility model.

Where an invention concerns a new biological material which cannot be described in a way to enable the exploitation by a person skilled in the art, the applicant shall, in addition to the other requirements, deposit a sample of the biological material with a depositary institution and submit a receipt and the viability proof. Moreover the applicant must provide in the application, relevant information of the characteristics of the biological material and indicate the scientific name (with its Latin name) and the title and address of the depositary institution, the date on which the sample of the biological material was deposited, and the accession number of the deposit.

When applying for a design patent, the applicant shall submit written request, drawings, or pictures of the design, a brief description of the design and other relevant documents. Drawings or pictures shall be clear enough to show the product for which protection is sought.

3.2 Convention priority (Article 29)

As indicated previously, China acceded to the Paris Convention; therefore both foreign and Chinese applicants may enjoy the so called Convention priority. According to Article 29 of the Patent Law: 'If, within twelve months from the date the applicant first files an application for an invention or utility model patent in a foreign country, or within six months from the date the applicant first files an application for a design patent in a foreign country, he files an application for a patent in China for the same subject matter, he may enjoy the right of priority in accordance with the agreements concluded between the said foreign country and China, or in accordance with the international treaties to which both countries have acceded, or on the principle of mutual recognition of the right of priority. If, within twelve months from the date the applicant first files an application for an invention or utility model patent in China, he files an application for a patent with the patent administration department under the State Council for the same subject matter, the applicant may enjoy the right of priority'.

3.3 Grace period

The grace period is provided for in Article 24 of the Patent Law. According to this article, an application for invention, utility model, or design does not lose its novelty if within six months before the date of application any of the following events occur:

i) It is exhibited for the first time at an international exhibition sponsored or recognized by the Chinese government. Under Article 30 of the Implementing Regulations, an international exhibition sponsored or recognized by the Chinese government refers to the international exhibitions registered or recognized by the Bureau of International Exposition (BIE) as prescribed by the Convention Relating to International Exhibitions.

ii) It is published for the first time at a specified academic or technological conference. Under Article 30 of the Implementing Regulations, an academic or technological conference refers to any academic or technological meeting organized by a competent department concerned under the State Council or by a national academic or technological association.

iii) The content of the invention-creation is divulged by others without the consent of the applicant.

3.4 Amendments

Under Article 33, an applicant on its own initiative can amend the patent application, provided that the amendment to the application documents does not exceed the scope of the original description and claims. Similarly the amendment to the design patent application must not exceed the scope of the original drawings or pictures.

In regards to time and procedure, Rule 51 of the Implementing Regulations states that such amendments can be requested 'when a request for examination as to substance is made or when a response is made in regard to the first office action'. Besides, for a patent application for invention, the request for substantive examination is filed at the same time when filing the application, the applicant will be given a three-month period from the date of receiving the 'Notice of Entering Substantive Examination' to make voluntary amendment.

For patent application for utility model or design, the request of amendments shall be filed with SIPO 'within two months from the date of filing'.

3.5 Withdrawal of the application

Article 32 of the Patent Law provides that an applicant may withdraw his patent application any time before the patent is granted.

3.6 Preliminary examination

Once the SIPO receives an application for a patent, it shall notify the applicant of the filing date and application number (Rule 38 of the Implementing Regulations). According to practice it is usually referred as preliminary examination phase the one going from the application to the publication which occur eighteen months after the application is file, unless the applicant requires an earlier publication.

During the preliminary examination phase of the invention patent SIPO will check if all the required documents are included in the application, if all documents were submitted in a timely manner and if the application fees were paid correctly. The applicant then has an opportunity to correct any problems identified by the examiner. If the applicant is unable to overcome the problems, the application is rejected.

For utility model and design patent applications, the preliminary examination is the only examination process required. Besides the formality check which is same for invention patents, in utility model and design patents the examiner will check the existence of novelty and reject the applications where the novelty requirement is found lacking.

3.7 Publication and granting of utility model and design

In contrast to invention patent applications; utility model and design patent applications only pass the preliminary examination phase before publication and granting. Indeed according to Article 40 of the Patent Law, if no reason for refusal is found during the preliminary examination, the utility model and design shall be published and granted for protection from the date of application.

3.8 Substantive examination

The applicant of an invention patent shall file a request for substantive examination at any time within three years from the application date. If the applicant fails to file such a request within the due time without any good reason, the application is deemed to have been withdrawn (Article 35 of the Patent Law). The purpose of substantive examination is to determine the patentability of an invention, based on novelty, inventiveness, and practical applicability.

3.9 Office action

If during examination it is found that the application does not conform to the requirements provided by the Patent Law, SIPO shall notify the applicant requesting explanations and/or amendments within a certain time frame. If the applicant does not reply to the office action, the patent application will be deemed withdrawn. If the reply is not satisfactory, the patent will be rejected.

3.10 Patent Prosecution Highway and accelerated examination

Where SIPO has signed a bilateral or multi-lateral agreement with a patent authority of a country that includes prioritized or accelerated procedures, such agreements are to take precedence before the above scheme. For example, SIPO has agreements with a number of countries (Japan, Korea, US, Germany, and Russia) under the pilot Patent Prosecution Highway (PPH) scheme.

With Administrative Measures issued on 19 June 2012 and coming into effect on 1 August 2012, the SIPO has introduced a fast track system for the examination procedure of patent applications in China.

Such accelerated processes are only allowed for certain types of patents:

- Important applications relating to energy conservation and environment protection, new generation information technology, biology, high end equipment manufacture, new materials, and new energy automobiles;
- Important applications promoting the development of green technologies, such as those relating to low carbon emission and conservation of resources;
- Applications for the same invention first filed in China and then in other countries or regions; and
- Other applications which materially affect national or public interests and require prioritized examination.

3.11 Publication and granting

If the reply is satisfactory or no office actions were ever issued, the patent will be granted, the certificate issued, recordation will occur and an announcement will be made.

3.12 Re-examination

If the applicant is dissatisfied with the decision made on rejecting the application, he may, within three months from the date of receipt of the notification, file a request with the patent review board for review. If the patent applicant is dissatisfied with the review decision made by the patent review board, he may take legal action before the People's Court within three months from the date of receipt of the notification. Currently the competent Court to decide cases against the PRB is the Beijing IP Court.

3.13 Termination

According to Article 44 of the Patent Law, the patent right is terminated if the patentee fails to pay the annual fee or waives the patent right by written declaration. In addition the earlier termination can be due to invalidation under Article 45 of the Patent Law.

If a patent right is terminated before the duration expires, the patent administration department shall register and announce such termination.

3.14 Invalidation

Starting from the date the patent administration department announces the grant of a patent right, anyone who believes that a patent does not possess the requirements for granting and does not conform to the relevant provisions of the Patent Law, may file an invalidation request with the patent review board (Article 45 of the Patent Law).

The patent review board will examine the request and make a timely decision. Both the applicant and the patentee will be notified of the decision made to invalidate the patent right. The decision on declaring a patent right invalid will be registered and announced by the patent administration department (Article 46 of the Patent Law).

If dissatisfied with the patent review board's decision, the person who initiated the invalidation or the patentee, may take legal action before a people's court. This must be undertaken within three months from receipt of the invalidation notification.

The patent which is declared invalid will be deemed as non-existent from the beginning. The decision on declaring a patent right invalid shall have no retroactive effect on any written judgment or written mediation already issued and executed. However, compensation shall be made for any loss caused to another person mala fides by the patentee.

3

PATENT LITIGATION IN CHINA

Alan Xu

1. Status of Patent Lawsuits in China

Chinese patent law was first enacted in 1984 when China adopted the national policy of reform and opening-up. Most of the terms, concepts, and principles under the patent law were directly transplanted from Western countries and were adapted to China's special national conditions.

As Figure 3.1 shows below,[1] the number of patent litigations filed from 2009 to 2014 has been increasing, reaching a peak in 2012–19: 680 patent cases were filed in the latter year which is almost double the number of patent cases filed in the United States[2] in 2012. Thus China has become the global leader in patent litigation. Considering that Chinese patent law was only implemented in 1984, these filing numbers are remarkable achievements and indicate that patents are playing an increasingly important role in market competition.

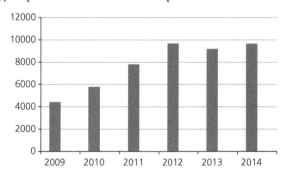

Figure 3.1 Patent lawsuits filed from 2009 to 2014

---

[1] The numbers were excerpted from *Intellectual Property Protection by Chinese Courts (2009–2013)* and *Intellectual Property Protection by Chinese Courts (2014)*.
[2] Brian Love, Christine Helmers, and Markus Eberhardt, *Patent Litigation in China: Protecting Rights or the Local Economy?* (comparing the number of patent suits filed in China and the US), available at http://digitalcommons.law.scu.edu/cgi/viewcontent.cgi?article=1920&context=facpubs.

However, as Figure 3.2 suggests,[3] most of the patent lawsuits from 2013 to 2015 were involved with design patents, which accounted for almost 2,755 cases, while only 603 patent cases were related to inventions. This phenomenon is consistent with the current situation that most of the patent infringement cases in China are to fight against counterfeits that directly copy the patentee's products.

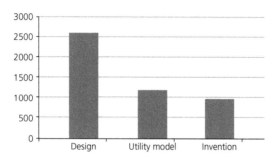

Figure 3.2 Patent lawsuits adjudicated from 2013 to 2015

For all patent litigations from 2013 to 2015, 234 cases involved international companies, which accounted for almost 5 per cent of all the patent lawsuits.

As we can see from Figure 3.3 above, when it came to patent lawsuits with international companies, most of the litigious disputes were about inventions, with a percentage of 56 per cent. This is also consistent with the current situation, that international companies are having more technical advantages than their Chinese competitors.

Figure 3.3 Patent litigations involved with international companies

2. Legal Framework of Chinese Patent Infringement System

2.1 Claim interpretation

It cannot be overstated that in patent law, 'the name of the game is the claim'.[4] Patent claims are the touchstones of patent protection, what is often referred to as

---

[3] Cao Jingtao and Li Hui, *Analysis for the Adjudicated Cases of Patent Litigation Involved with International Company (2013–2015)*, available at http://www.zhichanli.com/article/28953.
[4] Giles S. Rich, *The Extent of the Protection and Interpretation of Claims—American Perspectives*, 21 INTERNATIONAL REV, INDUS.PROP. & COPYRIGHT L. 497,499,501 (1990).

the 'metes and bounds' of the patentee's protected interest. Claims are comprised of words, and the words must be given meaning (or interpreted). Therefore, patent claim interpretation is the first step for the analysis of patent infringement—to identify the scope of patent rights.

2.1.1 Who is the interpreter?

When it comes to claim interpretation, the first question is who is the interpreter? Just like the methods for examining novelty and inventive step, claim terms shall be interpreted from the perspective of the hypothetical person having ordinary skilled in the art, rather than a judge or technical expert. The general rule is that claim terms are assigned their ordinary and customary meaning to the person skilled in the art.

2.1.2 Evidence for the interpretation

Article 59 of the Patent Law provides that 'The scope of protection of the patent right for an invention or utility model shall be determined by the terms of the claims. The description and the appended drawings may be used to interpret the claims.' The second part of Article 59 emphasizes the importance of description and drawings in interpreting the claims. Actually it's widely recognized by the courts that there are two different types of interpretive evidence: intrinsic and extrinsic. The former comprises of the claims, specification, and prosecution history; the latter includes such things as expert testimony, dictionaries, and treatises, all of which are external to the patent documents.[5]

2.2 Standard of determining patent infringement—All elements rule

Before the judicial interpretation was enacted in 2009 (below), many scholars argued that Article 59 provided evidence that China had adopted the all elements rule. As a matter of fact, the all elements rule was judge-made law. In 2001, the Supreme Court published a draft of judicial interpretation, recommending applying the all elements rule for the trials of patent infringement cases. In 2002 the all elements rule was first used and explained by Qingdao Intermediate People's Court and Shandong High People's Court.[6] The courts held that after determining the scope of patent protection, to decide whether there was a patent infringement or not, all the elements of the patent claims should be compared with the technical features of the accused product. From then on more and more courts invoked the all elements rule to analyse patent infringement.

---

[5] *Shenzhen Blue Eagle Hardware and Plastics Co., Ltd. v Luo Shizhong* (Case Number: (2011) Min Ti Zi No. 248).

[6] *Qingdao Gold Shield Electrically Operated Door Co., Ltd. v Beijing Hanweida Transportation Equipment Co., Ltd., et al* (Case numbers: (2002) Qin Zhi Chu Zi No. 3).

In 2009, in order to avoid ambiguity, the Chinese Supreme Court promulgated *Interpretation of the Supreme People's Court on Several Issues concerning the Application of Law in the Trial of Patent Infringement Dispute Cases*, Article 7 of which states:

> When determining whether the alleged infringing technical solution falls into the scope of protection of a patent, the people's court shall examine all the technical features described in the claim asserted by a right holder.
>
> Where the alleged infringing technical solution contains technical features identical or equivalent to all the technical features described in a claim, the people's court shall determine that it falls into the scope of protection of the patent; or where, compared with all the technical features described in a claim, the technical features of the alleged infringing technical solution are lack of more than one technical feature as described in the claim or contain more than one technical feature which is neither identical nor equivalent to any technical feature as described in the claim, the people's court shall determine that it does not fall into the scope of protection of the patent.

Article 7 above is very clear that the all elements rule has been officially established as the applicable law when determining patent infringement. If one or more elements cannot be found in the accused infringing product/process, there shall be no patent infringement.

And it should be pointed out that the all elements rule is not only applicable for literal infringement but also the basic principle for the analysis of infringement under the doctrine of equivalents.[7]

2.2.1 Literal infringement

Literal infringement is found where the accused subject matter (product/process) falls precisely within the express boundaries of the claims. In other word, to establish literal infringement all the identical technical features of the claims shall be present in the accused product/process.[8]

One might expect instances of literal infringement to be relatively rare, assuming that patent claims provide clear, advance notice to competitors of what is and is not permissible imitation. However, in practice, examples of literal infringement are quite common. This follows from the uncertainty of claim interpretation, i.e. the ambiguity of the literal scope of the claims. The meanings of one or more terms contained in the claims are hotly disputed in practically every patent infringement case.

---

[7] *Chengdu Youta Pharmaceutical Co., Ltd. v Jiangsu Wanggao Pharmaceutical Co., Ltd., et al* (Case Number: (2010) Min Ti Zi No. 158).

[8] *Beijing Power Machineries Institute v Zhongshan Vatti Gas Appliance Stock Co., Ltd.* (Case Number: (2011) Gao Min Zhong Zi No. 1639).

2.2.2 *Doctrine of equivalents*

The doctrine of equivalents was first introduced in a retrial case by the Supreme Court in 2001.[9] In this case, the Supreme Court elaborately explained what was and constituted equivalency. And then many courts adopted the doctrine of equivalents to determine patent infringement, but there was also the indication that some of the courts had abused the application of equivalency.

To regulate the application of the doctrine of equivalents, in 2009, the Supreme Court promulgated *Several Provisions of the Supreme People's Court on Issues Concerning Applicable Laws to the Trial of Patent Cases*, Article 17 of which provides that:

> The first Paragraph of Article 59 which states that the scope of protection of the patent right for an invention or utility model shall be determined by the terms of the claims means that the scope of protection of patent shall be determined by the scope of the essential technical features disclosed in the claims, including the scope that is equivalent to essential technical features.

> Equivalent technical features refer to those that as compared with the feature described, performs substantially the same function in substantially the same way, produce substantially the same effect, and can be associated by a person skilled in the art with the features described.

This judicial interpretation set forth the uniform standard for infringement under the doctrine of equivalents and is on various occasions referred to as the test of 'Function/Way/Result'. It shall be pointed out that infringement under the doctrine of equivalents is not about whether the technical effect of the accused product/process is equivalent to the claims. Instead, the specific comparison shall be made between the elements of the patent claims and the technical features of the accused product/process. Equivalency means the technical features of the accused product/process, although not identical to patent claims, can perform substantially the same function and produce the same effect so a person skilled in the art can easily figure it out without contributing creative labour.

2.2.3 *Prosecution history estoppel*

The principle of prosecution history estoppel, even though not officially written into the laws, is widely recognized by court decisions.[10] Thus it is also judge-made law and although it is not technically binding to judges, every court accepts and uses it.

---

[9] *Ningbo Oriental Machine Factory v Jiangyin Golden Bell Metal Products Co., Ltd.* (Case Number: (2001) Min San Ti Zi No. 1).

[10] *Zhongyu Electronics (Shanghai) Co., Ltd. v Shanghai Nine Eagles Electronic Technology Co., Ltd.* (Case Number: (2011) Min Ti Zi No. 306).

Prosecution history estoppel is the legal limitation on the doctrine of equivalents and is based on the notion that if a patent applicant surrendered certain subject matter in the prosecution procedure in order to obtain its patent, it cannot thereafter rely on the doctrine of equivalents to obtain exclusionary rights over that subject matter relinquished. By reading the patent and its prosecution history in order to determine what the patentee surrendered, competitors should be provided with a reasonable degree of certainty that so long as they operate within the confines of the surrendered subject matter, they will not be found to infringe under the doctrine of equivalents.

2.3 Defence to patent infringement

As a practical matter, when sued for patent infringement, the accused infringer will almost always try to defend itself. The common defence to patent infringement is the prior art defence and legitimate source defence.

2.3.1 *Prior art defence*

Article 62 of the Patent Law states that 'In a dispute over patent infringement, if the accused infringer has evidence to prove that the technology or design it or he exploits is an existing technology or design, no patent infringement is constituted.' Thus if the technology used by the accused product/process is prior art, there would be no patent infringement.

To successfully defend itself using the prior art defence, the defendant will need to prove that all the accused infringing technical features of the product/process were disclosed by a single prior art. In other words, the defendant shall demonstrate that the accused infringing technical features of the product/process were identical or equivalent to the corresponding elements disclosed in a single prior art.[11] The defendant is not allowed to use and combine the technical features disclosed in two or more prior arts; therefore the standard of prior art defence is similar to the test for novelty in the prosecution procedure.

2.3.2 *Legitimate source defence*

The legitimate source defence is defined by Article 70 of the Patent Law, which states that 'Whoever uses or sells or offers to sell a patented product for the purpose of production and business operation without knowing that the product was produced and sold without permission of the patentee is not required to bear the liabilities for compensation provided that it or he can prove that the product is obtained from a legal source.' The legitimate source defence is distinctly Chinese in

---

[11] *Yancheng Zetian Machinery Co., Ltd. v Yancheng Greater Machinery Co., Ltd.* (Case Number: (2012) Min Shen Zi No. 18).

character. It was introduced into patent law because legislators thought that China was an undeveloped country and the legitimate source defence was to protect domestic companies.

To win the legitimate source defence the defendant will need to prove that (1) it acts in good faith and does not know the product/process has infringed the patent; and (2) it can provide a relevant contract, payment voucher, and invoice to indicate the product/process was purchased through a legitimate channel.[12]

Since the legitimate defence, which is applicable only to end user and seller, only exempts the liability for compensation; its application will not seriously restrict the patentee's rights.

However, Article 25 of the *Interpretation (II) of the Supreme People's Court on Several Issues concerning the Application of Law in the Trial of Patent Infringement Dispute Cases*, promulgated on 25 January 2016 and becoming effective on 1 April 2016, provides that:

> Where a party uses, offers to sell, or sells a patent-infringing product for the purpose of production and operations without the knowledge that such product is manufactured and sold without the permission of the patentee, and proves such product has legal sources, the people's court shall support the request of the right holder that the above use, offering to sell or sale should be stopped, **except that** the user of the alleged infringing product can prove that it has paid reasonable consideration for such product.

Thus the new judicial interpretation goes further than patent law. If the end user or the seller can prove it has paid reasonable consideration for the infringing products, the patentee cannot stop it from using or offering to sell or selling the infringing products. This is a significant restriction on the patentee's rights. If the patentee cannot stop the infringing products circulating on the market, it will obviously have adverse effect on its business.

3. How to Litigate a Patent Case in China

Before deciding to sue for patent infringement, a patent right holder shall keep in mind that patent litigation is a long and complicated fight against counterfeits or competitors, and getting to know the features of patent litigation in China could help you to make an effective strategy to protect your intellectual property rights.

---

[12] *Guangdong Yajie Hardware Co., Ltd. v Yang Jianzhong, et al* (Case Number: (2013) Min Ti Zi No.187).

3.1 Evidence collection

In some ways patent litigation is all about evidence. The party who is claiming patent infringement has the evidentiary burden of proof.[13] Unlike common law system, China does not have a disclosure procedure[14] and evidence preservation orders are only available in exceptional circumstances, so the patent right holders generally has to collect and produce all the evidence to prove infringement and damages.

Under the Chinese legal system all the evidence shall be cross-examined by the other party and only original evidence will be accepted by the courts. Oral evidence is given less weight and non-original evidence shall be notarized to be accepted as valid evidence. Therefore it is very common that most of the evidence will be notarized for patent litigation in China.

The common ways to collect evidence for patent infringement include the following.

3.1.1 Webpage notarization

In this information age most infringers establish official websites or open online shops on e-commerce platforms such as Alibaba, Amazon, and JD. To promote or advertise its products the infringing products will be displayed on official websites or online shops. Therefore notarization for the promotional products is necessary for the collection of evidence.

Sometimes online shops will also post the sales record for the infringing products in order to advertise the products and attract more consumers, so if there are a large amount of sales, the sales record shall be notarized as well. The sales record can be used to convince the court to grant high compensations.[15] If the sales record indicates that the profit made by the accused infringer clearly exceeds the limitation of statutory damages, the court has the power to determine the compensation above the statutory damages.

3.1.2 Notarized purchase of infringing product

If the infringing products can be found on the public market, then in practice, purchase of the product under the supervision of public notary is advised. If the patentee chooses not to make the notarized purchase, then it should keep complete evidence (such as a contract, invoice, or receipt) to prove it did purchase the products from the accused infringer.

---

[13] Article 64 of Civil Procedure Law.

[14] To determine the damages the Courts in Guangdong Province have used a new method analogous to disclosure procedure that will be discussed later. Although this new method adopted the advantages of discovery procedure, technically it's not discovery procedure.

[15] *Hangzhou Naiad Refrigeration Electric Factory v Dongguan Chongheng Industrial Co., Ltd.* (Case number: (2016) Hu Min Zhong No. 12).

3.1.3 Onsite investigation and notarized purchase of sample

Sometimes the infringing products are not available on the public market and are only supplied to specific customers. This is especially the situation where the infringing product is a spare part of another product /machine or it is not a popular consumer good and only has limited customers.

Under these circumstance on-site investigation to identify the infringing product is necessary and then obtaining samples under the supervision of public notary is a common way to collect evidence.

However, if the infringing products cannot be obtained by the three ways mentioned above, then the patentee has to file an application with the court for evidence preservation, this will be discussed later.

3.2 Venue and filing of lawsuit

3.2.1 Venue

When the evidence is ready, the next question is where to find a competent court to file the lawsuit. Not all Chinese courts can hear patent litigation and only the Intermediate People's Courts and Intellectual Property Courts[16] authorized by the Supreme Court have jurisdiction over patent infringement cases.

Under Chinese law the courts, where the defendant is domiciled or the infringement took place, have jurisdiction over the patent infringement case. However, according to the analysis of Brain J. Love, Christian Helmers, and Markus Eberhardt, patent cases are highly concentrated in a small number of jurisdictions and almost 57 per cent of patent infringement cases were litigated in China's three largest cities: Beijing, Shanghai, and Guangzhou.[17] We are not surprised by these statistics, as judges and lawyers in big cities have more experience in patent infringement cases and are more capable of trying cases that involve complicated technical issues.

If the manufacturer of the infringing products is not located in Beijing, Shanghai, Guangzhou, or another big city, a practical tip is to purchase the infringing products in the cities where the patentee wants to file civil action and then sue the seller and the manufacturer. If the infringing products cannot be found in the

---

[16] So far there are eight-seven courts that have jurisdiction over patent cases. Intermediate People's Courts authorized by the Supreme Court are generally the courts located in the provincial capitals or the municipalities directly under the central government. There are also three Intellectual Property Courts in Beijing, Shanghai, and Guangzhou that were authorized to hear only intellectual property cases including patent.

[17] Brian Love, Christine Helmers, and Markus Eberhardt, *Patent Litigation in China: Protecting Rights or the Local Economy*? available at <http://digitalcommons.law.scu.edu/cgi/viewcontent.cgi?article=1920&context=facpubs>.

physical stores in big cities, but are available from online shops, another useful tip is to place an order with the online shop and instruct the online shop to deliver the infringing product to a designated address in a big city. Although whether the delivery address can be considered as the place of infringement is controversial, in practice some of the courts in the cities of delivery address did agree to accept the case.[18]

3.2.2 *Evidence preservation*

Under Chinese patent law there are two kinds of evidence preservation: pre-trial evidence preservation and evidence preservation during litigation. Pre-trial evidence preservation can be only available when the following elements are satisfied:[19]

- The applicant is the patentee or the licensee;
- There is high possibility of patent infringement;
- The acts of the respondent may bring irreparable harm to the applicant;
- The balance of rights and interests between the applicant, respondent and public will not be broken;
- The applicants provides valid warranty.

Evidence preservation during litigation is when the application is filed after the court accepts the patent infringement case. It is available pursuant to Article 81 of the Civil Procedure Law when the plaintiff has difficulty in collecting such evidence by itself or when the evidence may be destroyed, so its condition is less stringent than pre-trial evidence preservation.

In practice, in order not to disrupt the balance between the plaintiff and defendant,[20] the courts often require the plaintiff to submit preliminary evidence to prove that the evidence to be preserved was actually under the defendant's control and request at its own discretion the plaintiff to provide warranty. Most of the evidence preservation applications were rejected because the plaintiff failed to provide adequate preliminary evidence.

As a matter of fact most judges are reluctant to do evidence preservation, because the defendant often refuses to cooperate with the court, but the law is not clear about the adverse consequences that can be imposed upon the defendant if it refuses to cooperate.

---

[18] *Shenzhen Liang Electronics Co., Ltd. v Guangdong Tongfang Lighting Co., Ltd.* (Case Number: (2015) Yue Gao Fa Li Min Zhong Zi Nos. 127 and 128).

[19] Ma Yunpeng, *Analysis of Substantive Factors in Pre-trial Act Preservation against Patent Infringement, CHINA PATENTS & TRADEMARKS*, No. 2, 2015.

[20] Burden of proof borne by the plaintiff is one of the principles of Civil Procedure Law.

3.3 Court hearing

3.3.1 Infringement analysis report issued by Judicial Appraisal Center

The hearing of patent cases is similar to other civil cases; except that in patent cases the comparison between the patent claims and the infringing product/process is an essential part of the hearing.

Expert evidence presented by the parties themselves, although admissible, has been given little weight. If the judge feels that he/she can understand the technical issues he/she will conduct the hearing directly and organize both parties to explain and debate whether there is patent infringement or not.

However, if the judge cannot or is not confident in understanding the complicated technical matters; the court will appoint a Judicial Appraisal Center to do the patent infringement analysis. The Judicial Appraisal Center has a list of qualified experts and the parties are given the opportunity to choose experts from the list, but in the event that the parties do not agree on the choice of experts, the court will make the appointment, albeit that the parties may veto an expert on grounds of connections to the other party or known or presumed bias.

Generally the Judicial Appraisal Center will arrange an informal hearing for both parties to present their arguments before it draws the conclusion for the infringement analysis. The Judicial Appraisal Center will produce a technical report for the court's reference about whether or not there is a patent infringement.

The analysis report issued by the Judicial Appraisal Center will be introduced as evidence and will be cross-examined by the parties. The court will rely on the analysis report to confirm or deny the infringement, unless the report has obvious flaws or mistakes.

3.3.2 Technical investigator

One reform approved by the Supreme Court and carried out in the Beijing, Shanghai, and Guangzhou IP Courts, is the establishment of the technical investigator system. Based on the existing systems of expert consultation, expert jury, and technical assessment, the Supreme Court decided to explore and implement the technical investigator system which is part of the judicial reform.

The technical investigators are defined as ancillary judicial personnel who shall participate in the court activities according to the court's instructions. Technical investigators are divided into four types, namely, employed as civil servants, employed but not as civil servants, communicating investigator, and part-time investigator.

The responsibilities of technical investigators include, without limitation, to identify the technical focus issues, attend the hearing and assist the judge to arrange the judicial evaluation. The technical investigators can deliberate about the merits of the case but do not have the right to vote. However, their opinions can be used by the court to determine the technical issues or facts.

With the help of the technical investigator, the parties concerned can put more energy on arguments over technical opinions, rather than spending lots of time in explaining technical terms. This saves a large amount of time and increases the efficiency of the court trial. It remains to be seen whether this technical investigator system will be adopted by more courts in future.

3.4 Injunction

Under common law system injunctions (preliminary/interim or permanent injunctions) are an essential component of effective patent enforcement. However, in China, final/permanent injunctions are more readily available, but it is difficult to obtain a preliminary injunction.

After the court hearing, if the judge believes that patent infringement can be established, the court will issue a permanent injunction ordering the defendant to stop the infringement. So in China, permanent injunction is a common remedy for a plaintiff winning the lawsuit.

The substantial conditions to obtain a preliminary injunction under Chinese laws are more or less the same with common law systems, that is, the applicant shall prove the following factors:[21]

• There is a high possibility of patent infringement made by the respondent;
• Refusing to grant the injunction may cause a irreparable harm to the applicant;
• The applicant shall provide warranty;
• The injunction will not harm the public interest.

One prominent difference for the Chinese preliminary injunction system is that if the respondent is dissatisfied with the injunction order it can only file an application to request the court reexamine the injunction. Generally the court will arrange a hearing to reexamine the injunction, but the injunction order is effective during the reexamination procedure unless the court officially overturns it.

The difficulty in obtaining a preliminary injunction lies in the fact that patent infringement cases often involve complicated technical issues and the judges are not confident in issuing an injunction. Or the judges do not want to take the risk of issuing an injunction order within forty-eight hours,[22] because Chinese courts have

---

[21] Sun Hailong and Yao Jianjun, *A Comparative Study of System of Patent Preliminary Injunction in China and United States*, CHINA PATENTS & TRADEMARKS, No. 3, 2008.
[22] The court shall make a ruling about whether to grant the preliminary injunction or not within forty-eight hours pursuant to Article of 66 of Patent Law.

established an internal evaluation system for judges and if the injunction is later proved wrong, it will have a negative effect on the judge's chances of obtaining a promotion or bonus.

3.5 Monetary damages

If patent infringement was confirmed, the court can grant the patent holder economic compensation, which shall be measured based on the economic loss incurred by the patent holder or the profit made by the infringer from the infringement. However, in practice it is extremely difficult to prove the patent holder's loss or the infringer's profits, so the court will determine the compensation based on statutory damages that vary from RMB 10,000 to 1 million.

As a matter of fact for most patent cases, the monetary damages granted by the court are insufficient to compensate the patent holder for their loss, let alone act as a deterrent to potential infringers. The Chinese monetary damages system is widely criticized, especially by international companies, because it cannot efficiently crack down on counterfeits as long as the infringer benefits from the infringing act. It is also fiercely criticized by scholars and Chinese companies, because if the patent system cannot protect the patentee, no one has motivation to invest in new technology and products; which will eventually impede technological progress.

4. Existing Problems of the Chinese Patent System and the Potential Reforms

4.1 Existing problems of the Chinese patent system

In April 2014 the Standing Committee of National People's Congress issued a report concerning the problems discovered during the implementation of Patent Law. In this report the Congress summarized two main problems for patent enforcement existing under the Chinese patent system:

- **Difficulty in protecting the patent rights holder.** This problem includes: (a) lengthy patent procedures (patent invalidation and infringement); (b) difficulty for the patentee to collect and produce evidence of infringement; and (c) the high cost for taking legal action.
- **Insufficient remedy.** This problem is outstandingly reflected by the fact that compensation that is granted by the court does not cover the damages incurred by the patentee. Sometimes even to the extent that the patentee has won the lawsuit, but ultimately lost the market.

4.2 Potential reform of the Chinese patent system

In response to Congress inquiries, the Chinese Supreme Court issued a report in 2015, recommending reform of the current patent system. The recommended solutions included:

4.2.1 Establishment of the National Intellectual Property High Court

The National Intellectual Property High Court will be the appellant court for all patent cases, so it can establish an identical standard for hearing and adjudicating patent cases and reduce procedural times.

4.2.2 Establishment of discovery procedure

Under the current patent system, the courts in Guangdong province are exploring a new method to determine damages in patent infringement cases, which in some way combines the discovery procedure with the proof obstruction system.

This new method consists of three steps:

- If the plaintiff knows the profits made by the defendant but cannot prove it, the plaintiff can request the court to ask the defendant to submit such evidence, such as the financial accounting books.
- The defendant refuses to cooperate by providing nothing, or by providing fake or incomplete accounting books.
- The court can uphold the plaintiff's position and presume that plaintiff's method in calculating the profits is supported.

Technically this new method is not a discovery procedure because it has to be used together with the proof obstruction system (that is, the defendant refuses to obey the court order). Moreover, it is very common for Chinese companies to prepare two accounting books: one is genuine and kept for internal use and another is fake only for outside inspection. It is difficult for the court or even professional accountants to discover which accounting books are fake.

Furthermore, this new method only applies to the determination of damages and cannot be used for other evidence, especially not for proof of infringement. It is not a secret that some of the patent right holders were forced to withdraw their lawsuits when the infringing products could not be purchased on the public market and the court refused to do evidence preservation. Without evidence to prove the infringement, how can a patent right holder win an infringement case?

In order to solve the difficulty for the patent right holder to collect and produce evidence, the Supreme Court suggested learning from the common law system, adopting the discovery system and under some circumstances imposing the obligation on the defendant to produce evidence.

It is the consensus view of legislators, judges, and lawyers that the status of low compensations has to be changed. In a high profile case adjudicated by the Beijing Intellectual Property Court,[23] compensation of RMB 49 million was granted to the patentee. Moreover, the defendant was also required to compensate the plaintiff for its attorney fees, which amounted to RMB 1 million and was calculated on the basis of the time spent by the plaintiff's attorneys. It is the first time that a Chinese court has supported a plaintiff's claim for attorney fees for time-based billing. It is predicted that high compensation might be supported by more judges in the future.

4.2.3 Perfection of the system for compensatory damages

Considering the low compensation in patent cases, the Supreme Court has suggested introducing the punitive damages system and increasing the standard of statutory damages.

The punitive damages system was first introduced into Trademark Law in 2013, but was not adopted by patent law, so the Supreme Court suggested establishing punitive damages in patent law. The punitive damages system applies to willful or repeated infringement and can prominently increase the amount of compensation.

Due to the difficulty in proving damages incurred by the patentee or profits obtained by the infringer, the increase of statutory damages allows the court more discretion in awarding the plaintiff greater compensation. The amendments made to the Patent Law have increased the maximum statutory damages from RMB 1 million to RMB 5 million.

4.2.4 Perfection of preliminary injunction

The judicial interpretation regarding the application of injunctions drafted by the Supreme Court is under deliberation. This new judicial interpretation will set up the conditions for applying preliminary injunctions and ensure that the patentee receives a prompt and efficient remedy, in order to avoid the situation where the patentee wins the lawsuit but ultimately loses the market.

---

[23] *Beijing Woqi Data System Co., Ltd. v Hengbao Stock Co., Ltd.* (Case Number: (2015) Jing Zhi Min Chu Zi No. 441).

4

TRADEMARKS AND RELATED RIGHTS IN CHINA

Dong Zhu and Xiuqin Lin

1. Overview

The use of trademark is an outcome of a commodity economy. Early in the Song Dynasty in China, which is about 1,000 years ago, one needle-maker in Jinan used a figure of a white rabbit on his product as a sign of origin, see Figure 4.1.[1] But there was no trademark law originated within ancient China. The modern trademark registration regime in China was introduced in 1904, at the end of the Qing Dynasty, to meet the requirements imposed by foreign countries.[2] From then on several trademark laws had been passed during the first half of the twentieth century.[3] However, the current Trade Mark Law (TML) in China was passed in 1982 and went into force in 1983 under the background of the reform and opening policy.[4] The first amendment of TML was made in 1993 to fulfil the international obligations as a member of the Paris Convention and Madrid Agreement.[5] In order to join in WTO, the People's Congress amended TML in 2000 for the second time to meet the minimal requirement of the TRIPs Agreement.[6] The latest amendment

---

[1] Zheng Chengsi, 'History of Trade Mark and Trade Mark Protection', (1997) 5 Chinese Trade Mark 39, 39.

[2] In 1904, the government of Qing Dynasty issued 'Experimental Regulations on Trademark Registration'(商标注册试办章程) to set up a trademark registration regime. See Qu Chunhai, 'The Evaluation on Late Qing Dynasty Historical Facts of the Experimental Regulations on Trade Mark Registration', (2012) 4 Historical Archives 87.

[3] For a detailed study of the modern trademark law history in China, see Zuo Xuchu, *Legal History of Trade Mark Law in China (Modern Times)* (Intellectual Property Press, Beijing 2005).

[4] Ren Zhonglin, 'Introduction to Trade Mark Law (Draft)', (1982) 14 Gazette of the State Council 616.

[5] China became a member of Paris Convention in 1985, and Madrid Agreement in 1989. Liu Minxue, Minister of SAIC, 'Introduction to Trade Mark Law Amendment (Draft)', (1993) Gazette of the Standing Committee of the National People's Congress, 1, available at <http://www.npc.gov.cn/wxzl/gongbao/1992-12/22/content_1481237.htm> accessed on 30 August 2016.

[6] Wang Zhongfu, Minister of SAIC, Introduction to Trade Mark Law Amendment (Draft), (2001) 7 Gazette of the Standing Committee of the National People's Congress 534.

of TML was made in 2013 to cater for the enforcement of the National Intellectual Property Strategy, and the new law came into force on 1 April 2014.[7] It was deemed as an initiative update of the current rules compared to the former amendments.[8] Accordingly, the Trade Mark Law Implemental Regulations (TMLIR) has been amended in 2014.

Figure 4.1 White Rabbit Trade Mark Used by Liu's Needle Shop in Jinan, Song Dynasty

In order to be protected by TML in China, one qualified trademark should be registered in the Trade Mark Office (TMO) (Sec. 2 TML).[9] For foreign applicants, an agent established in accordance with the Chinese law shall be appointed to deal with the applications and other related matters (Sec. 18(2) TML). Any issues concerning registration arising after a TMO's decision (approval or disapproval) could be filed to the Trade Mark Review and Adjudication Board (TMRAB).[10] Any parties, if not satisfied with the decisions of TMRAB may file an administrative lawsuit against TMRAB to Beijing IP Court. Through registration, the

---

[7] For a brief introduction to the third amending of Trade Mark Law, see Jin Weiwu, 'Review and Summary of the Third Amending of Trade Mark Law', (2013) 10 Intellectual Property 3.

[8] Zhou Bohua, Minister of SAIC, 'Introduction to Trade Mark Law Amendment (Draft)', (2013) 5 Gazette of the Standing Committee of the National People's Congress 723.

[9] Formerly, TMO was a branch of the State Administration for Industry and Commerce (SAIC) under the State Council, and now it is a branch of the new National Intellectual Property Administration (CNIPA) since 2018. The main functions of TMO are registering and administering trademarks, protecting trademark rights and handling trademark infringement and counterfeiting cases; handling trademark disputes; the recognition and protection of well-known trademarks; registering, recording, and protecting special signs and official signs; researching, analyzing, and releasing trademark registration information; providing information for government decision-making and to the public, etc.

[10] TMRAB is another branch of CNIPA, its main function is handling trademark disputes including revision of the TMO decisions of refusing the application, cancelation of registration, hearing the invalidation cases.

registrant can enjoy an exclusive right to use the trademark for ten years (Sec. 39 TML).[11] Anyone who uses a registered trademark without authorization therefore may cause public confusion constitues an infringing activity. The trademark owner can file a lawsuit against the infringer seeking for both injunction and damage remedies.

For those unregistered trademarks, the trademark holder can file lawsuits against the producers or sellers of the counterfeit goods based on Anti-Unfair Competition Law (AUCL).[12] Moreover, AUCL also provides protection to well-known product names, get-ups, trade names and domain names (Sec. 6 AUCL) when someone is trying to deceive the public by using such trade symbols, and therefore could cause likelihood of public confusion.

In this chapter, we are not going to give a thorough introduction to Chinese trademark law, neither will we deal with the procedure maters in detail. Instead, we focus on some of the key issues concerning trademark protection in China. Part 2 discusses the key requirements of trademark registration. Part 3 focuses on trademark infringement, especially on such issues as trademark use, likelihood of confusion, and liability of online platforms. In Part 4, we discuses the civil remedies provided for trademark infringement. Part 5 deals with the special protection of well-known trademarks. Not only legislation but also judicial practice are the key concerns in our discussion.

2. Trademarks that Can be Registered

A trademark refers to a sign of origin, which can be used to identify and distinguish trademark owners' goods or services from those of others. The phrase trademark is used in a broad sense in China, except for the mark used on goods as a sign of origin; it also includes service marks, collective marks, as well as certification marks (Sec. 3(1) TML). For a mark that could be registered as a trademark, the registrant should follow the requirements laid down by TML. This part will discuss these requirements in turn.

2.1 Elements of a trademark

In theory, any sign that could function as an indicator of the origin can be registered. But this is not the case according to TML. A sign that can be registered

---

[11] The registrant of a trademark can file an application to renew the registration before expiration (on later than six months after expiration), and the registrant will be given another ten-year protection each time (Sec. 40 TML).

[12] In China, AUCL was passed in 1993, and the first amendments of this law was finished in the end of 2017. The new version of AUCL has come into force since 1 January 2018.

as trademark in China could be any word, device, any letter of the alphabet, any number, three-dimensional symbol, colour combination, and sound, or any combination thereof (Sec. 8 TML). Before 2013, only visual marks, both two-dimensional and three-dimensional, could be registered as trademark.[13] For colour, only a combination of different colours can be registered. A single colour is not allowed to be registered as trademark, because the legislator worried that registration of a single colour might result in monopolies in the limited kinds of colours.[14]

Since 2013, the elements of a trademark have been expanded to include sound. The first registered sound trademark was the opening song of China Radio International, which was approved on 14 April 2016.[15] After Tecent's application of registration of the prompt sound of QQ program was denied by TMO and TMRAB, the first administrative case concerning registration of sound trademark in China is now pending in Beijing IP court.[16] It can be seen from this case that the administrative departments in China are very cautious about the registration of sound trademark. But what position would the court choose has been unclear until now. So, it is noteworthy to follow the new developments of these cases, in order to figure out the attitude of the administrative and judicial authorities towards the registration of sound trademark.

2.2 Marks that cannot be used as trademark

Unrelated to the basic function of trademark as a sign of origin, some marks are not permitted to be used as trademarks based upon the policy concerns such as protecting public interests in China.[17]

In accordance to the Paris Convention, the use of trademarks identical or similar to public symbols are prohibited,[18] such as (Sec. 10(1) (a)–(e) TML):

(1) the state name, national flag, national emblem, national anthem, military flag, army emblem, military song, or decorations of the People's Republic of China; those identical with a state organ's name, symbol, or the names of the specific locations that are seats of central state organs; or those identical with the names or designs of landmark buildings;

---

[13] See Sec. 8 TML 2001.

[14] Lang Sheng (ed.), *Interpretation of the Trade Mark Law of the People's Republic of China* 22 (Law Press, Beijing 2013).

[15] Xing Zheng, 'SIAC Issued the First Sound Trade Mark in China', available at <http://finance.people.com.cn/n1/2016/0214/c1004-28122202.html> accessed 15 March 2016.

[16] Liu Suya, 'After 6 "Di"s was Rejected, Tencent sues TMRAB', Beijing Evening News, 20 July 2016.

[17] Hang Hui, 'Public Interests in Trade Mark Law and its Protection', (2015) 10 Science of Law 74, 80–81.

[18] See Article 6.3 of Paris Convention.

(2) the state names, national flags, national emblems or military flags of foreign countries;

(3) the flags, emblems, names or others of international inter-governmental organizations;

(4) an official mark or inspection seal that indicates control and guarantee;

(5) the symbols or names of the Red Cross or the Red Crescent.

Of course, these are not absolute exemptions, for example, the symbols of foreign countries, international organizations, and the official marks that indicate control and guarantee can be used as trademarks upon authorization (Sec. 10(1)(b)–(d) TML).

Only the use of which is identical or similar to these public symbols as a whole is prohibited. In the 'Chinese JIN Wine' (中国劲酒) case, the court held that Sec. 10(1)(a) of TML does not prohibit the use of 'China' or 'Chinese' as an element of a trademark, however, whether the use of 'Chinese JIN Wine' can cause harmful effects according to Sec. 10(1)(h) of TML was another issue to be concerned.[19]

Another important policy concern in China is the moral and political influence of the use of a certain mark. If the use of certain marks would be harmful to the public interests, such as those which could be discriminatory or fraudulent in a way that easily confuses the public, and those detrimental to socialist morals or customs, or can cause other harmful effects, cannot be used as trademarks as well (Sec. 10(1)(f)–(h) TML). For example, the registration of 'ER FANG JIA NIANG' (二房佳酿) as a trademark for wine is not permitted, because 'ER FANG' in Chinese means a concubine, its use may be in conflict with the monogamy promoted by the Marriage Law.[20] Another example is 'Bin Laden', known as the leader of the notorious terrorist organization Al Qaeda, and its use would definitely bring bad political influences to Chinese society because it may represents mercilessness and brutality.[21]

One of the hottest issues on the public interest protection in TML arose from whether the registration of 'WeChat' (微信) as its trademark by a third party other than Tencent in the area of communication services would cause 'harmful effect' to the public.[22] WeChat programme, provided by Tencent, is now one of the world's most popular social media software, and has been used by millions of people in China. In the WeChat case, TMRAB held that the registration of WeChat as a trademark by a third party may cause cognitive difficulties to the public, because they could not use WeChat to refer to the programme provided by Tencent any

---

[19] Supreme People's Court, *Jin Pai Co. Ltd. v TMRAB* [2010] Xing Ti Zi No 4.

[20] SAIC, Rules for Trade Mark Review and Adjudication 2005.

[21] Ibid.

[22] See Hang Hui, 'Public Interests in Trade Mark Law and its Protection', (2015) 10 Science of Law 74.

more, if it belongs to that third party, therefore it is the 'harmful effect' caused to the public. Beijing IP Court affirmed on the same ground.[23] However, Beijing High People's Court also affirmed but did not agree with the lower court's reasoning. The court held that the evidence provided was not sufficient to uphold the 'harmful effect' that may be caused by the registration of WeChat as trademark, and warned that the broadening interpretation of the 'unhealthy influences' should be treated with caution. Finally, the court denied the registration of WeChat for its lack of distinctiveness.[24] That is to say, even Tencent could not be a qualified trademark registrant of 'WeChat'. Therefore, the court closed the door of registration of 'WeChat' as a trademark, and at the same time, opened a gate for any other people to use 'WeChat' freely to refer to other similar social software.

Geographical names are also not allowed to be used as trademarks. The reason for forbidding a geographical name used as trademark is that geographical names usually refer to the geographical origin of the goods or services, therefore, cannot be used to distinguish producers or service providers from the others. According to TML, the geographical names at or above the county level and foreign geographical names well known to the public are also enjoined from using as trademarks. Whereas, when a geographical name has another meaning or is being used as an element of a collective mark or certification mark, it can be registered. For those geographical names which have been registered the trademarks would remain valid (Sec. 10(2) TML). In the 'Red River' (红河) case, Beijing High People's Court dealt with the issue on the basic understanding of the 'other meaning' of a geographical name. The court held that the other meaning of a geographical name refers to the existing meaning other than a name of some place, which makes the name eligible to be used as a sign of origin. In this case, 'Red River' is not only a county name, but also the name for a river running through Yunnan Province, therefore the trademark could be valid.[25] Moreover, where a trademark includes a geographical indicator that does not describe the location or the origin of the goods at issue and may cause public confusion, it shall also not be used (Sec. 16(1) TML).

2.3 Distinctiveness and non-functionality

The basic function of trademark is to indicate the origin of the goods or services attached, which requires the trademark to be distinguishable so the consumers can easily find out what they want by just referring to the trademark. TML requires a

---

[23] Beijing IP Court, *Trunkbow Asia Pacific (Shandong) Co. Ltd. v TMRAB* [2014] Jing Zhi Chu Zi No 67.

[24] Beijing High People's Court, *Trunkbow Asia Pacific (Shandong) Co. Ltd. v TMRAB* [2015] Gao Xing Zhi Zhong Zi No 1538.

[25] Beijing High People's Court, *Yunan Honghe Guangming Corp. v TMRAB* [2003] Gao Xing Zhong Zi No 65.

trademark seeking registration shall be as distinctive to the public as to be thus distinguishable (Sec. 9 TML). So, distinctiveness is the key requirement for trademark registration. Distinctiveness requires a registered trademark should not be identical or similar to other trademarks. To evaluate the distinctiveness of a trademark, such factors should be taken into account as the meaning of the mark, the looking of the mark, the goods used to designate the mark, the relevant public's cognitive habits, and areas of the trademark used, etc.[26] In the 'International Sommelier Guild' case, the Supreme People's Court held that whether a mark is distinctive depends on the common recognition of the relevant public of the products which the mark is used on.[27]

Distinctiveness is a matter of degree. Those marks that lack distinctiveness are not permitted to be registered. For example, (1) generic terms to a class or group of goods, (2) descriptive terms that merely indicate the quality, materials, function, quantity, or other features of the goods, and (3) other marks lack of distinctiveness, such as marks made up of simple lines or graphs, too complicated combinations of words and/or numbers, a single letter or number in the form of common use, common get-up, non-original slogans, etc. (Sec. 11(1) TML).[28] In the WeChat case mentioned above, Beijing High People's Court denied the registration of 'WeChat' on the ground that 'WeChat' in Chinese is composed of two single characters, which mean an easy way of communication, therefore, it is only a description of the service provided.[29]

However, it does not mean that those marks lack of distinctiveness cannot be registered in any case. If they have acquired distinctiveness through use as a sign of origin, namely a secondary meaning other than their original meaning, they might be registered (Sec. 11(2) TML). For example, 'LIANG MIAN ZHEN' (两面针) for toothpaste, although the phrase 'LIANG MIAN ZHEN' (zanthoxylum nitidum) is the most important ingredient of that kind of toothpaste, it acquires secondary meaning as a trademark from the long period of use by the producer as a sign of origin.[30] Such factors can be considered in the process of dealing with acquired distinctiveness issues of certain marks, as in what way does the related public see the mark, how the mark is used by the owner, and how long has it been used as a sign of origin, etc.[31]

---

[26] Lang Sheng (ed.), *Interpretation of the Trademark Law of the People's Republic of China* 29 (Law Press, Beijing 2013).
[27] Supreme People's Court, *TMRAB v International Sommelier Guild* [2001] Gao Xing Zhong Zi No 1744.
[28] SAIC, Rules for Trade Mark Review and Adjudication 2005.
[29] Beijing High People's Court, *Trunkbow Asia Pacific (Shandong) Co. Ltd. v TMRAB* [2015] Gao Xing Zhi Zhong Zi No 1538.
[30] SAIC, Rules for Trade Mark Review and Adjudication 2005.
[31] Lang Sheng (ed.), *Interpretation of the Trademark Law of the People's Republic of China* 23 (Law Press, Beijing 2013).

The doctrine of non-functionality was introduced in 2001 when registerable trademarks were expended to three-dimensional designs. The purpose of trademark law is to make sure that a trademark can function as a sign of origin. However, protection of technical features of a product is the task of patent law.[32] Based upon this principle, trademark protection should not be expanded to functionality of a trademark. For three-dimensional designs, those (1) only indicate the shapes inherent to the goods, such as a book; (2) merely dictated by the need to achieve certain technical effects, such as the shape of the power plug; or (3) merely dictated by the need to give the goods substantive value, such as the shape of jewellery, cannot be registered as trademark (Sec. 12 TML). Unlike other countries, there is no general non-functionality requirement for all the marks to be registered in China. So, it is unclear if the courts can apply this doctrine when dealing with other marks such as marks made of colours.

2.4 Prior rights

TML requires a registered trademark shall not be in conflict with the prior legitimate rights of others (Sec. 9 TML), in order to protect the rights that existed before the trademark registration. These prior rights should be valid before the date of the trademark application, including trademark, trade name, design patent, copyright, name, portrait, etc.[33]

The word 'right' as in prior rights here is not used in a technical sense. All interests protected by law before the application date of the trademark could be the prior rights.[34] So, an applicant is not allowed to rush to register in an unfair manner when a mark is already in use by another party and enjoys substantial influence (Sec. 32 TML). In the 'KUNG FU PANDA' (功夫熊猫) case, Beijing High People's Court denied Beijing First Intermediate People's Court and held that prior rights are not limited to the legitimate rights recognized by law, but also include the anonymous interests although not listed but still protected by law. The prior right protected in this case was a merchandising right to the tile of the film, *Kung Fu Panda*.[35] Within three months from the date of publication after a preliminary examination and approval, any holder of prior rights can file an opposition to TMO to deny the registration (Sec. 33 TML). Within five years from the date of registration, any holder of prior rights is entitled to request TRAB to invalidate the trademark's registration

---

[32] Yuan Bo, 'Registration of Three-dimensional Trade Mark: Non-functionality and Distinctiveness', (2013) 3 Chinese Trade Mark 77, 78.

[33] SAIC, Rules for Trade Mark Review and Adjudication 2005.

[34] Lang Sheng (ed.), *Interpretation of the Trademark Law of the People's Republic of China* 67 (Law Press, Beijing 2013).

[35] Beijing High People's Court, *DreamWorks Animation SKG Inc. et al. v TMRAB* [2015] Gao Xing (Zhi) Zhong Zi No 1969.

(Sec. 45(1) TML). For the malicious piracy of well-known trademark, the owner shall not be bound by this five-year period limitation.

Besides, a prior right holder should enjoy a good reputation in order to be protected.[36] For example, it is unfair to deny the registration based upon a less famous unregistered trademark, because a nationwide exclusive right could be granted through registration. This is in line with the rule of the priority right of a trademark user. If some person uses a trademark before the registration within a small area, the register cannot enjoin him from using the trademark within the original scope; therefore the two trademarks should not be deemed to conflict with each other (Sec. 59(3) TML).

3. Trademark Infringement

3.1 Overview of trademark infringement

In China, TML is designed to provide protection to 'the exclusive right to use a registered trademark'.[37] The exclusive right to use a registered trademark is limited to the mark which has been approved for registration and on the goods or services in connection with which the trademark is used (Sec. 56 TML). However, trademark infringement is not limited to the use of the identical trademark without the consent of the trademark owner. TML lists all kinds of trademark infringements as follows (Sec. 57 TML):

(1) using a sign that is identical to a registered trade mark for goods or services which are identical to those for which it is protected without the authorization of the owner of the registered trade mark;

(2) using a sign that is similar to a registered trade mark in connection with the goods or sevices which are identical to those for which it is protected, or using a sign that is identical with or similar to a registered trade mark in connection with the goods or sevices which are identical with or similar to those for which it is protected, without the authorization of the owner of the registered trade mark which is likely to cause public confusion;

(3) selling goods that violate the exclusive right to use a registered trade mark;

(4) counterfeiting, or making, without authorization, representations of another party's registered trade mark, or selling such representations;

(5) altering another party's registered trade mark without authorization and selling goods bearing such an altered trade mark;

---

[36] Li Yang, 'Interpretation of the Prior Right in Trade Mark Law from the Perspective of Intellectual Property', (2006) 5 Science of Law 41, 46–47.

[37] For a discussion of the difference between 'trade mark right' and 'the exclusive right to use a registered trademark', see Liu Jiaqi, 'Rethinking and Reconstruction of the Concept of Trade Mark Right', (2009) 7 Intellectual Property 65.

(6) helping any others to infringe the exclusive right to use its registered trade mark with intention to provide convenience for infringing the exclusive right to use its registered trade mark;

(7) other acts which may cause prejudice to another party's exclusive right to use its registered trade mark.

According to the Supreme People's Court, other infringing acts include: (1) using of a trademark as a trade name on the identical or similar products significantly therefore is like to cause confusion; (2) copying, imitating, and translating other registered well-known trademark or its main part therefore is likely to cause consumer confusion and damages to the trademark owner; (3) using of identical or similar trademark as domain name and doing business under this domain name therefore is likely to cause confusion.[38]

In China, whether the use of a trademark as another commercial symbol is an infringing act under TML is not uncontroversial. Rule 76 TMLIR holds that the use of a trademark as the name or get-up of a product can be deems as trademark infringement according to Sec. 57(2) TML (Rule 76 TMLIR). Whereas, Sec. 58 TML articulates that the use of a registered trademark as a trade name to deceive the public is an unfair competition, therefore the trademark owner can only file a lawsuit based upon AUCL. So, the line between trademark infringement and unfair competition cannot be easily drawn in China.[39]

As to a trademark infringement, the trademark holder can file a lawsuit to the court. At the same time, the administrative authorities can deal with trademark infringements even without the application of the trademark holder. The administrative authorities for industry and commerce are authorized to investigate infringing acts on their own initiatives; where a crime is suspected, the administrative authority shall promptly turn over the case to the judicial department (Sec. 61 TML).[40]

3.2 Trademark use

In theory, trademark use refers to any forms of the use of the trademark as a sign of origin. Trademark use does not involve normative use and indicative use of a trademark. For example, a trademark owner cannot prohibit other people from using a common name, logo, or model contained in the relevant registered trademark, nor

---

[38] Supreme People's Court, Interpretation on Issues concerning the Application of Law in the Trial of Civil Trade Mark Dispute Cases, Rule 1.

[39] Li Yang, *Fundamental Principles of Intellectual Property Law*, 867 (Beijing: Chinese Social Science Press, 2010).

[40] According to Criminal Law (CL), crimes of infringing on trademarks include counterfeit of registered trademark (Sec. 213 CL), sale of products with counterfeit of registered trademark, (Sec. 214 CL) as well as production and sale of counterfeited marks (Sec. 215 CL).

could he/she prohibit other people from using trademarks to indicate the quality, ingredients, raw materials, functions, weight, quantity, geographic name or other features of the product (Sec. 59(1) TML); a three-dimensional registered trademark holder is not entitled to prohibit other parties from reasonably using a similar shape of the product by its own nature, or essential to achieve a similar technical effect (Sec. 59(2) TML).

It is necessary to point out here that the concept of trademark use is quite narrow in China. Trademark use only includes such acts as attaching trademarks on goods, packages, or containers thereof and commodity trading instruments, or use of trademarks in advertisements, exhibitions, and other commercial activities (Sec. 48 TML). The use of trademark as other commercial symbols may fall into other categories of infringing acts other than trademark use or unfair competition. Moreover, selling of counterfeited goods is not a form of trademark use, because 'selling goods' has been treated separately as another kind of infringing act for a long time in China.[41] So, trademark use is restricted to the attaching of the mark to the goods in the production phase. This is somewhat different from the other countries. In the EU and the US, for example, selling goods also belongs to trademark use.[42] The alienation of sale from trademark use is problematic. In the judicial decisions, the courts in China tend to separate 'selling goods' from the confusion test and hold only trademark use in the production phase can cause confusion. The sale of goods infringing the trademark rights which are manufactured by the defendant is divided into two distinct issues, one is the use of trademark by the manufacture; the other is the selling of goods.

The current issue of trademark use in China arises from the Original Equipment Manufacture (OEM) cases. OEM refers to a international business mode when a brand owner commissions another manufacturer to produce goods according to its standard and retails these goods under its own trademark. China now is the world's factory. Some of the commissioners who are not trademark owners may order goods from China, these commissioners will sell counterfeit goods around the world. The issue raised in the OEM case is whether the OEM factory in China is liable for trademark infringement. In the early cases, based on the presumption that the use of trademark is limited in the circle of production, the defendants attached the trademark onto the goods without the authorization of the trademark owner but upon the request of the other person, most of the courts ruled that the defendant have infringed the plaintiff's right although the goods are not sale in China.[43] However, from the point of view of the effect of OEM, the goods are all

---

[41] Zhu Dong, 'The Nature of Sale Behavior in Trademark Infringement in China', (2013) 4 Science of Law 174, 175–76.

[42] Mary LaFrance, *Understanding Trademark Law*, 178 (2nd edn. LexisNexis, 2009).

[43] Yi Jianxiong, 'Choice of Attitude towards Disputes about the Infringement of Trademark in OEM', (2009) 3 Intellectual Property 23, 25.

sold abroad and not in the home market, the OEM company is not in competition with the trademark owner in China, therefore it is impossible to cause confusion of consumers. Some courts held that the function of trademark is to help the consumers figure out the origin of the goods sold in the market, so the confusion of consumers is the presumption in deciding a trademark infringement. The OEM goods are not intended to be offered for sale within the territory of China, so there is no issue about whether they are infringing products.[44] In the recent 'PRETUL' case, the Supreme People's Court denied the lower courts decision and confirmed that the mere act of attaching the trademark to the OEM goods couldn't be deemed as trademark use, because the OEM goods are not intended to be sold within China, and the trademarks attached to such goods do not function as a sign of origin.[45]

3.3 Likelihood of confusion

There was no likelihood of confusion doctrine in TML in China before 2013. For a long time, use of identical or similar trademark had been the key element of trademark infringement.[46] This is quite different from the basic logic of the likelihood of confusion doctrine. It focused on the mark itself and did not treat trademark as the container of good will, so was called the symbol protection doctrine.[47] But it did not mean that the courts in China did not consider likelihood of confusion at all in the judicial practices. During that period, the Supreme People's Court tried to introduce confusion into to the test of trademark infringement, but it was only one of the several factors considered in the similar trademark test.[48] From 2013 on, the likelihood of confusion doctrine has been introduced (Sec. 57(2) TML). This situation is somewhat similar to the EU situation.[49] But there are still some problems left unsolved. First, it seems that the likelihood of confusion doctrine only applies to similar marks, and it is irrelevant in the case of identical marks used on identical goods or services. A new issue arises whether likelihood of confusion is irrelevant when the infringer uses the same mark as the trademark owner. Second, the relationship between similarity and confusion is also controversial.[50] It seems

---

[44] Zhang Yurui, 'The Confusion of Consumer is not the Presumption of Trademark Infringement', *Intellectual Property in China* (Beijing, 14 September 2014) 8.

[45] Supreme People's Court, *Pujiang Yahuan Locks Co. Ltd. v Focker Security Products Int. Ltd.* [2014] Min Ti Zi No 38.

[46] See Sec. 52(1) TML 2001.

[47] See Li Chen, 'Trade Mark Infringement and Symbol Enclosure' (2006) 1 Henan Social Science 65, 66.

[48] See Supreme People's Court, Interpretation of the Supreme People's Court about the Law Application Issues as Hearing of the Civil Dispute Cases Involving Trade Mark, Rule 11.

[49] Council Directive Directive 2008/95/EC Article 5.

[50] See Wang Taiping, 'Standard of Trade Mark Infringement: Relationship between Similarity and Confusion', (2014) 6 Legal Research 162.

that the basic logic of judicial practice dealing with trademark infringement has been turned upside down since 2013. Now, the similarity of marks and goods or services has become one element in the test of confusion. However, it is not quite clear what the influence would be, so it is still worthy of attention.

Another contemporary issue under the confusion test in China is the application of reverse confusion doctrine. Reverse confusion stems from the US case law.[51] Although reverse confusion is not literally involved in TML, some resent cases show a willingness of the courts in applying the reverse confusion doctrine to protect registered trademarks that may be similar to the famous unregister trademarks. For example, in the 'XIN BAI LUN' (新百伦) case, Gouangzhou Intermediate People's Court held that NewBalance cannot use 'XIN BAI LUN', one Chinese translation of 'NewBalance' in China, because 'XIN BAI LUN' has been registered by a Chinese company. Although NewBalance is more famous and therefore could be recognized as a well-known trademark, it lost the chance to challenge the registration of 'XIN BAI LUN' as it did not file an invalidating application to TMRAB within five years of the registration of 'XIN BAI LUN'. The court reasoned when NewBalance is allowed to use the phrase 'XIN BAI LUN' in China, the consumers would be confused to think that all the goods with the brand 'XIN BAI LUN' were produced by NewBalance due to its fame, therefore there would be no room for the Chinese company with the registered trademark 'XIN BAI LUN' to develop its own business. The court ordered NewBalance to pay damages amounting to 98 million RMB yuan.[52] But Guangdong High People's Court reduced the damages to 5 million RMB yuan.[53] In the 'FEI CHENG WU RAO' (非诚勿扰) case, Shenzhen Intermediate People's Court held that the famous TV matchmaking programme called 'FEI CHENG WU RAO' made by Jiangsu TV infringed a registered trademark owned by a small company in Guangdong Province. Abiding by the decision, Jiangsu TV finally changed the name of that TV show.[54] These cases reflect a strong policy concern of the courts and raised some hot issues concerning reverse confusion. Some scholars are quite critical towards these cases, they believe the reverse confusion doctrine were misused and worry that the application of this doctrine would protect the malicious pirate under guise of the first-to-file

---

[51] See Louis Altmana and Malla Pollacka, *Callmann on Unfair Competition, Trademarks and Monopolies* vol. 4 §22: 11 (Thomson/West, 4th edn., 2015).

[52] Guangzhou Intermediate People's Court, *Zhou Lelun v Xinbailun Trade (China) Co. Ltd. & Guangzhou Shengshichang Chain Co. Ltd.* [2013] Hui Zhong Fa Min Chu Zi No 547.

[53] Guangdong High People's Court, *Zhou Lelun v Xinbailun Trade (China) Co. Ltd. & Guangzhou Shengshichang Chain Co. Ltd.* [2015] Yue Gao Fa Min San Zhong Zi No 444. It raised another issue on the damages calculation in the reverse confusion cases.

[54] Shenzhen Intermediate People's Court, *Jin Ahuan v Jiangsu Broadcasting Corporation* [2015] Shen Zhong Fa Zhi Min Zhong Zi No 927.

doctrine.[55] Of course, it can be expected that the application of reverse confusion will be more controversial in the next few years in China.

3.4 Liability of online platform

According to TML, anyone who knowingly provides online marketplace to the infringer of a registered trademark should be deemed as 'providing convenience' to the infringer in Sec. 57 TML, therefore the online auction site could be liable as a contributory infringer when it knowingly provides Internet services to the third-party online sellers (Rule 76 TMLIR). Moreover, Sec. 36 of Tort Liability Law (TLL), stemmed from DMCA of the US, and was specially designed to deal with the torts that happened on the Internet.[56] Sec. 36(2) is the safe harbour rule,[57] which requires the ISPs to take necessary measures such as deletion, blocking, or disconnection after receiving the notification from the right holder; otherwise, they shall be jointly and severally liable for any additional harm with the network user.

Based on the legislative foundations as to the liability of the ISPs mentioned above, most courts in China tend to apply the safe harbour rule more literally, and treat it as the sole standard to establish liability for online auction sites. First, the online auction sites could have known or should have reasonably known the infringing acts of the third-party sellers only after being notified by the trademark holder.[58] Second, generally speaking, removal of the infringing links could fulfil the requirement of taking necessary measures upon notification.[59] In a word, as to the trademark infringements which happened on the online market place, the judicial practices in China show that the courts are reluctant to impose any further

---

[55] See Zhang Jin, 'Reflections on Localization of Reverse Confusion', (2016) 6 Chinese Patent and Trade Mark 70; Huang Wushuang, 'The "Fei Cheng Wu Rao" case under the Theory and Rules of Reverse Confusion', (2016) 1 Intellectual Property 26.

[56] See Yang Lixin, *Tort Liability Law* 243 (Law Press, Beijing 2011).

[57] Actually, safe harbour refers to a bundle of rules concerning the limitation on the liabilities of the ISPs, but Sec. 36(2) TLL only focuses on the notice-and-takedown regime, it indicates a narrow understanding of the safe harbour among Chinese legislators as well as the Chinese scholars. See Wang Qian, *Copyright Protection in Internet Environment* 230 (Law Press, Beijing 2011).

[58] For example, Shanghai First Intermediate People's Court, *AKTIESELSKABETAF 21. NOVEMBER 2001 v eBay Information & Network (Shanghai) Co. Ltd.* [2005] Hu Yi Zhong Min Wu (Zhi) Chu No 371; Zhuhai Intermediate People's Court, *Wisconsin Ginseng Agricultural Association v Yuezhu Pharmaceutical Co. Ltd., Lv Xiaotao, and Zhejiang Taobao Network Co. Ltd.* [2012] Zhu Zhong Fa Zhi Chu Zi No 1.

[59] For example, Jieyang Intermediate People's Court, *Guo Donglin v Lin Weimin & Zhejiang Taobao Co. Ltd.* [2013] Jie Zhong Fa Min San Chu Zi No. 31; Shanghai Second Intermediate People's Court, *Shanghai Shengfang Trade Co. Ltd. v Beijing Jingdong 360° E-commerce Co. Ltd. & Guangzhou Heshengfang Bio-tech Co. Ltd.* [2013] Hu Er Zhong Min Wu (Zhi) Chu Zi No. 236; Beijing Second Intermediate People's Court, *Yongli Holiday Village (International) Group v Xiong Xiabing et al.* [2014] Er Zhong Min Chu Zi No 2013.

obligations to the operator of the online auction sites such as monitoring the trademark infringing acts and preventing further infringements of the online sellers.[60]

Among the many cases on the secondary trademark liability of Taobao, the largest C2C online auction site in China, there was one significant case that should be mentioned. In the 'YI NIAN' (依念) case, Shanghai First Intermediate People's Court held that Taobao knew or should have known that the third-party seller was using the Internet service provided by Taobao to sell counterfeit goods based on the facts in this case, even though the notifications sent by Yinian could not be valid. Moreover, upon knowing the infringing acts of a specific seller, Taobao did nothing except removing the suspected links that definitely meant Taobao did not take necessary measures after knowing the infringing acts, because removal of infringing links could not effectively reduce the scale of infringing products sold on Taobao.[61] This case seems to be an exemption among the cases decided by most courts in China, for Taobao failed to shield itself from liability by relying on the safe harbour rule, both the trial court and the appellate court held Taobao liable even though Taobao had removed the infringing links after receiving the notification from the trademark holder. This case pointed out some possible directions to strengthen the online auction sites liability. By emphasizing the mind state and the necessity of the anti-counterfeit measures, the courts could do more balancing work.

4. Remedies

Remedies provided for trademark holders whose trademark is infringed include injunctions, damages as well as apology and elimination of consequences and restoration of reputation (Sec. 15(1) TLL). Of course, the most important ones are injunctions and damages, which will be discussed in detail in the part.

4.1 Injunctions

For the infringer of a registered trademark, the court can grant a injunction relief to the trademark holder to stop the ongoing infringing acts. Except for permanent injunction, preliminary injunction is also now available in China. In 2002, the

---

[60] Some US scholars have recognized the impact of introducing the safe harbour standard in the secondary trademark liability cases by analysing *Tiffany v eBay*, 600 F 3d 93 (2d Cir 2010). See Michael Pantalony, 'Contributing to Infringement: Intermediary Liability after Tiffany v. eBay and Louis Vuitton v. Akanoc', (2015) 105 Trademark Reporter 709, 712; Michelle C. Leu, 'Authenticate This: Revamping Secondary Trademark Liability Standards to Address a Worldwide Web of Counterfeits,' (2011) 26 Berkeley Technology Law Journal 591, 615.

[61] Shanghai First Intermediate People's Court, *Yinain (Shanghai) Fashion Trading Co. v Zhejiang Taobao Network Co. & Du Guofa*, (2011) Hu Yi Zhong Min Wu (Zhi) Zhong Zi No. 40. This case was published as a model case in (2012) 1 Gazette of Supreme People's Court 38–48.

Supreme People's Court issued a judicial interpretation to address this issue.[62] TML introduces preliminary injunction in 2013. When the infringer is engaged in or will soon engage in actions that infringe the trademark holder's exclusive right to use its registered trademark, unless they are stopped promptly, will cause irreparable injury to its legitimate rights and interests, the court can grant a preliminary injunction to stop such actions based upon the application of the trademark owner or any interested party before filing a lawsuit (Sec. 65 TML). The procedures of applying for a preliminary injunction are laid down in the Civil Procedure Law (CPL).[63] The Chinese courts were very cautious about the application of preliminary injunction. For a long time, there was no preliminary injunction granted since 2002. In the 'HONG SHI' (红狮) case, Beijing Second Intermediate People's Court granted a preliminary injunction for the first time in China in 2015.[64]

4.2 Damages

To award damages relief, two key elements should be reviewed by the court: they are (1) the trademark holder suffers actual losses from the infringing act, and (2) the infringer is negligent towards these losses. When the trademark holder claims for damages, the infringer challenged can raise a counter-plea on the ground that the trademark holder has never used the trademark before the case. The court may order the trademark owner to submit proofs of using the trademark over the past three years. If the trademark owner cannot provide the aforesaid proofs to establish actual losses caused by the infringing acts, the defendant shall not compensate for any claimed losses (Sec. 64(1) TML). In order to gain damages from the infringer, the trademark owner should also prove negligence of the infringer. However, as to selling of infringing products, negligence can be presumed.[65] Where a party unknowingly sells goods infringing upon another party's exclusive right to use a registered trademark, but can prove that it has obtained these goods lawfully and is able to identify the supplier, it shall not be held liable for damages (Sec. 64(2) TML).

The amount of damages for infringing the exclusive right to use a trademark shall be the actual losses that the trademark owner has been suffered as a result of the infringement. The amount of damages will also include reasonable expenses the trademark owner has suffered to prevent the infringement (Sec. 63(1) TML). The

---

[62] Supreme People's Court, Interpretation of the Issues Relating to Application of Law to Pre-trial Suspension of Acts of Infringement of Exclusive Right to Use Trade Marks and to Evidence Preservation.

[63] See Secs. 100–105 CPL.

[64] Beijing Second Intermediate People's Court, *Beijing Hongshi Painting Co. Ltd. v Beijing Hongshijingqi Trade Co. Ltd.* (2014) Er Zhong Min Bao No 10508.

[65] Chen Xiaoyan and Cheng Chunhua, 'Distribution of Burden of Proof and Standard of Proof in Trade Mark Infringement' (2014) 10 Intellectual Property 58.

reasonable expenses include any cost of transportation, investigation, identification, as well as attorney fees, and any other costs used to prevent infringing acts.[66]

In order to solve the difficulties in calculating actual losses, TML provides some alternatives of damage calculation in accordance with Copyright Law and Patent Law (Sec. 63(1) TML). Where the actual losses cannot be determined, the amount of damages for trademark infringement could be the profits that the infringer has earned as a result of the infringement.[67] Where neither the actual loss of the trademark owner nor the profits earned by the infringer can be determined, the amount of damages could be determined based on the amount paid for a licensing royalty for the trademark right. Furthermore, where the actual losses suffered by the trademark owner, the profits earned by the infringer, or the licencing royalties of trademark infringement cannot be determined, the court could award damages up to 3 million RMB yuan according to the facts of the case (Sec. 63(3) TML). For those cases in which the evidence show that the amount of damages are definitely higher than 3 million RMB yuan, the court can decide the exact figure of money on its own judgment beyond the limit of statutory damage.[68] It is clear that TML provides an order of these damage calculation methods. However, most of the courts in China in the judicial practice tend to apply the statutory damages directly on the ground that the former methods of damage calculation are difficult to apply, even the trademark holder did not provide any evidence to prove actual losses, profits of infringer, or established royalties.[69] The current judicial practices are criticized for lacking of certainty, and might free the trademark holders from burden of proof.[70]

Since 2013, punitive damage was introduced by TML to punish the infringer.[71] Punitive damage can be granted in the case of a malicious infringement and an existence of serious circumstances, the amount of damage could be more than one up to three times of the actual losses, profits of the infringers, or royalties (Sec. 63(1) TML). However, there has been no case applying punitive damages in trademark

---

[66] Lang Sheng (ed.), *Interpretation of the Trademark Law of the People's Republic of China* 123 (Law Press, Beijing 2013).

[67] When determining the amount of damages, if the account books and information related to the infringement are held by the infringer, and where the rights owner has presented as much proof of its claims as is practically possible, the court may order the infringer to submit such account books and information. If the infringer refuses to submit such account books and information, or submit a false version thereof, the court may determine the amount of damages with reference to the trademark holder's claims and proofs (Sec. 63(2) TML).

[68] Supreme People's Court, 'The Opinions on Several Issues concerning Intellectual Property Trials Serving the Overall Objective under the Current Economic Situation', Fa Fa [2009] No. 23.

[69] Song Jian, 'Discussion of Damages in Intellectual Property—Based on Empirical Data' (2016) 5 Intellectual Property 12.

[70] Zhang Xiaoxia, 'Double-edge of the Burden of Proof in Damages' (2016) 5 Intellectual Property 28.

[71] Zhou Bohua, Minister of SAIC, 'Introduction to Trade Mark Law Amendment (Draft)', (2013) 5 Gazette of the Standing Committee of the National People's Congress 725.

cases by the courts in China till now.[72] The reason may be the courts in China now tend to grant statutory damage and seldom calculate damages according to the methods stated above. As a result, the relationship between punitive damage and statutory damage needs further discussion.

5. Protection of Well-known Trademark

The protection of well-known trademark was introduce in 2001, with the aim of providing addition protection to the unregistered trademark and expanding the scope of exclusiveness of registered well-known trademarks.[73] These years, the basic understanding of the nature of well-known trademark protection has experienced a significant change. For years, the phrase 'well-known trademark' was used as a keyword in the advertisements, and the number of well-known trademarks granted was deemed as an important indicator of local economic development.[74] Therefore, many Chinese companies were eager to gain well-known trademark certificates from the government, and accordingly, the government was willing to grant those certificates even without any requirement of the trademark owner. These practices are not squared with the basic idea of well-known trademark protection, and have been corrected by the latest amendment of TML since 2013. Accordingly, the specialized law on well-known trademarks in China, Provisions on the Determination and Protection of Well-known Trade Marks (PDPWTM) announced by SAIC in 2003 was amended in 2014.[75]

5.1 Definition and determination

The protection of well-known trademark is an obligation articulated in Article 6(2) of the Paris Convention and Article 16 of TRIPs Agreement. However, there is no definition of well-known trademark in these conventions. In China, a well-known trademark refers to a trademark, registered or unregistered, wildly known to the relative public within the territory of China (Art. 2(1) PDPWM & Art. 1 EWTMP). The relative public includes the consumers of the related goods or services indicated by the said trademark, producers and service providers, as well as the sellers and relevant people involved in the circulation (Art. 2(2) PDPWM).

---

[72] Gong Lintian, 'Trade Mark Punitive Damage: It is not Easy to Say Love You', available at <http://www.zhichanli.com/article/38763>, accessed 28 October 2016.

[73] Lang Sheng (ed.), *Interpretation of the Trademark Law of the People's Republic of China* 33 (Law Press, Beijing 2013).

[74] Yuan Zhenfu, 'Preventing Alienation of Well-known Trade Mark', (2009) 9 Electronics Intellectual Property 23, 24.

[75] The Supreme People's Court also issued the Explanation about the Law Application Issues as Hearing of the Civil Dispute Cases Involving Well-known Trade Mark Protection (EWTMP) in 2009.

Here are the factors that shall be considered in defining a well-known trademark (Sec. 14(1) TML):

(1) the degree of public recognition of the mark within its trading areas;
(2) how long the mark has been used;
(3) the duration and extent of advertising and publicity of the mark, and the geographical extent of the trading areas in which the mark is used;
(4) the record of protection as a well-known trademark;
(5) other factors which can be used to prove well-known of the mark.

It is worth noting that these are just relevant factors which can be used in the determination of a well-known trademark, not all of them should be taken into account in a specific case (Art. 13(1) PDPWM & Art. 4 EWTMP).

A well-known trademark is defined upon requirement of the trademark owner on a case-by-case basis (Art. 4 PDPWM).[76] The phrase 'well-known trademark' cannot be used in advertising, exhibitions or other commercial activities; neither could it be used on the goods, packaging, or containers (Sec. 14(5) TML).[77] Determination of a well-known trademark can be achieved both through administrative and judicial authorities in China.[78] The TMO, TRAB, and the courts appointed by the Supreme People's Court are authorized to identify well-known trademarks. During the examination of a trademark registration and in the course of investigating cases involving illegal use of trademarks handled down by the authorities for industry and commerce, upon a claim filed by the parties involved, the TMO may determine whether a trademark is well-known (Sec. 14(2) TML). In the process of handling a trademark dispute, the parties may, in accordance with Sec. 13 TML, ask the court to decide whether the disputed trademark is well-known; TMRAB may, in accordance with the needs of a specific case, make a determination on its own initiative as to whether the disputed trademark is well-known (Sec. 14(3) TML). In civil and administrative trademark cases, the courts appointed by the Supreme People's Court may make a decision, based on the specific circumstances and needs of each case, as to whether the disputed trademark is a well-known trademark (Sec. 14(4) TML).

---

[76] Before 2013, the administrative authorities could actively grant well-known trademark without the request of trademark owner in a specific case. So, this is a significant change in the determination of well-known trademark when the passive doctrine and case-by-case doctrine were established as the dominant principles in this area.

[77] Anyone who disobeys this rule should be imposed a fine of 100, 000 RMB yuan.

[78] The courts were granted the authority to recognize well-known trademark from 2001 in China. Before then, only the administrative authorities could determine whether a mark was well-known in China.

5.2 Protection

TML provides some extra protection to the well-known trademark.

First, for a registered well-known trademark, both registration and use of the mark which is a reproduction, imitation, or translation of such well-known trademark should be prohibited. That is to say, the exclusiveness of a registered well-known trademark has been expanded to the goods which are not identical to or dissimilar with which the registrant of well-known trademark has been used, if it might mislead the public and cause injury to the interests of the registrant of the well-known trademark (Sec. 13(3) TML). According to the Supreme Peoples' Court, for the protection of a registered well-known trademark in China, dilution doctrine could be applied. For those marks considerably related to a well-known trademark from the perspective of the relative public, therefore, would cause blurring of distinctiveness of the well-known trademark, tarnishing of the trademark holder's reputation, and by which the goodwill of the trademark holder would be misappropriated, both of the use and registration should be prohibited (Rule 9(2) EWTMP).[79] In the 'Cartirena' (卡地亚那) case, Yunnan High People's Court held that the defendant's mark 'Cartirena' used on the wedding photography service diluted the well-known trademark 'Cartier', although it is used on jewelleries.[80]

Second, for an unregistered well-known trademark, TML provide protection similar to a registered trademark in China. Where a mark is a reproduction, imitation, or translation of a third-party's unregistered well-known trademark, no registration shall be granted and the use of the mark shall be prohibited, where the goods are identical or similar, which may cause public confusion and damage the interests of the registrant of the well-known trademark (Sec. 13(2) TML). However, the use and registration of a well-known trademark on dissimilar goods are not prohibited.[81]

Moreover, where a party uses a well-known trademark (registered or unregistered) as a trade name therefore may confuse the public, is unfair competition, the dispute shall be handled in accordance with the AUCL (Sec. 58 TML).

---

[79] But it seems that the dilution doctrine is engraved under the confusion doctrine. See Deng Hongguang, 'Slowing Down the Application of Dilution Doctrine in Well-known Trade Mark Protection in China' (2010) 2 Legal Science 105.

[80] Yunnan High People's Court, *Cartier International N V v Yunnan Cartirena Wedding Photography Co. Ltd.* (2009) Yun Gao Min San Zhong Zi No 35. This case was elected as one of the top fifty typical IP cases in 2009 by the Supreme People's Court, available at <http://www.chinacourt.org/article/detail/2010/04/id/405451.shtml> accessed on 30 October 2016.

[81] Lang Sheng (ed.), *Interpretation of the Trademark Law of the People's Republic of China* 34 (Law Press, Beijing 2013).

6. Concluding Remarks

Trademark law in China is imported from aboard under the background of globalization. Currently, both the legislation and judicial practices of trademark protection in China are experiencing significant changes. One of the most significant recent changes is that trademark protection is becoming much stronger, such as the scope of registerable marks are enlarged to involve sound, the enforcement is more efficient after rules of preliminary injunction and punitive damages being introduced. Moreover, more and more specific issues are arising within the Chinese context, such as protection of public interests in trademark law, the meaning of trademark use in OEM cases, the application of reverse confusion doctrine, and the liability of online auction sites. Most of these issues are still controversial among Chinese scholars and judges. For practitioners, these new trends of the trademark law development are worthy of attention. For academics, these issues are so exciting that the process of arguing on the subject definitely provides a good opportunity for the development of Chinese trademark law research.

5

INTELLECTUAL PROPERTY
COURTS IN CHINA

*Duncan Matthews**

1. Introduction

When the first specialized Intellectual Property (IP) court in the People's Republic of China opened in Beijing on 6 November 2014, it marked a milestone in the process of China's judicial reform. This was followed, before the end of 2014, by two further specialized IP courts in Shanghai and Guangzhou, capital city of Guangdong Province. As a result, while jurisdiction over IP cases still lies with the general courts in other regions of China, in Beijing Municipality, Shanghai Municipality, and Guangdong Province general courts no longer hear civil and administrative cases where the subject matter is specifically related to IP.[1]

The rationale for setting up specialized IP courts was set out by the Supreme Court of the People's Republic of China in its 2014 *White Paper on Intellectual Property Protection by Chinese Courts*, namely that establishing IP courts is a fundamental measure in terms of judicial reform in China as a whole.[2] Similarly, the Central Committee of the Communist Party of China (CCCPC) has stated that it considers the establishment of IP courts to be a significant step in the reform of the national scientific and technological base.[3]

---

[*] Professor of Intellectual Property Law, Centre for Commercial Law Studies, Queen Mary University of London. With thanks to Jingwen Guo for research assistance and translation.

[1] The Guangzhou IP court has jurisdiction over the entire Guangdong Province, while the Beijing and Shanghai IP courts have jurisdiction over smaller geographical areas because they are courts that cover the respective Municipalities.

[2] The Supreme People's Court of the People's Republic of China (中华人民共和国最高人民法院), *Intellectual Property Protection by Chinese Courts in 2014* (中国法院知识产权司法保护2014) (White Paper, 2015) ch 2, available at http://www.wipo.int/wipolex/en/details.jsp?id=15689.

[3] The Central Committee of the Communist Party of China, *Decision of the CCCPC on Some Major Issues Concerning Comprehensively Deepening the Reform* (中共中央关于全面深化改革若干重大问题的决定) (White Paper, 2013) ch 3, para 13, available at http://www.china.org.cn/chinese/2014-01/17/content_31226494.htm.

This chapter provides an overview of China's IP court system, highlighting the process by which the IP courts were set up and assesses how efficiently the courts are operating. The chapter argues that, while specialized IP courts have had a positive effect overall, unresolved issues remain, particularly in terms of the role of technical investigation officers, the operation of the Guiding Cases system, the absence of specialist IP courts of appeal, the lack of jurisdiction over criminal matters in the specialized IP courts, and the need for more effective policies to ensure the recruitment and retention of high calibre judges.

2. Background to the Establishment of China's IP Courts

When establishing specialized IP courts in 2014, China drew on its previous experience of setting up intellectual property tribunals in general jurisdiction courts. In addition, China already had experience of implementing the 'three-in-one' adjudication model on IP litigation, whereby the general courts are seized to hear disputes relating to civil, administrative and criminal law matters. This process began in the late 1980s, as US-China IP disputes came to the fore, and China faced pressure to improve the protection and enforcement of intellectual property rights within its territory. As a result, China began to explore innovative ways of dealing with IP litigation.

On 5 August 1993 intellectual property tribunals, the earliest specialized IP trial fora in China, were set up within the Beijing Intermediate and High People's Court. The following year, the Shanghai Pudong New Area People's Court established its own IP tribunal, the first to be established within the Chinese lower court system. By 1996 an IP tribunal had also been established within the Supreme People's Court, symbolizing the extent of China's intention to build an independent system of adjudication with respect to IP issues into its four-tier court system.[4] By 2012, according to statistics presented in the *2012 Work Report of the Supreme People's Court on Intellectual Property Trials*, a total of 420 IP tribunals had been set up within China's general court system.[5]

A further measure designed to facilitate specialized adjudication in IP cases was implementation of the 'three-in-one' adjudication model. The application of law

---

[4] Xiuting Yuan (袁秀挺), 'Chinese IP Courts: the Vision and the Road (中国知识产权法院的愿景及其实现路径)' (2015) 1 Journal of Science, Technology and Law (科技与法律) 23, 25.

[5] The Supreme People's Court of the People's Republic of China (中华人民共和国最高人民法院), *Work Report of the Supreme Peoples' Court on Intellectual Property Trials—Released on the Eleventh Session of the Standing Committee of the Thirtieth National People's Congress* (2012) (最高人民法院关于知识产权审判工作情况的报告—2012 年12月25日在第十一届全国人民代表大会常务委员会第三十次会议上) (White Paper, 2013) ch 1, available at http://www.npc.gov.cn/npc/xinwen/2013-01/06/content_1750233.htm.

had not been harmonized and different IP tribunals were adopting different approaches when applying the law. This situation was complicated further by the different approaches taken by the courts in proceedings related to civil, administrative, and criminal law, leading to the risk that judges could make contradictory decisions on IP matters.[6] A judge of the criminal tribunal, for instance, might hold that a defendant's conduct was illegal when measured against accepted standards of criminal law and award supplementary compensation in the criminal trial whilst, conversely, the civil tribunal might determine that the conduct in suit did not necessitate the payment of compensation. In order to resolve this problem, a 'three-in-one' adjudication model was devised and initially adopted by the Shanghai Pudong New Area People's Court in 1996.[7] By the end of 2013, the 'three-in-one' adjudication model, incorporating civil, administrative, and criminal matters within the same court proceedings, had been adopted by seven High People's Courts, seventy-nine Intermediate People's Courts and seventy-one Basic People's Courts across China.[8]

Building on the initiatives taken with IP tribunals, the establishment of specialized IP courts was first suggested in 2001 by Boming Wu (吴伯明), a member of CPPCC (National Committee of the Chinese People's Political Consultative Conference), who proposed to establish China's IP courts in the Fourth Session of the Ninth CPPCC.[9] This initiated a debate on the necessity and feasibility of a specialized IP court system and, by 2008, significant progress had been made with the State Council announcing, in its *Outlines of the State Intellectual Property*

---

[6] Xiaoqing Feng (冯晓青) and Li Wang (王丽), 'From Specialised Tribunals to Specialised Court: New Development of China's IP Judicature (从专门法庭到专门法院:我国知识产权司法的最新进展透析)' (2015) 35 (3) Academic Forum of Nandu (Journal of the Humanities and Social Sciences) [南都学坛(人文社会科学学报)] 59, 61–2.

[7] In 1995 one civil case, one administrative case, and one criminal case which all related to the infringement of a trademark called 'Fei Ying', owned by Shanghai Jilie Limited Company, were brought to the Shanghai Pudong New Area People's Court. The three cases were each heard separately by the intellectual property tribunal, the administrative tribunal, and the criminal tribunal respectively. However, the court found that the crux of the three cases was that they all dealt with the infringement of intellectual property rights and that, if the IP-related civil, administrative, and criminal cases were integrated and dealt with by the intellectual property tribunal, it would improve the quality and efficiency of adjudication as the intellectual property tribunals are experienced in hearing cases related to IP issues. As a result, the Shanghai Pudong New Area People's Court adopted a 'three-in-one' adjudication model. See Xueyou Sheng (盛学友), 'What does "There-in-one" Bring to us-Investigating Shanghai Intellectual Property New Mechanism ("三合一"给我们带来什么-探访上海知识产权"三审合一"新机制)' (2009) 24 Law and Life (法律与生活) 45.

[8] The Supreme People's Court of the People's Republic of China (中华人民共和国最高人民法院), *Intellectual Property Protection by Chinese Courts in 2014* (中国法院知识产权司法保护2014) (White Paper, 2015) ch 2, available at http://www.chinacourt.org/article/detail/2014/04/id/1283299.shtml.

[9] *Yuan* (n 4) 26.

Strategy, the intention to explore the establishment of specialized IP courts with jurisdiction in particular over highly technical patent cases.[10]

Subsequently, on 13 November 2013, the *Decision of the CCCPC on Some Major Issues Concerning Comprehensively Deepening the Reform*, was adopted at the Third Plenary Session of the Eighteenth Central Committee of the CPC (Communist Party of China), highlighting the need for China to strengthen the protection of intellectual property rights, improve mechanisms to stimulate innovation, and explore the possibility of establishing IP courts as part of the wider strategy of reforming the national scientific and technological base.[11] Motivated by the CCCPC's Decision, several prominent municipalities immediately declared their intention to set up specialized IP courts.[12] Then, on 6 June 2014, an official plan for establishing IP courts was adopted by the Central Committee of the CPC.

By 31 August 2014, the Standing Committee of the Twelfth National People's Congress had enacted a decision on the establishment of IP Courts in Beijing, Shanghai, and Guangzhou. This was followed subsequently by the Supreme People's Court promulgation of the *Provisions of the Supreme People's Court on the Jurisdiction of the Intellectual Property Courts of Beijing, Shanghai and Guangzhou over Cases*, which set out the extent of the jurisdiction of the IP courts.[13]

3. Rationale for the Establishment of Specialized IP Courts

According to the official sources outlined above, establishing specialized IP courts was considered an important element in the reform of the judicial and technological system in China. More specifically, the rationale for the establishment of specialized IP courts can be further sub-divided under the five headings outlined below.

3.1 Policy reasons

At a national level, the quality of adjudication regarding IP disputes in China is directly related to national economic development, technological innovation, and the nation's status in terms of international relations. China began to explore effective

---

[10] The State Council of the People's Republic of China (中华人民共和国国务院), *Outlines of the State Intellectual Property Strategy* (国家知识产权战略纲要) (White Paper, 2008) para 45.

[11] *The Central Committee of the Communist Party of China* (n 3).

[12] *Feng and Wang* (n 6), 60.

[13] Provisions of the Supreme People's Court on the Jurisdiction of the Intellectual Property Courts of Beijing, Shanghai and Guangzhou over Cases (最高人民法院关于北京、上海、广州知识产权法院案件管辖的规定关于北京、上海、广州知识产权法院案件管辖的规定), promulgated by the Adjudication Committee of the Supreme People's Court, 27 October 2014, issued 3 November 2014 (hereinafter Provisions on Jurisdiction), available at http://www.chinacourt.org/law/detail/2014/10/id/147980.shtml.

ways of reforming its judicial system in the field of IP law after observing the approach taken by other countries in the region and taking into account its obligations under the World Trade Organization (WTO) Agreement on Trade-Related Aspects of Intellectual Property Rights (the TRIPS Agreement).[14] Furthermore, the introduction of a specialized IP court system was seen as an effective response to bilateral pressure to improve the protection and enforcement of intellectual property rights.[15]

3.2 The increasing number of IP cases

China also faced an increasing number of civil and administrative cases with respect to IP issues, putting a strain on the existing court system. According to the Supreme People's Court *White Paper* on *IP Protection Provided by Chinese Courts*, the number of filed cases increased by 19.52% from 2013 to 2014, reaching a total number of over 130,000.[16] Furthermore, due to the uneven nature of technological and economic development in different regions of China, most IP cases arose in the Beijing-Tianjin-Hebei region, the Shanghai-centred Yangtze River Delta region and the Guangzhou-centred Pearl River Delta region.[17] Given that the general courts are set up according to the layout of administrative divisions, this meant that IP litigation was distributed disproportionately amongst the administrative divisions.[18] As a result, it made sense to establish specialized IP courts in the regions where IP litigation most often occurred. The decision to focus on creating IP courts in regions with a propensity for IP litigation was therefore a pragmatic one in terms of the allocation of judicial resources.

However, not all commentators agreed that the setting up of specialized IP courts in China was entirely necessary. Xiuting Yuan argued that the number of IP cases

---

[14] Thailand, for instance, set up the Central Intellectual Property and International Trade Court to deal with IP and trade-related matters. See *Yuan* (n 4) 30.

[15] The United States had removed Taiwan from the Special 301 Watch List in 2009 after it set up an IP court system. The IP court system in Taiwan shares many common features with the specialized IP courts in Mainland China, including the 'three-in-one' adjudication model and the role of technical investigation officers. See *Yuan* (n 4) 30; also see Jiming Yi (易继明), 'Why to Establish IP Courts (为什么要设立知识产权法院)' (2014) 4 Journal of Science, Technology and Law (科技与法律) 573, 577.

[16] The Supreme People's Court (n 2).

[17] In 2012, the top 1–7 in the ranking list of China's courts based on the number of filed civil first instance cases are: Guangdong Province (23,672), Zhejiang Province (16,171), Beijing (8,492), Jiangsu Province (8,526), Shandong Province (5,309), Hubei Province (4,758), and Shanghai (3,251). Jiangsu Province, Zhejiang Province, and Shanghai belong to Yangtze River Delta region. This data demonstrates that IP-related civil litigation is concentrated in the Beijing-Tianjin-Hebei region, the Yangtze River Delta region and the Pearl River Delta region. See Editing Committee of Yearbook for Judicial Protection of Intellectual Property in China (中国知识产权司法保护年鉴编辑委员会), *Yearbook for Judicial Protection of Intellectual Property in China* (中国知识产权司法保护年鉴) *(2012)* (Law Press China, 2013) 66–154.

[18] *Yi* (n 15) 574.

was insufficient to justify the setting up of specialized IP courts in China because IP litigation accounts for a small proportion of the total number of cases heard by Chinese courts as a whole, amounting to approximately 1.14% of all cases heard by Chinese courts in 2013.[19] Xiuting Yuan questioned whether the increase in the number of IP cases had been significant enough to justify the establishment of specialized IP courts, arguing that cases related to property, employment, banking and finance and family matters should perhaps then also be heard by specialized courts.[20]

However, a combination of factors has driven the establishment of specialized IP courts and these factors are not accounted for only by the numerical increase in IP cases. The distinctive characteristics of IP litigation, such as the concentration of IP disputes in particular geographical locations in China and the difficulties encountered by general courts when considering highly technical facts in IP cases, makes this a field of the law that warrants special treatment within the court system.

In reality, faced with the challenge of a rapidly increasing number of IP cases, China had two choices, first to simply increase the number of judges in the general courts or, second, to reform the existing judicial system by establishing specialized IP courts. Superficially, employing more judges in general courts would have been a much more efficient method of dealing with the challenge faced due to an increase in the number of IP cases. However, China also needed to address the policy imperative of improving the quality of adjudication in IP disputes. Taking these factors into account in their totality, arguments in favour of the establishment of IP courts in China prevailed.

3.3 The complexity and technical nature of IP disputes

The complexity of IP cases, in term of both legal and technical issues, proved to be an important factor in the creation of specialized IP courts in China. The difficulties associated with deciding on highly technical facts and identifying technical issues posed a great challenge to general courts and proponents of specialized IP courts pointed out that judges with experience of hearing cases involving a particular subject matter are more likely to reach reliable judgments than judges sitting in general courts. By way of comparison, in the United States for instance, Judge Friendly has noted that courts are often faced with a large number of patent cases involving a range of high technologies 'which are quite beyond the ability of the

---

[19] *Yuan* (n 4) 28: 'With regard to the number of IP cases, in recent years it is increasing rapidly (on average, by 30% per year); however, it is still small compared to the number of other cases. According to the 2013 Statistical Bulletin of China's Courts, 8,876,733 first instance cases were heard and the number of IP cases (including administrative, civil and criminal cases) was 100,800 which occupied just 1.14%.'

[20] Ibid.

usual judge to understand without the expenditure of an inordinate amount of educational effort by counsel and of attempted self-education by the judge, and in many instances, even with it'.[21] As a consequence, the technical complexity of underlying facts is seen as a key driver leading to demands for specialized IP courts.[22]

3.4 Lack of judicial consistency

Another important factor that accounts for the establishment of specialized IP courts in China is that un-harmonized standards of adjudication on IP-related cases can have a negative impact on the creation new technologies. Ambiguity in legal instruments, the absence of a reliable body of established case law, and an uneven quality of judges leads to different standards being adopted in terms of the application and interpretation of IP law. Different courts may well make different judgments even when the facts and legal issues are similar in cases. Such inconsistency and lack of predictability can have an adverse impact on the reputation of the courts and on the predictability of IP law. As discussed above, the setting up of IP tribunals in China's general jurisdiction courts was the first step in the process of specializing IP trials. However, the operation of these IP tribunals is less than straightforward. Due to the geographical concentration of IP cases around Beijing, Shanghai, and Guangzhou, judges working in IP tribunals in regions where fewer IP disputes occur are sometimes asked to hear other types of civil cases, such as family law cases, in order to ensure they have an appropriate caseload.[23] As a result, judges in these regions do not have significant experience in hearing IP cases, indicating that the setting up of IP tribunals does not automatically result in improvements to the quality of adjudicative decisions. Furthermore, even though IP tribunals are now well established in China, there is no compelling evidence that this system has been particularly helpful in terms of harmonizing standards of adjudication.

---

[21] Henry Friendly, *Federal Jurisdiction: A General View* (CUP, 1973) 156–7. This statement cited by Richard L. Revesz, 'Specialised Courts and the Administrative Law-making System' (1990) 138 (4) U Pa L Rev 1111, 1117–18.

[22] *Feng and Wang* (n 6) 61. On the other hand, Xiuting Yuan, a former IP judge, has argued from the opposite point of view and said that the difficulty of finding technical facts can be solved by using expert witness and other professional advisors without employing more staff in courts and even setting up specialized IP courts. He also indicated that this difficulty seems to be exaggerated. According to Xiuting Yuan, 'I worked as a IP judge for several years. Based on my experience and my observations, technical issues are generally not concerned with trade mark cases while they are involved in a few copyright cases. In a considerable amount of patent cases, there is no dispute between litigants with regard to technical issues. Two parties in a litigation always have a consensus on the facts of infringement and merely have different opinions on the issue of liability... this phenomenon may be related to the quality of patents in China. The proportion of IP cases involving disputes on technical issues is not more than 20%.' See *Yuan* (n 4) 29.

[23] Ibid.

3.5 The problem of circuity of action

Circuity of action involving intellectual property rights is another significant reason why commentators advocate the existence of specialized IP courts in China.[24] This situation arises due to the bifurcated nature of Chinese IP legal proceedings whereby there may well be a civil proceeding, for instance an infringement action, and an administrative proceeding, such as a validity challenge, running concurrently. This can lead to problems in the sense that patentees or trademark owners may have to spend longer than necessary claiming remedies for IP infringement.[25] Patent disputes in China, for example, usually involve not only the courts but also the Patent Re-examination Board of the State Intellectual Property Office (SIPO) which, since 28 August 2018, has been renamed the China National Intellectual Property Administration (CNIPA) because the re-examination of patents granted by SIPO (and now by CNIPA) is considered an administrative function to be dealt with the body that originally granted the patent in the first place.[26]

Since November 2014, with the establishment of the Beijing IP Court, an administrative suit against decisions made by the Patent Re-Examination Board of SIPO (now CNIPA) or by the Trade Mark Review and Adjudication Board is brought before the Beijing IP Court instead of the Beijing No. 1 Intermediate Court, as was previously the case. Any private entity can bring an administrative action before the Beijing IP Court challenging SIPO's (now CNIPA's) decisions.[27] If the Beijing IP Court rejects the claim, the complainant can appeal to the Beijing High People's Court. If the Beijing IP Court overturns the administrative decision made by the Patent Re-Examination Board of SIPO (now CNIPA)—and it can only require the

---

[24] See Guangman Li (李光曼) and Xing Zhao (赵兴), 'Concerning Reflections and Suggestions of "Three-in-one" IP Adjudication-Based on the Establishment of IP Courts (关于知识产权审判"三合一"的反思与建言-以知识产权法院设立为背景)' (2015) 1 Journal of Jiangxi Police Institution (江西警察学院学报) 118, 120; see also Minglin Li (黎明琳) and Yuzhu Wang (王玉柱), 'Analysis on Judicial Practice of IP Courts and IP Protection in Shanghai Municipality (知识产权法院与上海知识产权保护的司法实践分析)' (2016) 2 Legal System and Society (法制与社会) 136, 136.

[25] Yinliang Liu (刘银良), 'Demonstrations on Establishment of IP Courts in China (我国知识产权法院设置问题论证)' (2015) 3 Intellectual Property (知识产权) 3, 4.

[26] In addition to patents, utility models, and designs, CNIPA now also handles trademarks (formerly administered by the State Administration of Industry and Commerce, SAIC) and geographical indications (formerly handled by the Administration of Quality Supervision, Inspection and Quarantine, AQSIQ).

[27] After the Beijing IP Court was established, an administrative suit against the decisions on affirmation of intellectual property rights made by Patent Re-Examination Board of SIPO or Trade Mark Review and Adjudication Board shall be brought to the Beijing IP Court instead of the Beijing No. 1 Intermediate Court. Since 28 August 2018 CNIPA, the successor organization to SIPO, has taken over responsiblity for the registration and administrative adjudication of trademarks. Although the Patent Re-Examination Board and the Trade Mark Review and Adjudication Board are still separated, both of them now come under the CNIPA organizational structure. Prior to this, the Trade Mark Review and Adjudication Board was a part of the State Administration for Industry and Commerce of the People's Republic of China.

Board to make a new decision—it has no authority to amend or correct such a decision. If the Patent Re-Examination Board further makes a similar administrative decision, the private entity will have to bring a new administrative suit against this new decision to the Beijing IP Court in order to quash it again. This will be the case even though the new administrative decision will be the same as the previous one brought before the Beijing IP Court and the issues in suit will be essentially the same as in the previous trial.[28] As a result, the Patent Re-Examination Board of SIPO (now CNIPA) can still make a similar administrative decision on the same issue, requiring the private entity to later bring a new administrative action against this new decision. Consequently, a circuity of action occurs, leading to inefficiencies in the allocation of administrative and judicial resources. In this regard, improving the efficiency of IP trials with respect to civil or administrative disputes is considered by the Beijing High People's Court as a measure necessary to reduce the negative effects brought by the circuity of actions.[29]

Although, one of the main objectives of the establishment of the IP court system was to solve this problem and improve the efficiency of IP proceedings, it has not yet been resolved.[30] The fundamental reason for this problem is that, due to the bifurcated system, Chinese courts are not entitled to declare a patent or trademark invalid, either in a civil case or an administrative case. Instead, the validity of intellectual property rights is considered a matter to be dealt with by SIPO (now CNIPA), an administrative body. In order to avoid circuity of actions involving intellectual property rights entirely, the specialized IP courts would need jurisdiction

---

[28] According to Article 71 of Administrative Procedure Law of the People's Republic of China 2015, when courts make a judgment to order an administrative body to make new administrative action, it cannot make a similar action based on the same facts and reasons. However, in practice, it is quite common for an administrative body to make similar decisions over and over, which leads to circuity of action. See Bixin Jiang (江必新) and Changmao Shao (邵长茂), *Interpretation and Application of Amended Provisions on New Administrative Procedure Law* (新行政诉讼法修改条文理解与适用) (China Legal Publishing House[中国法制出版社] 2015) 283.

[29] See the Beijing High People's Court (北京市高级人民法院), *Work Report of the Beijing High People's Court on the Judicial Protection of Intellectual Property Rights-released on the Twenty-first Session of the Standing Committee of the Fourteenth Beijing Municipal National People's Congress on Sep.23, 2015* (北京市高级人民法院关于知识产权司法保护情况的报告-2015年9月23日在北京市第十四届人民代表大会常务委员会第二十一次会议上) (White Paper, 2015) ch 2, available at http://www.bjcourt.gov.cn/article/newsDetail.htm;jsessionid=1F7E05B038440BB7AFFCF677770BF8E7?NId=55001088&channel=100001012.

[30] Guangliang Zhang (张广良) 'On the Thinking of Localisation of Designing Intellectual Property Court System (知识产权法院制度设计的本土化思维)' (2014) 6 The Jurist (法学家) 55, 60; Jiming Yi (易继明), 'What Kind of IP Courts should be Established (设立什么样的知识产权法院)' (2014) 4 Journal of Science, Technology and Law (科技与法律) 747,751; also see He Guo (郭禾), 'Reform of the Patent Invalidation System and its Cooperation with IP Court Construction-Discussing from the Fourth Amendment of Patent Law (专利权无效宣告制度的改造与知识产权法院建设的协调-从专利法第四次修订谈起)' (2016) 3 Intellectual Property (知识产权) 14, 15–19; also see *Liu* (n 25) 7–11.

to decide whether a patent or trademark was valid.[31] At the present time, China's specialized IP courts do not have such powers over validity matters.

4. Main Features of the Specialized IP Court System

One of the main factors driving the establishment of specialized IP courts in China has been a desire to unify standards of adjudication with respect to IP matters. The three specialized IP courts in Beijing, Shanghai, and Guangzhou must now interface with the general courts and other judicial organizations to achieve adjudicative consistence. Accordingly, the Supreme People's Court has promulgated two official documents to regulate such matters.[32]

4.1 Scope of jurisdiction

The specialized IP courts in Beijing, Shanghai, and Guangzhou have first instance jurisdiction over civil and administrative cases related to patents, new plant varieties, layout design of integrated circuits, know-how, and computer software.[33] In addition, administrative cases regarding copyright, trademark, and unfair competition, in terms of first instance jurisdiction to hear actions against the administrative decisions of departments of the State Council or local governments (at or above county level) are transferred to the specialized IP courts.[34]

Unlike the Shanghai and Guangzhou specialized IP courts, the Beijing IP court also has an exclusive first instance jurisdiction to hear cases against administrative actions made by a department under the State Council involving authorization and affirmation of intellectual property rights, and compulsory licences (including the royalties associated with the granting of compulsory licences) relating to patents, new plant varieties, and layout designs of integrated circuits.[35] The specialized IP courts are also responsible for hearing appeals against the Basic People's Courts' civil and administrative judgments or awards relating to

---

[31] Some commentators propose to amend the Chinese Administrative Procedure Law in order to solve this problem. See *Liu* (n 27) 8. Yongshun Cheng (程永顺) participating at the seminar *Commercial Law in China: Intellectual Property in Business* organised by the Centre for Commercial Law Studies, Queen Mary University of London, on 15 December 2016 stated that an administrative procedure is an inadequate means of resolving validity matters relating to intellectual property rights.

[32] Two official documents are *Provisions on Jurisdiction* and *Notice of the Supreme People's Court on Issues concerning the Jurisdiction of Intellectual Property Courts over Cases* (最高人民法院关于知识产权法院案件管辖等有关问题的通知) (hereinafter *Notice on Jurisdiction*).

[33] Provisions of Jurisdiction, art 1.

[34] Ibid.

[35] Ibid., art 6.

copyright, trademarks, technology contracts, unfair competition, and other intellectual property rights.[36]

In terms of jurisdiction rules with respect to the specialized IP courts in China, when compared to the general courts' jurisdiction with regard to IP litigation, the jurisdiction over IP-related criminal cases still remains with general courts, no matter whether these cases are dealt with at first or second instance. In addition, except in the case of the Beijing IP court which has jurisdiction to hear cases against administrative actions made by a department under the State Council concerning affirmation and other specified IP issues, the jurisdiction to deal with civil and administrative cases is not exclusive. This may result in a conflict of jurisdiction between a specialized IP court and a general court. Given that a defendant's place of residence, for example if he or she is located in Shanghai Municipality, may be different from the place where patent infringement has been committed, for example in Nanjing, both the specialized IP court in Shanghai and a Basic People's Court in Nanjing will have jurisdiction to hear this case in terms of civil law.[37] Due to the absence of clear rules on this matter, it is presumed that the claimant can choose which court he would like to bring a case before. Nevertheless, it has been suggested by Xudong Zhang that preference will be given to the specialized IP court when there is conflict of jurisdiction, giving priority to the availability of a specialized adjudication.[38]

In the United States, concern over the possibility of forum shopping has prompted commentators to support the establishment of a court with appellate jurisdiction over patent cases.[39] Dreyfuss, for example, has pointed out that forum shopping in IP disputes is caused by the huge difference on the ratio of decisions holding a patent valid and infringed to those holding a patent invalid among different District Court circuits, with the result that uncertainty as to which court is responsible may well have an adverse impact in terms of establishing legal certainty.[40] As with

---

[36] Ibid.

[37] According to Article 5 of *Provisions of the Supreme People's Court on Several Issues Concerning the Application of Law Related to Hearing Patent Disputes* (最高人民法院关于审理专利纠纷案件适用法律问题的若干规定), patent infringement cases shall be heard by the court where infringement occurred or where the defendant's settled place of abode is located.

[38] Xudong Zhang (张旭东), 'Inspection on China's Jurisdiction of Intellectual Property Civil Cases-from the Angle of Patent Cases (中国知识产权法院民事案件管辖规定检视-以专利纠纷案件为视角)' (2015) 9 Social Sciences of Beijing (北京社会科学) 81, 84.

[39] *Revesz* (n 23) 1116.

[40] Rochelle C Dreyfuss, 'The Federal Circuit: A Case Study in Specialized Courts' (1989) 64 NYUL Rev 1, 7: 'In the period 1945–1957, a patent was twice as likely to be held valid and infringed in the Fifth Circuit than in the Seventh Circuit, and almost four times more likely to be enforced in the Seventh Circuit than in the Second Circuit … Without knowing where a patent would be litigated, it became impossible to adequately counsel technology developers or users. In such a legal environment, the promise of a patent could hardly be considered sufficient incentive to invest in research and development.' This statement was cited by *Revesz* (n 23) 1116–17.

claimants in the United States, a rational approach for Chinese plaintiffs may well be to choose an IP-friendly court in order to increase the odds of the proprietor prevailing in the dispute.

4.2 The relationship between the specialized IP courts and general courts

As with general jurisdiction courts in China, specialized IP courts are supervised by the Supreme People's Court and by the High Court in the location of the IP court.[41] Given that appeals against a decision or award made by a specialized IP court at first instance will be heard by the intellectual property tribunal of the High Court where the IP court is situated,[42] it can be seen that there is no unified IP appeal court in China.[43]

5. Characteristics of the Specialized IP Courts in China

Based on lessons drawn from foreign IP court systems, notably Taiwan, and its own practical experience in establishing IP tribunals and implementing the 'three-in-one' adjudication model, China has set up an innovative specialized IP court system with a number of noteworthy characteristics, each of which will be discussed under the headings below.

5.1 The use of technical investigation officers

In order to address the challenge of how best to assess technical facts, the IP specialized courts employ technical investigation officers. China's specialized IP courts are not unique in using technical investigation officers to hear complex disputes, particularly in the field of patent litigation. Japan, South Korea, and Taiwan have adopted a similar approach to hearing IP disputes. The *Interim Provisions on Several Issues Relating to Technical Investigation Officers of IP Courts to Participate in Intellectual Property Court Proceedings*,[44] issued by the Supreme People's Court on 2014, sets out the responsibilities of technical investigation officers and determines the procedures for their participation in IP trials. Unlike expert witnesses and technical judges, technical investigation officers act as judicial assistants and give their opinions regarding technical issues, with the limitation that they do not have the

---

[41] Article 5 of *Decision of the Standing Committee of the National People's Congress on Establishing Intellectual Property Right Courts in Beijing, Shanghai and Guangzhou* (全国人大常委会关于在北京、上海、广州设立知识产权法院的决定).

[42] Provisions on Jurisdiction, art 7.

[43] The advantages of specialized IP appeals court are discussed in Section 6.

[44] *Interim Provisions on Several Issues Relating to Technical Investigation Officers of IP Courts to Participate in Intellectual Property Court Proceedings* (最高人民法院关于知识产权法院技术调查官参与诉讼活动若干问题的暂行规定) (hereinafter *Interim Provisions*).

power to make judicial decisions.[45] Technical investigation officers can attend collegiate panel deliberations and participate in many stages of civil and administrative
trials, including investigations, evidence collection, inspection, and preservation.[46]
With the judge's permission, they can question the litigants, *agents ad litem*, witnesses, appraisers, and inspectors with regard to case-related technical issues.[47]

However, the need to appoint technical investigation officers in specialized IP
courts is questioned for two reasons. First, although establishing technical facts is
generally the most difficult matter in IP trials, in other jurisdictions the court can
find technical facts by relying on the opinions of expert witnesses and professional
consultants without employing technical investigation officers.[48] Secondly, it can
be argued that the system of technical investigation officers may pose a threat to
the independence of the judiciary. When a judge hears a case with complex technical matters, that judge may become over-reliant on the technical investigation
officer's opinion, leading to a risk that the technical investigation officers in fact act
as technical judges.[49]

Furthermore, technical investigation officers differ from other trial participants
who serve to provide technical opinions (such as expert witnesses, technical advisors, and judicial authenticators) in that technical investigation officers are usually former employees of the courts. To put it in another way, they are the judges'
colleagues whereas other trial participants are third-party participants who provide
professional opinions on behalf of one of the parties or at request of the court.
Their role also differs from other trial participants in that technical investigation
officers are entitled to attend the collegiate panel, participate in its deliberations,
or participate in other court investigative activities, evidence collection, inspection,
and preservation.

The Chinese specialized IP courts themselves have indicated that technical investigation officers have had a positive impact on the courts' deliberations. In the
Beijing IP court, for example, there are currently twenty-five technical investigation
officers and they have participated in finding technical facts in 250 cases, providing
110 technical examination opinions.[50] The Beijing IP court has indicated that their

---

[45] *Interim Provisions*, arts 1 and 8. However, the related regulations do not state whether their
opinions shall be available to litigants.

[46] *Interim Provisions*, art 6.

[47] *Interim Provisions*, art 7.

[48] See *Yuan* (n 4) 29. Also see *Zhang G* (n 30) 63: 'Technical appraisal is available and the people
with technical knowledge are allowed to participate the trials. In addition, the system of expert commission is established in China. Thus, there is no need to introduce technical investigation officers.'

[49] *Zhang G* (n 30) 63.

[50] Closure rate = the sum of cases closed/the sum of cases filed. See Qing Li (李青),
'Judges' Brain Trust Making Adjudication More Professional-System of Technical
Investigation Officer Operating for One Year in the Beijing IP Court (法官"智囊"

work has been particularly beneficial in terms of improving the quality and efficiency of adjudication on technology-related cases and as a result the court has increased the completion rate of IP cases involving technology by 87%.[51] Since cases involving complex technologies have now been transferred from general courts within the Beijing Municipality, the Shanghai Municipality, and the Guangdong Province to the three specialized IP courts, judges in the IP courts need to deal with more complex technical matters than those in the general courts on a regular basis. In the Shanghai IP court, for instance, nearly 90% of filed cases involve disputes on technical issues.[52] The availability of reliable technical advice for the IP courts has therefore arguably become more important.

Conversely, the risks associated with employing technical investigation officers also deserve further attention. One risk is that it is entirely possible they may serve as technical judges alongside their role as technical investigation officers. As a result, it could be argued that using a technical investigation officer offers a lower degree of independence than using an expert witness or technical advisor acting on behalf of one of the parties. As technical investigation officers are court employees, a judge may well trust their professional opinion to a greater extent than advice provided by an expert witness or an independent technical advisor since a technical investigation officer is, in effect, his colleague.[53] In addition, it is difficult for a judge without professional knowledge to eliminate non-neutral opinions provided by technical investigation officers. Consequently, it is important to consider how China can reduce the risks associated with employing technical investigation officers if it is to review and build on the specialized IP courts system in the future.[54]

让裁判更专业-北京知产法院技术调查官制度运行一年)' *People's Court Daily* (人民法院报) (Beijing, October 2016) 4.

[51] Ibid.

[52] Yingying Chen (陈颖颖) and Yejie Wang (王烨捷), 'The Shanghai IP Court Employed 11 Technical Investigation Officers for the First Time (上海知识产权法院首聘11位技术调查官)' (*China Daily* [中国日报], 23 March, 2016), available at <http://www.chinadaily.com.cn/micro-reading/dzh/2016-03-23/content_14622415.html> accessed 9 January 2017.

[53] The most important reason why many lawyers in China are former judges is that a former judge has already built a professional network—he has strong connection with other judges in courts. It is quite common for a client to ask a lawyer if he knows anyone working in the court that will hear the client's case. If there is a private relationship between the judge and the lawyer hired by one of the parties, the judge may make a decision in a shorter time. Furthermore, due to the absence of binding case law, it is feasible for the judge to make a decision for the sake of this party's interest by exercising his discretion.

[54] Some commentators have suggested that it is more appropriate for the specialized IP courts to employ technical judges rather than technical investigation officers. See, for example, Xudong Zhang (above n 38) 85: 'It is supposed that China should follow Germany to combine legal judges and technical judges in order to improve the predictability and consistency of adjudication effectively and truly achieve the goals of specialisation on courts, adjudication and judges.'

5.2 Establishing a system of guiding IP cases

On 15 November 2010 the Supreme People's Court issued *The Provisions of the Supreme People's Court Concerning Work on Case Guidance*,[55] indicating that China would start to build a Guiding Cases system to serve as a significant element in China's judicial reform project.[56] In the absence of legal precedence in the Chinese system, the identification of guiding IP cases aims to assist with solving the problem of adjudicative inconsistency across China's lower courts. In order to clarify the use of guiding IP cases, on 27 April 2015 the Supreme People's Court announced that lower courts 'should quote the Guiding Cases as a reason for their adjudication, but not cite it as the basis of their adjudication'.[57]

In support of the Guiding Cases project, on 24 April 2015, the Supreme People's Court established a research base of guiding intellectual property cases in the Beijing IP Court. Underpinned by the research and adjudication resources of the Beijing IP Court, the system requires that the judge, collegiate panel, and adjudication committee member of the Beijing IP Court will consider guiding cases in the process of pre-trial preparation, hearing, and when writing the judgment.[58] It also requires the judge to identify related precedents, cite, and explain the relevance of guiding IP cases in their written judgments.[59] In addition, judges in the Beijing IP court are now required to state in detail, in the written judgment, how and why the collegiate panel reached its decision. This approach differs from the traditional format of written judgments in China.[60]

The Beijing IP court is also building a database, recording guiding cases, as a means of reference and resource for judges, lawyers, and scholars in the future.[61] In 2015,

---

[55] (最高人民法院关于案例指导工作的规定), promulgated by the Adjudication Committee of the Supreme People's Court, 15 November 2010, issued 26 November 2010, translated in Stanford Law Sch., China Guiding Cases Project, available at https://cgc.law.stanford.edu/wp-content/uploads/sites/2/2015/08/guiding-cases-rules-20101126-english.pdf.

[56] For detail introduction and analysis on China's guiding cases system, see Mark Jia, 'Chinese Common law? Guiding Cases and Judicial Reform' (2016) 129 (8) HLR 2213.

[57] Article 10 of *Detailed Rules for the Implementation of the 'Provisions of the Supreme People's Court Concerning Work on Case Guidance'* (最高人民法院关于案例指导工作的规定实施细则), promulgated by the Adjudication Committee of the Supreme People's Court, 27 April 2015, issued 13 May 2015, translated in Stanford Law School, China Guiding Cases Project (2015), available at <https://cgc.law.stanford.edu/wp-content/uploads/sites/2/2015/10/guiding-cases-rules-20150513-english.pdf>, (hereinafter *Rules on Case Guidance*). In terms of the binding force of guiding cases (a source of law or a source of reference), Mark Jia stated, 'the 2015 Rules did much to legitimate the use and citation of guiding cases in lower court decisions, while still supporting the view that guiding cases were binding de facto but not de jure'. See *Jia* (n 56) 2224.

[58] Research Team of the Beijing Intellectual Property Court (北京知识产权法院课题组), 'Thinking and Exploring about the Reform of Operation of Adjudicative Power—the Beijing Intellectual Property Court as a Sample Analysed (关于审判权运行机制改革的思考与探索-以北京知识产权法院为分析样本)' (2015) 10 Journal of Law Application (法律适用) 6, 9.

[59] Ibid.

[60] Ibid.

[61] Ibid.

the Beijing IP Court made over sixty judgments based on *stare decisis*, namely the legal principle of determining points in litigation according to precedent.[62] As Chi Su, the President of the Beijing IP court, has made clear the Guiding Cases system in effect changes the relationship between the judge and the lawyer.[63] For Chi Su, when judges encourage lawyers to cite related precedents, this makes the statements of lawyers more important in trials.[64]

However, it should be noted that the usage rate of guiding IP cases remains low. From 6 November 2014 to 20 August 2015, the Beijing IP Court heard 2,348 cases.[65] Yet only about 60 of these cases were decided according to precedents as part of the Guiding Cases project. This situation may be explained partly by the fact that only ten IP-related cases have been issued by the Supreme People's Court as part of the Guiding Cases project.[66] It seems that a number of challenges remain in the operation of guiding IP cases system. Firstly, the Office for the Work on Case Guidance of the Supreme People's Court is in charge of review and selection and determines which jurisprudence qualifies as a Guiding Case.[67] When compared to the judges working in the specialized IP courts, judges in the Supreme Court have far less experience of dealing with IP disputes, even though they are the ones tasked with selecting the guiding cases. Secondly, as the judges working in the Supreme Court are former judges of the general courts, they do not have the benefit of specialized IP training, nor do they necessarily have any particular experience of identifying appropriate precedents or making a comparison between a new case and the similar cases previously. Furthermore, the current format of written judgments increases the degree of difficulty in identifying similar prior cases.[68] It is not the final decision that matters but the reasoning written in the judgment of a

---

[62] Lijun Mao (毛立军), 'IP Courts: Providing Protection with the Comprehensive Development of Innovation (知识产权法院:为全面创新发展提供司法保护)' *The People's Political Consultative Daily* (中国政协报) (Beijing, 26 April 2016) 12.

[63] Ibid.

[64] Ibid.

[65] This statistic was given by Chi Su, the President of the Beijing IP Court, at a press conference organized by the Supreme People's Court. See the Supreme People's Court (最高人民法院), ' Chi Su, the President of the Beijing IP Court Published a Work Report on the Operation of the Beijing IP Court (北京知识产权法院院长宿迟发布北京知识产权法院工作运行情况)' (Website of the Supreme People's Court [最高人民法院网], 9 September 2015), available at http://www.court.gov.cn/zixun-xiangqing-15367.html>accessed 15 December 2016.

[66] The Supreme People's Court has published ten IP-related guiding cases. Nos. 20 and 55 Guiding Cases involve patent infringement; Nos. 29, 30, 46, 45, and 47 involve unfair competition; Nos. 30, 46, and 58 involve trademark infringement; Nos. 48 and 49 involve copyright infringement. All guiding cases are available at http://www.court.gov.cn/shenpan-gengduo-77.html?page=2 (the official website of the Supreme People's Court).

[67] Rules on Case Guidance, art 4.

[68] Jing Yang (杨静), 'Barriers to Operate Guiding Cases System and Their Overcoming—An Empirical Research on the Substantiation of Court Hearing in the Beijing Intellectual Property Court (知识产权案例指导制度的障碍与克服-北京知识产权法院庭审实质化实证研究)' (2016) 10 Journal of Law Application (法律适用) 69, 72.

precedent. However, Chinese judges do not generally reason their decisions in detail nor cite similar precedents in their written judgments. Consequently, it appears that establishing a meaningful Guiding Cases system to achieve greater adjudicative consistency in IP litigation will remain a long-term project for China.

6. Shortcomings in the Specialized IP Court System

Although the specialized IP court system in China is designed to improve the quality of adjudication, efficiency in hearing IP disputes, and to achieve greater adjudicative consistency, a number of shortcomings remain. These are: first, the absence of an IP appeal court; second, the absence of jurisdiction over criminal IP-related cases; and, third, an adequate mechanism for the recruitment and retention of high-calibre judges. Each of these shortcomings will be considered in turn, below.

6.1 Absence of IP appellate courts

In 2008, when China's intellectual property strategy was announced, it included a plan to explore the establishment of specialized IP appeal courts. Since that time, as we have seen, only three IP courts at intermediate level have been set up. Judges of different IP courts hear civil and administrative cases specified under Article 6 of *Provisions on Jurisdiction* and may adopt different standards of adjudication to deal with IP disputes since there is no inter-court coordination on hearings. Nor are there any activities with respect to sharing information about prior cases amongst China's specialized IP courts. Furthermore, the Beijing High People's Court, the Shanghai High People's Court, and Guangdong High People's Court are responsible for hearing appeals against judgments made by the three specialized IP courts respectively. The only mechanism for judges to apply uniform criteria in dealing with IP disputes is the Guiding Cases system. However, as outlined above, China's Guiding Cases system is faced with the challenge of low numbers of IP cases selected by the Supreme People's Court and the lack of detailed judicial reasoning in the cases published. Consequently, the standard of adjudication on IP cases remains fragmented.[69] This indicates that the existing system of IP courts in China is far from being an effective mechanism to help achieve adjudicative consistency.

---

[69] It should be acknowledged that the Guangzhou IP Court, which has cross-regional jurisdiction in Guangdong Province, unifies the standards of adjudication with respect to IP issues adopted by twenty-one intermediate courts in Guangdong Province. However, due to the absence of an IP appeal court, the improvement brought about by the current system is not as significant as might be expected. Furthermore, despite the absence of an IP appeal court, the Guiding Case system may help achieve the goal of unifying adjudicative standards in the future.

In other jurisdictions, the practice of setting up specialized IP courts generally includes a specialized IP court of appeal. In the United States, for instance, the Court of Appeals for the Federal Circuit hears all appeals in patent cases. In the EU, the embryonic Unified Patent Court (UPC) comprises a Court of First Instance (with local, regional, and central divisions) and a Court of Appeal. In China, establishing a system of specialized IP courts that includes a court of appeal has gained support from Chinese academic circles, although at present there is an absence of consensus on the issues such as the number of IP appeal courts required and how they should operate.[70] It should be noted also that, apart from the imperative of achieving adjudicative consistency, establishing an IP appeal court with judicial power to determine the validity of patents or trademarks could also address the issue of circuity of action, as discussed above.[71]

6.2 Absence of jurisdiction to hear IP-related criminal cases

The Intellectual Property Court of Taiwan was the first specialist IP court anywhere in the world with jurisdiction to handle civil, administrative, and criminal cases.[72] It is the court of first instance to hear civil and administrative IP-related cases and is responsible for dealing with civil and criminal appeals concerning IP disputes.[73] In Mainland China, the situation differs when one compares the 'three-in-one' adjudication model adopted by more than 200 general People's Courts, on the one

---

[70] One suggestion is to set up a single, unified, IP appeal court in Beijing, augmented by several circuit courts of appeals in the regions where IP cases are predominantly concentrated. See Handong Wu (吴汉东), 'IP Court Construction in China: Pilot Samples and Fundamental Direction (中国知识产权法院建设:试点样本与基本走向)' (2015) 10 Journal of Legal Application (法律适用) 2, 3; also see Xinming Cao (曹新明), 'Establishment of IP Courts: an Important Measure of Rule of Law and Judicial Modernisation (建立知识产权法院:法治与国家治理现代化的重要措施)' (2014) 5 Law and Social Development (法制与社会发展) 60, 62. Another suggestion is to set up several regional IP appeal courts to act as agencies of the Supreme Court. See *Li and Zhao* (n 24) 122.

[71] From January 2014 to September 2014, the Beijing No. 1 Intermediate People's Court heard 3,632 administrative cases involving affirmation and authorization of trademarks at first instance and the Beijing High Court heard 905 administrative appeals. According to research carried by the Beijing High Court, about 70% of the total administrative cases specified above were caused by civil disputes between private bodies. See Yan Zhao (赵岩) and Bo Zhou (周波), 'Beijing Courts Reported the Adjudication on Cases Involving Affirmation and Authorisation of Trade Mark (北京法院通报商标授权确权案件审理情况)' (*Beijing Courts [北京法院网]*, 30 October 2014), available at <http://bjgy.chinacourt.org/article/detail/2014/10/id/1470852.shtml>accessed 23 December 2016. The data indicates that a considerable number of administrative cases with the disputes on validity of intellectual property rights would not be filed if Chinese courts have judicial power to declare intellectual property rights valid or not.

[72] Li Zhu (朱理), 'Review and Lesson-drawing on Litigation System of Taiwan's Intellectual Property Court (台湾地区"智慧财产法院"诉讼制度考察与借鉴)' (2015) 10 Intellectual Property (知识产权) 64, 64.

[73] Article 3 of Intellectual Property Court Organisation Act (智慧財產法院組織法) (TPE). A noteworthy characteristic of Taiwan's IP court is that it has jurisdiction to hear civil appeals against the judgment made by the same court.

hand, and China's specialized IP courts on the other. The latter have no jurisdiction to hear IP-related criminal cases. This rule seems to go against the fundamental objective of unifying adjudicative standards with respect to IP issues in a country that has a twenty-year history of implementing the 'three-in-one' model. Due to the fact that civil, administrative, and criminal cases concerning alleged IP infringing conduct will be heard by different courts, the judge in a general court and that in an IP court may in effect apply different standards with regard to identifying an infringement.[74]

This might occur, for instance, because according to Chinese criminal law some acts of IP infringement are criminalized in view of their seriousness or because they constitute behaviour likely to cause specified effects, such as enabling the infringer to gain a large sum of illicit income or because the infringer has committed multiple infringements.[75] It should be noted that, as with IP-related civil and administrative cases, the first and also the key step for the judge hearing such criminal cases is to determine whether the intellectual property right has in fact been infringed. Given this, it seems that there is no convincing reason to justify the practice of requiring a judge in a general court, hearing a criminal law matter, and a judge in a specialized IP court to identify infringement separately. In particular, this could be problematic when judges in general courts hearing a criminal law matter have insufficient experience of adjudication in the field of IP issues. In practice, since the judges with most experience in hearing criminal law matters related to IP have moved from the general courts to the three specialized IP courts, this increases the risk that the quality of adjudication on IP-related criminal cases heard in general courts may be lower than prior to late 2014. This problem has been exacerbated by the withdrawal of the intellectual property tribunals in the Beijing, Shanghai, and Guangzhou Intermediate Courts, which have, of course, since late 2014 been replaced by the three specialized IP courts.[76] However, the general courts in Beijing, Shanghai, and Guangzhou still have jurisdiction to hear IP-related criminal cases. Adjudication on such criminal cases related to IP thus failed to benefit from a concentration of judicial resources when this expertise was moved to the three specialized IP courts.

---

[74] For instance, appeals against the decision of the basic People's Courts in criminal cases concerning crime of counterfeiting registered trademark (Article 213 of Criminal Law of the People's Republic of China 1997) shall be dealt with by intermediate courts. While IP courts have the jurisdiction to hear appeals against an administrative penalty decision due to trademark counterfeiting. The judge in the intermediate court and the judge in the IP court may apply different standards when it comes to determining whether a trademark look is identical to the actual registered trademark.

[75] See Arts 213 and 217 of Criminal Law of the People's Republic of China 1997.

[76] For example, the intellectual property tribunal in the Guangzhou Intermediate People's Court began to hear cases involving environmental resources from February 2015, and it will set up a new environmental resource tribunal when the Supreme Court approves its application for withdrawal from the intellectual property tribunal.

Although the proposal to add criminal jurisdiction to the specialized IP courts is gaining support in Chinese academic circles, the consequences of this in terms of the heavy workloads that would consequently be experienced by judges in IP courts warrant further attention. Taking into account the large number of civil and administrative cases, there are two possible solutions. The first solution would be that only appeals, not first instance trials, on criminal cases would be dealt with by specialized IP courts. In 2014, 10,803 IP-related criminal cases were heard at first instance, while only 521 appeals concerning IP-related criminal cases were heard by Chinese courts.[77] It therefore appears a possible solution in terms of striking a good balance between adopting the 'three-in-one' model in IP courts and the practicalities of increased workload that would be involved. In addition, taking the pre-trial detention and investigation into account, it is more appropriate for a basic court than a specialized IP court with cross-regional jurisdiction to handle criminal cases at first instance.[78] The second possible solution would be the so-called '2+1' model currently being explored by the Shanghai specialized IP court. By adopting this model, IP-related criminal cases would be heard by a collegial panel formed by the Shanghai IP Court and the Shanghai No.3 Intermediate Court that has jurisdiction to deal with criminal IP cases.[79]

6.3 Recruitment and retention of high calibre judges

Given that jurisdiction of the general basic and intermediate People's Courts in Beijing Municipality, Shanghai Municipality, and Guangdong Province to hear cases as specified by Articles 1, 5, and 6 of *Provisions on Jurisdiction* has transferred to the three specialized IP courts, judges in these specialized IP courts are already suffering from a heavy workload. In the Guangzhou IP court, for instance, between 21 December 2014 and 31 December 2015, thirteen judges heard a total of 3,393 cases, amounting to an average of 261 cases per judge in one year.[80] In the Beijing IP Court, the situation is even worse, not least because it has exclusive first instance jurisdiction to hear administrative cases against decisions made by a department under the State Council involving authorization and affirmation of intellectual property rights and compulsory licences.[81] The number of IP cases is still increasing

---

[77] *The Supreme People's Court* (n 2) ch 1.
[78] Zhu (n 71) 64.
[79] Shuyang Hu (胡姝阳), 'Shanghai is Exploring New Mechanism of IP Adjudication (上海探索知识产权专业审判新机制)' (*National Copyright Administration of the People's Republic of China [中华人民共和国国家版权局]*, 31 December 2015), available at <http://www.ncac.gov.cn/chinacopyright/contents/518/271736.html> accessed 20 December 2016.
[80] The Guangzhou IP Court, *Judicial Protection Provided by the Guangzhou IP Court in 2015 (广州知识产权法院司法保护状况[2015年度])* (White Paper, 2016) ch 1.
[81] *Provisions on Jurisdiction*, art 5.

rapidly and judges in the three specialized IP courts face an even heavier workload in the future. Consequently, there is a risk that the quality of adjudication may suffer adverse effects.

In terms of recruitment and retention of high calibre judges, remuneration is also an issue. Judges in the specialized IP courts have considerable experience in hearing IP cases. Judges in the Beijing IP Court, for instance, have on average ten years' experience as IP judges.[82] Yet judicial salaries are relatively low and arguably do not reflect accurately experience, ability, or workloads. Ying Jiang, the Chief Judge of No.1 Tribunal in the Beijing IP Court, has been quoted as stating that the salary of a judge in specialized IP courts remains the same as that received by a judge in the general court.[83]

Compared to the more potentially complex tasks of reforming the role of technical investigation officers, building a properly functioning Guiding Cases system and establishing an effective IP appeal court, ensuring effective recruitment and retention of judges in the specialized IP courts through appropriate remuneration packages seems a relatively simple task to achieve. Nevertheless, it is an issue that appears to have been overlooked by decision-makers in China. As judges of IP courts are the people who implement concrete measures to promote judicial reform in adjudication with respect to IP cases, their performance will ultimately have a significant impact on the operation of IP court system and the effect of judicial reforms in China.

7. Conclusion

In recent years, China has taken significant steps to reform its legal system for intellectual property protection and enforcement. That task is not yet complete and remains a work in progress. China has already set up intellectual property tribunals to implement the 'three-in-one' adjudication model in general courts and has established specialized IP courts in the three most heavily IP-litigated locations. However, as this chapter has illustrated, based on the Chinese courts' practical experience of hearing IP disputes and the lessons that can be drawn from the legal reforms undertaken thus far, further consideration may well be needed on a range of issues including, amongst others, the role of technical investigation officers, the

---

[82] *The Supreme People's Court* (n 65).

[83] Nianzu Shen (沈念祖), 'The Explorer of Judicial Reform Discloses the Secrets of First IP Court in China (司改探路者解秘全国首家知识产权法院)' (The Economic Observer [经济观察网], 19 November 2014), available at <http://www.cnipr.com/sj/zx/201707/t20170718_213268.html> accessed 3 December 2016.

operation of the Guiding Cases system, the absence of IP appeal courts, jurisdiction to deal with IP-related criminal cases, and the recruitment and retention of judges. Further reforms and developments are no doubt necessary and likely to occur in the near future.

Bibliography

LEGISLATION: CHINA

Administrative Procedure Law of the People's Republic of China 2015 (中华人民共和国行政诉讼), art 71.

Criminal Law of the People's Republic of China 1997 (中华人民共和国刑法), art 213 & 217.

Decision of the Standing Committee of the National People's Congress on Establishing Intellectual Property Right Courts in Beijing, Shanghai and Guangzhou (全国人大常委会关于在北京、上海、广州设立知识产权法院的决定).

Detailed Rules for the Implementation of the 'Provisions of the Supreme People's Court Concerning Work on Case Guidance' (最高人民法院关于案例指导工作的规定实施细则), arts 4 and 10.

Interim Provisions of the Supreme People's Court on Several Issues Relating to Technical Investigation Officers of IP Courts to Participate in Intellectual Property Court Proceedings (最高人民法院关于知识产权法院技术调查官参与诉讼活动若干问题的暂行规定), arts 1, 6, 7, and 8.

Notice of the Supreme People's Court on Issues concerning the Jurisdiction of Intellectual Property Courts over Cases (最高人民法院关于知识产权法院案件管辖等有关问题的通知).

Provisions of the Supreme People's Court on the Jurisdiction of the Intellectual Property Courts of Beijing, Shanghai and Guangzhou over Cases (最高人民法院关于北京、上海、广州知识产权法院案件管辖的规定), arts 1, 5, and 6.

Provisions of the Supreme People's Court on Several Issues Concerning the Application of Law Related to Hearing Patent Disputes (最高人民法院关于审理专利纠纷案件适用法律问题的若干规定), art 5.

LEGISLATION: TAIWAN

Intellectual Property Court Organization Act (智慧財產法院組織法) (TPE), art 3.

BOOKS

Friendly H, *Federal Jurisdiction: A General View* (CUP 1973).

Jiang BX (江必新) and Shao CM (邵长茂), Interpretation and Application of Amended Provisions on New Administrative Procedure Law (新行政诉讼法修改条文理解与适用) (China Legal Publishing House [中国法制出版社] 2015).

Editing Committee of Yearbook for Judicial Protection of Intellectual Property in China (中国知识产权司法保护年鉴编辑委员会), *Yearbook for Judicial Protection of Intellectual Property in China* (中国知识产权司法保护年鉴) (*2012*) (Law Press China 2013).

JOURNAL ARTICLES

Cao XM (曹新明), 'Establishment of IP Courts: an Important Measure of Rule of Law and Judicial Modernisation (建立知识产权法院:法治与国家治理现代化的重要措施)' (2014) 5 Law and Social Development (法制与社会发展) 60.

Dreyfuss R, 'The Federal Circuit: A Case Study in Specialised Courts' (1989) 64 NYUL Rev 1.

Feng XQ (冯晓青) and Wang L (王丽), 'From Specialised Tribunals to Specialised Court: New Development of China's IP Judicature (从专门法庭到专门法院:我国知识产权司法的最新进展透析)' (2015) 35 (3) Academic Forum of Nandu (Journal of the Humanities and Social Sciences) [南都学坛(人文社会科学学报)] 59.

Guo H (郭禾), 'Reform of the Patent Invalidation System and its Cooperation with IP Court Construction-Discussing from the Fourth Amendment of Patent Law (专利权无效宣告制度的改造与知识产权法院建设的协调-从专利法第四次修订谈起)' (2016) 3 Intellectual Property (知识产权) 14.

Jia M, 'Chinese Common law? Guiding Cases and Judicial Reform' (2016) 129 (8) HLR 2213.

Li GM (李光曼) and Zhao X (赵兴), 'Concerning Reflections and Suggestions of "Three-in-one" IP Adjudication-Based on the Establishment of IP Courts (关于知识产权审判"三合一"的反思与建言-以知识产权法院设立为背景)' (2015) 1 Journal of Jiangxi Police Institution (江西警察学院学报) 118.

Li ML (黎明琳) and Wang YZ (王玉柱), 'Analysis on Judicial Practice of IP Courts and IP Protection in Shanghai Municipality (知识产权法院与上海知识产权保护的司法实践分析)' (2016) 2 Legal System and Society (法制与社会) 136.

Liu YL (刘银良), 'Demonstrations on Establishment of IP Courts in China (我国知识产权法院设置问题论证)' (2015) 3 Intellectual Property (知识产权) 3.

Research Team of The Beijing Intellectual Property Court (北京知识产权法院课题组), 'Thinking and Exploring about the Reform of Operation of Adjudicative Power-the Beijing Intellectual Property Court as a Sample Analysed (关于审判权运行机制改革的思考与探索-以北京知识产权法院为分析样本)' (2015) 10 Journal of Law Application (法律适用) 6.

Revesz R 'Specialized Courts and the Administrative Law-making System' (1990) 138 (4) U Pa L Rev 1111.

Sheng XY (盛学友), 'What does "There-in-one" Bring to Us—Investigating Shanghai Intellectual Property New Mechanism ('三合一"给我们带来什么-探访上海知识产权"三审合一"新机制)' (2009) 24 Law and Life (法律与生活) 45.

Wu HD(吴汉东), 'IP Court Construction in China: Pilot Samples and Fundamental Direction (中国知识产权法院建设:试点样本与基本走向)' (2015) 10 Journal of Legal Law? Application (法律适用) 2.

Yang J (杨静), 'Barriers to Operate Guiding Cases System and Their Overcoming—A Empirical Research on the Substantiation of Court Hearing in the Beijing Intellectual Property Court (知识产权案例指导制度的障碍与克服—北京知识产权法院庭审实质化实证研究)' (2016) 10 Journal of Law Application (法律适用) 69.

Yi J (易继明), 'What Kind of IP Courts should be Established (设立什么样的知识产权法院)' (2014) 4 Journal of Science, Technology and Law (科技与法律) 747.

Yi J (易继明), 'Why to Establish IP Courts (为什么要设立知识产权法院)' (2014) 4 Journal of Science, Technology and Law (科技与法律) 573.

Yuan XT (袁秀挺), 'Chinese IP Courts: the Vision and the Road (中国知识产权法院的愿景及其实现路径)' (2015) 1 Journal of Science, Technology and Law (科技与法律) 23.

Zhang GL (张广良) 'On the Thinking of Localisation of Designing Intellectual Property Court System (知识产权法院制度设计的本土化思维)' (2014) 6 The Jurist (法学家) 55.

Zhang XD (张旭东), 'Inspection on China's Jurisdiction of Intellectual Property Civil Cases-from the Angle of Patent Cases (中国知识产权法院民事案件管辖规定检视-以专利纠纷案件为视角)' (2015) 9 Social Sciences of Beijing (北京社会科学) 81.

Zhu L (朱理), 'Review and Lesson-drawing on Litigation System of Taiwan's Intellectual Property Court (台湾地区"智慧财产法院"诉讼制度考察与借鉴)' (2015) 10 Intellectual Property (知识产权) 64.

COMMAND PAPERS

The Central Committee of the Communist Party of China, *Decision of the CCCPC on Some Major Issues Concerning Comprehensively Deepening the Reform* (中共中央关于全面深化改革若干重大问题的决定) (White Paper, 2013) ch 3, para 13.

The State Council of the People's Republic of China (中华人民共和国国务院), *Outlines of the State Intellectual Property Strategy* (国家知识产权战略纲要) (White Paper, 2008) para 45.

The Supreme People's Court of the People's Republic of China, *Work Report of the Supreme People's Court on Intellectual Property Trials* (最高人民法院关于知识产权审判工作情况的报告) *(2012)* (White Paper, 2013) ch 1.

The Supreme People's Court of the People's Republic of China (中华人民共和国最高人民法院), *Intellectual Property Protection by Chinese Courts in 2013* (中国法院知识产权司法保护状况 2013) (White Paper, 2014) ch 2.

The Supreme People's Court of the People's Republic of China (中华人民共和国最高人民法院), Intellectual Property Protection by Chinese Courts in 2014 (中国法院知识产权司法保护2014) (White Paper, 2015) ch 2.

The Beijing High People's Court (北京市高级人民法院), *Work Report of the Beijing High People's Court on the Judicial Protection of Intellectual Property Rights-released on the Twenty-first Session of the Standing Committee of the Fourteenth Beijing Municipal National People's Congress on Sep.23, 2015* (北京市高级人民法院关于知识产权司法保护情况的报告-2015年9月23日在北京市第十四届人民代表大会常务委员会第二十一次会议上) (White Paper, 2015) ch 2.

The Guangzhou IP Court (广州知识产权法院), *Judicial Protection Provided by the Guangzhou IP Court in 2015* (^广州知识产权法院司法保护状况[2015年度]) (White Paper, 2016) ch 1.

NEWSPAPER ARTICLES

Li Q (李青) 'Judges' Brain Trust Making Adjudication More Professional—System of Technical Investigation Officer Operating for One Year in the Beijing IP Court (法

99

官"智囊"让裁判更专业-北京知产法院技术调查官制度运行一年)' *People's Court Daily* (人民法院报) (Beijing, October 2016) 4.

Mao LJ (毛立军), 'IP Courts: Providing Protection with the Comprehensive Development of Innovation (知识产权法院:为全面创新发展提供司法保护)' *The People's Political Consultative Daily* (中国政协报) (Beijing, 26 April 2016) 12.

INTERNET SOURCES

Chen YY (陈颖颖) and Wang YJ (王烨捷), 'The Shanghai IP Court Employed 11 Technical Investigation Officers for the First Time (上海知识产权法院首聘11位技术调查官)' (*China Daily* [中国日报], 23 March, 2016), available at <http://www.chinadaily.com.cn/micro-reading/dzh/2016-03-23/content_14622415.html> accessed 9 January 2017.

The Supreme People's Court (最高人民法院), 'Chi Su, the President of the Beijing IP Court Published a Work Report on the Operation of the Beijing IP Court (北京知识产权法院院长宿迟发布北京知识产权法院工作运行情况)' (*the Supreme People's Court* [最高人民法院网], 9 September 2015), available at http://www.court.gov.cn/zixun-xiangqing-15367.html>accessed 15 December 2016.

Zhao Y (赵岩) and Zhou B (周波), 'Beijing Courts Reported the Adjudication on Cases Involving Affirmation and Authorisation of Trade Mark (北京法院通报商标授权确权案件审理情况)' (*Beijing Courts* [北京法院网], 30 October 2014), available at <http://bjgy.chinacourt.org/article/detail/2014/10/id/1470852.shtml>accessed 23 December 2016.

Hu SY (胡姝阳), 'Shanghai is Exploring New Mechanism of IP Adjudication (上海探索知识产权专业审判新机制)' (National Copyright Administration of the People's Republic of China [中华人民共和国国家版权局], 31 December 2015), available at <http://www.ncac.gov.cn/chinacopyright/contents/518/271736.html>accessed 20 December 2016.

Shen NZ (沈念祖), 'The Explorer of Judicial Reform Discloses the Secrets of First IP Court in China (司改探路者解秘全国首家知识产权法院)' (The Economic Observer [经济观察网], 19 November 2014), available at <http://www.cnipr.com/sj/zx/201707/t20170718_213268.html>accessed 27 November 2018.

6

COPYRIGHT AND COMPETITION

Law and Enforcement in the People's Republic of China

Guan H. Tang

1. Introduction

Copyright law serves a pro-competitive role not in a particular work as such but in the market for ideas, the fountain of creativity. On the one hand, the law grants a right holder a specific form of exclusivity to the copyrighted work, expression of idea so such work can be enjoyed in the larger market by the many. The copyright owner's work, together with inspired works created by others, would form and stimulate competition in the market for the underlying idea. On the other hand, in order to reinforce such competition, copyright law exemplifies certain infringing acts from liability by applying the merger or fair use doctrines in contexts, in which the copyright owner's exercise of exclusive rights might impede competition in a related market.[1] The delicate balance between the right of authorship and the right of access is the two dimensions of the public interest in the regime of copyright, as well as the ultimate goal of the system of copyright.[2] Certainly, copyright law's mission of safeguarding expression of ideas and individual rights, promoting learning and creativity, stimulating exchange of ideas, and trading the expression of ideas is shared by the system of competition, a mechanism designed to provide protection for competitors, consumers, freedom of competition, and economic efficiency.[3]

---

[1] Thomas F. Cotter, 'The Procompetitive Interest in Intellectual Property Law', [2006] 48 WM & MARY L REV 483.

[2] Guan H. Tang, *Copyright and the Public Interest in China* (Edward Elgar Publishing 2011) (hereafter Tang, *Copyright and the Public Interest*).

[3] Ioannis Lianos, 'Some Reflections on the Question of the Goals of EU Competition Law' CLES Working Paper Series (2013) 3, available at <https://www.ucl.ac.uk/cles/research-paper-series/research-papers/cles-3-2013> accessed 16 March 2017.

When the People's Republic of China (hereafter referred to as 'China') adopted its Reform and Opening-up Policy in 1978, no one could have predicted that China would become the second-largest economy by 2010.[4] From an isolated, centrally controlled, and strictly planned economy to the integration into the world economy and moving towards a free market with rapid and powerful improvement, China has made enormous efforts and has come a long way.[5] Prior to its official entrance to the global economy, i.e. the accession to the World Trade Organization (WTO) in 2001, China enacted and revised over 2,000 related laws, regulations, and measures in order to satisfy the WTO member global trading rules, and tremendous changes were made to its trade regime.[6] Yet China has to transition out of the government's role of directing and controlling markets progressively towards the implementation and enforcement of laws and regulations promoting free markets. The WTO acceptance also embraces China's commitments to more than twenty existing multilateral WTO agreements, consisting of the TRIPS, which confirms China's obligation to adhere to the international standard of intellectual property (IP) protection. Indeed, opening up to the international community has shaped China's legal system, including the statutory mechanisms of copyright and competition, concepts that are foreign to China traditionally and the substantive law came into force late in the country, with Chinese characteristics.[7]

2. The Current System

On 7 September 1990, the 15th Session of the Standing Committee of the National People's Congress ('NPC') approved China's first modern copyright statute, the Copyright Law of the People's Republic of China ('CCL'), which took effect in conjunction with Implementing Regulations on 1 June 1991. To enable accession to the WTO, revisions of the 1990 CCL and the 1991 Implementing Regulations were adopted correspondingly in October 2001 and August 2002. As result of a WTO US-China dispute over intellectual property rights ('IPR'), further amendments of the 2001 CCL were enacted on 1 April 2010, embracing the revision of Article 4 and the addition of Article 26.[8] The 2002 Implementing Regulations were amended in January 2011 and then again in January 2013. On 6 June 2014,

---

[4] National Bureau of Statistics of China, 'China Statistic Yearbook 2010', available at <http://www.stats.gov.cn/tjsj/ndsj/2010/indexch.htm> accessed 16 March 2017.

[5] 李成钢　　　 '世贸组织规则博弈:中国参与WTO争端解决的十年法律实践'商务印书馆2011; Chenggang Li, *The WTO Game Rules: Ten Years of China's Legal Practice in the WTO Dispute Settlement* (The Commercial Press 2011).

[6] See <http://www.chinadaily.com.cn/chinagate/com.html> accessed 16 March 2017.

[7] Tang, *Copyright and the Public Interest* (n 2).

[8] WTO Report of the Panel, *China—Measures Affecting the Protection and Enforcement of Intellectual Property Rights* (2009), available at <https://www.wto.int/english/tratop_e/dispu_e/362r_e.pdf> accessed 16 March 2017.

the Legislative Affairs Office of the State Council published the draft version of the third revision of the copyright law ('2014 Draft CCL') for public comment. It had been previously released by the National Copyright Administration ('NCA') for comments in March and July 2012 respectively. The 2014 Draft CCL consists of eight chapters and ninety articles, amending the 2010 CCL's six chapters and sixty-one articles. Two additional chapters of the 2014 Draft CCL are 'Technological Protection and Rights Management Information' (Chapter VI) and 'Protection of Rights' (Chapter VII).[9] The 2010 CCL recognizes that rights arising from creative works are of two kinds: property and personal.[10] Discussions in the context of competition focus on the power of securing private property rights, which is fundamental for a competitive market.[11]

As part of its ongoing evolution, China has been looking to establish a Chinese characteristics instrument for copyright protection. It employs a dual-track system, i.e. judicial protection and administrative enforcement. The Supreme People's Court ('SPC') is the highest judicial organ and all levels of local courts are subject to the supervision of the SPC, while lower level courts are subject to the supervision of the higher level courts.[12] The CCL offers a legal basis for administrative enforcement and defines certain responsibilities including civil liabilities, criminal liabilities, and exposure to administrative sanctions.[13] The most important regulatory stakeholders with respect to administrative copyright enforcement are the National Copyright Administration of the People's Republic of China ('NCAC') and the provincial and municipal Copyright Bureaus responsible for investigations into infringement cases, administration of foreign-related copyright issues, and developing arbitration rules and regulations. According to Articles 48 and 49 of the 2010 CCL and Articles 36 and 37 of the Implementing Regulations 2013, the local administrative authorities are entitled to take legal action against any copyright infringement proactively or under a request of the proprietor of copyright in line with the mentioned provisions and for any foreign proprietor, or under either the Berne Convention or the UCC, of which China has been a member since October 1992.[14]

---

[9] Although the 2014 Draft CCL has not been enacted to date, it is expected to come into force anytime in the near future. The public comment on 2014 Draft CCL was opened on 6 June and closed on 5 July 2014. For the full text of the 2014 Draft CCL together with an explanation see <http://www.gov.cn/govweb/xinwen/2014-06/10/content_2697701.htm> accessed 16 March 2017.

[10] 刘春田 '知识产权法 (第五版)' 人民大学出版社 2015; Chuntian Liu, *Intellectual Property Law 5th Edition* (China Renmin University Press 2015).

[11] Armen A. Alchian, *Property Rights and Economic Behavior* (LFI 2006).

[12] Article 127, Constitution of the People's Republic of China.

[13] Article 48, CCL 2010.

[14] Other relevant administrative authorities that may also enforce copyright law include the General Administration of Customs, the Ministry of Public Security (MPS), and the Bureaus (the police), Regional IPR bureaus, the State Food and Drug Administration (for pharmaceutical

Meanwhile, China endeavours to promote the judicial enforcement of IPR and the laws in general.[15] Chinese courts and administrative authorities every year carefully select ten typical IP cases, publish, and widely distribute them as the 'Top Ten of the Year', aiming to promote IP awareness among the masses and guiding the future decisions of the courts.[16] It should be noted that although China is not a country governed by case law, cases have always played an extremely important role in its making, enforcement, and promotion of laws due to the influence of its traditional culture of 'facts speak louder than words' on the one hand, and the current centralized governance of administration and courts on the other.[17] Moreover, China has established the 'Guiding Case System', since November 2010;[18] representative cases have ever since been carefully selected and published by the SPC for the three-fold purpose: 'to unify the application and reference of law, to enhance judicial efficiency and to promote the socialist rule of law together with the socialist core values'.[19] To date, ten sets and fifty-two SPC Guiding Cases in total, covering most concerned subject areas, have been released;[20] among four of the copyright related Guiding Cases two are copyright abuse disputes. In 2014, three IPR courts were set up in Beijing, Shanghai, and Guangzhou[21] to deal with civil and administrative IP-related cases in particular.[22] The IPR courts have set their aims to providing 'more skilled judges and more professional trials to ensure the judicial protection for IPR that has been a key role in technological advance, overall innovation, and economic development in the country'.[23] On 28 January 2015, as part of the legal

---

products), the Ministry of Culture (for copyright materials of cultural value), the Administration for Quality Supervision, Inspection and Quarantine (infringements of low quality goods), and their local level offices.

[15] 最高人民法院知识产权庭负责人孔祥俊做客人民网; The Supreme People's Court's IP Chief Judge Xiangjun Kong at the People's Daily Online, available at <http://ip.people.com.cn/GB/141384/148181/index.html> accessed 16 March 2017.

[16] Tang, *Copyright and the Public Interest* (n 2).

[17] Ibid.

[18] For a comprehensive study on the 'guiding case system' in English, see the Stanford Law School China Guiding Cases Project, available at <https://cgc.law.stanford.edu> accessed 16 March 2017.

[19] 最高人民法院发布加强案例指导工作情况; The Supreme People's Court Press Conference on the Guiding Case System, available at <http://www.court.gov.cn/zixun-xiangqing-14623.html> accessed 16 March 2017.

[20] 最高人民法院关于发布第10批指导性案例的通知; The Supreme People's Court Published Its Notice of the 10th Set Guiding Case, available at <http://www.court.gov.cn/shenpan-xiangqing-14240.html> accessed 16 March 2017.

[21] 全国人大常委会关于在北京、上海、广州设立知识产权法院的决定; The NPC Standing Committee Decisions on the establishment of IP courts in Beijing, Shanghai, and Guangzhou, available at <http://npc.people.com.cn/n/2014/0901/c14576-25574846.html> accessed 16 March 2017.

[22] 最高人民法院关于北京、上海、广州知识产权法院案件管辖的规定; The Provisions of the Supreme People's Court on the Jurisdiction of the Intellectual Property Courts of Beijing, Shanghai and Guangzhou over Cases, available at <http://www.court.gov.cn/fabu-xiangqing-13655.html> accessed 16 March 2017.

[23] Mr. Deyong Shen's speech at the opening of Guangzhou IP Court on 16 December 2014, available at <http://www.court.gov.cn/zixun-xiangqing-7079.html> accessed 16 March 2017.

reform strategy, China inaugurated the First SPC Circuit Court in Shenzhen, and a few days later, the Second SPC Circuit Court was opened in Shenyang.[24] The SPC Circuit Courts aim to ease the country's pressure of 信访, 'petitioning', and bring high quality, efficient, and professional decisions to local disputes,[25] which in most cases are between individuals and regional authorities, and are intense and sometimes lead to extreme actions.

Under the CCL, exclusive rights are afforded, which enable copyright holders to prevent unlawful use of their protected work, subject to limitations and exceptions. To prevent copyright abuse, exercises of such rights in the market have to fall within the permitted boundaries of the competition law. The terminology of 竞争法, 'competition law', refers to two substantive laws, the Law of the People's Republic of China Against Unfair Competition 1993 ('UCL'), and the Anti-Monopoly Law of the People's Republic of China 2008 ('AML');[26] whilst the former regulates conducts that may harm the legitimate fairness of competition, the latter measures conducts that may eliminate or restrict competition in the market.[27] With much to be improved, the UCL 1993 offers protection for trademark and famous designers,[28] and for trade secrets.[29] It also includes provisions for abuse of administrative power restricting competition,[30] and prohibition of commercial bribery.[31] The UCL accomplishes the IP system by providing protection in the following three catalogues: added protection for existing IPR, special protection for subject matter with no specific provision in current IP law, and 'catch-all' protection for neighbouring rights.[32] The main administrative enforcement body for the UCL is the State Administration for Industry and Commerce (SAIC).

---

[24] 司法改革的"中国速度"—最高人民法院巡回法庭诞生记; 'China Speed', The Judicial Reform and the Formation of the SPC Circuit Court, available at <http://www.court.gov.cn/zixun-xiangqing-13168.html> accessed 16 March 2017.

[25] 最高人民法院巡回法庭成立一周年记; On the Anniversary of Establishment of the SPC Circuit Court, available at <http://www.court.gov.cn/fabu-xiangqing-16626.html> accessed 16 March 2017.

[26] UCL is 'formulated with a view to safeguarding the healthy development of socialist market economy, encouraging and protecting fair competition, repressing unfair competition acts, and protecting the lawful rights and interests of business operators and consumers' (UCL, Article 1), and AML is 'enacted for the purpose of preventing and restraining monopolistic conducts, protecting fair competition in the market, enhancing economic efficiency, safeguarding the interests of consumers and the public interest and promoting the healthy development of the socialist market economy' (AML, Article 1).

[27] 刘水林:反垄断私人诉讼的协商制模式选择, 载 '法学'2016 年第6 期, 第129–138页; Shuilin Liu, 'The Choice of Cooperative Mode of Antimonopoly Private Litigation' [2016] 6 China Legal Science 129–38.

[28] Article 5, UCL.

[29] Article 10, UCL.

[30] Article 7, UCL.

[31] Article 22, UCL.

[32] 吴汉东:论反不正当竞争中的知识产权问题, 载 '现代法学'2013年第1期, 第37–43页; Handong Wu, 'On Intellectual Property Related Unfair Competition Problems', [2013] 1 Modern Law Science 37–43.

On 30 August 2007, the 29th session of the NPC passed AML, which came into force on 1 August 2008. On 31 July 2008, the SPC published a notice compelling the People's Courts at all levels to study the AML and to stress the complicated nature of competition cases, the merger of legal and economic issues on the one hand and their close link to IPR on the other, which would require professionalism of the courts.[33] The AML prohibits 'monopolistic conduct' of three main categories, i.e. monopolistic agreements, abuse of a dominant market position, and mergers that may have an effect of eliminating or restricting competition.[34] Article 17 states that undertakings with a dominant market position are prohibited to abuse their dominant market positions by carrying out following conducts:

- selling commodities at unfairly high prices or buying commodities at unfairly low prices;
- selling commodities at prices below cost without legitimate reasons;
- refusing to trade with counterparties without legitimate reasons;
- requiring its counterparty to trade exclusively with it or trade exclusively with the appointed undertakings without legitimate reasons;
- tying products or imposing unreasonable conditions for trading without legitimate reasons;
- applying dissimilar prices or other transaction terms to equivalent counterparties;
- other conducts identified as abuse of a dominant position by antimonopoly authorities.

It defines that 'Dominant market position' refers to the undertaking(s) having the ability to control the price, quantity, or other trading conditions of products in the relevant market, or to hinder or affect other undertakings to enter the relevant market.[35] With regard to IP, the AML stipulates:

> This law is not applicable to conducts by undertakings to implement their intellectual property rights in accordance with relevant IP laws and administrative regulations; however, this law is applicable to the conduct by undertakings to eliminate or restrict market competition by abusing intellectual property rights.[36]

Which establishes the principle that applies to anti-competitive abuses of IPR. It confirms the legitimate monopoly granted by the system of IPR protection and also set the boundaries of conducts for fair competition in the market. However, it is conceptual but explicit. As the only relevant provision leaves ambiguity in regulating IP-related anti-monopoly conducts. For instance, whilst excessive

---

[33] See 最高人民法院通知要求切实依法审理好各类反垄断案件; Notice of the SPC on Proper Trial of Various Types of Antimonopoly Cases, available at <http://old.chinacourt.org/html/article/200807/31/314776.shtml> accessed 16 March 2017.

[34] Article 3, AML.

[35] Article 17, AML.

[36] Article 55, AML.

competition beyond the scope of protection of IP law is prohibited, would such competition within the scope of IPR become exception to the anti-monopoly?

The AML authorizes the State Council to set up the Antimonopoly Commission to be in charge of organizing, coordinating, guiding anti-monopoly works, and performance,[37] and the three 'anti-monopoly authorities' to be responsible for the administrative enforcement of AML.[38] Whilst the SAIC's Anti-monopoly and Anti-Unfair Competition Enforcement Bureau reviews monopolistic agreements, abuse of dominant market position, and abuse of administrative power to eliminate or restrict competitions, the Ministry of Commerce's (MOFCOM) Anti-Monopoly Bureau regulates mergers and acquisitions, and the National Development and Reform Commission (NDRC) regulates monopolistic activities involving prices.

To implementing AML, the SAIC issued its Order Number 74, i.e. Regulation on the Prohibition of Conduct Eliminating or Restricting Competition by Abusing Intellectual Property Rights on 7 April 2015 (2015 Regulation).[39] The 2015 Regulation declares that IP laws and AML share the goals of facilitating competition and innovation, promoting economic efficiency, and protecting consumers and the public interest.[40] In the circumstances that IPR owners abuse their exclusive rights and such abuse of IPR have the effects of eliminating or restricting competition then the mechanism of AML will be imposed. It defines acts of abusing IPR to be exercising IPR to conduct monopolistic behaviours (except for the price monopoly conduct) including monopoly agreements and the abuse of a dominant position in the relevant market,[41] while the relevant market shall include both relevant product and geographical markets, relevant product market shall cover the market for technology and the market for the products incorporating specific IPR.[42] Abusive conducts shall be identified on a case-by-case basis, and in each case Article 15 of the 2015 Regulation requires that an authority shall:

- confirm the nature and forms of the exercise of IPR;
- determine the nature of relationships between operators;
- define the relevant market;
- affirm the market position possessed by operators; and
- assess the effects of competition on that relevant market.

Article 9, AML.
[38] Article 10, AML.
[39] 国家工商行政管理总局令第74号：　关于禁止滥用知识产权排除、限制竞争行为的规定; State Administration for Industry and Commerce Order No. 74: Provisions on Prohibition of Abuse of Intellectual Property Exclusion and Restriction of Competition, available at <http://www.saic.gov.cn/zwgk/zyfb/zjl/fld/201504/t20150413_155103.html> accessed 16 March 2017.
[40] Article 2, AML.
[41] Article 3, AML.
[42] Ibid.

Adopting more standard terminologies, the 2015 Regulation keeps in line with international conventions. The instructive steps offered should have a positive effect on improving administrative enforcement with regards to the relevant issues and, very likely, these clear steps may have benefitted from a long lasting, landmark court case, *Qihoo v Tencent*, which was concluded by the SPC. However, such instructions only provide answers to what, but not how, determines whether a conduct is abusive, especially in following the latter three steps set out in the 2015 Regulation as mentioned above.

3. Market Definition and Abuse of Dominant Market Position

Copyright related competition issues, i.e. disputes over a copyright owners' abusive conduct of their dominant market position, have become topical along with the fast-growing technological development in China,[43] especially in the software and IT-dependent industries. According to the 2016 Report on Copyright Protection in the Online Environment, there were 2,118 online civil copyright cases in 2015 and among them there were a big percentage of competition disputes.[44] As a subject matter of the CCL, the protection for software is explicitly under copyright law. Software is defined as 'computer programs and relevant documents' and the enforcement is governed by the Regulations on Computers Software Protection.[45] Software related competition conducts therefore have been merely relying on Article 55.[46] The most discussed, as well as often incoherent issues arising in the area include the definition of relevant market and the abuse of dominant market position, of which the latter is fundamental since a business operator at the dominant market position may be free from the constraints of competition, and pricing, or making other business decisions without fair consideration of any competitors or counterparties.[47]

---

[43] 李浩成：知识产权滥用反垄断立法规制的现状与重构，载'政法论丛'2013年第3期, 第98–104页; Haocheng Li, 'Regulating Intellectual Property Rights Abuse in Anti-monopoly Law: Present and Reform', [2013] 3 Journal of Political Science and Law 98–104.

[44] Which was on the request of the National Copyright Administration and released by China Academy of Telecommunication Research (CATR) on 26 April 2016, available at<http://www.ncac.gov.cn/chinacopyright/upload/files/2016/4/27161449900.pdf> accessed 16 March 2017.

[45] By the Decree of the State Council of the people's Republic of China No. 339.

[46] 王先林：我国反垄断法适用于知识产权领域的再思考，载'南京大学学报(哲学·人文科学·社会科学版)'2013年第1期, 第34–43页; Xianlin Wang, 'Rethink Applying Antimonopoly Law in Intellectual Property' [2013] 1 Journal of Nanjing University (Philosophy, Humanities and Social Sciences) 34–43.

[47] 王晓晔：标准必要专利反垄断诉讼问题研究，载'中国法学'2015年第6期, 第217–238页; Xiaoye Wang, Research of Anti-monopoly Litigations Problems in Standard Essential Patents, [2015] 6 China Legal Science 217–38.

These key questions have been highlighted, examined, and responded to by the SPC in *Beijing Qihoo Technology Ltd v Shenzhen Tencent Technology Ltd*.[48] *Qihoo v Tencent 2013(5)* was the first anti-monopoly case heard in the SPC and the final judgment, given on 8 October 2014, dismissed the claimant's appeal and sustained the Guangdong High People's Court (HPC) decision. However, it was not the first case ruled by the SPC related to conducts of competition between Tencent and Qihoo. Earlier on 28 February 2014, the SPC ruled in *Qihoo v Tencent 2013(4)* to uphold the Guangdong HPC's findings of an unfair competition dispute between the two parties, in which Tencent was successful in the unfair competition allegation against Qihoo.[49]

The two SPC concluded cases, *Qihoo v Tencent 2013(5)* and *Qihoo v Tencent 2013(4)*, were influential to lower courts' trials and evolved from clashes of interests in exercising copyright on the Internet in 2010, when Qihoo and Tencent, China's two leading Internet Service Providers ('ISPs'), each accused the other of abuse of copyright, indecently using software to block users from accessing the other's software. Both Qihoo and Tencent were profiting from selling online advertising and offering value-added services to their users, of which the base was built via their free core products; Qihoo's 360 Antivirus software and Tencent's QQ instant messaging (IM) software. While 360 Antivirus had 223 million monthly active users, the active user accounts for QQ IM amounted to 853 million.[50] In September 2010, Qihoo publicly alleged QQ of collecting information through scanning users' computers and released its 360 Bodyguard software that allowed its users to control their information, as well as the number of commercials that QQ could display. Tencent swiftly struck back by making its QQ IM incompatible with all Qihoo software; users were not allowed to log in to their QQ IM account if they had Qihoo software installed, and had to choose between QQ IM and 360 Antivirus. That is known as the 'choose one from two' incident.[51] In less than forty-eight hours, Qihoo lost around 10 per cent of its users. The two companies entered the so-called '3Q War'.[52] Before long, thousands of users complained that the two companies' conflict affected their rights of using the

---

[48] 北京奇虎科技有限公司与腾讯科技(深圳)有限公司等滥用市场支配地位纠纷案(2013)民三终字第5号 &(2011)粤高法民三初字第1号民事判决书; SPC Civil Three Final Judgment (2013) Number 5, and Guangdong HPC Civil Three First Judgment (2011) Number 1.

[49] 北京奇虎科技有限公司等与腾讯科技(深圳)有限公司等不正当竞争纠纷案(2013)民三终字第4号 and(2011)粤高法民三初字第2号民事判决书; SPC Civil Three Final Judgment (2013) Number 4, and Guangdong HPC Civil Three First Judgment (2011) Number 2.

[50] About Tencent, available at <http://www.tencent.com/en-us/at/abouttencent.shtml> accessed 16 March 2017.

[51] See, for example, 'China Internet users forced to choose in software row', available at <http://www.bbc.co.uk/news/mobile/world-asia-pacific-11691324> accessed 16 March 2017.

[52] '3Q大战',战火愈演愈烈; Report on the '3Q War' by SIPO, available at <http://www.sipo.gov.cn/ztzl/ywzt/zlwzn/zlss/dxal/201306/t20130604_801820.html> accessed 16 March 2017

Internet.[53] Several government departments, including the Ministry of Industry and Information Technology (MIIT) and the PMS, interfered in the 3Q War. In November 2010, the MIIT ordered both parties to allow compatibility on computers. Although the two companies followed the MIIT order, both started their journey of litigation, under the UCL and the AML respectively.

In 2010 Tencent launched its action with the Guangdong HPC against Qihoo, asserting that Qihoo breached the UCL, 'business operator shall not fabricate or spread false information to injure his competitors' commercial credit or the reputation of his competitors' commodities'.[54] In 2011 Qihoo sued Tencent in the same court, alleging that Tencent had a dominant position in the provision of IM services in China, and that Tencent has abused its market dominance by engaging in the 'choose one from two' incident to eliminate and hinder competition in violation of the AML. Qihoo lost out to Tencent in both cases before the Guangdong HPC and appealed respectively to the SPC, where both judgments were given in favour of Tencent.

In the unfair competition appeal, *Qihoo v Tencent 2013(4)*, the SPC fully agreed with the court of first instance, offered an analysis on the line between the software owner's rights under the CCL and the limitation on conducts in business set by the UCL, and rejected Qihoo's defence of its conducts being technological innovation and in the scope of free competition. The SPC supported Tencent's claim, deemed Qihoo breaching of Article 14 of UCL and ordered Qihoo to pay Tencent a damage of five million Yuan Renminbi. Qihoo's defence of helping users to enforce their right to know and to protect users' privacy was rejected by the court. It should be noted that the Internet users' right to know and right to privacy had not been specifically and legitimately confirmed before 7 November 2016, when the Cybersecurity Law of the People's Republic of China was adopted. The new law, coming into force on 1 June 2017, states that 'where network products and services have the function of collecting users' information, their providers shall explicitly notify their users and obtain their consent' and 'if any user's personal information is involved, the provider shall also comply with this Law',[55] i.e. the provider shall explicitly notify their users and obtain their consent.[56] What differences would these provisions make regarding the providers' conducts in a competitive market? How would the courts enforce such provisions in general, as well as in cases similar to *Qihoo v Tencent 2013(4)*? Those questions are certainly worth exploring.

---

[53] For an example of a blog written in English see 'A shocking and annoying battle between Tencent and Qihoo', available at <https://blogs.ubc.ca/jiayuli/2010/11/05/a-shocking-and-annoying-battle-between-tencent-and-qihoo> accessed 16 March 2017.

[54] Article 14, UCL.

[55] Article 22(3), Cybersecurity Law.

[56] Article 41(1), Cybersecurity Law.

In the anti-monopoly appeal, *Qihoo v Tencent 2013(5)*, the SPC upheld the Guangdong HPC's ruling that Tencent was not in a dominant market position and had not abused its market power, whilst correcting significantly the court of first instance's analytical approach. Offering detailed reasoning, the final judgment gave answers to the main issues concerned, including as follows

- How to define the relevant market and what is the role of market definition in cases of such nature?
- What are the aspects and approaches that the court should take into consideration in determining whether the defendant has a dominant market position?
- Whether the defendant constituted abuse of dominant market position?

The SPC explained that market definition is usually an important analytical step in anti-monopoly cases. In a case of abuse of dominant position, a reasonably defined market would be key for assessing the market position of a business operator, analysing the competitive effects of its conduct, and determining the legality of its conduct and other main issues. The SPC pointed out that it was not necessary to explicitly and clearly define a relevant market in all cases of abuse of dominant market position, although market definition would be helpful to make clear the market scope of competitive behaviours and the competitive constraints faced by business operators. It would depend on specific situations of a case whether a relevant market could be clearly defined, especially availability of relevant evidence and data and complexity of competition. In a case of abuse of dominant position, 'market definition is not the purpose but a tool for evaluating the market power of the business operator being litigated and the competitive effects of its conduct'. The SPC held that even if a market is not clearly defined, the market position of the business operator being sued and the potential competitive effects of its conduct could also be evaluated through the direct evidence of exclusion or restraint to competition. Based on the direct evidence of the impact of the 'choose one from two' had on competitors and other IM providers' promotional activities during that period of time, the SPC concluded that Tencent's conduct had potential favourable effects to consumers and competition and did not constitute an abuse of dominant position.

In addition, the SPC stated that if qualitative analysis was sufficient to clearly define a relevant market, complicated quantitative analysis is not necessary. Market definition could be conducted in either a qualitative or quantitative way. Qualitative analysis is usually the starting point to define a relevant market. When qualitative analysis is sufficient for reaching a definite conclusion, it is not necessary to carry out complicated quantitative analysis. Qualitative analysis includes analysis of demand substitution and supply substitution based on factors such as product characteristics, use, and price. Quantitative analysis involves applying the methods of mathematical economics or econometrics. 'Method is not a purpose but a tool'; for market definition, qualitative analysis should be adopted first, and if it is sufficient for definition, quantitative analysis is not necessary. Only if a relevant market could not be clearly defined qualitatively and quantitative analysis is feasible (e.g. relevant data is available), it is then necessary to consider quantitative analysis. The SPC found that qualitative analysis was sufficient in this case.

It is recognized that monopoly power can make output lower, prices higher, and innovation less than in a competitive market.[57] In assessing Tencent's market power, the SPC applied the hypothetical monopolist test ('HMT'), examining the degree of substitutability among the target product and other products through a change of certain variables of the target product or service, assuming other conditions remain unchanged. The SPC stated that the HMT test may be generally applied as an analytical approach to market definition and may be used to define both a relevant product market and a relevant geographic market. The main consideration for defining a relevant geographic market is whether the business operators in other geographic markets will constitute effective competitive constraint to the hypothetical monopolist in the target geography in case of any change to such competitive elements like price and quality. It may be carried out not only through qualitative analysis, but also through quantitative analysis if conditions permit. The SPC noted that the Guangdong HPC had mistaken worldwide as the relevant geographic market and concluded that it was mainland China only. The SPC further highlighted that the Small but Significant Non-transitory Increase in Price (SSNIP) test adopted by the Guangdong HPC was inappropriate in this case as QQ IM software and other IMs services on the market are mostly provided free of charge. The SPC pointed out that competition in the provision of IM services was highly dynamic, the definition of the relevant market was not as clear as that of more traditional markets, the court should not rely too much on the implication of market share in assessing market dominance but other factors such as market entry, the competitive constraints resulting from internet platform competition, and direct evidence of the effects of Tencent's conduct on competition. The SPC found Tencent's high market share in the IM services market, over 85 per cent in terms of active usage, formed no dominant market power.

Indeed, *Qihoo v Tencent 2013(5)* offers important guidance to anti-monopoly litigation and also significant reference for the AML enforcement. The SPC's innovative approaches of taking on economic analysis of the facts specific to the case and of drawing conclusion from competitive-effect-based analysis instead of market definition analysis have become prominent in Chinese courts establishing abuse of dominant position regarding copyright-related competition dispute and beyond. In addition, the judgment provides specific reasoning for the discussion of each

---

[57] Mark Furse, *Antitrust Law in China, Korea and Vietnam* (OUP 2009).

issue, which is certainly welcome and hopefully may be able to prompt the Chinese courts' reasons for judgment. Nevertheless, the SPC's denial of Tencent's dominant market position together with the narrative of Tencent's conduct of 'choose one from two' are rather unconvincing, in spite of Qihoo's presentation of strong evidence, including that Tencent owning over 85 per cent of the IM market share.

4. Burden of Proof in Court

In line with the Chinese civil law, 'it is the duty of a party to an action to provide evidence in support of the party's allegations', i.e. a claimant has the burden of evidence in general.[58] Thus in any copyright-related competition civil litigations, claimants bear the burden of proof. On the one hand, the claimant has to provide evidence of defendant's dominant market power and its abuse of such position, and on the other hand, the claimant would also be obliged to prove that the defendant copied original elements from the claimant's copyrighted work in a civil dispute over copyright infringement.

Beijing Sursen Electronic Technology Co. Ltd. v Shanda Interactive Entertainment Ltd. and Shanghai Xuanting Entertainment Co. Ltd. (commonly known as '*Sursen v Shanda*') was the first court case decided under the AML, and its ruling on evidence had a strong influence on subsequent court decisions. Both the court of first instance, the Shanghai First Intermediate People's Court (IPC), and the court of appeal, the Higher People's Court, rejected the claimant's claim regarding the defendant's conduct of abusing its dominance in the online literature market.[59] The claimant Sursen was a successful digital book publisher who owned www.du8.com (读吧网), whilst Shanda, a leading Chinese provider for on-line games and publisher of digital books and other on-line entertainment material, was the owner of www.qidian.com (起点中文网). In 2008, author Zhu Hongzhi, using the pen name 'I eat tomato', published on www.qidian.com a series of novels called 'Star Change', which were commissioned by the defendants and soon became one of the most popular novels on the Internet. Later on, the claimant commissioned two authors, Kou Bin and Li Yapeng, who used the pen name 'Don't eat tomato', to write a series of novels entitled 'Star Change Sequel', which were then published on www.du8.com in May 2008 and also gained widespread popularity. The contents of the 'Star Change Sequel' bore noticeable similarities to Star Change's, including

---

[58] Article 64, Civil Procedure Law of the People's Republic of China.

[59] 北京书生电子技术有限公司诉上海盛大网络发展有限公司等垄断案 (2009) 沪高民三 (知) 终字第135号民事判决书 (2009) 沪一中民五 (知) 初字第113号民事判决书; *Beijing Sursen Electronic Technology Co. Ltd. v Shanda Interactive Entertainment Ltd. (Shanda) and Shanghai Xuanting Entertainment Co. Ltd.*, Shanghai High People's Court Civil Three Final Judgement (2009) Number 135, and Shanghai First Intermediate People's Court Civil Five IP Judgement (2009) Number 113.

the story line and the names of the characters. The claimant and the defendants were the copyright holders of the named works according to the agreement in the commission contracts that was recognized by the CCL.

The defendants contacted Bin Kou and Yapeng Li directly and accused them together with the claimant breaching their copyright in the 'Star Change' series, and demanded them to cease writing the 'Star Change Sequel' series. On 1 January 2009, Bin Kou and Yapeng Li respectively published a letter of apology on www.qidian.com and stated that they would no longer write the 'Star Change Sequel' series for the claimant's www.du8.com since the series were indeed inspired by the original story of 'Star Change'.

Sursen filed a complaint to the Shanghai First IPC, alleging that the defendants had abused their dominance by causing Bin Kou and Yapeng Li to cease writing novels for publication on www.du8.com. Specifically, Sursen said that the defendants had abused their dominant market position in the Chinese online literature market by restricting the authors of 'Star Change Sequel' from transacting with Sursen via conduct of duress. In addition, Sursen claimed that the 'Star Change Sequel' did not infringe 'Star Change' copyright and the defendants' accusation of copyright infringement was an invalid claim, and therefore could not constitute the 'legitimate reasons' required by Article 17(4) of the AML.

On 23 October 2009, the Shanghai First IPC dismissed Sursen's allegation and ruled that the claimant had failed to establish that the defendants possessed a dominant position in the market for online literature. In the interim, the court deemed that it was irrelevant and unnecessary to discuss whether there was a copyright infringement in this case. Sursen appealed to the Shanghai HPC. On 15 December 2009, the appeal court heard the case and supported the judgment of the first instance in full. The court held that two pieces of evidence submitted by Sursen for proving the defendants' dominant position were insufficient, several press articles published online on the topic of Chinese literature industry with statistics saying that the defendants had over 80 per cent shares of the market, and a statement on the defendants' website proclaiming that they occupied approximately 80 per cent market share of the online Chinese literature industry. The court of first instance pointed out that the defendants' statement online was most likely made for marketing purposes and was unlikely to be a properly calculated market share. The HPC agreed, and added that any promotional materials would be insufficient evidence and also the data in online publications may not be 'objective, fair or accurate'. Both courts gave rather detailed discussions on how the defendants' conduct of interfering with the two authors and of demanding the two authors to cease writing 'Star Change Sequel' were for a 'legitimate reason', defending their copyright vested in 'Star Change'. The courts also offered sections of analysis of how a 'relevant market' and a 'dominant position' should have been interpreted under the then new AML, and emphasized that having a dominant market position itself is not illegal, and only is when such dominant market position is being abused, in which circumstances sufficient evidence must be presented to the court and Sursen certainly failed to do so.

As the first court judgment enforcing the AML, *Sursen v Shanda* set the criterial standard for sufficient evidence to be presented in a competition case, 'objective, fair or accurate'. It held that the defendants did not have a dominant position in the online literature market in China since the claimant failed to provide sufficient evidence proving that the alleged market shares in the promotional materials were equivalent to the factual ones. While discussions on how to define 'relevant market' and 'dominant position' in *Sursen v Shanda* were substantive and lengthy, the court did not decide what the relevant market was. Indeed, litigators and the People's Courts have been finding it challenging with respect to identifying relevant market share in many cases. The SPC did make it clear in *Qihoo v Tencent* that definition of relevant market share is not always mandatory.

Nonetheless, hardly any claimants have succeeded in civil anti-monopoly cases due to the difficulties in collecting evidence and the heavy burden of proof required in such cases.[60] On 3 May 2012, the Provisions of the Supreme People's Court on Several Issues concerning the Application of Law in the Trial of Civil Dispute Cases Arising from Monopolistic Conduct ('2012 Provisions') were issued and took effect on 1 June 2012, offering judicial interpretation of the AML and setting out the general guidelines for the People's Courts at all levels in handling civil anti-monopoly cases, especially the burden of proof in such cases.[61]

The 2012 Provisions require a claimant to be responsible to prove both the defendant's dominance and its abuse thereof, stating that 'in case that the accused monopoly activity falls into the scope regulated by Article 17.1 of the Anti-Monopoly Law, the claimant shall produce evidence proving that the defendant has a dominance position in the relevant market and that the defendant abuses his market dominance position',[62] which demand a claimant to provide evidence that is sufficient in three aspects: specific definition of the relevant market, a market dominance position of the defendant, and conducts of abusing the market dominance by the defendant. Nevertheless, the defendant is obligated to prove that an agreement that the claimant claims is a monopolistic agreement prohibited by Article 13 of the AML, including a price-fixing or joint boycotting agreement, does

---

[60] Interview with Chef Judge of the SPC, available at <http://news.xinhuanet.com/legal/2012-05/08/c_111910772_3.htm> accessed 16 March 2017.

[61] See <http://www.chinacourt.org/law/detail/2012/05/id/145752.shtml> accessed on 16 March 2017.

[62] Article 8, AML.

not have the effect of excluding or restraining competition.[63] In addition, the 2012 Provisions permit a claimant to use the information published by the defendant as evidence of defendant's dominance, and the defendant then has to demonstrate the reasons justifying its conduct,[64] i.e. in such a case the burden of proof is shifted to the defendant to present evidence that there has been no prohibited restriction or exclusion of competition. In cases where the defendant is a public utility enterprise or other business operators that possess an exclusive monopolistic position based on a public utility enterprise, the court can, according to the market structure and competitive status in the market, conclude that such a defendant has a dominant market position unless such determination can be rebutted by other evidence presented by the defendant. Moreover, either claimant or defendant may apply to the court for the appearance of one to two experts to explain the technical issues involved in the case,[65] i.e. the 2012 Regulations confirm expert aid in the preparation of market survey or economic analytical reports on specialized issues involved.

The 2012 Provisions expect to reduce claimant's burden of proof in civil competition disputes. For example, when copyright infringement is involved in such cases, the claimant should present evidence to show that the defendant copied from the work, which may be that the defendant had access to the claimant's copyrighted work and that there are substantial similarities between the defendant's infringing work and the claimant's infringed work. If the claimant shows that the defendant had prior access to the claimant's work and that there is a substantial similarity between the infringed and infringing works, a presumption of copying arises shifting the burden to the defendant to rebut the presumption or to show that the alleged infringing work was independently created. Such inversion of burden of proof has been confirmed in *Guiding Case No. 49, Shi Honglin v Taizhou Huaren Electronic Information Co. Ltd.*, one of the 10th Set of the Guiding Cases issued on 15 April 2015.

Shi Honglin v Taizhou Huaren was a software copyright infringement case first filed with the Taizhou IPC and then appealed in the Jiangsu HPC, where the first instance decision was overturned. The appeal court found the defendant infringed the claimant's copyright, and ordered it to cease producing and selling the relevant products.[66] The Jiangsu HPC explained that when disputes occur upon exercising copyright to computer software, one of the ways to determine whether or not infringement exists should be to compare the source codes from

---

[63] Article 7, AML.
[64] Article 10, AML.
[65] Article 12, AML.
[66] (2007) 苏民三终字第0018号民事判决; Jiangsu High People's Court Civil Three Final Judgement (2007) Number 0018.

the copyright holder of the software and the party accused of the copyright infringement to see if they were identical or substantively identical. Where there was evidence to prove that one party had possession of evidence and refused to provide it without good cause, if the other party claimed that the content of the evidence was adverse to the party in possession of the evidence, it could be presumed that such a claim was true. As source code is generally in the possession of the developer, in the event that the party accused of copyright infringement refuses to provide the source code without good cause for a direct comparison, and such source code cannot be directly read from the product involved in the infringement due to technological limitations, if the copyright holder of the software has proved that the software from the person accused of the copyright infringement is identical with or similar to the software from the copyright holder in terms of flaws in design and other aspects, and that the content of the source code in the possession of the party accused of copyright infringement, which such party refuses to provide without reasonable justification, is adverse to the party, the court may rule that the source code from both parties is substantively identical, and the party accused of copyright infringement is to assume civil liability under the relevant provision.[67] Indeed, *Shi Honglin v Taizhou Huaren* has made it possible to expand the scope of the shift of burden to certain litigations in one of the most fast moving and competitive markets in China, the computer software market.

Noting that the 2012 Provisions, aiming to lift the heavy burden of proof of claimants' in civil competition cases, accept information disclosed by the defendant as the claimant's evidence of proving dominance, would the court's decision of burden of proof differed if *Sursen v Shanda* was trailed after the provisions came in effect in June 2012? That may be answered soon in the ongoing *LETV v Baidu*, a high profile case filed with the Beijing Haidian District People's Court in February 2016, in which the claimant alleged the defendant's use of LETV's screenshots had confused consumers and abused Baidu's dominant market position. As a country adopting the continental legal system, Chinese statutes and codes are designed to cover most (but cannot cover all) eventualities, and courts have a very limited role of applying the law to the case in hand. The Jiangsu HPC's flexible approach of law interpretation in *Shi Honglin v Taizhou Huaren*, together with the SPC's acknowledgement of such approach are inspiring, even though what the practical changes that the *Guiding Case Shi Honglin v Taizhou Huaren* would bring forward is currently unknown.

---

[67] Article 75, Several Provisions of the Supreme People's Court on Evidence in Civil Proceedings.

5. Technological Protection Measures

In line with WCT Article 11 and WPPT Article 18, technological protection measures (TPM) for copyright are confirmed by the CCL and may be used to restrict the unauthorized access of copyrighted works.[68] Like in other jurisdictions, TPM of copyrighted works in China nowadays are not only for 'disabling end users from availing themselves of some of the copying technology's potential for reproducing and redistributing copyrighted works',[69] but also for preventing unfair competition in the fast moving market, particularly in the software industry. *Zhongshan Haiyin Computer Ltd v Shenzhen Saiyin Yuangu Development Ltd.*, a Top Ten IP Case of the Year that was initiated by Saiyin at the Shenzhen IPC and petitioned with the Guangdong HPC's court by Haiyin in 2008, is known in China not only for the court's pioneering clarification on the two critical elements of copyright infringement, 'access to prior work' and 'substantial similarity', but also for their sound discussion of TPM in a competitive market.[70] While the Haiyin's copyright infringement was found, the Guangdong HPC rejected its plea under provisions of the AML and the UCL, saying that competition law would be inappropriate to be taken into account in this particular case as it was evidently an infringement dispute concerning TPM for copyright. The court then carried out a scrutiny discussing the TPM used in the source code by Saiyin, were fair and lawful protection for its copyrighted work, software specifically, which undertook no wrong doings, constituted no monopoly, and did not bring any harm to a competitive market. However, *Haiyin v Saiyin* did not explain where the line should be drawn between fair and unfair competition regarding copyright holders' use of TPM.

Such discussions were provided in another guiding case issued in 2015, the *Guiding Case 48, Beijing Jingdiao Technology Co. Ltd. v Shanghai Naiky Electronic Technology Co. Ltd.* The claimant claimed that it had independently developed the Jingdiao CNC Engraving System, including JDPaint software with Eng format data, a technical means of preventing copyright infringement. In early 2006, the claimant found the defendant's illegal deciphering of Eng format encryption, development, and sales of control system, which could read Eng format data files. The claimant sought a court order restraining the defendant from further infringement and ordering it to pay compensation. The court found that the computer software

---

[68] Article 48(6), CCL.

[69] Jane C. Ginsburg, *Legal Protection of Technological Measures Protecting Works of Authorship: International Obligations and the US Experience*, 29 The Columbia Journal of Law & the Arts 11 (2005–2006).

[70] 海茵公司与深圳市赛银远古实业发展有限公司侵犯计算机软件著作权案(2008) 粤高法民三终字第7号; Guangdong High People's Court Civil Three Final Judgement (2008) Number 7.

copyright owner set a special file format for the software's output data to restrict machines of competitors from reading data saved in this special file format and expand its competitive edge from software to machines for the tie-in sales of software and machines; such acts were not the technical measures taken by copyright owners to protect software copyright as provided for in the CCL. The research and development of software by other parties to read files saved in a format set by the copyright owner did not constitute infringement upon computer software copyright. On 20 September 2006, the Shanghai First IPC held the defendant had not sought to circumvent or sabotage technical means to protect copyright in computer software and had not infringed. And on 13 December 2016, the Shanghai HPC dismissed the claimant's appeal.

Jingdiao v Naiky makes it clear that the CCL prohibits trafficking of programmes and devices, which includes no manufacturing of the devices nor the very act of circumventing. Such ruling is appropriate and it will hopefully help courts at all levels to give more coherent decisions in future. It should be noted that laws applied in *Haiyin v Saiyin* and in *Jingdiao v Naiky* were focused on copyright provisions, and the defence of competition laws was declined in both cases. That is probably because the current competition laws offer no stipulations on right holders' technological measures in a competitive market. After all, courts in China have a very limited role of applying the law to the case in hand and have no authority to make law as such. However, current provision of TPM in the CCL is abstract and imparts no precise further measures. The lack of specific and good legislation may be changed once the 2014 Draft CCL come into effect.

The 2014 Draft CCL, as mentioned earlier, consists of an addition of a chapter on technological protection and rights management information. It defines TPM as 'effective technologies, devices or components that rights holders adopt in order to prevent or limit their works, performances, audio products or radio and television programs being reproduced, scanned, enjoyed, operated, altered, or disseminated through networks',[71] which is consistent with WCT and WPPT and confirms the TPM's legitimate control of reproduction and access over a copyrighted work in China. The 2014 Draft CCL authorizes that right holders may adopt TPM to protect their copyright and related rights, and also sets the anti-circumventing rules: 'without permission, no organisation or individual may wilfully avoid or destroy technological protection measures, may wilfully produce, import or provide to the public installations or components mainly used to avoid or destroy technological protection measures, may wilfully provide technology or services to other persons to avoid or destroy technological protection measures, except where laws or administrative regulations provide otherwise'.[72] Although the terminologies

---

[71] Article 68, CCL.
[72] Article 69, CCL.

may differ from the international conventions', the inclusion of the provisions for IPM is welcome. Nonetheless, definition of circumvention devices should also be provided and the liability for making and using such devices should be clarified. In addition, amongst the five catalogues of legitimate bypassing of TPM,[73] the latter two catalogues of act of circumvention, i.e. authorized security monitoring, and research on encryption or research on reverse engineering computer programs, need to be further explained and regulated to avoid abuse of such permitted acts. It is worth noting that prior to the 2014 Draft CCL TPM provisions, Chinese courts have confirmed TPM as an effective means of protection for copyright and the decision, as shown in *Haiyin v Saiyin* and in *Jingdiao v Naiky*, on the scope and extent of TPM together using TPM for fair competition is in harmony with the international standard. The courts have also mentioned the use of licence agreement in practicing TPM, whilst licensing of copyright in general is currently in development.

The 2014 Draft CCL introduces provisions regarding the licensing of copyright. It provides that a licence agreement should be registered with the special registration agency established by the Copyright Administration Department of the State Council and non-registration will render exclusive licenses void against third parties acting in good faith.[74] Where there is no explicit agreement on whether a licence agreement is exclusive, it is deemed to be non-exclusive,[75] and where the licence has no express provision for the calculation of royalties, the market rate or standard set out by the Copyright Administration Department of the State Council should be applied.[76] These provisions demand the level of royalty payable to be clearly stated in licence agreements as silence on this point could lead to royalties being deemed payable by the administration authority, and licence agreements to be recorded with the administration authority as failing that exclusive licensees will be at risk of third parties taking free of their rights. To have works available for trade in the market, right holders have to materialize their copyright, via licensing in many cases, and collective management of copyright is thus vital.

---

[73] Article 71, CCL: 'Under the following circumstances, technological protection measures may be avoided, but the technology, devices or components for avoiding technological protection measures may not be provided to other persons: (1) providing works, performances, audio products or radio and television programs to small numbers of teachers or researchers for classroom teaching or scientific research, and it is impossible to obtain the said work, performance, audio product or radio and television program through regular channels; (2) with no aim of profit, providing already published works to blind people in unique methods that blind persons can perceive, and it is impossible to obtain the said work through normal channels; (3) State organs implementing their duties according to administrative or judicial procedure; (4) bodies with security monitoring qualifications testing the security of computers and their systems or networks; (5) research on encryption or research on reverse engineering computer programs.'

[74] Article 59, CCL.

[75] Article 54, CCL.

[76] Article 53, CCL.

The current provision for collective management of copyright is merely the 2010 CCL, Article 8, which is abstract and hazy. The 2014 Draft CCL expands collecting society provisions in Articles 61–67, giving definition to 'collective administration organization' (CAO), and stating the rights and management of CAOs. However, along with the development of collecting society in China,[77] the absence of supervision of fees charged by CAOs may become problematic in the defence of fair competition.

6. Conclusion

It may have been noted that in other more established jurisdictions copyright abuse cases are mostly licensing related, for instance, use of copyright to exact concessions from the licensee, restriction of the licensee's ability to deal with the copyright owner's competitors, limiting another's ability to compete, and anti-competitive use of the judicial system,[78] while claims in China have mainly arisen in a copyright owner's monopolistic dealing in competition, i.e. abusive conduct of the dominant market position. Generally speaking, competition cases may be complicated not only because the legal and economic issues arising within but also because they are likely to involve more than one area of law; in China, civil competition litigations have been mostly related to IPR, often seen in software and IT-dependant industries. However, claims of such nature are seldom successful to date, which may result from the matters presented above. While courts are still deciding how to give clear explanation for market definition and abuse of dominant market position, the burden of proof on the claimant in a copyright abuse case is still not only heavy but also incoherent. Even though the SPC states that it is not required that the claimant define what the relevant market is or to quantify the harm, failing that may result in disallowance of such claim. The absence of stipulation in competition law also makes it more challenging for claimants' allegation to be upheld. Besides, the court's exhaustive explanation of TMP and its move to dismiss accusations under competition law shows the limitation of the TMP legislation being vested in the 2010 CCL, which calls for the prompt enactment of the 2014 Draft CCL on the one hand, and the consideration of introducing TMP to competition law on the other. And more importantly, specified regulations for Article 55 AML should be provided to perfect the People's Courts enforcement of the law in the case of copyright abuse, as well as abuse of IPR in general.

---

[77] To date, three main collecting societies are the Music Copyright Society of China, set up in 1992, the Written Works Copyright Society of China, and the Sound and Visual Copyright Society of China that both established in 2008.

[78] John T. Cross and Peter K. Yu, *Competition Law and Copyright Misuse* (2008), available at<http://www.peteryu.com/drake.pdf> accessed 16 March 2017.

Looking closely into the 10th Set Guiding Cases issued by the SPC, the sessions of reasoning in court decisions have been presented and expanded, even if conclusions may be unpersuasive at times; the active advocate of the SPC reasoning may lead to well-written, reasoned judgment in the future, a small step towards the rule of law. In addition, it seems that the Chinese courts are taking a tolerant approach towards dominant undertakings in the Chinese market. Such an approach is illustrated in one of the SPC recently issued the Top Ten IP Cases, *Yu Zheng v Qiong Yao*,[79] in which the court granted exclusive rights for the protection of a TV series plots such as 'baby swap' to one of the most celebrated contemporary novelists, known for her dramatic love stories by her pen name 'Qiong Yao', who issued an open letter to the copyright authorities online, and was widely forwarded and supported by peers, scholars, and fans.[80] The court's decision on protecting story plot is somewhat contrary to existing judicial opinions in other systems, for instance the UK and the US. Questions arising include: has it gone too far? What impact may it have on the succeeding rulings? Would it uplift monopoly power in the market place and discourage start-ups? Nevertheless, the court's lenient approach to certain civil copyright acts may be seen as the Chinese courts' attempt at safeguarding private rights on the one hand, and supporting the voice of the grassroots on the other. In a country traditionally lacking respect for individual rights and the masses, and an interrupted market economy for decades, such an approach is refreshing and constructive, notwithstanding it might in some cases 'over-correct a defect' for now. Needless to say, such an approach may also be interpreted as echoing the 13th Five-Year Plan for National Economic and Social Development of the People's Republic of China that set the country's milestone goal of 'building moderately prosperous society' by 2020, a part of the realization of the 'Chinese Dream' reiterated by Chairman Xi Jinping.[81]

Whilst the opportunities exist for an increasingly unlocked and enhanced environment for commerce, investment, production, technology, and innovation, the challenges arising in the regime of copyright and competition law are primarily from transformation of the imperfect statutory provisions and incoherent rulings to establishing an effective and of international standard enforcement system. With

---

[79] 于正等与琼瑶侵害著作权纠纷上诉案(2015)高民(知)终字第1039号民事判决书; SPC Civil IP Final Judgement (2015) Number 1039.

[80] 卢海君   张雨潇: '扒剧'行为、著作权法保护与文化产品的竞争——以琼瑶诉于正案为例 '中国出版' 2014年13期 第25–27页; Haijun Lu and Yuxiao Zhang, 'Copying Plots, Copyright Protection and Cultural Products Competition', [2014] 13 China Publishing Journal 25–27.

[81] For an English version of the 13th Five-Year Plan, see <http://en.ndrc.gov.cn/newsrelease/201612/P020161207645765233498.pdf> accessed 16 March 2017. For an English version of the Report on the Implementation of the 2015 Plan for National Economic and Social Development and on the 2016 Draft Plan for National Economic and Social Development, see <http://english.gov.cn/news/top_news/2016/03/19/content_281475310332486.htm> accessed 16 March 2017.

the continuous endeavours of courts at all levels, the establishment and development of an original Guiding Case mechanism at the right place in practice, and the forthcoming and further amendments of copyright and competition laws, more effective enforcement systems of copyright and competition are foreseeable, which would create a more tenable, fair, and competitive environment for creativity and trade, and hopefully beyond.

7

SEPS AND COMPETITION LAW

From the Perspective of *Huawei v IDC* Case

Xiaoye Wang* and Yajie Gao**

1. Introduction

Standard Essential Patents ('SEPs') refer to the indispensable and unsubstitutable patents to a technical standard. Or put it another way, SEPs are patents that have to be applied when enforcing a technical standard. Technical standard is a compulsory requirement for relevant undertakings, if it has been widely used so as to become an industrial standard or state compulsory standard, and products or services that cannot meet such a 'threshold' are prohibited from entering into the market. Due to the openness of the standard, technology licence related to SEPs concerns public interest. On the other hand, however, SEP is similar to general patent, both of which are private properties. In order to pursue economic interests, SEPs-holders may raise patent royalties unfairly or exclude other competitors with help of a 'lock-in' effect deriving from the SEP. Industry standards are widely acknowledged to be one of the engines driving the modern economy. Standards can make products less costly to produce and more valuable for consumers. They can increase innovation, efficiency, and consumer choice; foster public health and safety; and serve as a 'fundamental building block for international trade'.[1] Against this background, how to compromise protection of SEPs-holders' legitimate rights and interests and openness and social publicity of SEPs has become an important issue to be resolved in the intersection of anti-monopoly law and intellectual property rights ('IPRs') law.

---

* Professor at Hunan University and at Chinese Academy of Social Sciences, Expert of Consultation Group of Antimonopoly Commission of the State Council

** 2017 PHD candidate of the Queen Mary University of London

[1] The US Department of Justice and the Federal Trade Commission, *Antitrust Enforcement and Intellectual Property Rights: Promoting Innovation and Competition* (April 2007) 33 (hereafter The US DOJ and FTC, *Antitrust Enforcement and Intellectual Property Rights: Promoting Innovation and Competition*).

Since implementation of the *Anti-Monopoly Law of the People's Republic of China* ('AML'), there have been a number of cases involving SEPs. On 9 February 2015, the National Development and Reform Commission ('NDRC') fined Qualcomm Incorporated ('Qualcomm') RMB 6.088 billion for charging unfairly high royalties for its SEPs, which set the highest record for an administrative fine in China.[2] As one of the three competition authorities in China, the Ministry of Commerce ('MOFCOM') has also dealt with several cases concerning SEPs, such as Google's acquisition of Motorola Mobile ('Motorola') cleared subject to conditions on 19 May 2012[3] and Microsoft Corporation's ('Microsoft') acquisition of Nokia's Devices and Services business ('Nokia') cleared subject to conditions on 8 April 2014.[4] *Case Huawei Technology Co. Ltd. v InterDigital Technology Corp.*[5] (*'Huawei v IDC'*) is China's first antitrust litigation involving SEPs that has been accepted and decided by the Chinese courts with final judgment. In this case, Huawei (the plaintiff) is a manufacturer of wireless communication devices, while IDC (the defendant) holds numerous SEPs in 2G, 3G, and 4G standards within area of wireless communication technology. The plaintiff and the defendant had held multiple negotiations on patent royalties since November 2008. However, no agreement was reached for the reason that the royalties requested by IDC to Huawei were extremely higher than those requested to Apple Inc. ('Apple') and Samsung Corporation ('Samsung'). In July 2011, IDC filed lawsuits of SEPs infringement to a US federal court and the US International Trade Commission ('USITC') against Huawei, and requested for an injunction and cease of tort. On 6 December 2011, Huawei filed two complaints before the Shenzhen Intermediate People's Court of Guangdong Province, with one for cease of IDC's abuse of market dominance and compensation for damages, while the other for determination of royalties that should have been requested by IDC based on principle of fairness. In February 2013, the Shenzhen Intermediate People's Court came out with the first-instance judgment,[6] and the Guangdong High People's Court posted the final judgment in October 2013.[7] From the perspective of *Huawei v IDC*, this chapter discusses

---

[2] Administrative Punitive Decision of the National Development and Reform Commission (hereafter *NDRC*), FA GAI BAN JIA JIAN CHU FA (2015) No 1.

[3] Announcement of the Ministry of Commerce (hereafter *MOFCOM*) No 25 of 2012 'Announcement of Anti-Monopoly Review Decision on Conditional Clearance of Google's Acquisition of Motorola Mobility'.

[4] Announcement of MOFCOM No 24 of 2014 'Announcement of Anti-Monopoly Review Decision on Conditional Clearance of Microsoft's Acquisition of Nokia's Devices & Services Business'.

[5] The respondents in this case include InterDigital Technology Corporation, InterDigital Communication Inc., InterDigital Inc., and IPR Licensing Inc., all of which are subsidiaries wholly owned by InterDigital Corporation and called 'InterDigital Group' by the public. All the respondents in this case were abbreviated as 'IDC' by the court.

[6] (2011) SHEN ZHONG FA ZHI MIN CHU ZI No 857 and (2011) SHEN ZHONG FA ZHI MIN CHU ZI No 858.

[7] (2013) YUE GAO FA MIN SAN ZHONG ZI No 306 and (2013) YUE GAO FA MIN SAN ZHONG ZI No 305.

several key issues concerning SEPs related anti-monopoly litigation. Section 2 talks about whether a proprietor of SEPs enjoys dominant market position, which is also the foundation of Huawei's charge against IDC for its abuse of dominance. Section 3 deals with how the court determines fair, reasonable, and non-discriminatory ('FRAND') royalties of SEPs, which is the core of *Huawei v IDC*. Section 4 discusses the right of SEPs-holders to request an injunction, and this is also a novel issue in China's AML enforcement. This chapter ends with several inspirations and thoughts as a result.

2. Whether a Proprietor of SEPs Holds Dominant Market Position?

Huawei sued IDC on the grounds that the latter abused its dominant market position as proprietor of SEPs. However, in order to decide whether an undertaking has abused its dominance or not, determination of dominance by law enforcement agency is the prerequisite. Dominant market position reflects the relationship between an undertaking and the market, which confers on an undertaking the freedom to set price or make business decisions without consideration of reactions from competitors or customers. The case of *Huawei v IDC* involves mainstream technological standards of wireless communication, such as 2G, 3G, and 4G (especially 3G), which relate to international spectrum resources distributed uniformly by the International Telecommunications Union ('ITU') and need coordination and cooperation between governments all over the world. Hence, almost all the countries and regions have adopted these standards. Any proprietor of SEPs naturally enjoys dominance in the technological SEPs licensing market in this regards. However, in *Huawei v IDC*, IDC refused to admit its dominant market position, let alone the abuse, though it holds a lot of SEPs in the 2G, 3G, and 4G standards. Accordingly, whether a proprietor of SEPs enjoys dominant market position in the relevant SEPs licensing market becomes the first issue to be resolved.

2.1 Definition of relevant market

In order to determine whether an undertaking has obtained dominant market position, relevant market should first be defined scientifically and reasonably. Only

---

The Guangdong High People's Court dismissed the appeal and almost upheld the original judgment made by the Shenzhen Intermediate People's Court. The former reversed one of the latter's conclusion that IDC engaged in tie-in sales related to standard essential patents (hereafter *SEPs*). Since packaged sales of essential patents on a global scale is in line with the efficiency principle when cooperating with transnational companies, to name Huawei as an example. This chapter makes no difference when referring to judgments made by the two courts mentioned above in the main text, but would mention the exact case number in the citation.

through defining relevant market could both existing competitors and potential competitors be recognized so as to calculate market share and concentration degree of relevant undertakings and then decide whether market position/conducts of undertakings would have side effect on competition. Defining relevant market is usually the starting point in analyzing competitive activities.[8] When defining relevant market, relevant product and geographic scope affected by relevant product of a case should be taken into consideration, which are called 'relevant product market' and 'relevant geography market' respectively.[9]

As for relevant product market, what competition authorities mainly focus on is demand substitution of consumers. According to Article 3 of the *Guidelines of the Anti-Monopoly Commission of the State Council on Defining Relevant Markets*, 'A relevant product market shall mean a market compromising of a group or a category of products which are regarded as interchangeable or substitutable by consumers for the reason of products' characteristics, intended use and prices.' In *Huawei v IDC*, acting as a manufacturer of wireless communication devices, Huawei has to obtain IDC's license for using 3G wireless communication SEPs set and released by 3GPP, 3GPP2, and other international standard setting organizations ('SSOs').[10] The court observed that 'technical standard' is a set of unified technical specifications with the aim of securing the interchangeability, compatibility, and universality of products or services. It is a mandatory request for manufacturing undertakings.[11] Accordingly, technical standardization unifies technical specifications on one hand, and eliminates competition in relevant technical market on the other hand. In the context of technical standardization, there wouldn't be any technical competition which could have happened before or without the standardization. Due to functional diversities among different SEPs within a standard, manufacturers need to negotiate with proprietors of all the SEPs for use. In this case, every single essential patent within a standard could be recognized as an independent relevant product market. *Huawei v IDC* concerns IDC's essential patents within 3GPP and 3GPP2 wireless communication technical standard. There is no alternative technology in the market either. So it is no doubt that relevant product market in this case is every single essential patent owned by IDC within the 3GPP and 3GPP2 technical standards. We could also find similar expression in the EU Commission's ('Commission') decision on Samsung ('Samsung Case'), '... the relevant product markets encompass the licensing of the technologies as specified in the UMTS standard technical specifications, on which each of Samsung's UMTS SEPs reads.... for manufacturers of UMTS standard-compliant mobile devices in

---

[8] Guidelines of the Anti-Monopoly Commission of the State Council Concerning the Definition of Relevant Markets, Article 2.

[9] Xiaoye Wang, *Anti-Monopoly Law* (Law Press 2011) 85–88.

[10] (2013) YUE GAO FA MIN SAN ZHONG ZI No 306, 40.

[11] Ibid, 41–42.

the EEA, there are no substitutes to the technologies as specified in the UMTS standard technical specifications, on which each of Samsung's UMTS SEPs reads'.[12]

Geographic scope of relevant product should also be considered when defining relevant geographic market. On the one hand, Huawei manufactures and sells wireless communication devices in the Chinese market. The products should comply with three standards, which are CDMA2000, WCDMA, and TD-SCDMA, within the Chinese 3G wireless communication area. On the other hand, Huawei also exports wireless communication devices to the U.S., which applies CDMA2000 and WCDMA standards on the basis of international standards (3GPP and 3GPP2). It means that Huawei couldn't sell its products to either PRC nor the US if it cannot obtain SEPs licence from IDC. So, even if IDC licenses SEPs of the 3GPP and 3GPP2 standards globally, relevant geographic markets of this case are PRC and the U.S. for the reason that Huawei only needs to obtain the licence for these areas. In summary, relevant markets in this case are every single essential patent within 3G wireless communication standard of IDC in both PRC and the U.S. Since proprietor of all these SEPs is IDC, relevant market could be regarded as an aggregate of IDC's SEPs within 3G wireless communication standard in PRC and the U.S.[13]

Nevertheless, IDC didn't agree with the court's observation of defining its SEPs within 3G technical standard as relevant product markets for the reason that: 'According to particularity of SEPs, no terminal product could be produced only basing on technologies covered by IDC's essential patents.'[14] It means that IDC treated terminal product covered by 3G standard as relevant product market. Put it in another way, the demanding party is terminal consumer of wireless communications devices instead of Huawei. The proposition put forwards by IDC couldn't stand. Though protection of consumers is an important purpose of anti-monopoly law, it doesn't mean that the law protects terminal consumers as a whole abstractly. As for who exactly the 'consumer' is in a particular case, it depends on specific circumstances. Parties closely connected with the case economically should be considered. They could be household consumers or productive consumers. In cases concerning technology licence, procurement of raw materials, or semi-manufactured products, the demanding party should be the licensee of related technology or consumer of related raw materials or semi-manufactured products. Cause of action of this case is that Huawei requested IDC to license its SEPs within 3G wireless communication technology standard on FRAND conditions. So the demanding party in this case is Huawei. It is odd for IDC to treat terminal consumers as the demanding party in this case, since the terminal consumers are neither in need of obtaining right to

---

[12] *Samsung-Enforcement of UMTS Standard Essential Patents* (Case 39939) Commission Decision of 29.4.2014, paras 41–42 (hereafter *Samsung-Enforcement of UMTS Standard Essential Patents*).
[13] (2013) YUE GAO FA MIN SAN ZHONG ZI No 306, 40–41.
[14] (2011) SHEN ZHONG FA ZHI MIN CHU ZI No 858, 13.

use IDC's essential patents, nor will they seek for legal remedies concerning IDC's patent licence.

The analysis mentioned above proves that definition of relevant market in *Huawei v IDC* is clear and scientific. The focus of the court was that IDC's essential patents within 3G wireless communication standard obtained by Huawei constituted an indispensable link of its production and operation activities. That is to say, even if there are hundreds of standards within a smartphone or a computer, and hundreds of thousands of essential patents within every standard, every single SEP could constitute a relevant product market, since every single SEP is indispensable for the potential licensees' production activities. As pointed out by the Commission in Decision on Google's acquisition of Motorola, 'The specificity of SEPs is that they have to be implemented in order to comply with a standard and thus cannot be designed around, i.e. there is by definition no alternative or substitute for each such patent. Therefore, each SEP constitutes a separate relevant technology market on its own.'[15]

2.2 Market position of IDC

It is much easier to determine whether IDC holds a dominant position in the 3G wireless communication SEPs licensing market after the relevant market is defined. As pointed out by the court:

> In this case, IDC is proprietor of essential patents within WCDMA, CDMA2000 and TD-SCDMA standards in 3G communication field all over the world, including PRC and the U.S. Due to the uniqueness and un-substitutability of every essential patent within 3G standard, IDC has 100% market share in the licensing market of every essential patent within the 3G standard, empowering it to hinder or restrict other undertakings from entering into relevant market.'[16]

That is to say, in the SEPs licensing market, proprietors do enjoy dominant market position. During NDRC's investigation into the Qualcomm case, Qualcomm 'failed to deliver any evidence to prove that it didn't have dominant position in wireless SEPs licensing market'.[17] In Huawei's litigation against Zhongxing Telecommunication Equipment Corporation ('ZTE') dealt with by a German court, there wasn't any controversy concerning the proprietor's dominant market position between these two parties.[18]

---

[15] *Google/Motorola Mobility* (Case M.6381) Commission Decision of 13.2.2012, paras 54, 61 (hereafter *Google/Motorola Mobility*).

[16] (2013) YUE GAO FA MIN SAN ZHONG ZI No 306, 43.

[17] Administrative Punitive Decision of the NDRC [2015] No 1.

[18] Case C 170/13 *Huawei Technologies Co. Ltd. v ZTE Corp., ZTE Deutschland GmbH* [2015] ECLI:EU:C:2015:477, para 43 (hereafter *Huawei Technologies Co. Ltd. v ZTE Corp., ZTE Deutschland GmbH*).

However, in Huawei's litigation against IDC, IDC put forward an opposite proposition according to Article 19[19] of AML. It was of the opinion that the number of SEPs owned by IDC was far less than half of all the SEPs due to the huge number of essential patents included in 2G, 3G, and 4G wireless communication standards. So it didn't hold dominant market position.[20] IDC also supplemented that exercise of its rights would definitely be affected by the whole wireless communication market and development of wireless communication technology, although it is a proprietor of essential patents.[21] This proposition cannot stand either. It is clear that relevant product market in this case is not all the essential patents included in 3G wireless communication standard, but only those owned by IDC. Since there is no alternative to IDC's essential patents in the relevant market, there is no doubt that IDC accounts for 100 per cent of every single essential patent licensing market share. Similarly, in the Samsung Case, the Commission concluded preliminarily that Samsung holds a dominant position in the markets for the licensing of the technologies as specified in the UMTS standard technical specifications, on which each of its UMTS SEPs reads, on foundation of two reasons mentioned below. First, Samsung holds a 100 per cent market share in each of the relevant markets. Second, the widespread adoption of the UMTS standard in the EEA is due, to a significant extent, to Decision 128/1999/EC. (PS: Decision 128/1999/EC required Member States to take all actions necessary in order to allow the co-ordinated and progressive introduction of UMTS services on their territory by 1 January 2002. In line with the requirements of Decision 128/1999/EC, the UMTS standard was implemented in most Member States by that date.)[22]

3. FRAND Royalty of SEPs

If considered by the court of having dominant position in SEPs licensing market, according to Article 17 of AML, IDC shouldn't abuse its dominance, including but not limited to being prohibited from 'selling commodities at unfairly high prices'; 'refusing to enter into transactions with their trading counterparts', 'conducting tie-in sale of commodities', 'adding other unreasonable trading conditions to transactions', or 'applying differential prices and other transaction terms among their trading counterparts who are on an equal footing' without justifiable reasons, etc. Acting as a proprietor of essential patents, IDC has made FRAND (fair, reasonable, and non-discriminatory) commitment to SSOs, obliging itself to license SEPs to third parties under FRAND conditions. The focal issue in this case is to

[19] Anti-Monopoly Law of the People's Republic of China (hereafter *PRC*), Article 19 (hereafter *AML*).
[20] (2011) SHEN ZHONG FA ZHI MIN CHU ZI No 858, 13.
[21] Ibid.
[22] *Samsung-Enforcement of UMTS Standard Essential Patents* (n 12), paras 45–46.

determine FRAND royalty requested by IDC to Huawei. How did the court determine FRAND royalty? What's the relationship between FRAND commitment and anti-monopoly law? Should FRAND royalty be determined in accordance with contract law?

3.1 Determination of FRAND royalty

From judgment of *Huawei v IDC*, we could find that the central idea of FRAND royalty are reasonable and non-discriminatory principles, while the former one is the key. It comprises both reasonableness of royalty itself and reasonableness of comparison among royalties requested to different licensees.[23]

When analysing FRAND royalty, the court took several elements into consideration: (1) As regards how much the royalty should be, the court could consider profits derived from exploitation of relevant patents or alternative patents, and the percentage of profits mentioned above in the licensees' profits or revenues derived from sales of relevant products. Since the final profits of a product are decided by technology, capital, operation work, and other elements, the patent royalty should only account for part instead of all of profits. Besides, in view of a proprietor's inability to provide all the technologies contained in a product, it should only be entitled to profits in proportion to the percentage of his or her patents in all technologies. (2) What a proprietor contributes is the innovative technology. So it should only be rewarded in accordance with relevant patents, instead of additional benefits simply due to a patent being included into the standard. (3) Proprietor of SEPs should only request royalty for the essential patents, excluding non-SEPs, since it is not reasonable. (4) The patent royalty shouldn't exceed a certain percentage of product profits, and patentees should distribute such royalty of proper percentage among them reasonably.[24] Nevertheless, the court realized that elements mentioned above did bring help to determine whether licence of SEPs is reasonable or not, but the method to determine royalty accordingly is only an idealized choice. In practice, one high-tech product may consist of numerous technical standards. For example, there are hundreds of standards within a computer. Furthermore, thousands of essential patents might be included in one standard. What's worse is that practical experience of evaluating quality of these essential patents and their contribution to terminal products is in shortage. All of them make it a huge difficulty for a court to assess whether the royalty of an SEP is fair and reasonable.[25]

---

[23] (2013) YUE GAO FA MIN SAN ZHONG ZI No 305, 46.

[24] Ibid, 46–47.

[25] Jianjun Zhu and Wenquan Chen, 'Justiciability of Conflicts Concerning SEPs Royalty Rate' [2014] The People's Judicature 4, 9 (hereafter Zhu and Chen, 'Justiciability of Conflicts Concerning SEPs Royalty Rate').

In this context, the court focused on analysing the 'non-discriminatory' principle of FRAND commitment. Or put it in another way, acting as the proprietor, whether IDC requested almost the same royalty or royalty rate to similar counterparties. The judgment pointed out that, 'If the royalty rate requested by the proprietor to a certain licensee is lower than that to another, then the latter would have reason to believe that it is treated discriminately through comparison. Proprietor of SEPs has breached the non-discrimination commitment accordingly.'[26] In this case, the court compared transactions between IDC and RIM, LG, Intel Corporation, Beijing New Coastline Mobility, HTC, et al. For two reasons to be listed below, the court mainly compared royalties requested by IDC to Apple and Samsung. Firstly, acting as manufacturers of wireless communication devices, both Apple and Samsung are similar to Huawei, who is in need of SEPs licensed by IDC. Secondly, both Apple's and Samsung's sales volume of mobile phone top the global list, ranking far above Huawei. Royalty rate requested by IDC to the two companies could be a sound reference for royalty rate that should have been requested to Huawei.[27] However, considering a huge difference still exists between the way royalty rate was achieved between IDC and Apple or Samsung, the court mainly compared the royalty rate requested by IDC to Huawei to that requested by IDC to Apple. While the royalty rate requested to Samsung was achieved through litigation, the royalty rate requested to Apple was achieved through equal and voluntary negotiation.[28] The court found that royalty requested by IDC to Apple from 2007 to July 2014 was USD 56 million, accounting for 0.0187 per cent (royalty rate) of Apple's total sales revenue (at least USD 300 billion) during these seven years.[29] Nevertheless, taking the fourth order offered by IDC to Huawei in 2012 as an example, any royalty rate concerning 2G, 3G, and 4G technical products requested by IDC to Huawei during 2009 to 2016 (seven years in total) accounted for 2 per cent of Huawei's sales revenue.[30] Normally speaking, the profit rate of ordinary industrial product is around 3 per cent. If Huawei accepted the royalty offered by IDC, then the royalty itself would hollow out almost all of Huawei's profits. So the court was of the opinion that royalty rate requested by IDC to Huawei was unreasonably high, and compared the royalty rate requested by IDC to Apple, concluding that the royalty rate requested by IDC to Huawei shouldn't be higher than 0.019 per cent.[31]

---

[26] (2013) YUE GAO FA MIN SAN ZHONG ZI No 305, 70.

[27] Ibid, 72.

[28] Ibid, 72–75.

[29] Ibid, 74.

[30] Ling Zhang and Jinzi Wen, 'Shenzhen Released "White Paper on IPRs Protection", while Case *Huawei v IDC* Becoming a Classic One' (24 April 2014), available at <://news.eastday.com/eastday/13news/auto/news/china/u7ai1314419_K4.html> accessed 15 June 2016.

[31] Taiwan Science & Technology Policy Research and Information Center, 'Guangdong High People's Court Determined the Royalty Rate Requested by IDC to Huawei not Exceeding 0.019%' (24 April 2014), available at <http://iknow.stpi.narl.org.tw/Post/Read.aspx?PostID=9585> accessed 15 June 2016.

IDC argued that the court determined the royalty rate which should be requested by IDC to Huawei through comparing the lump sum royalty requested by IDC to Apple, converting to certain percentage of Apple's sales revenue, was incorrect.[32] The court did accept the difference between lump sum royalty and royalty rate based on sales revenue. However, the court could only resort to the annual report of IDC, sales revenue of other licensees, and other information available so as to decide FRAND royalty that IDC should have asked from Huawei, when IDC refused to disclose any information in this regard.[33] Both the method and conclusion of the court are correct. On the one hand, if the court determined the royalty that Huawei should pay to IDC on foundation of the lump sum royalty paid by Apple to IDC, then the pre-condition is that sales revenue of both Huawei's and Apple's technical products making use of SEPs licensed by IDC are the same. However, huge difference exists between the sales revenue of Huawei and Apple. On the other hand, it is only the licensor who has access to confidential information as regards whether there is any price discrimination among different licensees or not due to information asymmetry. If the licensor didn't disclose information in this regard, the court would have to try its best to investigate and solve the problem. In fact, even if the lump sum royalty were compared, IDC cannot deny the fact that it overcharged Huawei, since the royalty requested to Huawei is much higher than that to Apple.

On the basis of FRAND commitment made by IDC, the court further analyzed the non-legitimacy of excessive royalty charged by IDC to Huawei. Firstly, IDC admitted in its annual financial report that the revenue from patent licence was going down from 2009 to 2011, since royalty correlated with product pricing. However, compared with the licence agreements between IDC and Apple, Samsung or other undertakings, the royalty charged by IDC to Huawei soared, which was obviously unfair.[34] Secondly, besides the excessive royalty, there is also a cross-licence provision, with IDC requiring Huawei to license all its patents to IDC for free.[35] Cross-licence is not necessarily unreasonable, according to the court. However, besides the excessive royalty, IDC also requested Huawei to license all its patents to IDC for free under circumstance that both the number and quality of Huawei's patents are much higher than that of IDC's, thus worsening IDC's unfair pricing. All the analysis mentioned above illustrated that the court had fully considered the FRAND principle in SEPs licensing, and royalty that Huawei should pay to IDC was determined as such.

---

[32] (2013) YUE GAO FA MIN SAN ZHONG ZI No 306, 56.
[33] Ibid, 70–71.
[34] Ibid, 71.
[35] Ibid, 71–72.

3.2 FRAND royalty and anti-monopoly law

As a legitimate exclusive right, patent entitles the proprietor two basic rights, with prohibiting third parties from obtaining or making use of the patent for the first, and setting licence conditions as one would like to for the second. Especially when it comes to determination of royalty, the proprietor could set it all by itself in reward for the previous R&D and innovation.[36] However, as for SEPs, if a standard is widely used and, for example, becomes an industrial standard or even an international standard, then it will bring about lock-in effect. That is to say, competitive technology would be excluded from the scope covered by the standard, and production of relevant product has to apply patents essential to the standard. Proprietor of SEPs obtains dominance in the licensing market naturally and could easily earn more money accordingly. In this situation, if the proprietor is allowed to choose any licensee or to impose adverse licence conditions at its will, such as charging excessive royalty, then it would bring serious side effects to business activities of the counterparties, and commercial exploitation of technical standards would be severely restricted or even decrease sharply, leading to products of technical standardization inaccessible to consumers, which is totally against the purpose and original intention of technical standardization. In order to avoid dominant market position being abused by the proprietor, SSOs usually request the proprietor to commit FRAND terms when licensing its patents to all the producers, exploiters, or relevant sales personnel in the future before the essential patents are included in the standard. This kind of commitment is called 'FRAND Commitment' or 'RAND Commitment'.[37] For example, according to *Intellectual Property Rights Policy* issued by the European Telecommunication Standards Institute ('ETSI') in 2008:

> When an essential IPR relating to a particular standard or technical specification is brought to the attention of ETSI, the Director-General of ETSI shall immediately request the owner to give within three months an irrevocable undertaking in writing that it is prepared to grant irrevocable licenses on fair, reasonable and non-discriminatory terms and conditions under such IPR.[38]

On the one hand, it is no doubt that voluntary FRAND commitment would definitely bring benefits to the proprietor, helping manufacturers obtain more sales opportunities. For undertakings engaging in R&D, the commitment would facilitate wider application of the patents so as to make it easier for the proprietor to broaden

---

[36] For example, Patent Law of the PRC, Articles 11(1), 12; The Agreement on Trade-Related Aspects of Intellectual Property Rights TRIPS, Article 28.

[37] The US DOJ and FTC, *Antitrust Enforcement and Intellectual Property Rights: Promoting Innovation and Competition* (n 1) 36.

[38] ETSI Rules of Procedure, Annex 6: ETSI Intellectual Property Rights Policy (26 November 2008) Article 6.1, available at <http://www.etsi.org/WebSite/document/Legal/ETSI_IPR-Policy.pdf> accessed 15 June 2016.

its product/technology market, and obtain more economic benefits within the protection period. Nevertheless, on the other hand, FRAND commitment is also a kind of restriction to the proprietor, prohibiting it from requesting excessive royalty at its will, refusing to license without good reasons, or imposing discriminatory or other unreasonable trading conditions. In a nutshell, FRAND commitment requests the proprietor neither to abuse the dominant position acquired through its patent being included in the standard, nor to grab unreasonable economic interests by virtue of the dominance. As pointed out by Alexander Italianer, former Director General for Competition of European Commission:

> Ownership of intellectual property rights essential to standards can confer market power. This is why commitments to license these rights in the context of standardization agreements are extremely important in preventing IPR holders from making the implementation of a standard difficult. This could happen by refusing to license or by requesting excessive fees after the industry has been locked in to the standard, or by charging discriminatory royalties.[39]

Judge Richard Posner of the United States Court of Appeals for the Seventh Circuit also mentioned that, '[t]he purpose of the FRAND requirements is to confine the patentee's royalty demand to the value conferred by the patent itself as distinct from the additional value—the hold-up value—conferred by the patent's being designed as standard-essential'.[40]

From the analysis mentioned above, we could regard FRAND commitment as agreement between SSOs and proprietor of SEPs, aiming to restrict conducts of proprietors. That is to say, due to the dominant market position obtained in SEPs licensing market, the proprietor might abuse the position, and coerce/ 'kidnap' potential licensees to accept un-FRAND provisions accordingly, thus constituting concern of the market competition. This logic corresponds with anti-monopoly law's regulation on undertakings with dominant market position. Or put it in another way, when an undertaking is partly or even totally not constrained by competition, it might take action which has no possibility of being taken in an effective competitive market.[41] That is to say, there should be a supervision mechanism targeted at undertakings with dominant position from under-competitive market so as to prevent the abuse of such a dominant position. In order to bear due responsibilities, SSOs request proprietors to make FRAND commitment. It is also one type of trade-off among rights and interests of various members within SSOs. Considering that it is not possible for one proprietor to obtain all the patents within a standard,

---

[39] Alexander Italianer, 'Innovation and Competition' (21 September 2012), available at <http://ec.europa.eu/competition/speeches/text/sp2012_05_en.pdf> accessed 15 June 2016.

[40] *Apple, Inc. v Motorola, Inc.*, 869 F Supp 2d 901, 913 (ND Il 22 June 2012), appeal pending, Nos 2012-1548, 2012-1549 (Fed Cir) (hereafter *Apple, Inc. v Motorola, Inc.*).

[41] Comparing to AML (n 19), Article 17.

members of a SSO could be the licensor sometimes, while acting as the licensee at other times. Furthermore, SSOs are always welcoming new members. That's the reason why IPRs policy of SSOs reflects rights and interests of both the licensor and the licensee inevitably. Or put it in another way, FRAND commitment should guarantee the patentee's right to obtain fair and reasonable royalty so as to maintain the motive of innovation and active participation in technical standardization, on the one hand.[42] On the other hand, FRAND commitment requests the proprietor to bear FRAND responsibilities with the purpose of prohibiting patent hold-up, to name excessive royalty as an example. Similar to general proprietors, those of SEPs are free to participate in economic activities or to sign agreement in principle. Nevertheless, the abuse of dominant position is forbidden.

FRAND commitment is one type of restriction to the proprietor, but not the decisive one. Since SEP-holders have to abide by anti-monopoly law anyway, no matter whether FRAND commitment has been made or not. The reason behind this is simple. A competitive market is the pre-condition for autonomy of will in private law. Refusing to deal or requesting excessive royalty is lawful in a competitive market, but turns out to be unlawful if monopoly or dominant position exists. Hence, there is always the possibility for proprietor of SEPs to be sued in the court or under investigation of competition agencies, as long as patent hold-up exists.

3.3 FRAND royalty and contract law

If the proprietor requests excessive royalty, refuses to license, sets discriminatory price, ties in or imposes other unreasonable licence terms, then it is going be recognized as against FRAND commitment. Then someone would be of the opinion that the court should solve disputes between Huawei and IDC on basis of contract law, since IDC has made FRAND commitment to SSOs and should bear the responsibility of licensing its SEPs to Huawei under FRAND conditions. However, this opinion needs to be discussed further.

It is undeniable that there indeed is a FRAND royalty case judged on basis of contract law in other jurisdictions, such as the case of *Microsoft v Motorola* decided by District Court, WD Washington in April 2013.[43] Motorola accused Microsoft of infringing its patents essential to an ITU advanced video coding technology standard called the 'H.264 Standard' and an Institute of Electrical Electronics Engineers ('IEEE') wireless local area network ('WLAN') standard called the '802.11 Standard', and requested Microsoft to pay royalty of 2.25 per cent of sales

---

[42] Rajendra K. Bera, 'Standard-Essential Patents (SEPs) and "fair, reasonable and non-discriminatory" (FRAND) licensing', available at <http://papers.ssrn.com/sol3/papers.cfm?abstract_id=2557390> accessed 15 June 2016.

[43] *Microsoft Corp. v Motorola, Inc.*, No C10-1823JLR, 2013 WL 2111217 (WD Wash. April 25, 2013) (hereafter *Microsoft Corp. v Motorola, Inc.*).

revenue of Windows and Xbox. On 9 November 2010, Microsoft initiated an action against Motorola, claiming that Motorola had breached the RAND commitments made to the IEEE and the ITU. Microsoft claimed itself beneficiary of the commitment. Judge in charge of this case was James L. Robart.

Judge Robart referred to the case *Georgia-Pacific Corp. v United States Plywood Corp.* judged in the 1970s,[44] presuming that the licensor and the licensee had negotiated on royalty and series of elements which should be taken into consideration when calculating reasonable royalty. All these elements are called 'Georgia-Pacific Elements'. Since *Microsoft v Motorola* concerned RAND royalty of SEPs instead of the general patents, Judge Robart brought huge modifications to the traditional Georgia-Pacific Elements, especially from the following perspectives.

Firstly, technical standardization can bring public interests. SSOs should actively promote the wide use of technical standards, which help expand production, promote price competition, and benefit the economy as a whole. FRAND commitment is a kind of promotion measure.[45] Public interest requires the proprietor to license its SEPs under RAND conditions instead of negotiating relevant terms with the counterparty privately.

Secondly, license of SEPs might lead to patent hold-up or royalty stacking, since technical products, such as computers or smart phones, often apply countless technical standards, and one technical standard often includes hundreds of thousands of essential patents. So royalty stacking is of great concern. In order to maximize profits, almost all of the proprietors would charge excessive royalty to the licensees, leading to the licensees not being able to afford such SEPs. The result is lack of access to the public of the products concerned. Considering the fact that thirty-five American undertakings own 2,500 patents essential to the H.264 standard and the number of standards owned by other nineteen undertakings was not clear, while 802.11 is a technical standard developed by more than 1,000 undertakings, Judge Robart observed that:

> There are at least 92 entities that own 802.11 SEPs. If each of these 92 entities sought royalties similar to Motorola's request of 1.15% to 1.73% of the end-product price, the aggregate royalty to implement the 802.11 Standard, which is only one feature of the Xbox product, would exceed the total product price.[46]

Thirdly, in order to avoid patent hold-up and royalty stacking, Judge Robart regarded comparable patent pool as (calculation) parameter for the royalty of 802.11

---

[44] *Georgia-Pacific Corp. v United States Plywood Corp.*, 318 F Supp 1116, 1120 (SDNY 1970), modified and aff'd, 446 F 2d 295 (2d Cir 1971) (hereafter *Georgia-Pacific Corp. v United States Plywood Corp.*).

[45] *Microsoft Corp. v Motorola Inc.* (n 43), para 13.

[46] Ibid, paras 72, 92, 112, and 456.

standard and H.264 standard. When calculating royalty of 802.11 SEP, Judge Robart was of the opinion that Marvel should pay US ¢3 per chip, since the royalty producer Marvell has to pay to ARM (proprietor of 802.11 SEP) accounts for 1 per cent of the price of one chip and Microsoft has to pay Marvel 3 USD per chip to produce Xbox.[47] Besides, Judge Robart also took into consideration of Via 802.11 patent pool, research data of InteCap (a consulting company), the number of SEPs held by Motorola, importance of these patents to the standard etc, and decided that the 'range' of royalty requested by Motorola for 802.11 SEP should be US ¢0.8–19.5 per product, while the reasonable royalty paid by Microsoft should be US ¢3.471 per Xbox. Basing on the same method of calculation, Judge Robart concluded that the computed RAND royalties fall in the range of US ¢0.555–16.389 for H.264. It was reasonable for Microsoft to pay US ¢0.555 per product.[48] Judge Robart cut the RAND royalty requested by Motorola to Microsoft significantly. Microsoft was ordered to pay Motorola USD 1.8 million for the SEP royalty every year, which was less than 1/2000 of USD 4 billion requested by Motorola to Microsoft before.[49]

Closed with a judgment of 207 pages, *Microsoft v Motorola* was the first case concerning RAND royalty of SEPs judged by the court in American history. It was regarded as a landmark accordingly.[50] Judge Robart contended that RAND royalty and its 'range' were determined to make clear whether Motorola had born the RAND commitment it had made to SSOs. Though it was a contract case,[51] and *Microsoft v Motorola* was dealt with from perspective of contract law, the court calculated RAND royalty in the same way with competition concern analysis in antimonopoly cases. For example, taking into consideration public interests related to SEPs, patent hold-up, and royalty stacking brought by SEP-holders' elimination and restriction of competition, especially Motorola's patent hold-up, the court determined RAND royalty that should be charged through comparing patent pool. Furthermore, on condition that Microsoft had applied patents but never paid the relevant royalty to the proprietor, the court still treated the excessive royalty requested by Motorola against contract law as the main issue, which was obviously

---

[47] Ibid, para 93.
[48] Dennis Crouch, 'SO THAT'S WHAT "RAND" MEANS?: A Brief Report on the Findings of Fact and Conclusions of Law in *Microsoft v Motorola*' (27 April 2013), available at <http://patentlyo.com/patent/2013/04/so-thats-what-rand-means-a-brief-report-on-the-findings-of-fact-and-conclusions-of-law-in-microsoft-v-motorola.html> accessed 15 June 2016.
[49] Ibid.
[50] Aaron Vehling, 'Motorola Urges 9th Circ. To Overturn Landmark RAND Ruling' (18 November 2014), available at <https://www.law360.com/articles/607864/motorola-urges-9th-circ-to-overturn-landmark-rand-ruling> accessed 15 June 2016 (hereafter Vehling, 'Motorola Urges 9th Circ. To Overturn Landmark RAND Ruling').
[51] *Microsoft Corp. v Motorola, Inc.* (n 43), para 3.

not according to general contract relationship.[52] Therefore, some scholars contended that even if conducts in breach of RAND commitment didn't constitute dishonesty to the SSOs, it could still be recognized as monopoly directly.[53]

There are still several confusions in theory, where legal issues concerning FRAND or RAND royalty of SEPs were treated as contract ones. Firstly, although SSOs request proprietors to license their SEPs under FRAND terms, these kind of agreements don't stipulate what measures the SSOs could take if FRAND commitment were breached. Secondly, SSOs request proprietors to license their essential patents in accordance with FRAND terms, but there is no definition of FRAND commitment in the agreement. In fact, it is not possible for a SSO to set fair and reasonable royalty for each essential patent, since it is not able to evaluate the quality of hundreds of standards within a technical product and thousands of patents contained in each standard, let alone the reasonable distribution of royalty among tens of thousands of essential patents. In another word, the FRAND commitment made by proprietors to SSOs is only theoretical and lacks operability. Thirdly, in terms of the relationship between proprietor of SEPs and potential licensee, contract concerning the royalty is not established if they haven't entered a licensing agreement from the perspective of continental law system, even if the proprietor has made FRAND commitment to the SSO.[54] For example, in *Motorola v Microsoft*, the German court was of the opinion that there wasn't any agreement concerning royalty of SEPs requested by Motorola.[55] In *Huawei v ZTE*, neither the German court nor the European court making preliminary judgment was of the opinion that the parties had entered into any agreement concerning FRAND royalty.[56] Actually, in *Microsoft v Motorola* judged by the American court, acting as the respondent, Motorola rebutted the conflict being treated as a contract case, since it had never entered into any agreement with Microsoft regarding the royalty. Not satisfied with the judgment favourable to Microsoft made by Judge Robart, Motorola contended that the case did not belong at the Ninth Circuit, because it involved important

---

[52] William H. Page, 'Judging Monopolistic Pricing: F/RAND and Antitrust Injury' (2014) 22 Tex Intell Prop LJ 181, available at <http://scholarship.law.ufl.edu/facultypub/588/> accessed 15 June 2016.

[53] Joseph Kattan, 'FRAND Wars and Section 2' (Summer 2013) Antitrust 30, 32.

[54] For example, Article 85 of General Principles of the Civil Law of the PRC stipulates that, 'A contract shall be an agreement whereby the parties establish, change or terminate their civil relationship.'

[55] The case was originally filed by Microsoft against Motorola in the Western District Court of Washington on 9 November 2010, claiming that Motorola had violated its reasonable and non-discriminatory licensing agreement to which Microsoft was a third-party beneficiary. While the US domestic contract litigation had been proceeding, Motorola sued Microsoft in Germany for patent infringement in July 2011. The German district court granted Motorola an injunction prohibiting Microsoft from selling allegedly infringing products in Germany based on German patent law. Then, Microsoft sought an anti-suit injunction against an injunction of patent infringement in Germany. See: *Microsoft Corp. v Motorola Inc.* (n 43).

[56] *Huawei Technologies Co. Ltd. v ZTE Corp., ZTE Deutschland GmbH* (n 18), para 54.

patent law issues that must be resolved by the Federal Circuit, which has sole jurisdiction over patent cases.[57]

It is worth mentioning that even if conflicts concerning FRAND royalty shouldn't be treated as a contract case, it doesn't mean that the case has no connection with civil law. On the contrary, principles of 'fair trade' and 'good faith' that should be respected in civil activities are also applicable to SEPs licence and other antimonopoly cases. For example, all the abuses explicitly prohibited by Article 17 of AML are qualified with 'unfair' or 'without justification'. In reality, anti-monopoly law is a type of fair trade law,[58] which is the reason why a lot of agencies in charge of anti-monopoly enforcement are called 'fair trade commission'.[59] It means that anti-monopoly law is closely connected with civil law, since both of them aim at advocating and promoting fairness and justice. Nevertheless, it is better to deal with a breach of FRAND commitment in accordance with anti-monopoly law, instead of contract law or civil law, since proprietors of SEPs making such FRAND commitment don't have any competitors in the relevant technical market after all. Because of the effect of competition elimination on relevant market, patent holdup should be treated the same as exploitative or other exclusive conducts of general monopolists, both in theory and practice. Under this situation, even if SEPs proprietors have made FRAND commitments to SSOs, anti-monopoly law still applies if it is not enough for such 'agreement' to protect public interests.[60]

4. Injunction Sought by SEPs Proprietors

In *Huawei v IDC*, the court observed that acting as proprietor of 3G SEPs, IDC abused it dominant market position through charging excessive royalties. IDC was also found to have asserted related patents against Huawei in Investigation Number 337-TA-800 before the USITC and seeking injunctions barring Huawei from using, making, importing, offering for sale, and/or selling various accused products in the U.S. with 3G and 4G capabilities in the United States District Court for the District of Delaware. The court concluded that the injunction sought by IDC constituted abuse of dominant market position, since it was only a measure taken by IDC to push Huawei to accept the unreasonable licence conditions, while Huawei was acting in good faith. It was against the FRAND commitment IDC had made and should be stipulated by anti-monopoly law.[61] Since there was no provision in

---

[57] Vehling, 'Motorola Urges 9th Circ. To Overturn Landmark RAND Ruling' (n 50).
[58] Such as the Fair Trade Act of Taiwan, PRC.
[59] Such as the Japan Fair Trade Commission and the Korea Fair Trade Commission.
[60] William H. Page, 'Judging Monopolistic Pricing: F/RAND and Antitrust Injury', 22 Tex Intell Prop LJ 181 (2014), 133, available at <http://scholarship.law.ufl.edu/facultypub/588/> accessed 15 June 2016.
[61] (2013) YUE GAO FA MIN SAN ZHONG ZI No 306, 50.

AML treating seeking unreasonable injunction as abuse of dominant market position until then, the judgment of *Huawei v IDC* was of great significance to the development of China's anti-monopoly law.

4.1 Limitation to the injunction sought by SEPs proprietors

In light of traditional civil law, a rights holder is entitled to request the court for cessation of infringement or compensation for damages, if relevant rights, including IPRs, are infringed. That's the reason why objects of various property rights have the characteristic of exclusivity.

However, due to the intangibility of IPRs, a request for cessation of infringement to IPRs is not like that of general rights, which can be limited to a particular scope. Proprietors would make use of it to grab improper economic interests, or eliminate or restrict competition so as to stifle innovation. This could mostly be found in industries closely related to technology standardization, such as wireless communication, semi-conductor, and software, since patent hold-up is more likely to happen in these areas. On the one hand, proprietors try their best to make FRAND commitment to SSOs in order to have their technologies included in the standard. On the other hand, however, they might refuse to license, or request excessive royalty, even through litigation on purpose, which is called 'patent troll'. Under this situation, if a licensee could only apply the patent after being licensed, then a proprietor might impose the licensee to accept unreasonable contractual terms through requesting the court to issue an injunction or compensation for damages so as to obtain excessive royalties. Right of injunction or compensation for damages shouldn't be regarded as a proprietor's absolute right. For potential licensees, compared with costly litigation, it is more cost-effective to accept excessive royalties. Gradually, right of injunction or compensation for damages would twist methods of negotiation for royalties, and raise royalty to unreasonable high level in the end. In the decision of Samsung Case, the Commission concluded that Samsung's seeking of injunctions against Apple was capable of: (i) excluding the rival manufacturer of UMTS-compliant mobile devices from the market; and (ii) inducing the licensee to accept disadvantageous licensing terms, compared to those which the licensee may have accepted in the absence of injunctions being sought.[62]

Due to the motivation of 'patent hold-up' behind tort or injunction litigation, which is against FRAND commitment, and the original intention of technical standardization as well, public interests, including those of consumers, would be harmed in the end. Some anti-monopoly agencies and courts have already recognized the necessity to limit right of proprietors to request for tort or injunction litigation. For example, *Policy Statement on Remedies for Standards-Essential Patents Subject to Voluntary F/*

---

[62] *Samsung-Enforcement of UMTS Standard Essential Patents* (n 12), para 62.

RAND Commitments published by U.S. Department of Justice ('US DOJ') and U.S. Patent and Trademark Office ('US PTO') jointly on 8 January 2013 pointed out that A patent owner's voluntary F/RAND commitments may also affect the appropriate choice of remedy for infringement of a valid and enforceable standards essential patent. In some circumstances, the remedy of an injunction or exclusion order may be inconsistent with the public interest.[63]

4.2 Pre-condition of application for and defence of injunction

The court emphasized efforts made by Huawei to negotiate sincerely with good faith with IDC (Huawei expected IDC to license its SEPs under FRAND commitment) when concluding that IDC abused its dominant market position through applying an injunction to an American court and the USITC. This showed that the court recognized the right enjoyed by the proprietors to apply for an injunction.

An SEP-holder is entitled to take reasonable steps to protect its interests by seeking injunctions against a potential licensee in, for example, the following scenarios: (1) a potential licensee is in financial distress and unable to pay its debts; (2) a potential licensee's assets are located in jurisdictions that do not provide for adequate means of enforcement of damages; or (3) a potential licensee is unwilling to enter into a licence agreement on FRAND terms, with the result that the SEP-holder will not receive FRAND compensation for the use of its SEPs, etc.[64] The right to claim for injunction or cessation of infringement is essential to the proprietor, without which the legitimate rights and interests of the proprietor might be damaged due to the speculating mentality of licensees or potential licensees. For example, a potential licensee in need of a license may in some circumstances refuse to pay the royalty or unreasonably delay negotiations to the same effect, which could be categorized as 'reverse patent hold-up'.[65] It is no doubt that 'reverse patent hold-up' makes it harder for the proprietor to get reasonable compensation for its innovation and invention, and could also stifle the initiative to participate in the technical standardization, which would bring serious long-term damages to industry development and social welfare. Then, under what circumstances could a proprietor's application for injunction or cessation of infringement be upheld by the court? Furthermore,

---

[63] The US Department of Justice and Patent and Trademark Office, *Policy Statement on Remedies for Standards-Essential Patents Subject to Voluntary F/RAND Commitments* (8 January 2013) 6–7 (hereafter The US DOJ and PTO, *Policy Statement on Remedies for Standards-Essential Patents Subject to Voluntary F/RAND Commitment*).

[64] *Samsung-Enforcement of UMTS Standard Essential Patents* (n 12), para 67.

[65] The United States, *INTELLECTUAL PROPERTY AND STANDARD SETTING* (17–18 December 2014) 13, available at <http://www.oecd.org/officialdocuments/publicdisplaydocumentpdf/?cote=DAF/COMP/WD(2014)116&docLanguage=En> accessed 15 June 2016.

what kind of 'good faith' should the potential patentees responding to injunction application have?

In the decision of Orange-Book-Standard (Az KZR 39/06) issued on 6 May 2009, the Federal Court of Justice of Germany (German: *Bundesgerichtshof,* BGH) listed two pre-conditions for defence against an injunction that might be put forward by potential licensees. Firstly, the potential licensee has made an unconditional and irrevocable offer to proprietor of SEPs in line with commercial customs and relevant laws and regulations, and agreed to stick to such an agreement. Secondly, the potential licensee has paid to or promised to pay to the SEPs proprietor through an escrow account for the royalty that should be paid.[66] The judgment triggered considerable controversy in Germany, especially the requirement for potential licensees to pre-pay royalty. The decision was welcomed by the majority of commentators. The court had managed to balance the parties' interests, safeguarding interests of the patentee by avoiding application of SEPs without due authorization/license.[67] The opponents contended that the court didn't take the key issue into consideration, which is SEP. The potential licensee might be hijacked by the proprietor if a court required it to make acceptable and unconditional offer to the proprietor or promise to pay the royalty, since right to use is essential for the potential licensee to enter the market.[68] Mr. Advocate General Wathelet contended that it was obviously excessive protection for the proprietor if the Orange-Book-Standard were applied to SEPs directly. Considering that the Orange-Book-Standard was a *de facto* industrial standard, the owner of the patent at issue had not given any commitment to grant licences on FRAND terms. It could be understood that an action for injunction sought by the proprietor would not be regarded as abusive as long as the royalty demanded is not clearly excessive.[69]

The judgment of the Orange-Book-Standard made by the Federal Court of Justice of Germany is not widely recognized worldwide. This is because the mainstream view of the competition authorities in both the EU and U.S. is that injunctive relief is not proper as long as the proprietor could be fully compensated in accordance with FRAND commitment.[70] For example, in the Samsung Case, the Commission

---

[66] *Orange Book Standard,* Case No KZR 39/06, Decision of the Federal Supreme Court (Bundesgerichtshof) [6 May 2009], para 29-b; IIC 3/2010, 369-75 (hereafter *Orange Book Standard*).

[67] Philipp Maume, 'Compulsory Licensing in Germany' 13, available at <http://ssrn.com/abstract=2504513> accessed 15 June 2016.

[68] Hanns Ullrich, 'Patents and Standard- A Comment on the German Federal Supreme Court Decision Orange Book Standard', IIC 3/2010, 337–51.

[69] Case C-170/13 *Huawei Technologies Co. Ltd. v ZTE Corp., ZTE Deutschland GmbH* [2014] ECLI:EU:C:2014:2391, Opinion of AG Wathelet, paras 48–51 (hereafter *Opinion of AG Wathelet of Huawei Technologies Co. Ltd. v ZTE Corp., ZTE Deutschland GmbH*).

[70] The US DOJ and PTO, *Policy Statement on Remedies for Standards-Essential Patents Subject to Voluntary F/RAND Commitment* (n 63) 1.

observed that, an SEP-holder is generally entitled to seek injunctions as part of the exercise of its IP rights, which in itself cannot constitute abuse of dominant position. The exercise of an exclusive right by its owner may, however, in exceptional circumstances and in the absence of any objective justification involve abusive conduct.[71] The Commission preliminarily concluded that the exceptional circumstances in this case are: (i) The UMTS standard has been widely implemented in the EEA. The industry is thus locked-in, with the risk that each holder of UMTS SEPs may hold up implementers either by refusing to license the necessary IP or by demanding excessive royalties; and (ii) The SEP-holder has agreed to license its UMTS SEPs on FRAND terms, and expects to obtain remuneration for its SEPs by means of licensing revenue rather than using these patents to exclude others.[72] In one word, if a technical standard has been widely used, such as becoming industrial standard, the injunction application is not fair as long as a proprietor has made a FRAND commitment and potential licensees haven't explicitly refused to accept such a commitment. Besides, the holding of IPR itself cannot constitute an objective justification for the seeking of an injunction by a SEP holder against a potential licensee that is not unwilling to enter into a licence agreement on FRAND terms.[73] Mr. Advocate General Wathelet also expressed a similar opinion in this regard. A mere willingness on the part of the infringer to negotiate in a highly vague and non-binding fashion cannot, in any circumstances, be sufficient to limit the SEP-holder's right to bring an action for injunction.[74]

A preliminary ruling recently issued by the European Court of Justice ('ECJ') made clear the pre-conditions for proprietors to apply for injunctions and potential licensees to file a defence accordingly.[75] ECJ and Mr. Advocate General Wathelet shared similar opinions, which was to compromise the Orange-Book-Standard and the Samsung Case.[76] The most obvious difference of ECJ's observation from Orange-Book-Standard is that, it is for the proprietor of the SEPs, (1) to alert the alleged infringer by designating the SEPs and specifying the way in which it has been infringed in writing; and (2) to present the infringer a specific written offer for a licence on FRAND terms, specifying in particular the amount of the royalty and

---

[71] *Samsung-Enforcement of UMTS Standard Essential Patents* (n 12), paras 55–56.
[72] Ibid, paras 56–61.
[73] Ibid, para 66.
[74] *Opinion of AG Wathelet of Huawei Technologies Co. Ltd. v ZTE Corp., ZTE Deutschland GmbH* (n 69), para 50.
[75] Request for a preliminary ruling under Article 267 TFEU from the Landgericht Düsseldorf (Germany), made by decision of 21 March 2013, which was received at ECJ on 5 April 2013. This request for a preliminary ruling concerns whether judgment made by the German court corresponded with EU laws. ECJ came out with the preliminary ruling on 16 July 2015. See *Huawei Technologies Co. Ltd. v ZTE Corp., ZTE Deutschland GmbH* (n 18).
[76] Ibid, para 55; *Opinion of AG Wathelet of Huawei Technologies Co. Ltd. v ZTE Corp., ZTE Deutschland GmbH* (n 69), para 52.

the way in which that royalty is to be calculated after the alleged infringer has expressed its willingness to conclude a licensing agreement on FRAND terms.[77] The limitation put forward by ECJ to proprietors of SEPs is reasonable since (1) it is not certain that the infringer of one of those SEPs will necessarily be aware that it is using an SEP both valid and essential to a standard in view of the large number of SEPs composing a standard;[78] and (2) where the SEP-holder has made commitment to SSOs to grant its patents to third parties on FRAND terms, it can be expected to restrict the licence terms accordingly. Furthermore, in the absence of a public standard licensing agreement, and where licensing agreements already concluded with other competitors are not made public, the proprietor of the SEP is better placed to check whether its offer to the alleged infringer complies with the condition of non-discrimination.[79]

Differing from the Samsung Decision made by the Commission, ECJ emphasized good faith the alleged infringer should have when negotiating with the proprietor for royalties before the injunction is applied. Firstly, it is for the alleged infringer to respond to the offer in accordance with recognized commercial practices and in good faith with no delaying tactics. Should the alleged infringer not accept the offer, it must submit to the SEP-holder in question, promptly and in writing, a specific counter-offer that corresponds to FRAND terms.[80] Furthermore, where both parties cannot agree on the counter-offer provided by the alleged infringer, they should request an independent third party to decide licence conditions in question without delay. It is for the alleged infringer to provide appropriate security, in accordance with recognized commercial practices in the field, for example by providing a bank guarantee or by placing the amounts necessary on deposit in this situation.[81] That is to say, the proprietor of a SEP who has committed to grant a licence to third parties on FRAND terms does not abuse its dominant position by seeking an injunction or requesting the alleged infringer to provide a guarantee for expected royalties, as long as the alleged infringer continues to use the patent in question, but does not diligently respond to the proprietor's offer in accordance with recognized commercial practices in good faith, such as the delaying tactics.[82]

Huge difference exists between opinion of the ECJ and *Policy Statement on Remedies for Standards-Essential Patents Subject to Voluntary F/RAND Commitments* jointly

---

[77] Ibid, paras 61–63.
[78] Ibid, para 62; *Opinion of AG Wathelet of Huawei Technologies Co. Ltd. v ZTE Corp., ZTE Deutschland GmbH* (n 69), para 81.
[79] Ibid, para 64; *Opinion of AG Wathelet of Huawei Technologies Co. Ltd. v ZTE Corp., ZTE Deutschland GmbH* (n 69), para 86.
[80] Ibid, para 65.
[81] Ibid, paras 66–68; *Opinion of AG Wathelet of Huawei Technologies Co. Ltd. v ZTE Corp., ZTE Deutschland GmbH* (n 69), paras 88–89.
[82] Ibid, para 77.

issued by US DOJ and US PTO in January 2013. The latter focuses more on competition twist and harm to public interests that might be brought by injunction,[83] while the former (ECJ) emphasizes the importance of striking a balance between IPRs protection and free competition.[84] FRAND commitment doesn't mean that the proprietor has given up the right to seek an injunction.[85] The authors agree with the opinion of the ECJ. Beside 'patent hold-up', there is also 'reserve patent hold-up', where the alleged infringer tries every effort to delay the negotiation with SEP-holder for royalties. 'Reverse patent hold-up' could also twist the competition and harm public interests, just like the effect of an injunction sought by the proprietor might have on the market. Both are not tolerated by anti-monopoly agencies and courts of course.

5. Several Inspirations and Thoughts

Huawei v IDC is the first anti-monopoly litigation concerning SEP in China. The Chinese courts concluded that IDC abused its dominant market position through charging excessive royalties to Huawei on the basis of AML, FRAND commitment IDC has made to SSOs, and similar cases closed by EU or U.S. anti-monopoly agencies and courts as well. The logic of analysis in this case is reasonable, and the method is also scientific, reflecting fairness and justice which should be maintained by law. The judgments of case *Huawei v IDC* have also triggered several inspirations and thoughts.

5.1 Application of AML to SEPs enforcement

Though SSOs generally request SEPs-holders to make FRAND commitment, practice shows that conflict between the proprietor's 'patent hold-up' and openness of the standard is inevitable. For example, SEPs-holders may refer to injunction or tort litigation in the name of IPRs protection, while potential licensees or alleged infringers would defend themselves on the basis of anti-monopoly. *Huawei v IDC* appears to be an IP case judged in accordance with anti-monopoly law. The court analyzed the nature and specialty of SEPs in the first place, recognized the dominant position held by IDC in the SEPs licensing market, and concluded that IDC had abused its dominance through charging excessive royalties and seeking injunction in America. It shows that competition law prevails when there is conflict between it and IP law, especially when it concerns SEPs. So SEPs-holders should foresee the potential investigation initiated by anti-monopoly agencies or anti-monopoly litigation brought by licensees when exercising patents improperly.

---

[83] The US DOJ and PTO, *Policy Statement on Remedies for Standards-Essential Patents Subject to Voluntary F/RAND Commitment* (n 63) 6–7.

[84] *Opinion of AG Wathelet of Huawei Technologies Co. Ltd. v ZTE Corp., ZTE Deutschland GmbH* (n 69), para 59.

[85] Ibid, para 61.

In some foreign jurisdictions, FRAND commitment is recognized as an agreement between the licensor/proprietor and the licensee: conflicts arising accordingly could be resolved in accordance with contract law. In reality, a proprietor is obliged to license its patent on fair and non-discriminatory conditions in accordance with anti-monopoly law, no matter whether it has made FRAND commitment or not, considering the competition in relevant technology market excluded by technical standardization. Of course, not all the cases related to SEPs should be decided as anti-monopoly ones, since patent law applies when a SEPs holder seeks for reliefs when there is 'reverse patent hold-up'. For example, the potential licensees delay the negotiation without good reasons or are reluctant to pay royalties. Put it in another way, application of law depends on nature and specific circumstances of a case, instead of agency in charge of the case.

5.2 Problem of Article 55 of the AML

IP law and competition law complement each other, since both of them aim to encourage competition and innovation, increase efficiency, and help broaden public interests. However, *Huawei v IDC* indicates that conflict still exists. In order to make clear the relationship mentioned above, Article 55 of AML stipulates that, 'This Law is not applicable to undertakings who exercise their IPRs in accordance with the laws and administrative regulations on IPRs; however, this Law shall be applicable to the undertakings who eliminate or restrict market competition by abusing their IPRs.' The problem here is, does the 'abuse' have to be out of scope of IPRs protection? From *Huawei v IDC*, we could find that enforcement of IPRs in accordance with IP laws cannot exempt the proprietor from application of anti-monopoly law. For example, the excessive royalty requested by IDC to Huawei and injunction sought by IDC in an American court when Huawei hadn't paid the royalty were not against patent law,[86] but recognized as abuse of dominant market position, according to anti-monopoly law. There is an application problem as regards sub-paragraph 1 of Article 55 of AML.

Before the 7th amendment in 2005, there was similar problem in *German Act against Restraints of Competition* (*'German Competition Act'*). Articles 17 and 18 of *German Competition Act* prohibit conducts which are out of the protection scope of IPRs law, while those within the scope could be exempted. However, the two articles were deleted by the 7th amendment, and there was no provision defining IPRs, either. Professor Josef Drexl explained it in a competition conference in Beijing that though people keep requesting competition agencies and courts to make clear the relationship between IPRs law and competition law, there is almost no special provisions concerning IPRs within competition law. This is not in compliance with

---

[86] Comparing to Article 12 of the Patent Law of the PRC, 'Any organization or individual that intends to exploit the patent of another person shall conclude a license contract with the patentee and pay the royalties.'

the importance and complexity of the problem. Even if there were such an article, what it emphasizes would be the characteristics of both set of laws, whereas the frontier still needs to be made clear in practice in the future.[87] This problem is initiated again by *Huawei v IDC*. So there is necessity for IPRs exemption regulated in Article 55 of AML to be discussed further by the Chinese legal society.

5.3 Issues to be resolved after *Huawei v IDC*

The highlight in *Huawei v IDC* is that, starting from FRAND commitment made by IDC, the court stressed the obligation IDC should bear when licensing its SEPs on FRAND conditions, and calculated the FRAND royalty rate IDC should have requested to Huawei through comparing with license conditions IDC offered to Apple. The analysis and final decision are innovative and reasonable. However, how will the court decide the royalty IDC should request for its SEPs if IDC hasn't licensed its SEPs to Apple or Samsung? Even if the court took lots of elements into consideration, such as profits that could be obtained from exercise of the patents or similar patents, percentage of the profits mentioned above in the total profits of products sold by the licensee, or the profits in sales revenue, the judge admitted the idealization of this method to calculate due FRAND royalty. Since it is very hard to be put into practice,[88] will an organization concerning technical standard, such as SSO, make more efforts in this regard, considering that it is not easy for both anti-monopoly agencies and courts to determine an accurate royalty of a SEP?[89]

Another issue is that potential licensee or the alleged infringer should also act in good faith, even if the SEP-holder is restricted when seeking for injunction or cessation of infringement, according to practice both home and abroad. Whereas various courts and anti-monopoly agencies define 'good faith' differently, such as the high requirements put forward by German Orange-Book-Standard,[90] and 'the potential licensee not unwilling to enter into a license agreement on FRAND terms' requested by the Commission to the alleged infringer in the Samsung decision,[91] etc. Then, what is 'willing to enter into a license agreement on FRAND terms'? Could oral acceptance of FRAND terms be categorized as 'good faith'? What other efforts should a potential licensee make if oral acceptance is not enough? Considering that increasing SEPs conflicts in high technology industry attract public attention nowadays, this issue is in urgent need of being resolved in practice.

---

[87] Josef Drexl, 'Abuse of Dominant Market Position and IPRs Law' in Xiaoye Wang (ed.), *Hot Issues on Anti-Monopoly Legislation* (Social Sciences Academic Press (China) 2007) 77.

[88] Zhu and Chen, 'Justiciability of Conflicts Concerning SEPs Royalty Rate' (n 25) 9.

[89] Mark A. Lemley and Carl Shapiro, 'A Simple Approach to Setting Reasonable Royalties for Standard-Essential Patents', Berkeley Technology Law Journal (Volume 28, Issue 2 Fall).

[90] *Orange Book Standard* (n 66).

[91] *Samsung-Enforcement of UMTS Standard Essential Patents* (n 12), para 66.

8

INTELLECTUAL PROPERTY RIGHTS AND CHINA'S COMPETITION LAW ENFORCEMENT

Implications for Foreign Rights Holders

*Mark Williams**

1. Introduction

In the decade since the enactment of the *Anti-Monopoly Law* (AML),[1] China[2] has astonished commentators by becoming one of the three major competition law jurisdictions. In merger control, China is now clearly one of the global triumvirate along with the US and EU, and in other aspects of competition law enforcement China's reach is increasingly being felt by both domestic entities and by major multinational corporations (MNCs).[3] Of increasing concern is China's application of its AML to the technology sector which is heavily dependent on the ownership and assertion of intellectual property rights (IPRs). China is cognizant of the fact that, comparatively, Chinese companies are IPR-late and to remedy this perceived weakness, seeks to adopt both the carrot and the stick approach to MNCs which have cutting edge technology protected by IPRs. China will offer the greater domestic market access that is mandated by the World Trade Organization (WTO) accession agreement if MNCs will enter joint ventures with domestic entities or will license domestic firms on favourable terms. The 'stick' of this two-pronged

---

* Professor of Law, Melbourne Law School, University of Melbourne.
[1] An official English version of the *Anti-Monopoly Law* (People's Republic of China) National People's Congress, 30 August 2007 is available at http://www.china.org.cn/government/laws/2009-02/10/content_17254169.htm.
[2] In this chapter, China refers to the mainland of the People's Republic of China and not to Hong Kong and Macau Special Administrative Regions or to Chinese Taipei which have their own separate legal systems.
[3] Thomas Horton, 'Antitrust or Industrial Protectionism? Emerging International Issues in China's Anti-Monopoly Law Enforcement Efforts' (2016) 14 *Santa Clara Journal of International Law* 109.

strategy is the implicit threat to allow the antitrust agencies to investigate, fine, and impose corrective measures on infringing MNCs by utilizing the anti-competitive abuse of IPRs provisions contained in the AML.[4]

This chapter seeks to consider whether China's current competition law provisions and its enforcement practices to date are in fact an adjunct to an industrial policy of coerced technology transfer or not. To achieve this, China's stated industrial strategy as envisaged in the China 2025 policy will be considered, and the provisions of the AML and subordinate legislation discussed. The use to which the specific abuse-of-IPR provisions have been put to date, as well as the use of other provisions in the AML, particularly the abuse-of-dominance provision to achieve similar aims, will be analysed. Consideration is also given to China's procedural methods in competition cases involving IPRs. The chapter concludes with an assessment of the likely future treatment of IPR-rich MNCs under China's competition regime.

2. China's Industrial Strategy

In May 2015, the Chinese government launched a new industrial strategy entitled *China Manufacturing 2025* (CM2025). This plan envisaged ambitious growth in ten developing industrial sectors. They are:

- Next generation IT
- High-end numerical control machinery and robotics
- Aerospace and aviation equipment
- Maritime engineering equipment and hi-tech vessel manufacturing
- Advanced rail equipment
- Energy saving vehicles and new energy vehicles
- Electrical equipment
- Agricultural machinery and equipment
- New materials
- Biopharmaceuticals and hi-tech medical devices.

In order to facilitate the development of these industries, the Chinese government will provide a raft of support measures to domestic enterprises such as direct research and development grants. Various other measures offered include direct product subsidies to stimulate domestic demand for the targeted products, mandated buy-local public procurement policies, the acquisition of foreign enterprises that hold advanced technology patents by Chinese state or private enterprises (often financially supported by state investment funds), the encouragement of the merger of competing

---

[4] Ibid.

state-owned enterprises (SOEs) to create national champions, and the application of pressure through the grant of extended market access to foreign enterprises on condition of technology sharing, licensing, or transfer to Chinese enterprises.

However, this policy is entirely at odds with the Decision of the Third Plenum of the 18th Congress of the Communist Party of China (CPC) on 12 November 2013. The Communiqué stated that the Plenum noted:

- it was necessary to comprehensively deepen reform
- we [the CPC] must closely revolve around the decisive function that the market has in allocating resources. Deepen economic structural reform, accelerate the perfection of modern market systems, macroeconomic regulation systems and open economic systems, accelerate the transformation of economic development methods, accelerate the establishment of an innovative country, and promote even greater economic efficiency
- economic structural reform is the focus point for comprehensively deepening reform, the core issue is handling the relationship between government and the market well, to ensure that the market has a decisive function in resource allocation and to give fuller rein to the function of government
- establishing **unified, open, competitive and ordered market systems** are the basis for **the market's decisive function in resource allocation.** We must accelerate the formation of a modern market system in which **enterprises do business autonomously**, with fair competition, free consumer choice, autonomous consumption, free flow of products and factors, and equal exchange, strive to eliminate market barriers, raise the efficiency and fairness of resource allocation. We must establish fair, open and transparent market rules, perfect mechanisms in which processes are mainly decided by the market, establish a uniform construction and land use market across town and country, perfect financial market systems and deepen science and technology structure reform
- the publicly owned economy and the non-publicly owned economy are both important component parts of the Socialist market economy, and are an important basis for our country's economic and social development. We must unwaveringly consolidate and develop the publicly owned economy, persist in the **dominant role of the public ownership system, give rein to the leading role of the state-owned economy, incessantly strengthen the vitality, control strength and influence of the state-owned economy.** We must unwaveringly encourage, support and guide the non-publicly owned economy to develop, and encourage the economic vitality and creativity of the non-publicly owned economy.[5]

---

[5] Chinese Communist Party, Communiqué of the 3rd Plenum of the 18th Party Congress (12 November 2013). <https://chinacopyrightandmedia.wordpress.com/2013/11/12/communique-of-the-3rd-plenum-of-the-18th-party-congress/> accessed 2 May 2017 (emphasis added).

Contrary to these sentiments, the CM2025 policy, adopted some two years later, proceeded to set out many highly proscriptive goals that should be achieved through state intervention and target-setting, rather than relying on market forces as advocated in the Plenum decision. CM2025 seeks to promote 'indigenous innovation' by setting market share goals for domestically and foreign-produced goods, whether the products concerned are made in China by a foreign-owned enterprise or imported after being manufactured overseas. The clear import of the policy is to favour domestically owned enterprises over foreign-owned ones to bolster Chinese 'self-sufficiency' in these product markets. This policy would seem to be contrary to allowing market forces and competition to play the decisive role in resource allocation, and rather falls back on state support and indirect market regulation via the discriminatory promotion of national champions to reduce China's perceived dependence on foreign innovation supported by IPRs.

CM2025 is the first of three proposed planning periods ending in 2049, the centenary of the founding of the People's Republic and the accession to power of the CPC. The aim is to establish China as a leading global manufacturing power, and requires China's industrial capacity to be overhauled and radically modernized. China's weakness lies in having few internationally competitive products, and companies which, tough very large as a result of significant market shares in the Chinese domestic market, are often internationally insignificant due to weak product ranges with few innovative features. Inevitably, there are exceptions, such as in the Chinese mobile phone sector.[6] But, even in the sectors where China's manufacturers are able to compete internationally, they are still dependent upon foreign capital goods and underlying patented technologies. CM2025 seeks to end such reliance on foreign owned technologies and IPRs through direct state intervention. Naturally, any state has the right to encourage research and development (R&D) through direct grants to research centres in universities or public and private institutions, but China goes much further. CM2025 mandates a comprehensive industrial policy plan which is reminiscent of Soviet state planning, rather than providing companies with open markets where competition between entities spurs innovation, provides expanded consumer choice, and where private profit is the motivating factor for taking the inherent risks of substantial investment in R&D.

Aside from the (doubtful) wisdom of this course of action and the perennially contradictory nature of CPC rhetoric and subsequent government activities, various other objections could be raised to the underlying philosophy of CM2025,

---

[6] David Shambaugh, 'The Illusion of Chinese Power' (Op-Ed, Brookings Institution, 25 June 2014), available at <https://www.brookings.edu/opinions/the-illusion-of-chinese-power/> accessed 2 May 2017.

including trade issues arising from China's WTO commitments.[7] The role of China's antitrust policy as an adjunct to CM2025 is also of concern. Whilst the CPC Plenum accepted that market forces and competition should be the primary allocator of resources, CM2025 does not appear to be congruent with that strategy. To the contrary, it provides the impetus for antitrust policies and enforcement activity to be used as a tool to help achieve China's industrial policy targets and the proscriptive (and arbitrary) market share targets for 'indigenous' Chinese technology. Waving through potentially anti-competitive domestic mergers, ignoring abuses of dominance by favoured domestic national champions, failing to act in response to collusive anti-competitive activity by domestic hi-tech enterprises, and the selective use against foreign rights owners of the AML provision that prohibits 'abuse of IPRs'[8] are all potential methods of achieving China's industrial policy aims as enunciated in CM2025.

The remainder of this chapter considers whether the AML and subsidiary legislation as well as the enforcement activity to date by China's antitrust agencies provides any evidence that supports these suspicions, and whether in the future it is likely that China will threaten or be tempted to use the AML provisions in this way to support its prized goal of technological autonomy.

3. The AML and Intellectual Property Rights

Article 1 of the AML states:

> This Law is enacted for the purpose of preventing and restraining monopolistic conduct, protecting fair market competition, enhancing economic efficiency, safeguarding the interests of consumers and interests of consumers and the interests of the society as a whole, and, promoting the healthy development of the socialist market economy.

Whilst preventing and restraining monopolistic conduct—so long as it constitutes abusive conduct—is an orthodox competition law goal, promoting the 'healthy development of the socialist market economy' (SME) is not. Here we can discern the basis upon which the AML could be used to achieve that overriding aim of the CPC: the development of China's SME in which the state retains decisive ownership and control of 'backbone' sectors, but where the government also guides the

---

[7] Shanghai Chapter of the European Union Chamber of Commerce, 'China Manufacturing 2025: Putting Industrial Policy Ahead of Market Forces' (7 March 2017).
[8] Article 55 of the AML provides:

> This law is not applicable to undertakings who exercise their intellectual property rights in accordance with the laws and administrative regulations on intellectual property rights; however, this Law shall be applicable to the undertakings who eliminate or restrict market competition by abusing their intellectual property rights.

development of the economy more generally. As such, aligning the use of the AML with CM2025—which clearly aims to guide and strengthen the SME—is entirely legitimate from a Chinese perspective.

Article 7 of the AML appears to support this interpretation. It provides:

> With respect to the industries controlled by the state-owned economy and concerning the lifeline of national economy and national security or the industries implementing exclusive operation and sales according to law, the state protects the lawful business operations conducted by the business operators therein. The state also lawfully regulates and controls their business operations and the prices of their commodities and services so as to safeguard the interests of consumers **and promote technical progresses.**

CM2025 explicitly seeks to promote the technical progress of Chinese enterprises, particularly state-owned enterprises (SOEs), to which much of the R&D funding, special access to finance, access to public procurement contracts, and other promotional policies are directed. Thus, again this provision of the AML supports the contention that the AML could be used as a basis to justify discriminatory enforcement practices which support the technical development of the SOE sector.

Turning to the specific prohibitions of the AML, article 17 is the most relevant to this discussion. Specially, the article provides:

> A business operator with a dominant market position shall not abuse its dominant market position to conduct the following acts:
> (1) selling commodities at unfairly high prices or buying commodities at unfairly low prices;
> (2) selling products at prices below cost without any justifiable cause;
> (3) refusing to trade with a trading party without any justifiable cause;
> (4) requiring a trading party to trade exclusively with itself or trade exclusively with a designated business operator(s) without any justifiable cause;
> (5) tying products or imposing unreasonable trading conditions at the time of trading without any justifiable cause;
> (6) applying dissimilar prices or other transaction terms to counterparties with equal standing;
> (7) other conduct determined as abuse of a dominant position by the Anti-Monopoly Authority under the State Council.

The article is substantially based on EU jurisprudence[9] and is thus superficially unsurprising, save for the 'catch-all' provision in article 17(7) which provides the enforcement agencies with great flexibility to determine whether any particular conduct of a dominant operator constitutes an abuse.

---

[9] Article 102 of the Consolidated Version of the Treaty on the Functioning of the European Union OJ C 326 contains a comparable provision prohibiting abuse of a dominant position by undertakings.

Prudently interpreted and without an industrial policy goal to achieve, the dominance provisions are relatively unexceptional, but when considered with such an objective in mind, it is easy to appreciate how such a provision could be used as a means to such end.

This is particularly so when coupled with the deeming provisions of article 19 that state that dominance shall be established as a rebuttable presumption if:

(1) the relevant market share of a business operator accounts for 1/2 or above in the relevant market;
(2) the joint relevant market share of two business operators accounts for 2/3 or above; or
(3) the joint relevant market share of three business operators accounts for 3/4 or above.

Thus the inherently flexible and open nature of the principal prohibition is coupled with deemed dominance, which may be particularly helpful in situations where the accused abuser has unique patented technology, so assisting a finding of dominance. The wide range and subjective nature of the categories of abuse, together with the ability of the authorities to unilaterally classify any particular conduct as an abuse, clearly opens the door to the AML serving as a useful adjunct to CM2025 in cases where foreign rights holders might refuse to licence IPRs, or where the price sought is deemed to be 'unfairly high'.

A further concern that antitrust law could be used as a lever to extract unjust benefits for Chinese enterprises is that the AML also contains a specific provision regarding the abuse of IPRs. Article 55 provides:

> This Law does not govern the conduct of business operators to exercise their intellectual property rights under laws and relevant administrative regulations on intellectual property rights; **however, business operators' conduct to eliminate or restrict market competition by abusing their intellectual property rights shall be governed by this Law** [emphasis added].

Again, superficially, this provision should not be of concern to foreign IPR holders. But an issue does arise when one considers the fact that it is unclear what the antitrust agencies would consider to be an 'abuse of IPRs'; the law is entirely silent as to what might constitute such an abuse. Presumably, reference would be made to the listed examples of abuse set out in article 17, as the market definition exercise to be conducted in such a case would consider the exclusivity granted to rights holders in many cases an indicia of dominance in the narrowly defined market for the patented product or invention. In cases concerning copyright and trademarks, the allegation would likely be more difficult to substantiate than in, for example, the licensing of standard essential patents in a hi-tech product market, where dominance might be easily inferred.

Turning now to subsidiary legislation, enforcement of the AML and the power to promulgate subsidiary legislation is granted to three executive agencies at ministry level, overseen by a State Council level Anti-Monopoly Commission (AMC).

The State Administration for Industry and Commerce (SAIC) and the National Development and Reform Commission (NDRC) share responsibility for enforcing the AML provisions on abuse of dominance. The distinction between their respective areas of competence is opaque; officially SAIC deals with 'non-price' infringements of the AML prohibition on monopolistic agreements and monopoly conduct undertaken through abuse of dominance, and NDRC is responsible for infringements that include anti-competitive pricing effects. In reality, this distinction is impossible to justify or to define and so both entities have de facto jurisdiction over most AML infringement cases. The third agency, Ministry of Commerce (MOFCOM), is responsible for merger assessment.

On 7 April 2015, the SAIC issued the *Provisions on the Prohibition of the Abuse of Intellectual Property Rights to Eliminate or Restrict Competition* (Provisions).[10] These rules had a long gestation period of over five years and nine drafts, and after considerable lobbying by (amongst others) the US government, other competition agencies, private law firms, and academic commentators, the resultant rules are largely compliant with international norms. However, they contain a number of provisions that could become contentious if implemented expansively.

Of particular importance is the concession in the Provisions that conduct will be found to violate the AML only when it eliminates or restricts competition; this had not been clear in earlier drafts. Further, the Provisions also make clear that in any assessment of dominance, ownership of an IPR is not the critical factor; there is no presumption of dominance, which must instead be determined following an assessment of all relevant factors in the product market. However, other elements contained in the Provisions may be greater cause for concern. In particular, article 7 adopts the 'essential facilities' doctrine of IPRs and prohibits a refusal to license on reasonable terms such an essential facility that would eliminate or restrict competition without a legitimate reason. Whether an IPR was an essential facility would be determined by a range of factors including:

(1) whether the IPR can be 'reasonably substituted' in the relevant market and is 'necessary' for other business operators to compete in the relevant market;
(2) whether the refusal to license will have a 'negative impact on competition or innovation in the relevant market to the detriment of consumer welfare or public interest'; and
(3) whether licensing such an IPR will cause 'unreasonable harm' to business operators.

Another aspect of possible concern is a provision that deals with essential patents. Article 13(1) provides that there will be AML liability for failure to disclose essential

---

[10] *Provisions on the Prohibition of the Abuse of Intellectual Property Rights to Exclude or Restrict Competition* (People's Republic of China) State Administration for Industry and Commerce, 7 April 2015.

patents, without requiring that the patent holder be an active voting participant in a Standard Setting Organization (SSO) with a written disclosure policy. Further, the article prohibits a dominant firm from, without 'legitimate reasons', deliberately failing to disclose essential patents while participating in a standard-setting process, and then asserting such patents against implementers after the patent has been adopted by the standard. However, liability under article 13(1) is explicitly limited to circumstances when such conduct results in the elimination or restriction of competition.

The fundamental problem with these provisions is that they are not limited to Standard Essential Patent (SEP) holders that are active voting participants in an SSO with an adopted published written disclosure policy; the provision is of general application. Furthermore, the article does not require that but for the SEP holder's failure to disclose a different technology would have been incorporated into the standard.

Thus, under article 13(1) there appears to be a general duty of full disclosure. This might discourage patent holders from participation in SSOs. This restriction on the freedom of action of IPR holders does not conform to generally accepted international norms, but from a Chinese perspective the advantages are clear, especially where foreign entities hold significantly more IPRs in a particular market, as the restriction would advantage potential Chinese licensees.

Under article 13(2), AML liability can be established for failure to license patents found to be essential on fair, reasonable and non-discriminatory (FRAND) terms, even in the absence of a voluntary commitment to do so. A dominant firm whose patent has become essential to a standard cannot 'without reasons' engage in conduct that 'eliminates or restricts competition' in violation of the FRAND principle.

Article 13(2) lists the following examples conducted by an IPR holder where licensing should be on FRAND terms:

• Refusal to license
• Tying
• Attaching other 'unreasonable trading conditions'.

Such a mandatory FRAND commitment on all essential patents could eliminate the right to exclusivity, thereby harming incentives to innovate. Again, from the Chinese perspective where most relevant patent holders are foreign, such concerns are potentially of secondary importance to achieving the goals set out in CM2025.

These eagerly anticipated regulations have not been used in any reported cases to date, and so the anxiety that has afflicted IPR-rich MNCs does not appear to have been justified. Of course, this does not mean that they will not be used aggressively in the future.

Another reason for the hiatus in the implementation of these rules may be that they are soon to be superseded by a new set promulgated by the AMC. In June 2015, the AMC commissioned the NDRC to create a new comprehensive set of implementing rules that would apply to all relevant acts of 'abuse of IPRs'; and SAIC to produce rules that would only apply to SAIC cases involving 'non-price' violations. A draft of the comprehensive rules was published on 31 December 2015 by the NDRC, though they did not make any mention of how the 'abuse of IPR' rules would apply to merger transactions. A further period of official silence began, broken on 23 March 2017 when MOFCOM issued a second draft of the proposed comprehensive rules.[11] No explanation was given as to why the mandate to create the unified IPR abuse rules had passed from NDRC to MOFCOM, however the 15 month void is likely to have occurred because of endemic bureaucratic infighting between the three AML enforcement agencies. The structure of AML enforcement is inherently flawed, with three operational agencies and the superficially powerful but practically weak AMC, the titular coordinating body.

It appears that this internal rivalry caused the relevant agencies to compete by producing multiple conflicting internal draft rules before a consolidated version was made public. As a knowledgeable commentator has opined:

> Both the NDRC and the SAIC prepared multiple drafts throughout 2015 and 2016, some of which were already subject to public consultation, and held several meetings with local regulators, domestic and multinational companies and chambers of commerce, law firms, and scholars. MOFCOM and SIPO also worked on drafts but these were not made public. It is understood that final submissions were made to the AMC by the four agencies in late 2016.[12]

The second draft guidelines generally follow the NDRC's first draft, but importantly adopt the SAIC's inclusion of the essential facilities doctrine which NDRC had omitted from its proposals. Safe harbour provisions were also included. A major addition was the inclusion of text relating to the application of the new rules in merger cases, including a rule extending the definition of a change of control or acquisition of decisive influence of an undertaking to include the transfer or exclusive licensing of IPRs, so requiring merger notification. Another rule provides specifically for behavioural remedies in such cases, a departure from established international norms, but common in many Chinese conditional merger clearance decisions.

As for other provisions in the second draft guidance, it appears to be a work of compromise, given the CPC endorsement of encouraging innovation on the one

---

[11] Anti-Monopoly Guidelines on the Abuse of Intellectual Property Rights (Draft for Comments) (People's Republic of China) MOFCOM, 23 March 2017.
[12] Allen & Overy, 'China's Draft IPR Guidelines Reach Final Consultation Stages' (4 April 2017), available at <https://www.jdsupra.com/legalnews/china-s-draft-ipr-guidelines-reach-62488/> accessed 2 May 2017.

hand, but seeking to ensure that Chinese IPR licensees are favourably treated on the other. Evidence of this uneasy compromise can be seen by:

- the acceptance that the mere existence of an IPR does not automatically confer dominance
- agreement that a 'rule of reason' analysis is required in determining anti-competitive effect in the alleged abuse under investigation
- the acceptance of safe harbour provisions.

These provisions are favourable to IPR holders including foreign owners. However, the aim to ensure that Chinese licensees are treated 'fairly' (or advantaged) can be seen in several other provisions, namely:

- the lack of clear acknowledgment that IPRs are inherently procompetitive
- the absence of text concerning the burden and standard of proof in establishing efficiency defences, so leaving substantial doubt as to how accused dominant undertakings may avail themselves of this 'defence'
- the fact that dominant IPR holders are prohibited justifying a refusal to license prospective licensees that are willing and able to pay reasonable fees
- the provision that existence of expired or invalid patents in a portfolio licence may be challenged as an abuse of excessive pricing.

When these guidelines have been finalized, potentially by the end of 2018, through a consensus between the anti-monopoly enforcement agencies and the State Intellectual Property Office (SIPO), they are likely to be implemented in all antitrust investigations. Only once several cases have been adjudicated will it be possible to ascertain the approach of AML enforcement regarding 'abuses' of IPRs and whether the fears of foreign IPR holders have been justified.

4. Selected IPR Cases Decided under China's AML

To consider whether foreign rights holders are justified in fearing that the AML will be used as an exploitative tool to force them to license or behave in ways not required by other competition law systems it will be instructive to consider two recent, high profile decisions by the Chinese authorities.

The *Huawei v InterDigital* case[13] was the first private litigation case in China where royalty rates were set by a court in a SEP royalty dispute. Huawei is the

---

[13] Michael Han and Li Kexin, '*Huawei v. InterDigital*: China at the Crossroads of Antitrust and Intellectual Property, Competition and Innovation' (Competition Policy International, 28 November 2013), available at <https://www.competitionpolicyinternational.com/huawei-v-interdigital-china-at-the-crossroads-of-antitrust-and-intellectual-property-competition-and-innovation/> accessed 2 May 2017, Paul Kossoff and Xiuting Yuan, 'Developments in Chinese Anti-Monopoly

largest manufacturer and supplier of electronic communication equipment in China and InterDigital is effectively a patent licensing entity and does not engage in manufacturing. In September 2009, InterDigital asserted to the European Telecommunications Standards Institute (ETSI) that it owned many essential patents and patent applications for 2G, 3G, and 4G wireless communication technologies, and had several outstanding patent claims filled in the US and in China. InterDigital, in its application to join ETSI, promised to undertake licensing of any of its patented technologies adopted in the standard setting process to designated SEPs on FRAND terms to other members of the ETSI, which included Huawei. Royalty negotiations had already begun on licensing terms in November 2008, but broke down as InterDigital was only prepared to accept a royalty rate from Huawei that was significantly higher than those it had offered to Samsung and Apple. InterDigital sought a US import ban on Huawei products and sought damages in an American court for patent infringement, on the basis that the use of its technology by Huawei was unlawful.

In December 2011, Huawei filed a private action against InterDigital alleging that, by engaging in certain patent practices, InterDigital had:

(1) abused its dominant market position, contrary to the AML, and
(2) as an owner of several SEPs for 2G, 3G, and 4G telecommunications technologies, had failed to negotiate licences on FRAND terms.

In February 2013, a Chinese trial court found in Huawei's favour and awarded damages of RMB ¥20 million (approximately USD $3.2 million) and ordered that InterDigital cease its unlawful behaviour. This decision was subsequently upheld on appeal in October 2013.

The affirmed lower court judgment held that:

(1) in respect to the abuse of dominance claim, InterDigital had abused its dominant position and thereby violated the AML by:
   (i) tying its SEPs with non-SEPs during licensing; and by
   (ii) seeking injunctive relief against Huawei before the US courts and seeking relief from the US International Trade Commission, while still in negotiations with Huawei, to require Huawei to accept unreasonable licensing terms including excessive royalties.
(2) In respect of the FRAND claim, InterDigital had failed to comply with the FRAND commitments in relation to its SEPs by:

Law: Implications of *Huawei v InterDigital* on Anti-Monopoly Litigation in Mainland China' (2015) 7 *European Intellectual Property Review* 438.

(i) commencing injunction proceedings and requiring Huawei to pay much higher royalties than those paid by Apple and Samsung; and

(ii) requiring that Huawei cross-license to InterDigital all its own patents obtained globally on a royalty-free basis.

The court also determined that the FRAND royalty rate for the InterDigital SEPs concerned should not exceed 0.019 per cent of the actual sales price of each product manufactured by Huawei.

This case highlights that the Chinese courts as well as the anti-monopoly agencies are prepared to both analyse the complex intersection of patent litigation and competition law and take a robust position to assist plaintiffs in suitable cases. The fact that InterDigital is a patent assertion entity (more pejoratively a patent troll) with no manufacturing or R&D capacity may also have influenced the decision in favour of Huawei, a very important innovator in the telecommunications sector both in China and globally. InterDigital's status as a patent assertion entity may have been particularly significant in respect of setting a low royalty rate, thereby both lowering a technological barrier, asserting that foreign entities are subject to the AML, and indirectly assisting China's pursuit of upgrading 'indigenous' technology in line with the goals set out in CM2025.

This conclusion is fortified by the comments in the press of one of the judges who decided the case. Juustice Qiu Yongqing, who presided over the case at the appellate level, is reported to have said that Huawei 'used antitrust law as a weapon to counter-attack' monopoly conduct by foreign technology MNCs, and that other Chinese firms should take note of the success Huawei had achieved via litigation in the Chinese courts. The judge went on to suggest that other Chinese companies should utilize antitrust litigation to overcome technology barriers and thereby better develop themselves.[14] This type of extra-curial encouragement to AML litigation to lower perceived entry barriers in hi-tech markets will understandably reinforce the anxieties of foreign MNCs.

Interestingly, InterDigital apparently settled a parallel investigation by NDRC into its industry-wide licensing practices by agreeing to adopt a similar pricing formula and pattern of conduct as mandated by the Huawei judgment. Thus, the significance of the judgment is not limited to benefiting Huawei only but is likely to be advantageous to the whole telecommunications manufacturing sector in China.[15]

The second case of particular interest to this discussion is the February 2015 NDRC Qualcomm decision. In November 2013, as a result of complaints concerning Qualcomm patent licensing practices made by the Mobile China Alliance and the

---

[14] See <http://finance.sina.com.cn/chanjing/gsnews/20131028/214517140841.shtml.>.
[15] The NDRC suspended its investigation under AML article 45, presumably as a result of commitments made by InterDigital. There is no official confirmation of the nature of the settlement.

Internet Society of China trade associations (representing Chinese mobile phone manufacturers and internet-related enterprises respectively), the NDRC raided a number of Qualcomm's offices to search and seize evidence relating to its investigation into alleged monopolistic practices engaged in by Qualcomm in breach of the AML. The subsequent investigation took 15 months to complete.

The NDRC found that Qualcomm had a dominant position in the markets of SEP licensing in respect of CDMA, WCDMA, and LTE wireless communication, and in the market of baseband chips. NDRC concluded that due to this dominant market position, Qualcomm was able to abuse its dominance in the relevant markets and engaged in the following abusive activities:

- **Charged unfairly high patent licensing fees.** Qualcomm refused to provide Chinese enterprises with its patent lists when granting licence to them and charged licensing fees for expired patents which are always included in its patent portfolio. At the same time, Qualcomm requested a free cross-licence of the Chinese licensees' own relevant patents, while refusing to deduct the value of such cross-licensed patents from its licensing fees or to offer any other consideration. In addition, for Chinese licensees who had been forced to accept Qualcomm's packaged licensing of non-SEPs, Qualcomm charged royalties on the basis of the net wholesale price of the device while imposing a relatively high royalty rate. The combination of these factors resulted in excessively high royalties.
- **Bundled sales of wireless communication non-SEPs without justification.** Qualcomm did not distinguish or offer separate licences in respect of its wireless communication SEPs and non-SEPs; instead, it took advantage of its dominant position in the market of licensing of SEPs relating to wireless communication to bundle the licensing of non-SEPs.
- **Imposed unreasonable restrictions on the sales of baseband chips.** Qualcomm conditioned its supply of baseband chips to Chinese customers on the signing of a patent-licence agreement. If a potential licensee did not sign the patent-licence agreement including the above unreasonable terms, or the licensee disputed such patent-licence agreement and brought legal action, Qualcomm would refuse to supply baseband chips to it. Because Chinese licensees were highly reliant upon Qualcomm's baseband chip products, they were forced to accede to the terms.[16]

It should be noted that the NDRC issued only a two page press release that gives little detail of its analytical methodology or the process followed during its

---

[16] For an industry commentary on the decision, see Linklaters LLP , 'NDRC issues decisoinin landmark case against Qualcomm and imposes record fine of RMB ¥6.088 billion' (February 2015) <www.linklaters.com/pdfs/mkt/beijing/A19534241.pdf>.

investigation, however it is understood that the NDRC worked closely with technical staff from the Ministry of Industry and Information Technology, the sector regulator.

As part of its decision the NDRC announced that Qualcomm had offered voluntary commitments to close the case which included promises:

(1) to charge royalties at the rate of 65 per cent of the net wholesale price of the cell phones sold for use within China;

(2) to provide patent lists when granting licences to Chinese licensees and not to charge licensing fees for expired patents;

(3) not to request a free cross-licence from Chinese licensees;

(4) not to bundle non-SEPs when licensing wireless communication SEPs without justification; and

(5) not to request that Chinese licensees enter into a patent-licence agreement including unreasonable conditions when selling baseband chips, and not to condition the supply of baseband chips to Chinese licensees on not challenging such patent-licence agreement.[17]

Most interestingly, as part of the press release the NDRC also announced that:

> The rectification commitments proposed by Qualcomm meet the requirements of NDRC. Qualcomm also indicated that it will continue to increase the investment and pursue a better development in China. NDRC welcomes Qualcomm's continued investment in China and supports Qualcomm in charging reasonable royalties for the use of its patented technologies.[18]

These promises by Qualcomm in respect of future conduct and continued investment in China appear to be part of an overall settlement package that presumably reduced the financial penalty that NDRC had initially decided to impose on Qualcomm for its past behaviour. However, even with these negotiated settlement terms, Qualcomm was fined the highest financial penalty to date imposed under the AML: 8 per cent of the value of sales in China in 2013 amounting to USD $975 million. This was considerably less than the maximum Qualcomm could theoretically have been fined, as the AML allows the global turnover of an undertaking to be used as the basis for determining fines of between 1 to 10 per cent of that annual turnover, as well as the confiscation of any 'illegal gains'.[19] It appears that the settlement included oral commitments not recorded in the official decision and certain findings may have been omitted from the decision to insulate Qualcomm

---

[17] Ibid.

[18] Ibid.

[19] See AML article 47 and for fining guidance generally see Baker & McKenzie, 'China Antitrust: Consultation on New and Clearer Penalty Guidelines', (Global Compliance News, 27 July 2016), available at <https://globalcompliancenews.com/china-antitrust-consultation-new-clearer-penalty-guidelines-20160727/> accessed 2 May 2017.

from private enforcement action, preventing potential plaintiffs in damages actions from relying on such findings.

Another issue that has caused loud but anonymous complaints from MNCs who have been the subject of, or threatened with, AML investigations is the lack of transparency and weak due process standards. Allegations of improper contact by the enforcement agency with domestic rivals of MNCs, and of engaging in 'fishing expeditions' to obtain confidential commercial information have been made. Further allegations include that enforcement agencies begin investigations with demands for swift confessions of guilt, and require public apologies for committing infractions, acceptance of the proposed financial penalties, undertaking 'voluntary' remedial conduct, and binding commitments about future behaviour. Such tactics, if proven, would be of considerable concern. And it is interesting that in fact, the vast majority of AML investigations to date have resulted in confessions of guilt, abject public apologies by major corporations, and the acceptance of imposed or negotiated remedies. Moreover, in the nine years that the AML has been operational, there has not been a single request for administrative reconsideration of a decision or an appeal to a court, even though both are available to subjects of AML investigations. This apparent acquiescence, unusual for large MNCs adversely affected by administrative decisions, suggests that the Chinese system is unusual and lends credence to allegations about serious due process and transparency deficiencies.

The case studies also demonstrate that the NDRC and SAIC are likely to concentrate their enforcement efforts on strategically important sectors for the Chinese economy, which clearly includes the technology sector. The Huawei and Qualcomm enforcement also provide the impetus and incentives for Chinese enterprises to be more assertive in their negotiations with foreign patent holders in licensing cases, as any perceived unfairness or discrimination would likely encourage either more complaints to the antitrust regulators, more private litigation, or both. This new environment will no doubt be a cause of concern for IPR-rich MNCs and, coupled with the government's clear industrial policy goals as expounded in CM2025, MNCs will be vigilant in cases where they perceive industrial policy goals are ousting China's official commitment to greater reliance on market mechanisms, as opposed to *dirigiste* Colbertism.[20]

---

[20] In the mid-seventeenth century, Colbert was Louis XIV's most important finance minister who encouraged a mercantilist external trade policy and the establishment of a self-sufficient domestic industrial policy guided by the state. Features of Colbert's policy included the establishment of state manufacturing capacity to produce a variety of goods, and investment in domestic infrastructure projects.

5. Prospects for AML Enforcement and Foreign Rights Holders

The combination of China's stated ambitions to upgrade its manufacturing base and the increased incidence of abuse of dominance allegations against foreign rights holders could be merely coincidental. The focus of the anti-monopoly agencies on drafting specific guidance on abuse of IPRs and their apparent readiness to utilize the AML in patent rights cases, along with apparent judicial encouragement of private abuse of dominance litigation appear to be part of a trend to increase scrutiny of largely foreign rights owners.

The Chinese government clearly wants to propel China's traditional strengths in manufacturing to a new level of sophistication, as confirmed by the ambitious objectives set out in CM2025. The important question considered here is whether the policy tools China will employ to attain these goals will go beyond extensive, but broadly orthodox industrial policy tools, to those which are unorthodox or incompatible with China's much broader aim of moving towards the market having a decisive influence in resource allocation and pricing. China's government appears to display a somewhat schizophrenic policy stance: on the one hand loudly proclaiming substantially pro-market reforms, but on the other promulgating a very bureaucratic planned approach to the manufacturing sector, to the extent of extolling the virtues of indigenous innovation and providing market share targets to be reserved for domestic producers. The key aim of promoting innovation is to be fostered by increased state-directed R&D funds, and is also manifested by leap-frogging basic research in some areas. Domestic companies/SOEs are ensured access on favourable terms to foreign technology through the combination of promises of increased market access to foreign rights holders, and the unspoken but implicit threat of enhanced antitrust scrutiny. This combination of trade policy 'carrots' and antitrust policy 'sticks' may succeed in achieving China's industrial policy aims. China's domestic market is so large and growing at such a sustained rate that many MNCs simply cannot ignore it as increasing sales in China is central to their future growth plans. This may explain why many will be prepared to accept perhaps lower than market royalty fees in return for increased market access, and may also explain the singular fact that MNCs accused of antitrust violations in China by the authorities confess without fail, provide remedial commitments to the agencies, and have not launched a single appeal against any antitrust decision since the implementation of the AML.

However, this Faustian pact is potentially unstable. If China's AML enforcers become too heavy handed they risk a significant reduction in foreign investment, R&D expenditure, and an even greater reluctance to concede voluntary technology transfer. Thus, China's authorities must tread a very difficult line between an excessively heavy-handed enforcement approach that scares away prized foreign technology firms, and a liberal, *laissez-faire* approach that runs the risk of not attaining China's industrial policy goals in the time allowed in CM2025. IPR-rich foreign undertakings are presumably fully aware of the risks and benefits of the Chinese market, and one must hope that the Chinese authorities appreciate the long term wisdom of adopting a conservative approach to usage of the concept of abuse of IPRs in enforcement of the AML. Over-vigorous use of this policy tool may result in unexpected and negative outcomes that will not be in China's long term interest as it seeks to become an innovative, developed, high income economy.

9

ANTI-COMPETITIVE AGREEMENTS AND INTELLECTUAL PROPERTY LICENSING IN CHINA

Ken Dai

1. Introduction

The Chinese competition legislation system is composed mainly of the *Anti-Monopoly Law of PRC* (the 'AML'),[1] the *Anti-Unfair Competition Law of PRC* (the 'AUCL')[2] and relevant guidelines and circulars. Based on the principle of good faith and recognized business ethics, the AUCL protects undertakings from suffering anti-competitive conducts so as to maintain a competitive market and protect the interests of consumers. The AML focuses more on competition itself, requiring enough competitors in the market in order to provide freedom of choice for counter-parties/consumers and improve economic efficiency and social welfare of consumers.

Generally speaking, undertakings in the market enjoy the freedom to choose whom and the conditions to establish a business relationship with in, which is the essence

---

[1] The *Anti-Monopoly Law of the People's Republic of China* ('AML') was promulgated on 30 August 2007 and came into effect as of 8 January 2008. It is the first systematic anti-monopoly law in China's legal history. The AML mainly stipulates four categories of monopolistic conducts, which are anti-competitive agreement, abuse of dominant market position, concentration of undertakings, and abuse of administrative power to exclude or eliminate competition.

[2] The *Anti-Unfair Competition Law of the People's Republic of China* ('AUCL') was promulgated on 2 September 1993 and came into effect as of 1 December 1993. Due to certain historical reasons, the AUCL includes articles concerning illegal conducts, such as counterfeiting a registered trademark of another person, undertaking's tie-in sale of commodities, or attaching any other unreasonable conditions to the sale of their commodities, which should be stipulated by advertising law and anti-monopoly law respectively. Taking into consideration of overlap with other laws and regulations, lack of rules against new anti-competitive conducts and limited deterrence of relevant legal responsibility, the Legislative Affairs Office of the State Council published the *Anti-Unfair Competition Law (Revised Draft Submitted for Review)* on 25 February 2016. One of the most heated discussion circles around whether 'superior bargaining power' should be included in the new AUCL.

of a free economy. However, what the border to rights and interests is what anti-monopoly law is to business agreements. From the AML's perspective, undertakings are prohibited from entering into anti-competitive agreements (including agreements, decisions ,and other concerted conducts designed to eliminate or restrict competition between competing undertakings or non-competing undertakings from upstream or downstream industries). Further, the AML is also applicable to the conducts of undertakings that eliminate or restrict competition by abusing their IPRs.

Nowadays, more and more cross-border transactions have been increasingly reached between undertakings from both at home and abroad in various forms, among which intellectual property ('IP') licensing is a classic. Usually, licensing is achieved through relevant agreements in practice. In an IP licensing agreement, the licensor keeps the ownership of the IPRs, while the licensee is entitled to make use of the IPRs under certain conditions. Whether the relationship between the licensor and the licensee is horizontal or vertical is unclear, and may depend on particular circumstances. Mostly, it appears in a vertical form. Some undertakings like Qualcomm Incorporated ('Qualcomm') grab a large part of their profits from licensing IPRs, while others like Huawei Technologies Co., Ltd. ('Huawei') and Zhongxing Telecommunication Equipment Corporation ('ZTE') may act as licensees or licensors in different situations. Not one of the undertakings can obtain all the cutting-edge technologies by itself, even Qualcomm. In order to maintain continuous growth and keep up with latest developments, master the core technologies or just for economic reasons, undertakings choose to request a licence of patents from the developed ones in a particular area. Clauses concerning grant-back, joint R&D, geographic restriction etc are very common in IP licensing agreements.

Strictly speaking, from the antitrust perspective, China has not had a set of laws or regulations targeting at intersection of anti-competitive agreements and IP licensing until the promulgation of the *Provisions on the Prohibition of the Abuse of Intellectual Property Rights to Eliminate or Restrict Competition* on 7 April 2015.[3] When it came to IP licensing agreements that would eliminate or restrict competition, the Chinese antitrust enforcement authorities could only count on Article 55 of the AML, which is quite general and vague. Of course, there are provisions in laws from other sectors dealing with IP-related agreements. However, those rules were enacted by the legislator to achieve other objectives, such as to promote import and export trade, etc. Taking the AML as a turning point, this article delves deep into the legislation and practice prior to the enactment of the AML firstly and then looks at relevant situations afterwards.

---

[3] State Administration for Industry and Commerce ('SAIC'): *Provisions on the Prohibition of the Abuse of Intellectual Property Rights to Eliminate or Restrict Competition*. Promulgation date: 7 April 2015. Effective date: 1 August 2015.

2. Legislation and Practice Prior to the AML

2.1 Legal framework

2.1.1 International treaty

The World Trade Organization ('WTO')'s *Agreement on Trade-Related Aspects of Intellectual Property Rights* ('TRIPS') negotiated at the end of Uruguay Round is an international agreement that establishes minimum levels of protection each government has to provide to the IPRs of fellow WTO members. TRIPS aims to narrow the gaps of various IPRs protected around the world, and bring them under common international rules.[4] As for application of TRIPS, China has to first transpose it into domestic law, such as *Patent Law of PRC* ('*Patent Law*').

Acting as a kind of property, IPR is distinct from the others because of its intangibility and replicability, which makes it very vulnerable. Besides, IPR is an exclusive right, meaning that the proprietor enjoys exclusive right of his or her IP, even monopolistic rights under some circumstances. That's the reason IPRs are more easily abused compared with general properties. IP law is a kind of interest-balance rule. It has to reward investors and innovators of new technologies, art, or literal works and innovative industry on the one hand, and provide access to contributions mentioned above to the public on the other hand. Conflicts and differences between developed countries with cutting-edge technologies and developing countries in the process of industrialization in respect of IPRs protection is widely recognized. TRIPS is fruitful of countless negotiations and a balance of rights and interests from all circles. It includes protection of trade-related IPRs, reflecting objects of developed countries, while controlling anti-competitive practices in contractual licences in Section 8 at the insistence of developing countries at the same time.

Generally speaking, member states agree that some licensing practices or conditions pertaining to IPRs that restrain competition may have adverse effects on trade and impede transfer and dissemination of technology.[5] A member state may adopt appropriate measures to prevent or control practices that may include exclusive grant-back conditions, conditions preventing challenges to validity and coercive package licensing in light of the relevant laws and regulations of that member state. Member states are free to specify in their legislation the licensing practices or conditions that may in particular cases constitute an abuse of IPRs having an adverse

---

[4] Intellectual property: protection and enforcement, Origins: into the rule-based trade system …', available at <https://www.wto.org/english/thewto_e/whatis_e/tif_e/agrm7_e.htm#skip> accessed 25 June 2016.

[5] World Trade Organization: *Agreement on Trade-Related Aspects of Intellectual Property Rights* ('TRIPS') (effective date: 1 January 1995; parties: all WTO members), Article 40(1).

effect on competition in the relevant market.[6] From a legal perspective, Article 40 aims to preventing IPRs holders from abusing their exclusive rights. We could also find more general rules or legal bases against the abuse from Articles 7,[7] 8,[8] 30,[9] and 31[10] of TRIPS.

2.1.2 Chinese laws and regulations

China's legal system consists of three levels. The first level consists of laws enacted by the National People's Congress and Standing Committee, which overrule the other levels.[11] The second level consists of administrative statutes published by the State Council.[12] Courts mainly count on legislation from the first and second levels to rule on specific cases. The third level consists of regulations, circulars, rules, and orders published by departments under the State Council within the scope of respective authority from now and then.[13] Courts may refer to rules from the third level when necessary, but will not rely on them. What's worth mentioning is that interpretation of questions involving the specific application of laws and decrees in court trials shall be provided by the Supreme People's Court ('SPC').[14] Judicial interpretation plays a pivotal role in China. Though inferior to legislative interpretation in aspects of nature and status, judicial interpretation could affect the society directly from points of the quantity and role played in the society, which makes it more important in people's daily life.

When it comes to the intersection of IP licensing and anti-competitive agreement, we have certain articles of the *Contract Law of PRC* ('*Contract Law*'), the *Foreign Trade Law of PRC* ('*Foreign Trade Law*'), and the Patent Law from the first level, the *Regulations of PRC on the Administration over Technology Import and Export* from

---

[6] Ibid, Article 40(2).

[7] Article 7 of TRIPS, 'The protection and enforcement of intellectual property rights should contribute to the promotion of technological innovation and to the transfer and dissemination of technology, to the mutual advantage of producers and users of technological knowledge and in a manner conducive to social and economic welfare, and to a balance of rights and obligations.'

[8] Article 8(2) of TRIPS, 'Appropriate measures, provided that they are consistent with the provisions of this Agreement, may be needed to prevent the abuse of intellectual property rights by right holders or the resort to practices which unreasonably restrain trade or adversely affect the international transfer of technology.'

[9] Article 30 of TRIPS, 'Members may provide limited exceptions to the exclusive rights conferred by a patent, provided that such exceptions do not unreasonably conflict with a normal exploitation of the patent and do not unreasonably prejudice the legitimate interests of the patent owner, taking account of the legitimate interests of third parties.'

[10] Article 31 of TRIPS is about compulsory licence.

[11] *Legislative Law of PRC (Revised in 2015)*, Article 7.

[12] Ibid, Article 65.

[13] Ibid, Article 80.

[14] Article II of the *Resolution of the Standing Committee of the National People's Congress Providing an Improved Interpretation of the Law* (promulgated and came into effect as of 10 June 1981).

level two and *Interpretation of the Supreme People's Court Concerning Some Issues on Application of Law for the Trial of Cases on Disputes over Technology Contracts* (*'Judicial Interpretation'*) before the promulgation of the AML in 2008.

2.1.2.1 Contract law Situations of invalidity of a contract[15] stipulated in General Provisions of the *Contract Law* could be applied to all contracts between equal parties, including technology contracts. Besides, the term 'mandatory provisions' mentioned in Article 52(5) of the *Contract Law* refers to the mandatory provisions on effectiveness[16] instead of mandatory provisions on management.[17] If parties of a contract violate mandatory provisions on effectiveness, then it would affect the validity of the contract.

Entering into a technology contract should reflect the basic principles, such as helping in the progress of scientific technology as well as transformation, application, and popularization of technological results. Any technology contract that illegally monopolizes technologies, impedes technological progress, or infringes upon the technological results of others is null and void,[18] in theory. However, several issues are in need of special attention. Firstly, a null and void contract is void ab initio. Secondly, a party of the contract could only apply to the court or arbitration institution to declare a contract null and void instead of to the other party directly and privately. After declaration of nullity, restoration to the original status might be required. To be more specific, one party should return technological materials or samples without keeping the replication to the other party. One could require the other to bear confidential responsibility as regards technological material/intelligence within a certain period or not to put the technology into practice. Moreover, if one party causes losses for the other, the amount of compensation for the loss shall be equivalent to the loss actually caused by the breach of contract and shall include the profit obtainable after the performance of the contract, but shall not exceed the sum of the loss that might be caused by breach of the contract and has been anticipated or ought to have been anticipated by the breaching party

---

[15] Article 52 of the *Contract Law*, 'A contract is invalid under any of the following circumstances:
  (1) either party enters into the contract by means of fraud or coercion and impairs the State's interests;
  (2) there is malicious conspiracy causing damage to the interests of the State, of the collective or of a third party;
  (3) there is an attempt to conceal illegal goals under the disguise of legitimate forms;
  (4) harm is done to social and public interests; or
  (5) mandatory provisions of laws and administrative regulations are violated.'

[16] Article 14 of *Interpretation II of the Supreme People's Court on Certain Issues concerning the Application of the Contract Law* (promulgated on 24 April and came into effect as of 13 May 2009).

[17] Most of 'mandatory provisions on management' are prohibitive or restrictive rules, in breach of which would not lead to invalidity of a contract. However, parties to a contract need to bear administrative liabilities.

[18] Article 329 of the *Contract Law*.

in entering into the contract.[19] If both parties breach the contract, then they shall bear respective liabilities accordingly.[20] Last but not least, if a technology contract is declared null and void due to infringement of the others' technological achievements, then several principles should be adhered to. If the technological contract is null and void for the reason that one infringes patent, the right to apply for a patent or right to practise patent of the other, then the contract should not be implemented if it had not been and the implementation should cease if it had been. If the one who adopts technology is fully aware of or should have known the infringement of the other, but still enters into and implements the contract, then contributory infringement should be determined and the two should bear joint and several liabilities. If the right to use and transfer of non-patent technological achievement is infringed, then the one offering technology should bear liability for tort. An adopting party with good faith could continue to apply technology but should pay reasonable royalties. For those who are fully aware of the tort but still adopt the relevant technology, they shall be deemed as contributory infringers with the aforesaid infringing party. In this case, joint and several liabilities is required, and continuous implementation is forbidden. For technological contract in breach of right of proprietary, such as right of invention, discovery, or other scientific and technological achievement, declaration of nullity of some provisions would not affect validity of the other provisions. That is to say, nullity of certain provisions would not affect the validity of the whole technology transfer contract. For those who are responsible for the tort, the court could require him or her to stop the infringement, eliminate the obstruction, and compensate for the damages.[21] It is noteworthy that the above mentioned technology contract under the *Contract Law* refers to a contract involving technology development, transfer, consulting and/or services, whose scope is much larger than licensing of patent. In other words, the provision on technology contract under the *Contract Law* applies to contracts with respect to technology, including patent, and non-patent technology.

In *Dayang Co. v Huanghe Co.*,[22] the SPC upheld a lower court's judgment, holding that the licensor's offering of dedicated production equipment to the licensee could include relevant technology. Since the patent licensing agreement did not constitute the 'contract that illegally monopolizes technologies, impedes technological progress'. What Article 329 of the *Contract Law* prohibits is requiring the licensee

---

[19] Article 113 of the *Contract Law*.
[20] Article 120 of the *Contract Law*.
[21] Article 118 of *General Principles of Civil Law of PRC*.
[22] *Dayang Co. v Huanghe Co.* (2003) MIN SAN ZHONG ZI No 8, available at http://www.itslaw.com/detail?judgementId=4214568c-b9d4-4d4c-a4e0-4793ed275866&area=1&index=1&sortType=1&count=2&conditions=searchWord%2B%E5%A4%A7%E6%B4%8B%E5%85%AC%E5%8F%B8%2B1%2B%E5%A4%A7%E6%B4%8B%E5%85%AC%E5%8F%B8&conditions=searchWord%2B%E9%BB%84%E6%B2%B3%E5%85%AC%E5%8F%B8%2B1%2B%E9%BB%84%E6%B2%B3%E5%85%AC%E5%8F%B8, accessed 23 May 2016.

to accept attached conditions which are not necessary for technology implemen-tation, including technology, service, raw materials, equipment, products, or per-sonnel not needed by the licensee.

In *Wu Yunjie and Guo Zhiming v Chongqing Paiwei Energy Management Co.*,[23] the SPC was of the opinion that only the provision concerning C/S structure software which infringed business secrets of a third party (Jia Li Da Co.) was null and void, not the whole software development agreement.

2.1.2.2 Foreign trade law Member states of WTO could take appropriate measures consistent with provisions of TRIPS to prevent the abuse of IPRs by owners or the resort to practices that unreasonably restrain trade or adversely affect the international transfer of technology.[24] Only legal persons or organizations, excluding natural person, engaging in foreign trade activities in compliance with provisions of the *Foreign Trade Law (1994)* were qualified for 'foreign trade operator'.[25] At that time, the Chinese legislator was of the opinion that domestic natural persons could not defend their rights very well due to lack of necessary knowledge or experience so as to exclude them from foreign trade activities directly. IPRs-related article in the *Foreign Trade Law (1994)* was very simple and general.[26] However, IPRs concerning trade have increasingly become an essential instrument taken by major trading nations around the world to safeguard state interests.

With the aim to expand the opening up to the outside world, developing foreign trade, maintaining the order of foreign trade, safeguarding foreign trade operators' legal rights and interests, and promoting the healthy development of a socialist market economy, the *Foreign Trade Law (2004)* was promulgated.[27] As of 1 July

---

[23] *Wu Yunjie and Guo Zhiming v Chongqing Paiwei Energy Management Co.* (2012) MIN SHEN ZI No 855, available at http://www.itslaw.com/detail?judgementId=df5406b4-0bd7-4ce1-88de-cd9d5b7ae391&area=1&index=1&sortType=1&count=3&conditions=searchWord%2B%E9%9D%9E%E6%B3%95%E5%9E%84%E6%96%AD%E6%8A%80%E6%9C%AF%E3%80%81%E5%A6%A8%E7%A2%8D%E6%8A%80%E6%9C%AF%E8%BF%9B%E6%AD%A5%E6%88%96%E8%80%85%E4%BE%B5%E5%AE%B3%E4%BB%96%E4%BA%BA%E6%8A%80%E6%9C%AF%E6%88%90%E6%9E%9C%E7%9A%84%E6%8A%80%E6%9C%AF%E5%90%88%E5%90%8C%E6%97%A0%E6%95%88%E3%80%82%2B1%2B%E9%9D%9E%E6%B3%95%E5%9E%84%E6%96%AD%E6%8A%80%E6%9C%AF%E3%80%81%E5%A6%A8%E7%A2%8D%E6%8A%80%E6%9C%AF%E8%BF%9B%E6%AD%A5%E6%88%96%E8%80%85%E4%BE%B5%E5%AE%B3%E4%BB%96%E4%BA%BA%E6%8A%80%E6%9C%AF%E6%88%90%E6%9E%9C%E7%9A%84%E6%8A%80%E6%9C%AF%E5%90%88%E5%90%8C%E6%97%A0%E6%95%88%E3%80%82, accessed 23 May 2016.

[24] Article 8(2) of TRIPS.

[25] Article 8 of the *Foreign Trade Law (1994)*.

[26] Article 27 of the *Foreign Trade Law (1994)*, 'Foreign trade shall be undertaken in compliance with law and under the principle of fair competition with the infringement upon the IPRs protected by law of PRC being strictly prohibited.'

[27] The *Foreign Trade Law (1994)* had been revised and adopted at the 8th Session of the Standing Committee of the 10th National People's Congress of PRC on 6 April 2004, and the revised edition was promulgated for implementation from 1 July 2004. Article 1 of the *Foreign Trade Law (2004)*.

2004, a whole chapter aimed at protecting IPRs related to foreign trade was introduced in accordance with WTO rules and legislation/enforcement experience of the US, EU, and Japan, etc. Under most circumstances, it is a competent department of foreign trade under the State Council (predecessor of Ministry of Commerce ('MOFCOM'))[28] instead of parties to a particular foreign trade relationship that could take actions on the basis of most-favoured-nation treatment, national treatment, or principles of reciprocity and equality.[29] Special attention should be paid to the fact that only when provisions in IPRs licensing agreement damage the order of fair competition in foreign trade could the foreign trade department under the State Council take necessary actions, which is consistent with the legislative purpose of the *Foreign Trade Law (2004)*,[30] illustrating its limited protective effects on intersection between anti-competitive agreements and IP licensing.

Where IPRs holders have any of the following acts, including (1) preventing licensees from challenging the validity of IP covered in licence contracts, (2) imposing forced package licensing; or/and (3) specifying exclusive grant-back conditions in license contracts etc, which damage the order of fair competition in foreign trade, the competent department of foreign trade under the State Council may take necessary measures to eliminate the damage.[31]

2.1.2.3 Patent law In principle, the holder of IPRs is free to decide whether to license its IPRs to other parties or not as long as it would not eliminate or restrict competition in the market or its pro-competitive effects outweigh private rights, though they are in sense of their nature. With respect to national industrial policy, national economic security, or even competitive position in international trade, states would compel proprietors to license certain IPRs when necessary.

Where a patentee's exercising of patent right is determined as monopoly in accordance with the law and the negative impact of such exercise on competition needs to be eliminated or reduced, the Patent Administration Department under the State Council ('Patent Administration Department') may grant a compulsory licence for the exploitation of an invention patent or utility model patent upon the application of any organization or individual possessing exploitation conditions.[32]

---

[28] Ministry of Commerce ('MOFCOM'), a department in charge of both domestic and international business, economy, and trade under the State Council, was established in 2003. The First Session of the Tenth National People's Congress decided to combine the previous Ministry of Foreign Trade and Economic Cooperation and State Economic and Trade Commission, establishing MOFCOM.

[29] For example, Articles 6, 26, 29, 30, 32, et al of the *Foreign Trade Law (2004)*.

[30] Article 1 of the *Foreign Trade Law (2004)*, 'With a view to expanding the opening-up to the outside world, developing foreign trade, maintaining the order of foreign trade, safeguarding foreign trade operators' legal rights and interests, and promoting the healthy development of the socialist market economy, this Law is formulated.'

[31] Article 30 of the *Foreign Trade Law (2004)*.

[32] Article 48(2) of the *Patent Law*.

Besides, when a national emergency or any extraordinary state of affairs occurs, or the public interest so requires,[33] for the purpose of public health with regard to patented drugs,[34] or if a patented invention or utility model had made significant technological advancement with remarkable economic significance, compared with an earlier patented invention or utility model and the exploitation of the former relies on the exploitation of the latter,[35] the Patent Administration Department may also grant necessary compulsory licence to exploit a related invention or utility model upon application of relevant parties. Furthermore, if an invention involved in a compulsory licence is a semi-conductor technology, the exploitation thereof shall be limited for purpose of public interest and for elimination or reduction of negative impact of the patentee's exercising patent right, such as licensing.[36] Of course, an organization or individual granted a compulsory licence for exploitation shall pay reasonable royalties to the patentee.[37] Until now, there is no case of compulsory licence in China. What's worth mentioning is that neither reasonable application nor compulsory licence applies to registered trademarks, as it concerns less about public interests.

2.1.2.4 Administration regulation over technology import and export On 10 December 2001, the State Council promulgated the *Regulations of PRC on the Administration over Technology Import and Export ('Administration Regulations over Technology Import and Export')*, which came into effect as of 1 January 2002. Strictly speaking, the *Administration Regulations over Technology Import and Export* has lost its legal ground, which is *Foreign Trade Law (1994)*,[38] though it was revised on 8 January 2011.[39] Conducts supervised by the *Administration Regulations over Technology Import and Export* include transfer of patents, transfer of the patent

---

[33] Article 49 of the *Patent Law*.
[34] Article 50 of the *Patent Law*.
[35] Article 51 of the *Patent Law*.
[36] Article 52 of the *Patent Law*.
[37] Article 57 of the *Patent Law*.
[38] Article 1 of the *Administration Regulations over Technology Import and Export*, 'With a view to regulating the administration of technology import and export, maintaining the order of technology import and export, and promoting national economic and social development, this Regulation is formulated pursuant to the *Foreign Trade Law (1994)* and other relevant laws.' However, the effectiveness of the *Foreign Trade Law (1994)* has already expired, and is replaced by the *Foreign Trade Law (2004)*.
[39] Pursuant to the *Decision of the State Council on Repealing and Revising Certain Administrative Regulations* promulgated on 8 January 2011, the expression of 'technologies falling under any of the circumstances prescribed in Article 16 or Article 17 of the *Foreign Trade Law (1994)*' under Article 8 and Article 31 herein shall be revised to read as 'technologies falling under any of the circumstances prescribed in Article 16 of the *Foreign Trade Law (2004)*'. Articles 16 and 17 of the *Foreign Trade Law (1994)* were about circumstances under which technology import or export might be restricted and prohibited respectively, while Article 16 of the *Foreign Trade Law (2004)* is about circumstances under which goods or technologies import or export might be restricted or prohibited.

application right, patent exploitation licensing, transfer of technological know-how, technological services, and technology transfer in other forms, referring to technologies from outside the territory of PRC to inside the territory of PRC, and vice versa.[40] The limitation here is that technology transfer in the form of IPRs licensing without crossing the border is not under the control of the regulations. The *Administration Regulations over Technology Import and Export* reflects more about industry policy than competition policy during the State's administration over technology imports and exports.[41]

The State encourages import of advanced, applicable technologies, and export of mature industrialized technologies.[42] In principle, achievements made from technological improvements shall belong to the party that made such improvements during the term of validity of a technology import contract.[43] Moreover, restrictive clauses include:

a) requiring the transferee to accept attached conditions not essential for technology import (including the purchase of non-essential technologies, raw materials, products, equipment, or services);

b) requiring the transferee to pay royalties or undertake relevant obligations for the technologies whose patent has expired or has been declared invalid;

c) restricting the transferee from making improvements to the technologies provided by the transferor or restricting the transferee from using improved technologies;

d) restricting the transferee from obtaining technologies similar to or competitive with the technologies provided by the transferor from other resources;

e) placing unreasonable restrictions on the channels or sources from which the transferee may purchase raw materials, parts and components, products or equipment;

f) placing unreasonable restrictions on the quantity, types or sale prices of the products manufactured by the transferee; or

g) placing unreasonable restrictions on the export channels of the products manufactured by the transferee using imported technologies, shall not be contained in any technology import contract.[44]

---

[40] Article 2 of the *Administration Regulations over Technology Import and Export*.

[41] Article 4 of the *Administration Regulations over Technology Import and Export*, 'Technology import and export shall be in line with State policies on industries, science and technology, as well as social development. It shall also be conducive to promoting China's scientific and technological progress and the development of foreign economic and technological cooperation, and to safeguarding China's economic and technological rights and interests.'

[42] Articles 7 and 30 of the *Administration Regulations over Technology Import and Export*.

[43] Article 27 of the *Administration Regulations over Technology Import and Export*.

[44] Article 29 of the *Administration Regulations over Technology Import and Export*.

Clauses mentioned above cover almost all anti-competitive situations in IPRs licensing. They are illegal per se, and no case-by-case analysis is needed, the determination of the Chinese legislators to protect the Chinese licensees could be reflected therefrom.

2.1.2.5 Interpretation of the Supreme People's Court In accordance with the *Contract Law*, the *Patent Law*, the *Civil Procedure Law of PRC*, and other relevant laws, and in consideration of trial practices, the *Interpretation of the Supreme People's Court on Some Issues Concerning the Application of Law in the Trial of Technology Contract Dispute Cases ('Interpretation of the SPC')* was promulgated on 16 December 2004 and came into effect as of 1 January 2005 in order to ensure the correct trial of cases involving technology contract disputes. Article 10 of the *Interpretation of the SPC* lists six circumstances that could be defined as 'illegal monopoly or hindrance to technology advancement' specified in Article 329 of the *Contract Law*, which could lead to technology contract null and void. They are:

a) restricting one of the parties concerned from carrying on any new research and development on the basis of the technology that is the subject matter of the contract or restricting the party from using the improved technology or carrying out exchange regarding the improved technology with unequal terms for both parties etc, including that one party is required to provide for free, or to transfer non-reciprocally, the technology improved by the party to the other party, or that one party monopolizes or shares, for free, the intellectual property rights to the improved technology;

b) restricting one of the parties concerned from obtaining from other resources the technology similar or competitive to that of the technology supplier;

c) hindering one of the parties concerned from sufficiently implementing the technology which is the subject matter of a contract in reasonable ways according to market demand, including obviously unreasonable restriction on the quantity, type, price, marketing channel, or export the market of the products produced or services provided by the technology receiving party through implementing the technology;

d) requesting the technology-receiving party to accept the conditions unessential to the implementation of the technology, including purchase of unnecessary technology, raw materials, products, equipment, or services, or acceptance of unnecessary personnel etc;

e) limiting unreasonably the channels or sources from which the technology-receiving party purchases raw materials, parts, and components, products, or equipment; and

f) prohibiting the technology receiving party from filing opposition to the validity of the intellectual property rights of the technology which is the subject matter of a contract, or imposing conditions on the filing of opposition.

Serving as private law, the *Contract Law* should respect autonomy of will. However, technology agreement refers to public interests (such as competition order in the market), that prevail when conflicts between the private and the public appear.

2.2 High-profile case: *Intel v Dongjin*

2.2.1 *Relevant parties*

The plaintiff Intel ('Plaintiff') is one of the world's largest and highest valued semi-conductor chip makers, headquartered in US. The Plaintiff has invested heavily in research in China. Around 100 researchers, 10 per cent of the total number of re-searchers of the Plaintiff are located in Beijing. In April 2011, the Plaintiff began a pilot project with ZTE to produce smart phones using the Plaintiff Atom processor for China's domestic market. China is one of the main markets for the Plaintiff.

As the defendant, Shenzhen Donjin Communication Technology Co. ('Defendant') is a Chinese telecommunication and network equipment manufacturer.

2.2.2 *Disputes*

In 2004, the Plaintiff accused the Defendant of copying parts of its Dialogic Systems Release 5.1.1 software used in circuit boards running touch-pad telephone systems at Shenzhen Intermediate People's Court and also sought for a permanent injunction of prohibiting the Defendant from manufacturing and selling prod-ucts in question and compensation of USD 7.96 million.[45] The main dispute was centred on compatibility of the Defendant's products with Plaintiff's software, as well as whether users of the Plaintiff's communications cards could switch to the Defendant's products without the need to change their existing programs. The marketing director of the Defendant said the Plaintiff's requirement had consti-tuted a technology monopoly, which was detrimental to the interests of consumers and did stifle fair competition.

In 2005, the Defendant's subsidiary in Beijing countersued the Plaintiff for IPRs monopolistic licensing. On 1 April 2005, Beijing No. 1 Intermediate People's Court accepted the case. Such subsidiary alleged that the Plaintiff's protocol of Dialogic System Release 5.1.1 software had strictly restricted its users by binding the software to its own hardware products. Hardware produced by third parties is out of reach of Plaintiff's customers. It is a classic kind of tie-in provision in a li-censing agreement. This counterclaim was sought for invalidation of the Plaintiff's protocol.

---

[45] 'Intel charged with tech monopoly', available at http://www.chinadaily.com.cn/english/doc/2005-04/05/content_431159.htm, accessed 30 May 2016.

2.2.3 Final settlement and its implication

On 14 May 2007, the Plaintiff announced that it had already settled the lawsuit with both the Defendant and its subsidiary. The Plaintiff's spokesman expressed the concern that continuous litigation would bring no good to its strategy,[46] which was also against its intent to exploit China's booming computer and microprocessor demand. Settlement of licensing between the Plaintiff and the Defendant had been achieved but was confidential. Though industry analysis, the settlement signalled that the Plaintiff would like to eliminate any potential political or business road-blocks during its ongoing investment in China.[47]

It has been observed that in the absence of the AML, to regulate the suspected anti-competitive IP licensing, undertakings could only challenge such conduct by applying the notion of technology monopoly.

2.3 Summary of legislation and cases before the AML

From relevant laws, regulations, judicial interpretations, and cases mentioned above before the promulgation of the AML, we could find that parties to IP licensing chose to seek for invalidity of the contract under most of the circumstances. The legal ground was certain provisions of the *Foreign Trade Law*, the *Contract Law* etc. Chinese legal professionals believed that related lawsuits were a great driving force for the legislation on intersection of IPRs and anti-monopoly. They also alerted Chinese high-tech companies to speed up innovation and create more products with their own IPRs, so as to make more products from China, instead of in China.

3. Legislation and Practice since the AML

3.1 Regulatory approach of the AML

To some extent, IPR is a kind of legal monopoly. IPRs holders are granted the exclusivity within a particular period and territory at the cost of short-term social interests. It could lead to a win-win result. On one hand, those with intelligent human resources are encouraged to spend more time on R&D activity so as to keep their cutting-edge position, leading the general direction of social development. On the other hand, the others with enough funding could pay for newest technology and put them into practice, which could affect people's daily life directly.

---

[46] 'Intel settles copyright fight with Chinese company', available at <http://www.itworldcanada.com/article/intel-settles-copyright-fight-with-chinese-company/8791>, accessed 30 May 2016.

[47] 'Intel settles copyright infringement suit with China firm', available at <http://www.chinaipmagazine.com/en/journal-show.asp?id=353>, accessed 23 May 2016.

Though there was great controversy as regards whether the AML applies to IPRs during discussion of the draft, the AML came out with a compromise. In principle, the AML does not apply to exercising IPRs in accordance with relevant laws and regulations. However, abuse of IPRs which might eliminate or restrict competition falls into the regulatory scope of the AML.[48] Such approach is consistent with the best practice in other matured competition jurisdictions, such as US and EU. Nonetheless, such stipulation is too general and vague, which has created the great uncertainty on the application.

The AML is applicable to legitimate exercise of IPRs. If an undertaking is accused of infringing Article 55(1) of the AML, then it needs to bear the burden of proof that practice of IPRs is in line with IPR laws and regulations. Nevertheless, the burden of proof is difficult, since most legal provisions are prohibitive rather than legitimate. To make a defence of legitimate practice work is really a technical piece of work.

The point of Article 55 depends on the second subparagraph, which is 'however, this Law (the AML) shall be applicable to the undertakings that eliminate or restrict market competition by abusing their intellectual property rights'. However, what practices could be defined as 'abuse' is not clear in written law. Abuse is very common in patent licenses, especially which are between non-competitors. So, patent licensing could constitute a horizontal or vertical anti-competitive agreement. Furthermore, the licensor might make use of its market position or superior bargaining power when licensing a patent to the licensee.

Compared with the relevant provisions under other laws and regulations, such as the *Contract Law* and the *Patent Law*, the AML makes it clear that abuse of IPRs is subject to antitrust enforcement both from the public and private sides. Anyone is entitled to make the complaints against the suspected monopolistic acts before the competent Chinese antitrust enforcement authorities.[49] Requirement for materials or evidence provided by such a complainant is much lower than that for a plaintiff in a civil litigation concerning disputes under the *Contract Law*. As for terms of reference, the competent department in charge of foreign trade could only take measures to eliminate negative effects instead of administrative penalty under the *Foreign Trade Law* and the *Administration Regulations over Technology Import and Export*.

---

[48] Article 55 of the AML, 'This law is not applicable to undertakings who exercise their intellectual property rights in accordance with the laws and administrative regulations on intellectual property rights; however, this law shall be applicable to the undertakings who eliminate or restrict market competition by abusing their intellectual property rights.'

[49] Article 38(2) of the AML, 'All units and individuals shall have the right to report to the authority for enforcement of the Anti-Monopoly Law against suspected monopolistic conducts. The latter shall keep the information confidential.'

3.2 SAIC provisions

In order to make it more certain for antitrust enforcement authorities to enforce the AML in IPRs area, upgrade transparency of enforcement, and help undertakings exercise IPRs properly, the State Administration for Industry & Commerce of PRC ('SAIC') has already initiated the draft work of guidelines for the AML enforcement in IPRs area as early as March 2009, only one year after the promulgation of the AML. Due to a lack of relevant experience, it seems to be too early to implement such a set of well-developed guidelines from all perspectives at that time. However, rules that could restrict or prohibited abuse of IPRs to eliminate or restrict competition are in great and urgent need. During the drafting of guidelines for anti-monopoly enforcement in IPRs area, SAIC was on the track of its own department regulations/provisions as a transitional enforcement tool.[50]

Acting as the sixth supporting regulation[51] ever since enforcement of the AML in 2008, the *Provisions on Prohibiting the Abuse of Intellectual Property Rights to Eliminate and Restrict Competition* (promulgated on 7 April 2015 and came into effect as of 1 August 2015, '*SAIC IPRs Provisions*') upgrade transparency of the AML enforcement and provide the public with more details as regards how one of the three antitrust enforcement authorities tackle[52] abuse of IPRs or non-patent technology more specifically,[53] through anti-competitive agreement and abuse of market position. It is the first anti-monopoly regulation targeting at abuse of IPRs, filling China's legislative loophole in this area. Although the *SAIC IPRs Provisions* are only working guidelines of a ministry under the State Council, one of whose

---

[50] *Provisions on Prohibiting the Abuse of Intellectual Property Rights to Eliminate and Restrict Competition* (promulgated on 7 April 2015 and came into effect as of 1 August 2015, '*SAIC IPRs Provisions*').

[51] The previous ones are:

1. *Provisions on the Procedures for the Administrative Organs for Industry and Commerce to Prevent Abuses of Administrative Powers to Exclude or Restrain Competition;*
2. *Provisions on the Procedures for the Administrative Organs for Industry and Commerce to Investigate Cases Concerning Monopoly Agreements and Abuses of Dominant Market Positions;*
3. *Provisions for Administrative Authorities for Industry and Commerce on Prohibiting Conclusion of Monopoly Agreements;*
4. *Provisions for Administrative Authorities for Industry and Commerce on Prohibiting Abuses of Dominant Market Positions; and*
5. *Provisions for Administrative Authorities for Industry and Commerce to Prevent Abuses of Administrative Powers to Eliminate or Restrict Competition.*

[52] Article 15 of the *SAIC IPRs Provisions* stipulate steps that might be taken by SAIC in analysing and determining whether a business operator has abused IPRs to eliminate or restrict competition. Article 16 lists factors which shall be taken into consideration by SAIC in analysing and determining the impact on competition by exercise of IPRs.

[53] The final version of the *SAIC IPRs Provisions* deleted Article 14 of its *Draft for Comments (promulgated on 11 June 2014, and the solicitation period lasted until 10 July 2014)*, which is about actions forbidden to be taken by the collective management organization of copyright.

duties is to review anti-competitive agreement and abuse of market position unrelated to price, they could still offer reference in practice more or less.

Through nineteen articles, the *SAIC IPRs Provisions* cover both conventionally monopolistic issues (such as anti-competitive agreements and abuse of market position) and innovative theories/policies (such as 'safe-harbour provisions',[54] essential facility[55], patent pool,[56] and standard patent[57]). Of note is that phrases such as 'eliminate or restrict competition' are everywhere, reflecting the enforcer's emphasis on anti-competitive conducts' effect on the market during the investigation and enforcement.

Article 4 of the *SAIC IPRs Provisions* rephrases general principles and exceptions concerning anti-competitive agreement stipulated in Articles 13,[58] 14,[59] and 15[60]

---

[54] Article 5 of the *SAIC IPRs Provisions*.
[55] Article 7 of the *SAIC IPRs Provisions*.
[56] Article 12 of the *SAIC IPRs Provisions*.
[57] Article 13 of the *SAIC IPRs Provisions*.
[58] Article 13 of the AML, 'Competing undertakings are prohibited from concluding the following monopoly agreements:

(1) on fixing or changing commodity prices;
(2) on restricting the amount of commodities manufactured or marketed;
(3) on splitting the sales market or the purchasing market for raw and semi-finished materials;
(4) on restricting the purchase of new technologies or equipment, or the development of new technologies or products;
(5) on joint boycotting of transactions; and
(6) other monopoly agreements confirmed as such by the authority for enforcement of the Anti-Monopoly Law under the State Council.

For the purposes of this Law, monopoly agreements include agreements, decisions and other concerted conducts designed to eliminate or restrict competition.'
[59] Article 14 of the AML, 'Undertakings are prohibited from concluding the following monopoly agreements with their trading counterparts:

(1) on fixing the prices of commodities resold to a third party;
(2) on restricting the lowest prices for commodities resold to a third party; and
(3) other monopoly agreements confirmed as such by the authority for enforcement of the Anti-Monopoly Law under the State Council.'

[60] Article 15 of the AML, 'The provisions of Articles 13 and 14 of this law shall not be applicable to the agreements between undertakings which they can prove to be concluded for one of the following purposes:

(1) improving technologies, or engaging in research and development of new products; or
(2) improving product quality, reducing cost, and enhancing efficiency, unifying specifications and standards of products, or implementing specialized division of production;
(3) increasing the efficiency and competitiveness of small and medium-sized undertakings;
(4) serving public interests in energy conservation, environmental protection and disaster relief;
(5) mitigating sharp decrease in sales volumes or obvious overproduction caused by economic depression;

of the AML. Articles 13.1.1–13.1.5 and 14.1–14.2 enumerate the most obviously illegal anti-competitive conducts, namely the horizontal and vertical monopoly agreements. When defending themselves according to Article 15, business operators should also prove that agreements shall not restrict the competition in the relevant market substantially and would enable consumers to share benefits derived therefrom.

The 'safe-harbour' mentioned in Article 5 of the *SAIC IPRs Provisions* is a huge step further on the basis of Article 15 of the AML. It stipulates monopolistic conducts under Article 13.1.6 ('other anti-competitive agreements between competing undertakings confirmed as such by the authority for enforcement of the AML under the State Council') and Article 14.3 ('other anti-competitive agreements between non-competing undertakings confirmed as such by the authority for enforcement of the AML under the State Council') of the AML. It means that all those situations expressly listed in black and white in Articles 13.1.1–13.1.5 and 14.1–14.2 of the AML are not eligible for 'safe-harbour'. Article 5 separates particular kinds of anti-competitive agreements from those ones illegal per se under certain conditions. Where the combined market share of two competing business operators is not more than 20 per cent in the relevant market that is affected by the exercise of IPRs, or there exist at least four alternative technologies on the relevant market that are accessible at reasonable costs and are under independent control; or where the combined market share of two non-competing business operators is not more than 30 per cent on the relevant market, or there exist at least two alternative technologies on the relevant market that are accessible at reasonable costs and are under independent control, Articles 13 and 14 of the AML do not apply. SAIC learns a lot from the relevant experience of the US and EU. It is a historic step forward in theory, of course. However, problems such as how to define the 'relevant market', 'alternative technologies accessible at reasonable costs and under independent control' etc are to be interpreted in practice. Legislation develops together with the social development. We have every reason to believe that SAIC would give out satisfying answers sooner or later, to provide a more improved instruction.

---

(6) safeguarding legitimate interests in foreign trade and economic cooperation with foreign counterparts; or

(7) other purposes as prescribed by law or the State Council.

In the cases as specified in Subparagraphs (1) through (5) of the preceding paragraph, where the provisions of Articles 13 and 14 of this Law are not applicable, the undertakings shall, in addition, prove that the agreements reached will not substantially restrict competition in the relevant market and that they can enable the consumers to share the benefits derived therefrom.'

3.3 Proposed guidelines

Though SAIC has promulgated and implemented the *SAIC IPRs Provisions* mentioned above, they cannot replace guidelines against abuse of IPRs to eliminate or restrict competition. On the one hand, acting as a ministerial regulation, *SAIC IPRs Provisions* could only be applied by SAIC during its own enforcement, not by NDRC or MOFCOM at all. On the other hand, due to legislative limitation and style, this regulation could only cover limited issues, and a lot more could not be regulated very well.[61] As such, it has been argued for a certain time that a wide guideline to regulate IP and antirust should be prepared by the Anti-monopoly Commission under the State Council (the 'AMC').

Actually, under the AML, the AMC is in charge of organizing, coordinating, and guiding anti-monopoly work and to perform duties, including but not limited to formulating and releasing anti-monopoly guidelines,[62] which could be relied on by all the three antitrust enforcement authorities. Acting as a coordinating organization, the AMC is not in charge of drafting guidelines itself. Instead, NDRC, SAIC (as early as 2009), MOFCOM, and the State Intellectual Property Office has initiated drafting guidelines against abuse of IPRs to eliminate or restrict competition under the direction of the AMC. The official version of the guidelines was due to be published by the end of 2016 on the basis of draft guidelines mentioned above. Until now, SAIC and NDRC have released their own drafts for the guidelines respectively.

3.3.1 Draft of SAIC IPRs guidelines

The 7th Draft of the *Guidelines for Anti-Monopoly Enforcement against Abuse of IPRs* ('*Draft of SAIC IPRs Guidelines*') was published by SAIC on 4 February 2016 to solicit public comments until 23 February 2016.[63]

Consisting of thirty-two articles in seven chapters, the *Draft of SAIC IPRs Guidelines* specifies basic principles for anti-monopoly law enforcement in the field of IPRs, and gives the prompt that 'the market position of the operator and the counterparty' and another eight factors could be considered in analysing and determining the influence of IPRs exercise by an operator on competition. Also, the guidelines

---

[61] Article 80(2) of the *Legislation Law*, 'Matters prescribed by department rules shall be matters for the application of laws or the administrative regulations, decisions, or orders of the State Council. Without the bases prescribed by laws or the administrative regulations, decisions or orders of the State Council, department rules shall not contain provisions that reduce the rights or increase the obligations of citizens, legal persons and other organizations, and shall not contain provisions that enhance the power or reduce the statutory duties of the department concerned.'

[62] Article 9 of the AML.

[63] *Guidelines for Anti-Monopoly Enforcement against Abuse of IPRs (7th Draft of SAIC) Issued to Solicit Public Comments*, available at <http://home.saic.gov.cn/fldyfbzdjz/gzdt/201602/t20160204_205344.html>, accessed 9 October 2018.

explain the definition of relevant market, IPRs-related monopoly agreement, IPR-related abuse of market dominance, and some specific issues (anti-monopoly analysis about standard setting, patent pool, and conduct of copyright collective management organization) in detail. In addition, the guidelines emphasize that where an operator is deemed to have abused IPRs, resulting in the elimination or restriction of competition, the competent antitrust enforcement authorities shall investigate the legal liability against the operator in accordance with the AML.

The *Draft of SAIC IPRs Guidelines* put agreements concerning IPRs between competing undertakings and non-competing undertakings within the same chapter. After giving the general principles, Chapter 3 firstly lists restriction provisions in agreement between competing undertakings that might eliminate or restrict competition, including price, output, R&D restriction, market division, and collective boycott. As for exclusive grant-back, it could be reached between both competing and non-competing undertakings, while the former one would bring more harm to competition. Price, geography, and consumer restriction in agreements between non-competing undertakings are forbidden under the *Draft of SAIC IPRs Guidelines*. The 'Safe Harbour' principle here is totally the same with that in the *SAIC IPRs Provisions*.

3.3.2 Draft of NDRC IPRs guidelines

3.3.2.1 Background During a press conference about price reform and supervision of NDRC held on 5 November 2015,[64] investigator (Mr. Dong Zhiming) of the Price Supervision Inspection and Anti-Monopoly Bureau ('PSIAMB') indicated that NDRC would race against time to promote research, draft, and promulgate six sets of guidelines, including those for prohibition against abuse of IPRs to eliminate or restrict competition, auto industry, leniency system, operator commitment, calculation of illegal income and fine, and exemption procedure for monopoly agreements. For the moment, laws, administrative statutes, and rules compatible with the AML are not well-developed, which do not meet the requirement of anti-monopoly enforcement. In order to clarify guiding rules concerning the anti-monopoly system further, provide market players with clearer reasonable expectation, and improve transparency of anti-monopoly enforcement, NDRC is studying relevant anti-monopoly guidelines under the direction of the AMC. Until now, all the six draft guidelines have been released.

3.3.2.2 General introduction On 31 December 2015, the *Anti-Monopoly Guidelines for Abuse of Intellectual Property Rights (Draft for Comments)* ('*Draft of*

---

[64] 'NDRC holds press conference for work of price reform and supervision', available at <http://www.scio.gov.cn/xwfbh/gbwxwfbh/xwfbh/fzggw/Document/1453975/1453975.htm>, accessed 30 May 2016.

NDRC IPRs Guidelines') were released to solicit public comments from 1 January 2016 to 20 January 2016.[65] The *Draft of NDRC IPRs Guidelines* is composed of the preface and three main parts. After providing the basic concepts, each part enumerates IPRs related conducts which are legal generally, but may be determined to be illegal if they would eliminate or restrict competition.

The preface reiterates the fundamental role played by Article 55 of the AML in reviewing the exercise of IPRs. The AML does not apply to the exercise of IPRs subject to IPRs-related laws and regulations, but applies to abuse of IPRs to eliminate or restrict competition. For the main body of the *Draft of NDRC IPRs Guidelines*, the first part is about basic issues. It stipulates principles of law enforcement, definition of relevant market, and the general analysis approach. As for principles of law enforcement, antitrust authorities should treat IPRs the same as other properties under the basic frame of the AML while specific characteristics of IPRs should be taken into consideration. An undertaking cannot be directly presumed to have dominant market position only because of its ownership of IPRs. Principles of fairness and transparency should be followed during the case-by-case analysis. The second and third parts of the *Draft of NDRC IPRs Guidelines* are about IPRs agreements that may eliminate or restrict competition and abuse a dominant market position involving IPRs respectively.

3.3.2.3 Analyses in detail For the first time, the *Draft of NDRC IPRs Guidelines* list explicit provisions often found in IPRs licensing agreement from all perspectives. Certain kinds of abuse of IPRs are stipulated under provisions of agreements concluded by competing undertakings and non-competing undertakings respectively. It does not mean that only these would appear in the former while those could only be found in the latter. Any IP licensing agreement could include such provisions, while the relationship between undertakings should be paid due attention.

Structure of the second part is similar to that of the AML (Article 13 for competing undertakings and Article 14 for non-competing undertakings). Generally speaking, IPRs agreement between competing undertakings is more likely to eliminate or restrict competition than that between non-competing undertakings. In judging whether a competing relationship between undertakings exists, exercise of IPRs by the parties before and after the agreement come into effect in the relevant market should both be analysed. Regarding IPRs agreements between competing undertakings, the *Draft of NDRC IPRs Guidelines* combines Articles 13.1.1–13.1.5 of the AML. This part covers IPRs agreement of joint

---

[65] *Anti-Monopoly Guidelines for Abuse of Intellectual Property Rights (Draft for Comments) Issued to Solicit Public Comments*, available at <http://jjs.ndrc.gov.cn/fjgld/201512/t20151231_770233.html>, accessed 30 May 2016.

R&D,[66] patent pool,[67] cross-licence,[68] or standard setting[69] between competing undertakings that might be recognized as would eliminate or restrict competition, though normally, these arrangements could save R&D costs, improve efficiency, promote innovation and competition. Besides giving definition of arrangements mentioned above, the draft guidelines also list elements that could be considered when coming out with the final decision. For example, if the cross-licensing is exclusive, and constitutes market entry barriers to a third party or impedes competition in the relevant downstream product market, then it might be recognized as likely to eliminate or restrict competition. To take standards setting as another example, if it could exclude other certain undertakings or relevant proposal of particular undertakings, then competition may probably be restricted. In addition, IPRs agreements between non-competing undertakings could also include these arrangements, and criteria mentioned above applies too. What's worth mentioning is that the 'non-competing relationship' element should be given enough attention.

Taken together with Articles 14.1–14.2 of the AML, IPRs agreement with grant-back,[70] non-challenge,[71] and other restriction provisions[72] between non-competing undertakings might be thought of eliminating or restricting competition, though sometimes they could also bring benefits. As for grant-back, what's prohibited is that the licensor or a certain third party appointed by the licensor could exercise technology improved by the licensee exclusively. Non-challenge provision prohibits the counterparty from challenging the validity of IPRs so as to avoid vexatious litigation and increase efficiency. But if the non-challenge provision requires all the licensees not to question the validity of IPRs, restricts exercise of other competitive

---

[66] Article II.A of the *Draft of NDRC IPRs Guidelines*, 'Joint research and development means that two or more undertakings jointly research and develop technology or products.'

[67] Ibid, 'Patent pool refers that two or more patentees jointly license their respective IPRs to others. Patent pool takes such forms as establishing dedicated company, entrusting certain member to manage or entrusting an independent third party to manage.'

[68] Ibid, 'Cross-licensing means that undertakings license their respective IPRs to each other.'

[69] Ibid, 'Standard setting means that undertakings jointly set the standards involving IPRs uniformly implemented in certain scope.'

[70] Article II.B of the *Draft of NDRC IPRs Guidelines*, 'Grant-back means that the licensees grant the follow-up improvements made upon the licensed IPRs or new fruits generated by using the licensed IPRs to the licensors. Exclusive grant-back means that only the licensors have the right to implement the improvement or new fruits granted back by the licensees.'

[71] Ibid, 'Under non-challenge clause, the licensors require the licensees not to challenge the validity of licensors' IPRs.'

[72] Ibid, IPRs agreements concluded by undertakings without a competing relationship may include clauses 1, restricting the licensees to use IPRs within a specific field; 2, restricting distribution channels, scope of distribution, or trading counterparts of products provided by the licensees through using the IPRs; 3, restricting volume of product produced or sold by using the IPRs; or 4, prohibiting the licensees from obtaining license or using competing IPRs from a third party, or prohibiting the licensees from producing or selling products which are competitive to products of the licensors.

IPRs, etc., then it may eliminate or restrict competition. The other restriction provisions, such as the restrictions on licensees to apply IPRs within certain fields through particular distribution channels only, are also very common in IPRs area. However, the content, degree, mode of exclusion, characters of product using IPRs and other criteria should also be on the schedule of investigation of the antitrust authorities. Price-fixing and restricting the minimum price of products for resale to a third party are regarded as illegal per se in China, as long as the agreements do not fall within Article 15 of the AML. Furthermore, if all the arrangements mentioned in this part meet the requirements in Articles 13.1.1–13.1.5 (for agreement between competing undertakings), they might also be prohibited.

The *Draft of NDRC IPRs Guidelines* is also equipped with its own 'safe harbour' principle. Though certain types of agreements are in principle exempted under Article 15 of the AML, case-by-case analysis is still needed to determine, unlike the 'safe-harbour' principle, exempting certain sets of agreement between undertakings meeting particular thresholds. IPRs agreements (such as IP licensing agreement) concluded by undertakings with relatively low market share usually do not severely eliminate or restrict competition. In order to increase efficiency of anti-monopoly enforcement and provide undertakings with a clear expectation, IPRs agreements could be presumed to be exempted under Article 15 of the AML if a) the combined market share of competing undertakings in the relevant market does not exceed 15 per cent; or b) the combined market share of non-undertakings in any relevant market involved in the agreements does not exceed 25 per cent. Similar to the 'safe harbour' in the *SAIC IPRs Provisions* (Article 5), agreements expressly stipulated in Articles 13.1.1–13.1.5 and 14.1–14.2 and those concerning price restriction are not eligible for the exemption.

3.3.2.4 Differences from the draft of SAIC IPRs guidelines It is worth mentioning that the safe harbour thresholds proposed in the *Draft of NDRC IPRs Guidelines* (15 per cent for competing undertakings and 25 per cent for non-competing undertakings) are lower than those in the *SAIC IPRs Provisions* (20 per cent for competing undertakings and 30 per cent for non-competing undertakings), which will no doubt bring great discussions by the public. In practice, one of the technical issues about market share standard is its calculation, especially in the relevant technology market. Should antitrust enforcement authorities take the average market share of undertakings concerned during a particular period as reference? When calculating market share in the relevant technology market of products involving IPRs, should volume of production or turnover act as the foundations? More questions still need to be answered in practice. It is a good example of a transplant from other legal systems, such as the 'safe harbour' in the US and EU.

Moreover, under the *SAIC IPRs Provisions*, if there exist at least four alternative technologies on the relevant market that are accessible at reasonable costs and are under independent control for agreements between competing undertakings, or at least two alternative technologies on the relevant market that are accessible at reasonable costs and are under independent control for agreements between non-competing undertakings, the 'safe harbour' principle could also apply. However, the *Draft of NDRC IPRs Guidelines* does not refer to alternative technologies. It is noteworthy that, only when the review of the effect on technology competition or R&D is required, market data is not accessible or market data could not reflect the importance of competition accurately, the alternative technology will apply under the *US Antitrust Guidelines for the Licensing of Intellectual Property*. There is not any similar limitation in the *SAIC IPRs Provisions*, not to mention the total lack of provisions of alternative technology in the *Draft of NDRC IPRs Guidelines*. One more thing, the 'safe harbour' in China only applies to anti-competitive agreements or conspiracy concerning abuse of IPRs, instead of anti-competitive agreements or conspiracy in general.

3.3.3 Draft of exemption guidelines

On 12 May 2016, NDRC released the *Guidelines on General Conditions and Procedures for the Exemption of Anti-Competitive Agreements (Draft for Comment)* (*'Draft of Exemption Guidelines'*) to solicit public comments until 1 June 2016.[73] It is the first time that Chinese antitrust enforcement authorities have implemented official working guidelines for case-by-case exemption. The *Draft of Exemption Guidelines* clarifies general conditions and procedure for anti-competitive agreement exemption based on Article 15 of the AML.

The *Draft of Exemption Guidelines* defines 'exemption application' and 'exemption consultation' respectively. 'Exemption application' refers to applications filed by undertakings after antitrust enforcement authorities have initiated investigation, while 'exemption consultation' means consultations made by undertakings to the authorities as regards whether agreements to be entered into by undertakings or industry association meet the exemption situations listed in Article 15 of the AML.[74] Generally speaking, it is up to undertakings and industry associations to decide whether agreements to be concluded satisfy the exemption conditions in Article 15 of the AML, and to decide all by themselves whether to initiate exemption application or consultation to antitrust enforcement authorities. Normally speaking, antitrust enforcement authorities would not communicate with undertakings or industry associations concerning such questions. However, there are two circumstances where antitrust enforcement authorities will accept exemption consultation

---

[73] *Guidelines on General Conditions and Procedures for the Exemption of Anti-Competitive Agreements (Draft for Comment)* Issued to Solicit Public Comments, available at <http://www.ndrc.gov.cn/gzdt/201605/t20160512_801562.html#rd?sukey=3903d1d3b699c208abbb713d238ffba03f3c173c8506c366b1dace5a669660e63fd85a879d78a149ee7da3a6e5448fa1>, accessed 25 May 2016.
[74] Article 2 of *Draft of Exemption Guidelines*.

about an agreement to be entered. Firstly, the agreement might have influences on several countries or regions, including China. Furthermore, the relevant undertaking or industry association decides to apply for exemption in other jurisdictions. Secondly, the national industry association would like to consult with the antitrust enforcement authorities for agreement with universality and significance in the name of the whole industry. Undertakings and industry associations having entered into agreement are presumed to have already decided by themselves as regards whether the agreement meets the provisions of the AML. Antitrust enforcement authorities will not accept exemption consultation after conclusion of an agreement and before initiation of an investigation.[75]

3.4 Standard essential patents

3.4.1 General introduction

When talking about IP licensing nowadays, one can never bypass standard essential patents ('SEPs'). Standard setting is the process of determining a common set of characteristics for goods or services.[76] Or to put it more formally:

> technical regulations and standards set out specific characteristics of a product— such as its size, shape, design, functions and performance, or the way it is labeled or packaged before it is put on sale. In certain cases, the way a product is produced can affect these characteristics, and it may then prove more appropriate to draft technical regulations and standards in terms of a product's process and production methods rather than its characteristics per se.[77]

Standardization of technology could promote compatibility and connectivity of products manufacture by differentiated manufacturers so as to decrease costs, upgrade efficiency, and promote continuous innovation.

In order to obtain a competitive advantage, undertakings participating in standard setting often choose to apply for patents with their own technologies. After being involved in the standard, relevant patent technologies would become SEPs. SEPs refer to essential and irreplaceable patents included in technology standard, or patents that have to be applied for implementation of technical standard. Technology standardization could reduce production costs, promote innovation, provide consumers with more choices, and remove international trade barriers brought by technology disparity. If a technological standard has been widely used so as to become the industrial standard or compulsory national standard, keeping products

---

[75] Article 3 of *Draft of Exemption Guidelines*.

[76] OECD Policy Roundtables—Standard Setting 2010, available at <http://www.oecd.org/daf/competition/47381304.pdf> p19, accessed 24 May 2016.

[77] See 'Technical Information on Technical barriers to trade', available at https://www.wto.org/english/tratop_e/tbt_e/tbt_info_e.htm, accessed on 24 May 2016.

and services below the standard out of the market, then the technical standard is compulsory requirement for undertakings.

For economic reasons, proprietors might raise royalties unreasonably or eliminate competitors in the industry through the foreclosure effect of his or her SEPs.[78] Since implementation of the AML, there have been several cases concerning SEPs, most of which were about abuse of market dominance. In most of the foreign legal regimes, a patent grants its investor an exclusive right to use the covered technology, and a standard-setting organization generally must obtain permission from the proprietor to include a patented technology in its standard. So, it will often request a proprietor to clarify its willingness to license its SEPs on fair, reasonable, and non-discriminatory terms ('FRAND'). If the proprietor refuses to accept FRAND terms, then the standard setting organization must exclude that technology out of the standard. Or put another way, the FRAND commitment serves to harmonize the private interests of proprietors and the public interests of standard-setting organizations.[79]

3.4.2 Situations in China

In China, it is the department of standardization administration under the State Council who is in charge of the unified administration of standardization throughout the country. National standards shall be formulated by the department of standardization administration under the State Council. Where, in the absence of national standards, technical requirements for a certain industry need to be unified, industry standards may be formulated. Industry standards shall be formulated by competent administrative authorities under the State Council. In the absence of both national and industry standards, safety and sanitary requirements for industrial products need to be unified within a province, an autonomous region or a municipality directly under the central government, local standards may be formulated by departments of standardization administration from respective level.[80] Moreover, for many industries all over the world, the majority of essential standards are set by standard setting organizations through cooperation, such as the International Telecommunication Union.

As early as 2012, the SPC released a judicial policy, namely the *Opinions on Giving Full Play to Functions of the Trial so as to Provide Judicial Protection to*

---

[78] Wang Xiaoye, 'Research on Anti-Monopoly Litigation of SEPs', China Legal Science (June 2015).

[79] See https://en.wikipedia.org/wiki/Reasonable_and_non-discriminatory_licensing, accessed 25 May 2016.

[80] Article 6 of the *Standardization Law of the People's Republic of China* ('*Standardization Law*', promulgated on 29 December 1988, and came into effect on 1 April 1989). What's more, the General Administration of Quality Supervision, Inspection and Quarantine ('AQSIQ') had revised the current *Standardization Law*, drafted an Amendment (*Draft for Review*), and submitted it to

Deep Reform of Science and Technology System and Speedy National System Construction.[81] Point 2(7) mentions that, as for patent patent infringement litigation concerning national, industrial, or local standard, courts should judge parties' legal liabilities reasonably on foundation of FRAND principle, combining industrial characteristics, standard nature, setting procedure etc., so as to promote the perfection of pre-disclosure of patent information, payment of royalties, and other standard setting procedures and rules. Article 24 of the *Interpretations (II) of the Supreme People's Court on Several Issues Concerning the Application of Law in the Trial of Cases Involving Patent Infringement Disputes* released on 21 March 2016 (effective date: 1 April 2016) also mentions FRAND terms. It is the first time China has expressed its attitude towards FRAND in the form of judicial interpretation. Firstly, the implementation of a patent belonging to a recommended national, industrial, or local standards should have a licence from the licensor as the pre-condition. Secondly, during the negotiation of terms of a licensing agreement, the licensor should respect FRAND principle, failure of which would deprive the licensor's right to require the licensee to cease the exploitation of the standards, if IP licensing contract cannot be concluded and the alleged infringer has no obvious fault in the negotiation. Last but not least, if the patentee and the alleged infringer cannot reach consensus on licensing and exploitation conditions, they could require the court to determine, during which FRAND principle should be respected. Furthermore, the court should also take into comprehensive consideration of the degree of innovation of the patent, the role the patent plays in relevant standards, the technical field to which the standards belong, the nature and scope of application of the standards, relevant licensing conditions, and other factors.

---

the State Council. The Legislative Affairs Office of the State Council studied and revised, in concert with the AQSIQ and the Standardization Administration of China, the *Draft for Review* and released the *Standardization Law of the People's Republic of China (Draft Revision for Comment)* (the 'Draft for Comment') for public comments on 22 March 2016 until 21 April 2016. The *Draft for Comment* clarifies that national standards shall be formulated for technical and administrative requirements that need to be unified nationwide. National standards shall be classified into compulsory standards and voluntary standards. Compulsory national standards shall be formulated for technical and administrative requirements that need to be unified to secure personal health and life and property security, state security, and ecological environment safety and meet the basic requirements for social and economic administration. Voluntary national standards shall be formulated by the competent administrative department for standardization under the State Council. Article 17(2) of the *Draft for Comment* stipulates that the use of standards for engaging in illegal activities such as imposing industry barriers, setting up regional blockades, engaging in unfair competition, etc. shall be prohibited.

[81] *Opinions on Giving Full Play to Functions of the Trial so as to Provide Judicial Protection to Deep Reform of Science and Technology System and Speedy National System Construction*, available at <http://www.court.gov.cn/zixun-xiangqing-4825.html>, accessed 25 May 2016.

3.5 Practice

Until now, IPRs guidelines are only at the draft stage to solicit public opinions, which have not yet come into effect. Almost all of the high-profile cases relate to abuse of dominant market position[82] or concentration of undertaking[83] concerning SEPs, instead of anti-competitive agreement, or maybe some of which have already been under investigation. Parties to SEPs licensing and exploitation agreement should respect FRAND commitment so as to get ready from the first step and better protect their SEPs if tort litigation were brought.

4. Conclusion and Looking Forward

Before the promulgation of the AML, parties to IP licensing agreements mainly counted on certain provisions of the *Contract Law*, the *Foreign Trade Law* etc. to restrict or prohibit abuse of IPRs. All those laws were enacted to achieve their own goals respectively instead of maintaining the competition order. Undertakings usually sought for invalidity of IP licensing agreement, though invalidity of anti-competitive provisions would not affect the validity of the other provisions generally. Only limited remedies were offered, making it difficult for a party to IP licensing agreement to protect his or her legal rights and interests.

The AML was the first Chinese law stipulating three traditional anti-competitive conducts, which are monopoly agreement, abuse of market dominance, and concentration of undertakings which have or will be likely to have the effect of restricting or eliminating competition. The AML does not apply to the proper practice of IPRs according to relevant laws and regulations, but does prohibit abuse of IPRs which eliminates or restricts competition.[84] Article 55 is only a general provision, reflecting the principal attitude of the legislator in this regards. It leaves great discretion to courts and antitrust enforcement authorities when deciding whether IP licensing, constituting abuse of IPRs, would be prohibited according to Articles 13 or 14 of the AML.

---

[82] Such as *Huawei v InterDigital* judged by Guangdong High People's Court, available at www.gdcourts.gov.cn/gdcourt/front/front!content.action?lmdm=LM41&gjid=20140417024309113155, accessed 26 May 2016 and the Qualcomm Case decided by NDRC, available at http://jjs.ndrc.gov.cn/fjgld/201503/t20150302_666170.html, accessed 25 May 2015.

[83] Such as MOFCOM's conditional clearance of Microsoft's acquisition of Nokia's Devices and Services Business available at http://fldj.mofcom.gov.cn/article/ztxx/201404/20140400542415.shtml, accessed 26 May 2016, Merck KGaA's acquisition of AZ Electronic Materials S.A., available at http://fldj.mofcom.gov.cn/article/ztxx/201404/20140400569060.shtml, accessed 26 May 2016, and Nokia's proposed acquisition of 100 per cent stock of Alcatel-Lucent, available at http://fldj.mofcom.gov.cn/article/ztxx/201510/20151001139743.shtml, accessed 25 May 2016.

[84] Article 55 of the AML.

Through summarizing experience, SAIC released the first IPRs provisions in 2015 among the three Chinese antitrust enforcement authorities to fill up loopholes left by Article 55 of the AML. Though only acting as working rules, the *SAIC IPRs Provisions* could provide some reference to NDRC and MOFCOM. The *SAIC IPRs Provisions* introduce essential facilities and 'safe harbour' principle for the first time. In order to provide a legal basis from upper level, both NDRC and SAIC have published draft of guidelines against abuse of IPRs as the first step under the direction of the AMC. Through combining the AML, recent cases concerning the most recent development of IPRs (including but not limited to joint R&D, patent pool, cross-licensing, standard-setting, grant-back, non-challenge clauses) and experience learned from the US and EU, IPRs guidelines of both SAIC and NDRC aim at targeting at the classic abuse of IPRs which eliminate or restrict competition. Until now, we do have several high-profile cases concerning SEPs in areas of concentration of undertakings and abuse of market dominance. In those cases, courts and antitrust enforcement authorities requested relevant undertakings to abide by FRAND principles during the SEPs licensing. With more and more undertakings becoming giant licensors of IPRs (especially patents), such as today's Huawei, China will become better developed in both legislation and enforcement in the intersection between anti-competitive agreement and IP licensing.

10

ABUSE OF DOMINANCE AND INTELLECTUAL PROPERTY IN CHINA

Fay Zhou, Anna Mitchell, and Xi Liao

The interface between antitrust and intellectual property (hereafter IP) is a complex topic, which has been heavily debated amongst practitioners and industry participants across jurisdictions.

Antitrust law seeks to promote consumer welfare by lowering barriers to entry and prohibiting certain actions which may harm competition, with respect to either existing or new ways of serving consumers. Indeed, the ultimate objective of competition law is to ensure unfettered competition in the market. The prohibitions against an abuse of a dominant market position seek to ensure this objective is achieved.

IP law, on the other hand, grants technology owners a monopoly to reward them for the development of, and investment in, the relevant technology and to incentivize further innovation. In particular, an IP right (like other property rights) confers exclusive rights on the holder, giving the holder the ability to exclude others from using that property, and allowing the holder of the IP right to appropriate the value of the property for himself. This is essential to encourage investment in products as, in the absence of such IP rights, rapid imitation of products would chill innovation, ultimately to the detriment of consumers.

The interplay between these two concepts presents complex, and often novel, legal, and policy questions, which require a balancing act between the incentives of the IP holder, and the prohibitions provided for in competition law. In particular, it is widely recognized that antitrust enforcement in relation to IP should be limited, focusing primarily on conducts and transactions capable of lessening competition amongst rival technologies. If it is not limited in this way, antitrust law may interfere with the principal goals of IP rights. For example, attempts to restrain licensing fees for fear of them being 'excessive' and therefore amounting to an abuse of a dominant position, in the short term, can undermine incentives to invest in the longer term. Such incentives to invest are key as, without receiving a reward for risky and costly investments, investors would not take the time, and spend the necessary resources, investing in new products. Innovation would slow down as a result and this, in turn, would ultimately lead to a decline in economic growth.

As a result of this ostensible tension between the two regimes, the traditionally-held view in Europe and the United States was that IP rights and competition law were incompatible.[1] However, the regimes share the common purpose of promoting innovation and enhancing consumer welfare and, as such, nowadays, they are more often viewed as complementary instruments, which can be used to enhance competition overall.

China is still a comparatively new player in the antitrust world but it has grown quickly and it is currently one of the most important emerging jurisdictions for antitrust enforcement. Recent enforcement of China's Anti-Monopoly Law (hereafter AML), particularly the rules against the abuse of a dominant market position, has started to intersect with IP law, bringing the interplay between IP law and antitrust law fully into the purview of the Chinese authorities. Intensifying enforcement action in China over recent years suggests that IP-centred, or related, business models and practices will face growing antitrust scrutiny over the next few years. However, due to a lack of clear guidance as to when conduct in the IP sector will breach the AML, entities currently do not have sufficient comfort that their practices are permissible under antitrust laws. Against this background, guidelines being drafted by the regulators that enforce the AML are a welcome step towards clarity and predictability and will assist entities in understanding the interplay between IP and antitrust in China going forwards. Once finalized, the guidelines will have far-reaching implications, as they will apply to the enforcement of all of China's competition authorities. They are also likely to be useful reference materials for courts presiding over private actions for damages.

This chapter seeks to review the developments in relation to an abuse of a dominant market position in the IP-space in recent years and to explore the issues calling for the detailed guidance between the IP and competition law regimes. Section 1 sets out the current rules on abuse of dominance under the AML; Section 2 describes the legislative framework in China for assessing an abuse of dominance in an IP context; Section 3 summarizes the key enforcement cases and private actions that relate to an abuse of dominance in the IP sector in China; Section 4 highlights the influence the enforcement actions and cases have had on the shaping of the IP-guidelines being drafted by the Chinese authorities; Section 5 discusses

---

[1] See, for example, 'Antitrust Enforcement and Intellectual Property Rights: Promoting Innovation and Competition' (United States Department of Justice and Federal Trade Commission Report, 2007).

how specific abuses of a dominant position are assessed in an IP-context under the guidelines and the case law; and Section 6 draws some conclusions.

1. Abuse of Dominance under the AML

Abuse of dominance is one of the cornerstones of competition law. It targets the unilateral conduct of dominant firms, which act in an abusive manner that restricts competition. As such, the focus is on the notion of a dominant undertaking, which has a special responsibility not to abuse its position of power.

1.1 Market definition

The typical starting point for assessing whether an undertaking is dominant is a definition of the relevant market in which the entity operates. Similar to many other regimes, including in Europe and the United States, 'relevant market' is defined under the AML as the product market and geographic market within which undertakings compete against each other during a certain period of time, with respect to specific products or services.[2] The relevant product market comprises all products of the same group or category which are regarded as close substitutes by customers, by reason of the products' characteristics, their intended use, and prices. The geographic market is defined by an area where customers procure closely substitutable products.

Relevant markets are primarily assessed based on demand-side substitutability (i.e. whether products are substitutable from a demand-side perspective), and, to a lesser extent, supply-side substitutability. The higher the degree of demand-side substitutability, the more likely it is that two products belong to the same relevant market. Similarly, if a supplier can switch production from one product to another within a short period of time without incurring significant investment costs, those products may form part of a single relevant market. When defining the relevant product market and geographic market, a number of factors need to be considered. For example, a product's overall features and end-uses, price, channels through which it is sold, etc. will be relevant in determining the product market and factors such as transportation costs, distribution networks, obstacles to cross-border trade, etc. will be taken into account when determining the geographic market.[3] When the market scope is unclear or cannot be easily ascertained, a hypothetical monopolist test can be applied to define the relevant market instead.[4]

---

[2] Article 12 AML [2008] (hereinafter AML).

[3] Anti-Monopoly Committee of State Council, 'Guidelines on the Definition of Relevant Market' (2009), Articles 8 and 9.

[4] Anti-Monopoly Committee of State Council, 'Guidelines on the Definition of Relevant Market' (2009), Article 7. This test provides that a market should be defined as the smallest set of products over which a hypothetical monopolist would need to have control in order to be able to

In an IP context, the market definition is even more complex, because, in addition to the general market definition principles which seek to define the relevant product and geographic markets, principles in relation to 'technology markets'[5] and 'innovation markets'[6] may also be relevant to the assessment of the relevant market. When defining 'innovation markets' and 'technological markets', it is still relevant to consider the product and geographic markets but industry-specific dynamics, such as the high rate of innovation, may also need to be taken into account.

1.2 Dominant position

Once the relevant market has been identified, it is necessary to determine whether an entity holds a dominant position on the relevant market.

Under the AML, a dominant undertaking is defined as being an entity capable of controlling the price or quantity of products or services or other trading terms in the relevant market or restricting or affecting other undertakings' entry into the relevant market.[7]

Several factors must be taken into consideration in order to evaluate whether a company can be classified as a dominant undertaking pursuant to this definition. For the purpose of the AML, these factors include: (1) the market shares of the relevant company and competition in the relevant market;[8] (2) whether the relevant undertaking has the ability to control the market; (3) the financial and technical capabilities of the company; (4) whether other companies are dependent on the allegedly dominant company; (5) the presence of barriers to entry; and (6) other factors relevant to the determination of a dominant market position.[9] The draft

---

profitably sustain prices by a small but significant amount (generally taken to be between 5 per cent to 10 per cent). In other words, a market is the smallest set of goods or services that is worth monopolising. This is similar to tests used in other regimes, such as Europe, the United States, and the United Kingdom.

[5] Comprising of the relevant technology and alternative technologies (see, for example, Anti-Monopoly Committee of State Council, 'Guidelines on the Definition of Relevant Market' (2009), Article 3).

[6] The market in which companies compete in the research and development of future new technologies or products.

[7] Article 17(2) AML. This is similar to the European concept of determining dominance for the purpose of Article 102 of the Consolidated version of the Treaty of the Functioning of the European Union [2012 C 326/47] (hereafter TFEU). In *United Brands v Commission*, the European Court of Justice laid out the test for determining a dominant position, noting that it is 'a position of economic strength enjoyed by an undertaking which enables it to prevent effective competition being maintained on the relevant market by affording it the power to behave to an appreciable extent independently of its competitors, customers and ultimately consumers' (Case C- 27/76 [1978] ECR 207).

[8] In an IP context, since technology and innovation markets are more susceptible to changes in technological developments, market shares may be less indicative of market power, depending on the individual case and the stage of technological development.

[9] Article 18 AML. Again, the factors are similar to an assessment of dominance in Europe, where the European Commission has said in its Guidance on the Commission's enforcement priorities in

guidelines relating to the application of the AML to IP rights published on 23 March 2017 by the Anti-Monopoly Commission of the State Council (the '2017 Draft IP Guidelines')[10] further provide that when calculating an undertaking's share in a relevant technology market, the share accounted for by the products manufactured using the technology in question, the percentage of the royalties derived from the technology in the total amount of royalties, and the number of alternative technologies should be considered.[11]

The AML embraces a rebuttable presumption of dominance based on market shares (as defined by the relevant market). According to this presumption, a company with an individual market share of 50 per cent or more will be presumed to be dominant; and two companies having a combined market share of at least two thirds, or three companies having a combined market share of more than 75 per cent, will be presumed to be collectively dominant (although companies with individual market shares of less than 10 per cent will not be presumed to be part of a collectively dominant group).[12]

The AML, however, does not provide an indication on how market dominance is determined when IP is involved. For example, whether one single product alone can be defined as a relevant market.

1.3 Abuse

Having a dominant position in itself is not a violation of the AML but once an entity has been found to be dominant (either individually or collectively), it must not engage in certain abusive conducts, as set out in Article 17 AML. Although the abuses in Article 17 are not explicitly labelled as such, they can be categorized as 'exploitative' and 'exclusionary conduct'.[13] This is in line with internationally

---

applying Article 82 of the EC Treaty to abusive exclusionary conduct by dominant undertakings [2009] OJ C 45/7 (hereafter EU Commission Guidance), that in addition to looking at an entity's market shares, in order to establish dominance, it is necessary to examine constraints imposed by the existing supplies from, and the position on the market of, actual competitors; constraints imposed by the credible threat of future expansion by actual competitors or entry by potential competitors; and constraints imposed by the bargaining strength of an undertaking's customers.

[10] See MOFCOM, '公开征求"关于滥用知识产权的反垄断指南(征求意见稿)"的意见' (Press Release, 23 March 2017) available at < http://fldj.mofcom.gov.cn/article/zcfb/201703/20170302539418.shtml> accessed 17 January 2018.

[11] Anti-Monopoly Commission, 'Anti-monopoly guidelines on abuse of intellectual property rights' (Draft, 2017), Article 4.

[12] Article 19 AML. This presumption is similar to the European principles. For example, in *AKZO v Commission*, the European Court of Justice held that a presumption of dominance exists where market shares exceed 50 per cent over time (Case C-62/86 [1991] ECR I-3359, [1993] 5 CMLR 215). Further, the European Commission has indicated in its guidelines that entities with a market share of below 40 per cent are unlikely to be dominant (EU Commission Guidance, para. 14 (n 9)).

[13] Exploitative abuses are conducts that directly or indirectly impose unfair purchase or selling prices, or other unfair trading conditions, on another entity. For example, an undertaking with a

accepted principles and the distinction between exploitative and exclusionary abuses is a common one which is used in other jurisdictions, including Europe and the United Kingdom.

Under the AML, prohibited 'exploitative' conduct includes excessive pricing,[14] whereas exclusionary conduct captures predatory pricing (selling products below cost), refusals to deal, exclusive dealing, tying/bundling (e.g. making the sale of one product conditional upon the sale of another, or bundling products together at a discount), and applying differential treatment to the same types of counter-parts, without a justified reason.

The prohibition in Article 17 AML also contains a catch-all clause prohibiting 'activities that abuse the dominant market position as recognised by the Anti-Monopoly Enforcement Authorities'.[15] The law expressly includes a 'rule of reason' approach, which means that a conduct will only be regarded as abusive if there is no reasonable justification for it.

1.4 Powers to enforce against abuse of a dominant position under the AML

In terms of the Chinese enforcement authorities who have the power to en-force against abuse of dominance under the AML, the powers are split between three PRC agencies: the National Development and Reform Commission (here-after NDRC) is responsible for investigating and sanctioning abuses of domin-ance that relate to pricing conduct; the State Administration for Industry and Commerce (hereafter SAIC) is responsible for investigating and sanctioning abuses of dominance that do not relate to pricing; and the third agency, the Ministry of Commerce (hereafter MOFCOM), is solely responsible for reviewing concentrations of undertakings, as part of which it will consider whether such concentrations give rise to potential anti-competitive effects by virtue of the cre-ation of a dominant position.

---

dominant market position may exploit its customers by using market power to charge excessive prices or to impose unjustifiably onerous or unfair terms. Exclusionary abuses are conducts that limit production, markets, or technical development to the prejudice of consumers. Such conducts make competitors' products or services less attractive or less available, rather than simply making the dominant company's product better or more available. As such, they are ultimately likely to have the effect of excluding competitors from being able to effectively compete on the relevant market.

[14] 'Excessive pricing' under Article 17(1) AML refers to 'selling products at unfairly high prices or purchasing products at unfairly low prices'.

[15] Article 17(7) AML.

2. Legislative Framework for Assessing Abuse of Dominance in an IP Context

2.1 Legislative background

Historically, antitrust regulation in relation to IP in China was scattered in a variety of laws and regulations, such as the Patent Law,[16] the Contract Law,[17] and the relevant judicial interpretations of the Supreme Court.[18] This has resulted in a lack of clarity in terms of what constitutes anti-competitive conduct in the IP sector.

The only provision of the AML which addresses the relationship between IP and antitrust is Article 55, which falls under Chapter VIII, named supplementary provisions of the AML. Article 55 provides that the AML does not, in principle, apply to undertakings exercising IP rights pursuant to law. However, if undertakings abuse their IP to eliminate or restrict competition, the AML applies. More specifically, Article 55 provides that the AML is not applicable to the undertakings which exploit IP rights according to the law, but it will kick in if undertakings misuse/abuse IP and eliminate or restrict market competition.[19]

The scope of Article 55 is unclear and, in particular, it is not certain whether Article 55 creates an additional abuse by a dominant undertaking of IP rights, in addition to Article 17, or whether it merely emphasizes that the AML also applies to IP. However, it is likely that it should be interpreted as the latter, since the AML does not provide for specific sanctions of Article 55, but rather sanctions are only imposed for anti-competitive agreements and an abuse of a dominant position under Articles 46 and 47 AML. Further, Article 55 does not provide a list of the IP rights that fall within its scope and, as such, it is likely that it is intended to capture all types of IP rights, including patents, trademarks, copyrights, and other forms of IP rights.

2.2 Supplementary guidelines and regulations

To supplement Article 55 and provide more clarity on the interplay between IP and antitrust in China, the AML enforcement agencies have made significant efforts to provide further guidance on the application of the AML to IP-related issues.

Back in 2009, the SAIC began to prepare guidelines in an effort to provide guidance on IP and antitrust and it has developed multiple versions of the guidelines

---

[16] The Patent Law of the People's Republic of China, the Presidential Order No 8. (2008).

[17] The Contract Law of the People's Republic of China, the Presidential Order No 15. (1999).

[18] Such as the Interpretations of the Supreme People's Court concerning Certain Issues Relating to the Application of Law in the Trial of Patent Infringement Dispute Cases, Fa Shi (2009) No 21.

[19] Article 55 AML.

since then. On 7 April 2015, in response to the need for guidance in enforcement practice, the SAIC turned the fifth version of its guidelines into an official, binding implementing regulation (hereafter SAIC IP Regulation).[20] The SAIC IP Regulation, which became effective on 1 August 2015, is a result of more than five years of research, consultations, drafting, and debates with stakeholders in relation to abuse of dominant position issues in the IP sector.

In 2015, in an effort to provide comprehensive and consistent guidance for all of the PRC antitrust enforcement agencies, the State Council's Anti-Monopoly Commission launched a broader legislative initiative, mobilizing the antitrust enforcement agencies (i.e. the NDRC, the SAIC, and MOFCOM), together with the State Intellectual Property Office (hereafter SIPO), which is responsible for granting patents and semiconductor layout designs, to develop a comprehensive set of guidelines applicable to all antitrust enforcement actions involving IP. Each of the four agencies were tasked with proposing rules on issues falling under their respective jurisdictions. In early 2016, they submitted their drafts to the Anti-Monopoly Commission for reconciliation and consolidation. Once enacted by the State Council's Anti-Monopoly Commission, these comprehensive guidelines are expected to supersede the SAIC IP Regulation and guide the enforcement activities of all three AML enforcement agencies.

2.2.1 *The SAIC IP Regulation*

As a currently effective implementing regulation, the SAIC IP Regulation provides some helpful clarifications on the interplay between IP and antitrust laws. In particular, the SAIC IP Regulation identifies certain behaviours that the SAIC will consider to be an abuse of a dominant market position, unless it can be justified. These are: (i) refusal to license essential IP; (ii) exclusive dealing; (iii) tying/bundling; (iv) imposing unreasonable trading conditions; and (v) discriminatory treatment to equivalent transactions.

More specifically, the SAIC IP Regulation provides detailed guidance in relation to the following types of abuses:

(i) **refusal to license**: the SAIC IP Regulation introduces the concept of an 'essential facility' for the first time in Chinese antitrust law.[21] In this context,

---

[20] The Provisions on Prohibition of Abuse of Intellectual Property Rights to Eliminate or Restrict Competition, Order (2015) No 74 of the State Administration for Industry and Commerce.

[21] The essential facilities doctrine is a well-established principle in Europe, with the obligation to provide access to 'essential facilities' being an extension of the abuse of a refusal to supply. The doctrine works on the assumption that if undertakings are denied access to an essential facility that is owned or operated by a dominant undertaking, then they may be restricted from competing in downstream markets. In an IP context, the European courts have fluctuated between interpreting the essential facilities doctrine widely and mandating that since IP rights are licensed, the application of the doctrine should be limited to exceptional circumstances (Joined Cases C-241/91P and C-242/91P, *RTE and ITP v Commission* ('Magill') [1995] ECR I-743; C-418/01, *IMS Health*

Article 7 of the SAIC IP Regulation provides that when considering an IP holder's refusal to license IP, the SAIC will take into account whether reasonable substitutes for the IP exist and whether the IP is necessary for the licensee to compete in the relevant market; whether the refusal will have an adverse impact on competition or innovation, to the detriment of consumer interest or public interest; and whether licensing the IP to the licensee will cause unreasonable harm to the IP holder.

The SAIC IP Regulation does not further elaborate on the circumstances under which IP owned by an undertaking would be found to constitute an essential facility and the undertaking's refusal to license the IP would breach the AML. However, the threshold for a finding of refusal to license essential facilities appears to be insignificant. This is likely to be of concern to owners of key IP rights, who may worry that they will be deprived of the freedom to decide whether and whom to license their IP to. On the face of it, the position under the SAIC IP Regulation is wider than in other jurisdictions. For example, in Europe, a refusal to license will only amount to an abuse of dominance in 'exceptional circumstances'; in the United States, the courts have imposed duties to supply on dominant firms only in highly specific situations.

(ii) **unreasonable trading conditions**: the SAIC IP Regulation prohibits the imposition by a dominant IP holder of unreasonable conditions on its licensees without justification. The regulation lists a non-exhaustive list of unreasonable conditions, including: (i) exclusive grant-backs of the licensee's improvement to licensed technologies; (ii) no-challenge clauses prohibiting a licensee from challenging the validity of the licensed IP; (iii) restrictions on the use of competing products or technologies after expiry of the licence agreement; (iv) obligations to pay royalties after the expiry or invalidation of the licensed IP; and (v) exclusive dealing. The prohibition against exclusive grant-backs and the no-challenge clause in particular, mirrors the European approach where technology licence agreements containing such clauses are not exempted from the European rules on restrictive agreements.[22]

GmbH & Co OHG v NDC Health GmbH & Co KG [2004] ECR I-539; *T-201/04, Microsoft Corp v Commission* [2007] ECR II-3601).

[22] See EU Commission Regulation (EU) 316/2014 on the application of Article 101(3) of the TFEU to categories of technology transfer agreements [2014] OJ L93/17 (hereafter TTBER) and the European Commission's Guidelines on the application of Article 101 of the TFEU to technology transfer agreements (2014/C 89/03). The TTBER also removes the benefit of the exemption from Article 101(1) TFEU for non-exclusive technology licences entered into between two undertakings for the manufacture or provision of goods or services incorporating the licensed technology, which contain termination clauses allowing the licensor to terminate the technology licence agreement if the licensee challenges the validity of the IP, since the European Commission considers that such termination arrangements can have the same deterring effect as no-challenge clauses. It is unclear whether the SAIC will consider that a termination clause is already covered in the SAIC IP Regulation, as a type of non-challenge practice.

(iii) **other IP-related abusive conduct:** exclusive dealing, tying, and discrimination in the exercise of IP are also prohibited under the SAIC IP Regulation. However, the clauses related to these types of conduct largely mirror the wording of the general provisions of the AML, and they have not been specifically applied in an IP context in the regulation.

The SAIC IP Regulation also addresses anti-competitive conduct in the context of patent pools. In relation to an abuse of a dominant position, the SAIC IP Regulation provides that, unless justified, patent pools with a dominant market position are restricted from engaging in several types of conduct, including preventing members from individually licensing outside the pool; preventing members or licensees from developing competing technologies on their own or in co-operation with third parties; requiring exclusive grant-backs; prohibiting licensees from challenging the validity of the pooled patents; or applying different trading conditions to equivalent transactions.[23]

The SAIC IP Regulation also contains provisions that are intended to regulate abusive conduct by dominant IP holders during the standard setting process. Under the SAIC IP Regulation, it will be considered an abuse of dominance if a patentee deliberately conceals patent information or waives the right of assertion during the standard setting process, but nevertheless asserts the patent after a certain standard has incorporated the patent.[24] It will also constitute an abuse if a holder of a standard essential patent (hereafter SEP)[25] refuses to license the SEP, ties in licensing, or imposes unreasonable conditions in violation of the 'fair, reasonable and non-discriminatory' (hereafter FRAND)[26] principle.[27]

Despite the fact that the SAIC IP Regulation covers a variety of potential abuses and it provides much welcome and detailed guidance in the IP-space, it has some

---

[23] Article 12 SAIC IP Regulation.
[24] Article 13 SAIC IP Regulation.
[25] A standard essential patent is a patent which is essential to implement a specific industry standard. This means that it is impossible to manufacture standard-compliant products, such as smart phones or tablets, without using technologies that are covered by one or more SEPs. SEPs can therefore confer significant market power on the SEP holder, which they would not have had absent the standard. The standards in question are agreed by standard-setting organizations such as the European Telecommunications Standards Institute, in which patent holders and manufacturers of standard-compliant products participate.
[26] FRAND stands for fair, reasonable and non-discriminatory and holders of an IP right usually have to agree to license a patent on FRAND terms before it will be accepted to become part of a standard body approved technical standard. In Europe, the European Commission published a new communication on SEPs at the end of 2017, noting that '*there is no one-size-fit-all solution to what FRAND is: what can be considered fair and reasonable differs from sector to sector and over time*'. (Communication from the Commission to the European Parliament, the Council and the European Economic and Social Committee, 'Setting out the EU approach to Standard Essential Patents' (COM (2017) 712 final) (hereafter EU Communication 2017)).
[27] Article 13 SAIC IP Regulation.

significant limitations. Firstly, it only applies to the SAIC's enforcement remit (i.e. to the enforcement of non-price related conduct), and it does not apply to the enforcement activities which fall under the scope of the NDRC (i.e. pricing related issues) or of MOFCOM (which is responsible for merger reviews, including reviewing transactions that involve IP, or that are in the IP sector). Secondly, it is not clear whether the SAIC IP Regulation, which was drafted by the SAIC, reflects the experience of its two sister agencies, and in particular, that of the NDRC, which has accumulated a significant amount of valuable experience as a result of its active enforcement activities in relation to IP.

2.2.2 *State Council draft IP guidelines*

The Anti-Monopoly Commission of the State Council published the 2017 Draft IP Guidelines on 23 March 2017 for public comment and, at the time of writing, there had not been a more advanced publicly-available version since this date. In relation to an abuse of a dominant market position, the 2017 Draft IP Guidelines:

- **provide guidance on market definition relating to IP**, including the possibility of defining a relevant technology and innovation market. The guidelines introduce the concept of a technology market,[28] in addition to the traditional concept of the relevant product market, and confirms that both of these markets should be defined by reference to a geographic dimension. However, the geographic scope of the two different markets could be different in each case. The guidelines also note that the impact of IP on innovation, research, and development should be taken into consideration depending on individual cases.[29]
- **confirm that ownership of IP alone does not confer a dominant market position upon the IP owner; rather, owning IP is only one of the many factors in determining whether the IP owner holds a dominant position.**[30] The confirmation of this position is in accordance with international practice. In addition, the guidelines reiterate that the analytical framework set out in Article 18 AML should be followed when evaluating whether an IP owner is dominant in the market.[31] In addition, the draft proposes that, due to the characteristics of IP, additional factors may also be taken into account when determining whether an undertaking has a dominant market position, such as the possibility for the counterparty to switch to alternative IP and the associated switching costs; the degree of the downstream market's dependence on the products involving the IP; and the counterparty's ability to constrain the IP owner.[32]

---

[28] See nn (5) and (6).

[29] Anti-Monopoly Commission, 'Anti-monopoly guidelines on abuse of intellectual property rights' (Draft, 2017), Article 3.

[30] Ibid, Articles 1 and 13.

[31] See Section 1.2. (Abuse of a dominant position under the AML.)

[32] Anti-Monopoly Commission, 'Anti-monopoly guidelines on abuse of intellectual property rights' (Draft, 2017), Article 13.

- **explain the conducts that may amount to an abuse of a dominant position by IP holders.** Potential abuses mentioned in the guidelines include (1) charging excessive royalties; (2) refusal to license a patent; (3) tying/bundling distinct IPs; (4) imposing unreasonable licensing conditions (such as requiring exclusive buy-backs or challenging the IP, preventing the licensee from using competitive IP or products, asserting rights over expired or invalid IP, and imposing restrictions on licensees regarding trades with third parties); (5) applying differential or discriminatory treatment to similar customers; and (6) seeking injunctive relief against patent users, including in the context of SEPs.[33] Further detail in relation to how these abuses will be assessed by the authorities under the guidelines is set out in Section 5 below.

- **reaffirm a 'rule of reason' approach for IP-related unilateral conduct which could amount to an abuse of a dominant position,** rather than considering it to be *'per se'* illegal. This is consistent with the general analytical approach set out in Article 17 AML. It is also broadly in line with the approach taken in other jurisdictions, where an abuse of a dominant position is usually analysed on its effects, rather than as a 'by object' restriction of competition law.[34] The guidelines acknowledge the positive effects of IP (such as efficiency and consumer welfare gains) and they acknowledge that an IP owner's conduct needs to be carefully reviewed. Therefore, IP-related unilateral conduct should not be presumed to be abusive, absent any anti-competitive effects. This stance in particular reflects the authorities' appreciation of the complex interplay between IP and antitrust law, and demonstrates a mature attitude towards the analysis of IP-related abuses of dominance.

In assessing whether conduct amounts to an abuse of a dominant position under the Draft IP Guidelines, the relevant market is particularly relevant to the assessment because IP holders typically either have a monopoly, allowing them to use IP rights exclusively and appropriate the value of that right for themselves. This is specific to IP rights, to encourage investment in products and reward technology owners for the development of, and investment, in technology and to further

---

[33] Injunctions in the context of SEPs are also covered by guidance published by the People's Supreme Court. On 22 March 2016, the People's Supreme Court published Judicial Interpretation No 2 regarding IP Dispute Cases. Article 24 of this judicial interpretation provides that, in relation to SEPs, courts would usually not uphold a licensor's application for injunctions against implementation of the standard by licensees, if, when licensing the SEP, the licensor did not comply with FRAND licensing obligations, resulting in no patent agreement, and the licensees did not commit gross negligence.

[34] Some conducts are considered to be so harmful to competition that they are only engaged in because their objective is to harm competition. These types of conducts are known as object restrictions under competition law principles. Where conduct does not have as its object the restriction of competition, it is necessary to demonstrate that it has a restrictive effect on competition, in order for it to breach competition laws.

incentivize innovation. It is for this reason that IP holders often have a dominant position and why the rules preventing an abuse of a dominant position are all the more relevant in IP markets. This is what the Draft IP Guidelines aim to address.

Once finalized, the State Council guidelines will be essential in assisting the business community and practitioners in understanding how antitrust laws will be applied in the IP sector going forward. They also bring China in line with more mature jurisdictions, such as the EU and US, both of which have well established guidance on the application of competition law to IP rights.[35]

3. Enforcement Cases and Private Actions in Relation to IP

Even prior to the 2017 Draft IP Guidelines being drafted, the AML enforcement authorities have been increasingly active in enforcing against IP-related cases in recent years and private antitrust litigation involving IP has significantly increased. High-profile cases include investigations against Qualcomm,[36] InterDigital,[37] and Microsoft,[38] and important private actions include the *Huawei v InterDigital* case.[39] Most of these cases involve allegations of abuse of dominance,[40] in particular in relation to SEPs, and they provide a useful insight into how the PRC authorities will interpret the interplay between IP and antitrust which, together with the various guidelines that are being drafted, assist in understanding how this complex topic is likely to be viewed in China in the future. The courts and the enforcement authorities have often taken similar positions in relation to key issues such as market definition and the importance of SEPs, as illustrated by several important decisions and cases.

---

[35] For example, the US Department of Justice and Federal Trade Commission, 'Antitrust Guidelines for the Licensing of Intellectual Property' (1995); as for the European Union, see the TTBER (n 20) and the EU Communication 2017.

[36] The Administrative Penalty Decision of the National Development and Reform Commission of the People's Republic of China, Fa Gai Ban Jia Jian Chu Fa (2015) No 1.

[37] NDRC, '国家发展改革委对美国IDC公司 涉嫌价格垄断案中止调查' (Press release, 22 May 2015), available at <http://www.sdpc.gov.cn/xwzx/xwfb/201405/t20140522_612465.html> accessed 17 January 2018.

[38] SAIC, '国家工商总局专案组对微软公司进行反垄断突击检查' (Press release, 29 July 2014), available at <http://www.saic.gov.cn/xw/yw/zj/201407/t20140729_210025.html > accessed 17 January 2018.

[39] Yue Gao Fa Min San Zhong Zi, No 305 (2013); Yue Gao Fa Min San Zhong Zi, No 306 (2013).

[40] Prior to these IP-related cases, earlier abuse of dominance cases under the AML related to the conduct of domestic companies active in various sectors, such as Wuchang Salt which was investigated for allegations of tying; investigations into local telecommunications companies for discrimination and margin squeeze; and investigations into local pharmaceutical companies for refusal to supply. In addition, local NDRC agencies probed local river-sand and pasteurized milk manufacturers for alleged excessive pricing.

3.1 Investigations by the NDRC

3.1.1 *Qualcomm*

On 9 February 2015, the NDRC issued a decision against the US semiconductor giant, Qualcomm, imposing a record penalty of RMB 6.088 billion (approximately USD 975 million), which equated to approximately 8 per cent of Qualcomm's 2013 China revenue, and imposed a set of remedies around the company's patent licensing practices. The *Qualcomm* case marked a new record for the highest individual fine in China and it by far exceeded the previous largest fine imposed by the NDRC under the AML in a single case[41] and against a single company.[42]

The NDRC's decision in the *Qualcomm* case came after fourteen months of investigation and after lengthy discussions involving a total of twenty-eight rounds of communications between officials and company representatives (eight of which were between the lead official and Qualcomm's president).[43] The investigation was reportedly prompted by complaints received by the NDRC in November 2013 from competitors and industry associations, most notably the Mobile China Alliance, which represents China's powerful mobile phone industry, and the Internet Society of China. After receiving the complaints and reviewing the accompanying evidence, the NDRC carried out simultaneous dawn raids at Qualcomm's offices in Beijing and Shanghai. Throughout the process, the NDRC co-operated closely with the Ministry of Industry and Information Technology, the Chinese telecom and internet regulator.

The case related to a collection of relevant SEP licensing markets and three separate downstream markets for certain types of baseband chips. In its decision, which was published on 2 March 2015, the NDRC defined separate markets for the licensing of each wireless communications SEP, which is consistent with the approach adopted by the court in *Huawei v InterDigital* and in line with European and United States practice.[44] The NDRC also considered that the licensing of SEPs

---

[41] Prior to the *Qualcomm* case (n 33), the largest fine imposed by the NDRC in a single case was RMB 832 million (approximately USD 136 million) imposed in the auto parts cartel. See NDRC, '日本十二家企业实施汽车零部件和轴承价格垄断被国家发展改革委罚款12.35亿元' (Press release, 20 August 2014) available at, <http://www.sdpc.gov.cn/fzgggz/jgjdyfld/jjszhdt/201408/t20140820_622757.html> accessed 17 January 2018.

[42] Prior to the *Qualcomm* case (n 33), the largest fine imposed by the NDRC against a single entity was RMB 290 million (approximately USD 47 million) imposed against Sumitomo Electric. See the Administrative Penalty Decision of the National Development and Reform Commission of the People's Republic of China, Fa Gai Ban Jia Jian Chu Fa (2014) No 9.

[43] See Xu Kunlin, 'Head of the Price Department of the National Development and Reform Commission: Personal Experience in High-Profile Antitrust Cases' (2015) 4 Oriental Outlook, available at <http://finance.sina.com.cn/china/20150620/213322484073.shtml> accessed 17 January 2018.

[44] See, for example, EU cases, see; *Samsung-Enforcement of UMTS Standard Essential Patents* Commission Decision AT.39939 [2014] OJ C 350/8, paras. 41–43; *Motorola-Enforcement of GPRS*

is national in scope as the licensing, use, and protection of IP are issued under national law.

The NDRC found that Qualcomm held a dominant position in each of the SEP markets by virtue of its 100 per cent market share; its ability to control the market; Chinese manufacturers' high dependence on Qualcomm's SEPs; and the significant difficulty in entering the market. Further, the NDRC held that Qualcomm exceeded the presumption of dominance by having market shares of more than 50 per cent, and that it was also dominant in the relevant downstream baseband chips markets. For the purpose of the assessment, the NDRC assessed market shares by value (rather than by volume) and held that the higher average selling pricing which Qualcomm was able to impose on its customers supported the conclusion that it held a dominant position.

Upon establishing that Qualcomm held a dominant position, the NDRC analysed a number of alleged anti-competitive conducts carried out by Qualcomm in abuse of its dominant position. The NDRC found that Qualcomm charged excessive royalties by: (i) requiring Chinese licensees to cross-license their patents to Qualcomm free of charge; (ii) bundling SEPs and other patents; (iii) imposing patent rates based on the net wholesale price of the device; (iv) failing to disclose complete lists of patents to other market participants; and (v) not modifying royalties upon expiry of a patent. Further, the NDRC found a violation of Article 17 AML by virtue of bundling SEPs and non-SEPs without justification and by imposing certain restrictions on its licensees (such as a covenant not to challenge the licence agreement).

Qualcomm ultimately offered a series of commitments to close the case and to avoid an even higher fine, including agreeing to lower its royalties by 35 per cent. However, as part of the commitments, Qualcomm is still entitled to base the calculation of its royalties on the net wholesale price, instead of the value of the smallest saleable unit (as was suggested by the Ministry of Industry and Information Technology). This was a heavily debated issue in the course of the proceedings, as it meant that Qualcomm could preserve some elements of its royalty formula and avoid a duty to license at the chip level, which might have led to patent exhaustion. Further, Qualcomm committed not to charge wireless communications device makers within mainland China for expired patents and to disclose complete lists of relevant SEPs. Pursuant to the commitments, Qualcomm is also required to negotiate in good faith with Chinese cross-licensees; to offer a fair compensation when seeking a cross-licence; and to stop bundling SEPs and non-SEPs without justification. The latter commitment is of particular significance for patent-rich

---

Standard Essential Patents Commission Decision AT.39985 [2014] OJ C 344/6 paras. 179–220 and *Broadcom Corp. v. Qualcomm Inc.*, 501 F 3d 297, 310 (3d Cir 2007).

licensees, who have had to bear additional opportunity costs when licensing their patent pool under a free-of-charge cross-licence agreement.

One novel feature of the *Qualcomm* case is that some of the remedies did not form part of the NDRC's decision, but they were given orally by Qualcomm as a means of avoiding possible follow-on litigation. Further, it is noteworthy that the NDRC reviewed excessive pricing practices to regulate the pricing of patent holders, which is an area in which the authorities in the US and—to a less extent—in the EU are reluctant to initiate cases.

3.1.2 InterDigital

The allegations made by the NDRC against InterDigital were broadly similar to those made in the Qualcomm case, with the NDRC focusing on unfairly high licensing fees for SEPs, as well as cross-licensing and bundling practices involving SEPs and non-SEPs.

Following the ruling of the Guangdong High Court in a parallel abuse lawsuit with regard to its patent licensing practice (detailed in Section 3.3.1), in May 2014, the NDRC formally suspended its investigation into InterDigital on account of the commitments InterDigital made. In this regard, InterDigital committed: (1) to comply with FRAND principles when licensing patents to Chinese manufacturers and to cease to charge excessive royalties; (2) not to bundle the SEPs and non-SEPs for the 2G, 3G, and 4G wireless telecommunication; (3) not to require royalty-free, reciprocal cross-licences from Chinese manufacturers; (4) to offer binding arbitration before seeking injunctive relief; and (5) to offer specific commitments in relation to the licensing negotiations with Huawei and ZTE, including abiding by the royalty rate determined by the Chinese courts, negotiating on arbitration clauses, withdrawing complaints and lawsuits.

3.1.3 Pharmaceutical industry

In addition to these two landmark investigations conducted by the NDRC, the NDRC appears to be focusing on IP-issues in other sectors, including in the pharmaceutical sector. In 2014, the regulator sent an industry-wide inquiry to international pharmaceutical companies relating to price differences for patent drugs in China compared to other jurisdictions. Continuing this wave of probing, in 2016 the NDRC began a market investigation into the healthcare sector (including in both the pharmaceutical and medical devices sectors), as part of which some questions asked by the NDRC appeared to be intended to test whether pharmaceutical companies are charging Chinese customers excessively high prices for their patent-expired drugs. Such questions appear to reflect an interventionist mindset, as it would be more appropriate for the price for off-patent drugs to be the subject of competition between the original drug manufacturer and the generic.

This investigation demonstrates that the NDRC is not limiting the focus of its enforcement of abuse of dominance as a result of holding IP rights to technology companies, and it is branching out into other sectors, in an attempt to ensure that all abuses of dominance in IP-related industries are carefully considered. This is in line with the enforcement focus in other countries with the abuse of dominance in the pharmaceutical sector as a result of holding patents having long been an enforcement priority for both the US and the EU antitrust regulators.

3.2 Investigations by the SAIC

On the SAIC side, prompted by complaints, the SAIC launched an investigation into Microsoft's alleged abuse of a dominant position in June 2014. The SAIC accused Microsoft of, amongst other things, compatibility, tying, and document verification in breach of the AML. It is believed that the SAIC conducted two dawn raids at premises of Microsoft and other companies, interviewed relevant personnel, and requested Microsoft to provide explanatory papers in relation to this investigation.[45] However, at the time of writing, it is unclear whether, and when, a decision in relation to the SAIC's probe will be issued.

3.3 IP Litigation

3.3.1 Huawei v InterDigital

In October 2013, the Guangdong High Court, in its capacity as the appellate court, ruled on the two lawsuits brought against InterDigital by Huawei in parallel in 2011.

InterDigital, an American company which designs and develops advanced technologies for wireless communications, holds several SEPs for the creation of international wireless communications standards. In July 2011, InterDigital filed a patent infringement complaint against Huawei to the United States International Trade Commission, and brought a parallel lawsuit in a United States District Court.[46]

In December 2011, Huawei, in turn, filed two complaints based on different causes of action against InterDigital before the Shenzhen Intermediate People's Court.[47] In one case, Huawei claimed that InterDigital had charged excessive royalties in

---

[45] See SAIC, '工商总局专案组对微软公司进行反垄断询问调查' (Press Release, 6 January 2016), available at <http://www.saic.gov.cn/xw/yw/zj/201601/t20160106_210623.html > accessed 17 January 2018.

[46] *InterDigital Communications LLC et al v Huawei Technologies Co. Ltd. et al*, No 1:11-cv-00654 (D Del 2011).

[47] Shen Zhong Fa Min Chu Zi, No 857 and (2011); and Shen Zhong Fa Min Chu Zi, No 858 (2011).

violation of the FRAND obligation InterDigital bore as the SEP owner, and, on this basis, it requested the court to lower the royalty rate.[48] In the other case, Huawei submitted that InterDigital had engaged in an abuse of a dominant position by imposing excessive royalties, discriminatory licensing terms and unreasonable licensing conditions, by tying, and by refusing to deal with Huawei by way of seeking an injunction before the United States International Trade Commission and the United States court.[49]

In the first case alleging violation of FRAND principles, Huawei petitioned to the court for a statutory determination of a FRAND royalty rate applicable to the licensing of SEPs to it by InterDigital. The court found that InterDigital voluntarily participated in forming the relevant ISO standards and committed to license its SEPs on FRAND terms. The court considered that, in so doing, InterDigital should have foreseen that its SEPs would have also been incorporated into Chinese standards due to consistency requirements. As such, the court considered that whilst InterDigital did not directly participate in the formation of the Chinese standards, it was nevertheless obliged to grant a licence to Huawei on a FRAND basis. The court further set a FRAND rate capped at 0.019 per cent of the actual product selling price. InterDigital appealed, and the Guangdong High Court upheld the Court of First Instance's ruling.

In the second case alleging an abuse of dominance, Huawei claimed that InterDigital had abused its dominant position in the licensing of SEPs for 3G wireless communications, and on that basis, Huawei requested RMB 20 million (approximately USD 3 million) in damages. The Court of First Instance held that InterDigital had violated its FRAND commitments and abused its dominant position by charging excessive royalties, refusing to deal with Huawei, tying, and discriminatory treatment. It further ordered InterDigital to cease the misconduct, and awarded the damages Huawei claimed. However, the court rejected InterDigital's claim that the package combining Chinese SEPs with non-Chinese SEPs licensed to Huawei by InterDigital constituted an abuse of a dominant position.

Both parties appealed, and the Guangdong High People's Court ruled in October 2013, affirming all of the Shenzhen court's rulings. Interestingly, InterDigital had argued that whilst it held a large number of SEPs under the WCDMA, CDMA200, TD-SCDMA standards for 3G communications technologies (which were at issue in the case), the relevant product market should also include the 2G and 4G standards as both are substitutable with the 3G standard. However, the Guangdong High Court rejected this argument, affirming the finding of the Court of First Instance. Specifically, the appellate court considered that a licensee could arguably

---

[48] Yue Gao Fa Min San Zhong Zi, No 305 (2013).
[49] Yue Gao Fa Min San Zhong Zi, No 306 (2013).

212

switch with relative ease from one technology to another at the time the standard was set, but such switching would become increasingly difficult as time passes because of the increasing resources the licensee would have put into the standard it had chosen. Huawei was considered to have already made a significant early-stage contribution in order to implement the 3G standard and such investment could not be withdrawn, whilst switching to another standard from the 3G standard would not only result in the loss of early-stage investment, but would also result in significant switching costs and market risks.

Following the Guangdong High Court's rulings, InterDigital petitioned to the Supreme People's Court for a re-trial. At the time of writing, the petition was being reviewed by the Supreme People's Court. It is anticipated that the decision of the Supreme People's Court will provide further clarification that can be used to interpret similar cases going forward.[50]

4. Influence of Investigation Decisions and Case Law on the Authorities' Guidelines

The enforcement decisions of the NDRC and the SAIC, and the case law from the courts, described in Section 3, have been instrumental in shaping the various versions of the SAIC IP Regulation and the more recent 2017 Draft IP Guidelines published by Anti-Monopoly Commission as part of the State Council's comprehensive guidance.

A clear example of this is the determination of dominance in an SEP context. Whether or not owning an SEP automatically equates to a dominant position in the relevant SEP market is an important issue which has often been considered by antitrust authorities. The 2017 Draft IP Guidelines appear to confirm that it does not consider that the holder of an SEP will necessarily have a dominant position in the relevant market. Rather, the guidelines provide that, in order to determine whether an SEP owner is dominant, it is necessary to consider: (1) the market value and application of the relevant standard; (2) the availability of alternative standards and the switching costs; (3) the degree of the industry's dependence on the relevant standard; (4) the evolution of, and compatibility between, the relevant standards; and (5) the possibility of the relevant technology incorporated into the standard being replaced.[51] These factors are to be considered in addition to the usual factors

---

[50] Vanessa Yanhua Zhang, '*Interview with Judge Chuang Wang, Presiding Judge of Intellectual Tribunal, Supreme People's Court of P.R. China*' [2016] 4(2) Antitrust Chronicle, available at <https://www.competitionpolicyinternational.com/wp-content/uploads/2015/11/Antitrust-Chronicle-Issue-5-2.pdf> accessed 17 January 2018.

[51] Anti-Monopoly Commission, 'Anti-monopoly guidelines on abuse of intellectual property rights' (Draft, 2017), Article 13.

to be taken into account when determining whether a non-SEP holder would have a dominant position.

The approach taken by the Anti-Monopoly Commission in this regard is just one example of the fact that the PRC antitrust enforcement authorities are trying to codify in their guidelines the already-established principles that have been adopted in the recent investigations and court decisions, as similar approaches were adopted in both the *Qualcomm* case[52] and the *Huawei v InterDigital* case.[53] In both cases, a comprehensive analysis of market definition in relation to SEPs was carried out and it was not presumed that the relevant entities had a dominant position simply by virtue of the fact that they owned an SEP. For example, as explained in Section 3.1.1 above, in *Qualcomm* case, the NDRC found that Qualcomm held 100 per cent share in the relevant SEP market, and further examined several other factors, including Qualcomm's ability to control the licensing royalty and terms, and to prevent or influence other competitors' entry into the relevant SEP market, downstream manufacturers' heavy reliance on Qualcomm's patents, and the high entry barriers. Similarly, in the *Huawei v InterDigital* case, the Guangdong High Court analysed InterDigital's position in the market based on a number of factors, and determined that, being the only player in the relevant market meant that InterDigital was able to hinder or influence other competitors' abilities to enter the relevant market.[54] In addition, since InterDigital was only active in patent licensing but did not engage in any real manufacturing activities, the court considered that it was not dependent on, or subject to, the cross-licensing of other SEP holders, and therefore, its dominance was not effectively constrained. On this basis, the court found that InterDigital held a dominant position in the relevant SEP market.

A similar position has also been adopted in the IP Tribunal of the Supreme People's Court, where a senior judge argued that not all SEP owners automatically hold a dominant position, since an SEP owner is faced with two types of competitive constraints: (1) competition between standards, since competing standards do not necessarily contain the same SEPs, meaning alternative technical solutions should also be considered; and (2) competition between standardized products and non-standardized products.[55] This demonstrates that, in addition to being significantly influenced by the enforcement actions of the antitrust authorities in determining the principles to be included in the State Council's IP-related guidelines, the relevant enforcement authorities have also been influenced by the principles established by other Chinese authorities.

---

[52] *Qualcomm* (n 33).
[53] *Huawei* (n 36).
[54] Ibid.
[55] Zhu Li, 'Legal issues with respect to standard essential patents: overlaps of patent law, contract law and competition law' [2016] Competition Policy Studies.

The principles set out in the guidelines also mirror the position adopted by case law in other jurisdictions, indicating the clear intention of the Chinese authorities to develop well-reasoned and comprehensive guidance that can be relied upon in interpreting how abuse of dominance in IP should be assessed.

5. Abuses of a Dominant Position in an IP Context

The potential abuses of a dominant position covered in the State Council's guidelines mirror those set out in Article 17 AML. Specifically, (1) charging excessive royalties; (2) refusal to license a patent; (3) tying/bundling; (4) imposing unreasonable licensing conditions (such as requiring exclusive buy-backs or challenging the IP; preventing the licensee from using competitive IP or products; asserting rights over expired or invalid IP; and imposing restrictions on licensees regarding trades with third parties); (5) applying differential or discriminatory treatment to similar customers; and (6) seeking injunctive relief against patent users, including in the context of SEPs, are all identified conduct that may amount to an abuse of a dominant position in an IP context.

5.1 Excessive royalties

In the *Qualcomm* case, the NDRC found that Qualcomm had directly or indirectly charged unreasonably high royalties.[56] This finding was built on the following specific claims: firstly, Qualcomm licensed a patent package to licensees without providing them with a patent list and despite the fact that many patents in the package had expired; secondly, as a condition of the licence, Qualcomm forced the licensees to give a royalty-free cross-licence; and thirdly, that Qualcomm used the net wholesale price of the devices as the basis to calculate applicable royalties. On this basis, the NDRC considered that the royalties Qualcomm charged were excessively high. Similarly, in the *Huawei v InterDigital* case, the Guangdong High Court found that InterDigital charged Huawei excessive royalties on the grounds that the royalties were clearly higher than were charged to other multinational device manufacturers.[57]

The factors considered by the NDRC and the Guangdong High Court have largely been codified into the 2017 Draft IP Guidelines. In the draft, it is explained that whether or not royalties are considered to be excessive should be determined by taking account of: (1) the method of calculating the royalties and the contribution of the IP to the value of the relevant product; (2) the licensing commitments attached to the IP; (3) the royalties charged historically and comparable royalties;

---

[56] *Qualcomm* (n 33).
[57] *Huawei* (n 36).

(4) whether the IP holder charges royalties beyond the IP's geographical or product scope; (5) in the case of licensing package, whether the IP holder charges royalties for expired or invalid IP; and (6) whether the IP holder forces, by injunctive relief, the licensee to accept the royalties it proposes.[58]

Excessive royalties have been considered by antitrust authorities in other jurisdictions, although they are typically not the focus of enforcement actions, since it is difficult to prove what amounts to an 'excessive' charge.[59] For example, in *SACEM*, the European Court of Justice (ECJ) was asked to give a preliminary ruling on whether a dominant association of authors, composers, and publishers of music in France infringed Article 102 TFEU by imposing royalties which were grossly higher than those imposed by similar copyright societies in other EU Member States.[60] The court considered that, to infringe Article 102 TFEU, the association must have imposed unfair conditions, by charging royalties that were appreciably higher than those charged in other Member States, when assessed on a comparable basis, and that the royalties charged in this case were excessive on that basis.

5.2 Refusal to license

The 2017 Draft IP Guidelines set out principles in relation to refusals to license. The guidelines confirm that an IP owner generally has no obligation to license its IP to a counterparty, which is a position that is likely to be warmly welcomed by the business community. However, the draft also notes that a dominant IP holder's refusal to license IP without justifications could hinder competition and harm consumer interest.

Pursuant to the draft, a case-by-case analysis in relation to whether a refusal to license is justified is required, and the following factors should be taken into consideration as part of the assessment: (1) the licensing commitments attached to the IP; (2) whether the IP is essential to entering the relevant market, and whether there is any alternative IP which is reasonably available; (3) the effect of the IP licensing on the IP holder's incentive to innovate; (4) whether the counterparty is unwilling or unable to pay reasonable royalties; and (5) whether the counterparty's use of the IP will result in an adverse impact on public interests.[61] Notably, the

---

[58] Anti-Monopoly Commission, 'Anti-monopoly guidelines on abuse of intellectual property rights' (Draft, 2017), Article 14.

[59] In the EU Commission Guidance, which sets out the enforcement priorities of the EU Commission in relation to abuses of a dominant position, the EU Commission focuses only on exclusionary abuses and does not focus on excessive pricing at all. Similarly, in 2015, the Hong Kong Competition Commission announced in its enforcement priorities paper that it would focus on exclusionary abuses of substantial market power, rather than on exploitative abuses such as excessive pricing (see Hong Kong Competition Commission Enforcement Policy [2015] para. 3.5).

[60] Case C-110/88, *Lucazeau v SACEM*, [1989] ECR 2811, [1991] 4 CMLR 248.

[61] Anti-Monopoly Commission, 'Anti-monopoly guidelines on abuse of intellectual property rights' (Draft, 2017), Article 15.

2017 Draft IP Guidelines notes that refusal to license is more likely to result in anti-competitive effects if the relevant IP constitutes an essential facility for production and operation.[62]

5.3 Tying and bundling

Tying and bundling was considered in both the *Qualcomm* case and the *Huawei v InterDigital* case.[63] In the *Qualcomm* case, the NDRC found that Qualcomm had forced customers to accept a licensing package which consists of both SEPs and non-SEPs as a condition of the licensing of SEPs.[64] The NDRC considered that SEPs and non-SEPs are of a different nature and are independent of each other, and that licensing them separately would not affect the application and value of these two types of patents.

The court in *Huawei* also addressed the issue of tying and bundling.[65] It ruled that InterDigital had engaged in tying in violation of the AML by bundling SEPs and non-SEPs. However, the court considered that the bundling of multiple SEPs would create efficiencies and would not result in the same competition issues as in the bundling of SEPs and non-SEPs (e.g. extending the dominance in the SEP market to the non-SEP market, thereby restricting competition).

5.4 Imposing unreasonable licensing conditions

In the *Qualcomm* case, the NDRC found that Qualcomm would only supply baseband chips to a customer on the condition that the customer also executed a patent licensing agreement with Qualcomm (which contained unreasonable clauses) and the customer would not challenge the patent licensing agreement.[66] The NDRC considered that this amounted to an abuse by Qualcomm, since Qualcomm had imposed unreasonable licensing terms on customers.

The 2017 Draft IP Guidelines seek to elaborate on this concept and explain in more detail the forms that unreasonable licensing terms can take. Arrangements that may be considered to be unreasonable include: (1) requiring an exclusive grant-back on the improved technology from the counterparty; (2) prohibiting the counterparty from challenging the validity of the licensed IP or initiating lawsuits against the licensor for IP infringements; (3) restricting the counterparty's use of competing technologies or products; (4) asserting rights on expired or invalid IP; (5) requiring the counterparty to the transaction to grant cross licences without

---

[62] Ibid.
[63] *Huawei* (n 36).
[64] *Qualcomm* (n 33).
[65] *Huawei* (n 36).
[66] *Qualcomm* (n 33).

offering reasonable consideration; and (6) forcing the counterparty to trade, or prohibiting the counterparty from trading with, a third party or imposing restrictive conditions on transactions between such counterparty and any third party.[67]

5.5 Applying differential treatment to similar customers

According to the 2017 Draft IP Guidelines, an unjustified imposition of different licensing terms on licensees in substantially the same position by a dominant company may eliminate or restrict competition. For example, an IP holder may charge competitors excessive royalties, or agree with different counterparties on different arrangements in the number of patents licensed and the geographic scope and duration of the licence, and this could amount to discriminatory anti-competitive conduct.[68]

The principle of discriminatory conduct is well-established in antitrust laws. In Europe, Article 102(c) TFEU specifically prohibits discriminatory abuse, which is defined as 'applying dissimilar conditions to equivalent transactions with other trading parties, thereby placing them at a competitive disadvantage'.[69]

5.6 Seeking injunctive relief

Injunctive relief refers to an injunction issued by the court at the request of the patent owner to restrict the use of a patent by another party. A section in the 2017 Draft IP Guidelines specifically addresses issues relating to injunctive relief, along with the other types of conduct which may amount to an abuse of a dominant position. Whilst the 2017 Draft IP Guidelines recognize that the patent owner is entitled to protect its interest by seeking injunctive relief against another party, they also caution that a dominant SEP holder can force the licensee to accept excessive royalties or other unreasonable licensing terms by seeking injunctive relief against the IP user, thereby restricting competition.

The 2017 Draft IP Guidelines further provide that, in order to determine whether the fact that an SEP holder seeks an injunctive relief has a restrictive effect on competition, the authority may examine: (1) the parties' respective behaviours during negotiation and the true intention reflected by such behaviours; (2) the commitments relating to injunctive reliefs made by the relevant IP holder; (3) the licensing conditions respectively proposed by the parties during negotiation; (4) the impact of the application for injunctive relief on the licensing negotiation; and (5) the

---

[67] Anti-Monopoly Commission, 'Anti-monopoly guidelines on abuse of intellectual property rights' (Draft, 2017), Article 17.
[68] Ibid.
[69] Article 102(c) TFEU (n 7).

impact of the application for an injunctive relief on the competition in the relevant downstream markets and on consumers' interests.[70]

In *Huawei v InterDigital*, the court also specifically addressed the fact that InterDigital petitioned to a US court for an injunction to prevent Huawei from using the SEPs owned by InterDigital.[71] The court reasoned that, by seeking an injunction, InterDigital was actually trying to force Huawei to accept the unreasonable licensing terms it had proposed, which in turn made the high royalties even more unreasonable and unfair.

6. Conclusion

Over nine years after the entry into force of the AML, China has firmly established its position as a heavyweight jurisdiction in the antitrust space, alongside the EU and the US. In recent years, the AML enforcement authorities have not only continued to take a harsh stance towards hard-core infringements of the AML, such as price-fixing and resale price maintenance, but they have also begun to make a foray into more complicated and sophisticated areas, such as the intersection between IP and abuse of market dominance.

Against the background of the Chinese government encouraging domestic innovation as part of its national policy, the interplay between IP and abuse of dominance becomes even more important. Through the high-profile investigations and the private litigation cases, the AML enforcement authorities and the courts have demonstrated that they will not shy away from addressing sophisticated issues, and they are willing to tackle complex areas of the law head-on.

In this regard, some concerns have emerged as a result of the case law that the authorities and the courts may have broader policy considerations in ensuring that domestic companies have access to IP rights on reasonable terms. For instance, the judge at the Guangdong Higher People's Court presiding over the *Huawei v InterDigital* case publicly stated that Huawei 'used antitrust law as a weapon to counterattack' dominant multinational firms and he encouraged other Chinese companies to learn from Huawei. He further suggested that Chinese companies should use antitrust litigation to overcome technology barriers they may face.[72] Such a statement will undoubtedly increase the confidence of domestic companies

---

[70] Anti-Monopoly Commission, 'Anti-monopoly guidelines on abuse of intellectual property rights' (Draft, 2017), Article 26.

[71] *Huawei* (n 36).

[72] '华为胜诉 意义何在' (International Finance News, 31 October 2013), available at <http://paper.people.com.cn/gjjrb/html/2013-10/31/content_1317541.htm> accessed 17 January 2018.

in using antitrust as a tool, and it may encourage them to bring more abuse of dominance cases in the IP sector.

Notwithstanding this, the principles proposed in the 2017 Draft IP Guidelines to regulate the interplay between abuse of dominance in the IP sector, are in line with the international practice, and the guidance overall provides a welcome step towards more clarity, which will without doubt help businesses understand how the intersection between IP and antitrust should be interpreted in China in the future.

11

COMPETITION LAW AND INDUSTRIAL POLICY IN CHINA

Burton Ong* and Tao Tao**

1. Introduction

Competition law and policy necessarily operate within jurisdiction-specific economic, political, and social contexts, resulting in legal frameworks which incorporate broader policy considerations that determine the specific contours of the legal prohibitions against anti-competitive conduct. As a rapidly developing economy with ambitious industrialization goals, China provides a good example of the nexus between competition law and industrial policy in the last decade when its cross-sectoral Anti-Monopoly Law ('AML')[1] came into force. This chapter aims to explore the interaction between China's competition law and industrial policy frameworks, focusing on how its competition authorities and courts have applied the AML to cases with broader national economic implications. The picture which emerges from our analysis is that China's AML is very clearly shaped by its domestic economic priorities, incorporating elements of industrial policy into its competition law regime to support its industrial engines of economic growth and pursuing broader developmental goals apart from the 'purer' competition goals (that focus, for instance, on enhancing consumer welfare) more frequently articulated by competition authorities from the more developed competition law jurisdictions.

To provide the necessary context to understanding China's competition law regime, Section 2 of this chapter provides an overview of the socio-political, cultural, and

---

* Faculty of Law, National University of Singapore.
** Rajah & Tann Singapore LLP, Singapore.
[1] The Anti-monopoly Law of the People's Republic of China ('中华人民共和国反垄断法'), adopted at the 29th Meeting of the Standing Committee of the Tenth National People's Congress and promulgated by Order No 68 of the President of the People's Republic of China on 30 August 2007. The AML entered into force on 1 August 2008. English version available at <http://www.npc.gov.cn/englishnpc/Law/2009-02/20/content_1471587.htm> accessed 2 April 2017.

historical background to the introduction of the AML in 2007, while Section 3 examines the concept of industrial policy within the Chinese context and how it has been embraced within China's competition law framework. Section 4 illustrates the confluence of competition law and industrial policy in China within the context of merger regulation, while Section 5 demonstrates how industrial policy considerations may have percolated into the judicial sphere as well—specifically within the sphere of intellectual property disputes involving Standard Essential Patents. Section 6 offers brief concluding observations.

2. The Competition Law Framework in China

In contrast to the developed competition law regimes of the US and the EU, the role that competition law has played in the modern China's legal landscape has only been significant in the last decade or so.

After the Communist Party of China defeated the Kuomintang in the Chinese Civil War and established the People's Republic of China ('PRC') in 1949, China adopted the planned economy model for more than two decades.[2] Under a planned economy, economic decisions were made by the central government and there was no competition among undertakings.[3] Needless to say, competition law was absent during this period of time since the idea of encouraging competition for business opportunities among undertakings was anathema to an economic system based on central planning.

This began to change in December 1978 when the 3rd Plenary Session of the 11th Central Committee of the Communist Party of China was held.[4] This meeting marked the start of economic reforms in China known as 'Reform and Opening Up' (改革开放, *Gaige Kaifang*).

During Deng Xiaoping's trip to the southern provinces in early 1992, Deng reiterated his commitment to the 'Reform and Opening Up' policy and emphasized the critical importance of economic development. More importantly, Deng confirmed that markets could contribute to China's economic development. In Deng's view, having a market-driven economy did not equate to capitalism, and a socialist

---

[2] Gao Ying (高莹), 'On the Establishment and Historical Significance of the Planned Economy System in the Early Days of the People's Republic of China' ('论建国初期计划经济体制的确立及其历史作用') (Wuhan University of Technology Master's Theses 2007) (Chinese).

[3] Xu Shiying and Tao Tao, 'Monopoly Agreements, Trade Associations and Competition Culture in China' in Thomas Cheng, Sandra Marco Colino, and Burton Ong (eds.), *Cartels in Asia: Law & Practice* (Wolters Kluwer Hong Kong Limited 2015) 257 (hereafter Xu and Tao, 'Monopoly Agreements').

[4] Xu and Tao, 'Monopoly Agreements' (n 3) 257.

state could also have a market-driven economy.[5] This view was endorsed at the 14th National Congress of the Communist Party of China held in October 1992, during which the concept of a 'socialist market economy' was fortified as the goal of China's economic reforms.[6] This was subsequently written into the Constitution in 1993.[7]

The 14th National Congress of the Communist Party of China also confirmed the 'basic role' of the market in the allocation of resources under the 'socialist market economy' system.[8] The role of the market in the allocation of resources was further elevated from being 'basic' to 'decisive' during the 3rd Plenary Session of the 18th Central Committee of the Communist Party of China.[9] This signalled an even greater role for the market in the development of the Chinese economy.

Against this backdrop of economic reforms, there was a need for a comprehensive legal framework to prohibit conduct that was harmful to market competition; before the enactment of the AML in 2007, laws which regulated how firms competed in the market were scattered across various different pieces of legislation.

2.1 Pre-AML competition-related laws

The 1993 Law Against Unfair Competition[10] touched upon various aspects of market competition, such as infringement of trademarks,[11] passing off,[12] false

---

[5] Deng Xiaoping (邓小平), 'Key Points in Speeches in Wuchang, Shenzhen, Zhuhai, Shanghai, etc.' ('在武昌、深圳、珠海、上海等地的谈话要点') in *Deng Xiaoping Selected Works III* ('邓小平文选（第三卷）') 373 (Chinese).

[6] 'Report of Jiang Zemin at the 14th National Congress of the Communist Party of China' ('江泽民在中国共产党第十四次全国代表大会上的报告') (Xinhua News Agency, 12 October 1992), available at <http://news.xinhuanet.com/zhengfu/2004-04/29/content_1447497.htm> accessed 2 April 2017 (Chinese) ('14th Party Congress Report').

[7] Amendment to the Constitution of the People's Republic of China 1993 ('中华人民共和国宪法修正案(1993)', adopted at the First Session of the Eighth National People's Congress and promulgated for implementation by the Announcement of the National People's Congress on 29 March 1993. English version available at <http://www.npc.gov.cn/englishnpc/Law/2007-12/05/content_1381974.htm> accessed 2 April 2017. After this revision, Article of 15 of the Constitution, which stated '*The State practises planned economy on the basis of socialist public ownership . . .*', was amended to '*The State practises socialist market economy . . .*'.

[8] 14th Party Congress Report (n 6).

[9] 'Communique of the 3rd Plenary Session of the 18th Central Committee of the Communist Party of China' ('中国共产党第十八届中央委员会第三次全体会议公报') (Xinhua News Agency, 12 November 2013, available at <http://news.xinhuanet.com/politics/2013-11/12/c_118113455.htm> accessed 2 April 2017 (Chinese).

[10] The Law of the People's Republic of China Against Unfair Competition ('中华人民共和国反不正当竞争法'), adopted at the Third Meeting of the Standing Committee of the Eighth National People's Congress and promulgated by Order No 10 of the President of the People's Republic of China on 2 September 1993. English version available at <http://www.npc.gov.cn/englishnpc/Law/2007-12/12/content_1383803.htm> accessed 2 April 2017 ('Law Against Unfair Competition').

[11] Article 5, Law Against Unfair Competition (n 10).

[12] Ibid.

advertisements,[13] violation of trade secrets,[14] injuring a competitor's business reputation,[15] etc. The Law Against Unfair Competition also has provisions aimed at protecting the competition process. For example, in relation to abuse of dominant positions, Article 6 of the Law Against Unfair Competition states as follows:

> **Article 6**: A public utility enterprise or any other business operator occupying monopoly status according to law shall not restrict people to purchasing commodities from the business operators designated by him, thereby precluding other business operators from fair competition.

In relation to bid-rigging activities, Article 15 of the Law Against Unfair Competition states as follows:

> **Article 15**: Bidders shall not act in collusion with each other so as to force up or down bidding prices.
>
> Bidders and tender-inviters shall not collude with each other so as to push out their competitors from fair competition.

In relation to predatory pricing, Article 11 of the Law Against Unfair Competition prohibits the selling of products below cost with the aim of driving out competitors, with a few exceptions:

> **Article 11**: A business operator shall not, for the purpose of pushing out their competitors, sell their commodities at prices lower than costs.
>
> Any of the following shall not be deemed as an unfair competition act:
>
> (1) Selling perishables or live commodities;
> (2) Disposing of commodities near expiration of their validity duration or those kept too long in stock;
> (3) Seasonal sales; or
> (4) Selling commodities at a reduced price for the purpose of clearing off debts, change of business or suspension of operation.

The Pricing Law,[16] which was enacted four years later in 1997, outlawed price-fixing activities generally. Article 14(1) of the Pricing Law states:

> **Article 14**: The manager may not commit any of the following illegitimate acts in pricing:
>
> (1) Colluding with others to manipulate the market price, thus harming the lawful rights and interests of other managers or consumers.
>
> . . .

---

[13] Article 9, Law Against Unfair Competition (n 10).

[14] Article 10, Law Against Unfair Competition (n 10).

[15] Article 14, Law Against Unfair Competition (n 10).

[16] The Pricing Law of the People's Republic of China ('中华人民共和国价格法'), adopted at the 29th Meeting of the Standing Committee of the Eighth National People's Congress and promulgated by Order No 92 of the President of the People's Republic of China on 29 December 1997. English version available at <http://www.npc.gov.cn/englishnpc/Law/2007-12/11/content_1383577.htm> accessed 2 April 2017.

The Law on Bid Invitation and Bidding[17] was enacted in 1999 and was focused on prohibiting one specific form of anti-competitive activity—bid-rigging activities. Article 32 of the Law on Bid Invitation and Bidding prohibits collusion among bidders, collusion between a bidder and the bid inviter, and bribery by a bidder. Article 32 provides as follows:

> **Article 32:** No bidder may collude with each other in the matter of their quotations or exclude others from fair competition so as to impair the lawful rights and interests of the bid inviter or the other bidders.
>
> No bidder may collude with the bid inviter in bidding so as to impair the interests of the State and the general public or the lawful rights and interests of others.
>
> Bidders are prohibited from bribing the bid inviter or members of the bid evaluation committee for the purpose of winning the bid.

As can be seen above, prior to the enactment of the AML, there was no single piece of legislation in China which comprehensively sets out the types of anti-competitive conduct which are prohibited and the exceptions to those prohibitions. The Pricing Law only dealt with price collusions but not non-price collusions such as market sharing or production controls. The Law on Bid Invitation and Bidding was only concerned with bid-rigging activities, whereas the Law Against Unfair Competition focuses on 'unfair' competitive behaviours as opposed to conduct which impairs the competitive process. The existence, and continued subsistence, of these conduct-specific laws within China's legal landscape does demonstrate the state's keen interest in exercising control over how commercial entities operate within the Chinese market, culminating in the passage of the AML on 30 August 2007 which formally came into force on 1 August 2008. Consisting of eight chapters and fifty-seven articles, the AML appears largely consistent with the prevailing competition law philosophies of the developed economies, with prohibitions directed at three main categories of anti-competitive conduct: monopoly agreements (Chapter 2), abuses of dominant positions (Chapter 3), and anti-competitive concentrations of undertakings (i.e. mergers control) (Chapter 4). It is interesting to note that although the AML was only passed in 2007, the first draft of the AML was in fact completed as far back as 1998.[18]

---

[17] The Law of the People's Republic of China on Bid Invitation and Bidding ('中华人民共和国招标投标法'), adopted at the 11th Meeting of the Standing Committee of the Ninth National People's Congress on 30 August 1999 and promulgated by Order No 21 of the President of the People's Republic of China on 30 August 1999. English version available at <http://www.npc.gov.cn/englishnpc/Law/2007-12/11/content_1383557.htm> accessed 2 April 2017.

[18] Ge Jiangtao (葛江涛), 'AML draftsman: the legislation process was a struggle' ('反垄断法'起草者：立法过程就是一场斗争') (Sina News, 27 October 2014), available at <http://news.sina.com.cn/c/2014-10-27/132831051078.shtml> accessed 2 April 2017 (hereafter Ge, 'AML draftsman') (Chinese).

2.2 Post-AML competition law institutions and regulations

With regard to the enforcement agencies of the AML, it has been observed that the enforcement agencies of the AML in China form a '1+3+x' structure.[19] '1' refers to the State Council Anti-Monopoly Commission ('SCAC'). '3' refers to the 3 main anti-monopoly enforcement agencies, i.e. the Ministry of Commerce ('MOFCOM'), the State Administration for Industry and Commerce ('SAIC'), and the National Development and Reform Commission ('NDRC'). 'x' refers to the various sectoral agencies which have certain enforcement powers under the AML.[20]

The SCAC is established under Article 9 of the AML to be the body in charge of organizing, coordinating, and directing anti-monopoly works. MOFCOM, SAIC, and NDRC are responsible for different aspects of the AML. The MOFCOM Anti-Monopoly Bureau is in charge of merger clearances. SAIC is in charge of enforcement against non-price monopoly agreements, abuses of dominant positions, and abuses of administrative power to eliminate or restrict competition. NDRC is in charge of enforcement against price monopoly agreements.[21]

Certain sectoral agencies also have certain powers to administer the AML within their respective jurisdictions. These sectoral agencies include the China Securities Regulatory Commission, China Banking Regulatory Commission, China Insurance Regulatory Commission, Ministry of Industry and Information Technology, State Electricity Regulatory Commission, Civil Aviation Administration of China, the Ministry of Transport, etc.[22]

Since the enactment of the AML in 2007, the State Council and each of the three AML enforcement agencies have published quite a significant body of administrative rules and regulations pertaining to the enforcement of its provisions. The volume, level of detail, and subject matter diversity of these publications reflects the degree of control which the state can exercise over the commercial life of undertakings operating within the China market.

The State Council's AML-related publications include:

---

[19] Zhou Zhenguo (周振国) and Li Kun (李坤), 'On the issues and improvement in the organization of the anti-monopoly enforcement agencies in our country' ('论我国反垄断执法机构存在的问题与完善') (Chinalawedu.com, 12 February 2015), available at <http://www.chinalawedu.com/web/23182/jx1502127603.shtml> accessed 2 April 2017 (Chinese) (hereafter Zhou and Li, 'Enforcement Agencies').

[20] Zhou and Li, 'Enforcement Agencies' (n 19).

[21] 'The State Council Anti-monopoly Commission has been established. The enforcement agencies have formed a tripartite structure' ('国务院反垄断委员会成立 执法机构'三足鼎立') (Sohu, 2 August 2008), available at <http://it.sohu.com/20080802/n258542693.shtml> accessed 2 April 2017 (Chinese).

[22] Zhou and Li, 'Enforcement Agencies' (n 19).

- *Regulations of the State Council on the Thresholds for Declaring Concentrations of Undertakings* (3 August 2008);[23] and
- *Guidelines of the State Council Anti-Monopoly Commission on the Definition of Relevant Market* (24 May 2009).[24]

MOFCOM's AML-related publications include:

- *Rules on the Calculation of Turnover for the Notification of Concentrations of Undertakings in the Financial Sector* (15 July 2009);[25]
- *Rules on Notification of Concentrations of Undertakings* (21 November 2009);[26]
- *Rules on the Review of Concentrations of Undertakings* (24 November 2009);[27]
- *Provisional Rules on the Implementation of Divestment of Asset or Business in Concentrations of Undertakings* (5 July 2010);[28]
- *Provisional Rules on the Assessment of Competitive Effects of Concentrations of Undertakings* (29 August 2011);[29]
- *Provisional Measures on the Investigation and Treatment of Failure to Notify Concentrations of Undertakings According to Law* (30 December 2011);[30]
- *Provisional Rules on the Applicable Standards for Simple Cases of Concentrations of Undertakings* (11 February 2014);[31]
- *Tentative Guidelines on Notification of Simple Cases of Concentrations of Undertakings* (18 April 2014);[32]
- *Guidelines on Notification of Concentrations of Undertakings* (6 June 2014);[33] and
- *Tentative Rules on the Imposition of Restrictive Conditions for Concentrations of Undertakings* (4 December 2014).[34]

---

[23] '国务院关于经营者集中申报标准的规定', available at <http://www.gov.cn/zwgk/2008-08/04/content_1063769.htm> accessed 2 April 2017 (Chinese).

[24] '国务院反垄断委员会关于相关市场界定的指南', available at <http://www.gov.cn/zwhd/2009-07/07/content_1355288.htm> accessed 2 April 2017 (Chinese).

[25] '金融业经营者集中申报营业额计算方法', available at<http://fldj.mofcom.gov.cn/article/c/200907/20090706411691.shtml> accessed 2 April 2017 (Chinese).

[26] '经营者集中申报办法',available at <http://fldj.mofcom.gov.cn/article/c/200911/20091106639149.shtml> accessed 2 April 2017 (Chinese).

[27] '经营者集中审查办法', available at <http://fldj.mofcom.gov.cn/article/c/200911/20091106639145.shtml> accessed 2 April 2017 (Chinese).

[28] '关于实施经营者集中资产或业务剥离的暂行规定', available at <http://fldj.mofcom.gov.cn/article/c/201007/20100707012000.shtml> accessed 2 April 2017 (Chinese).

[29] '关于评估经营者集中竞争影响的暂行规定', available at <http://fldj.mofcom.gov.cn/article/c/201109/20110907723357.shtml> accessed 2 April 2017 (Chinese).

[30] '未依法申报经营者集中调查处理暂行办法', available at <http://fldj.mofcom.gov.cn/article/c/201201/20120107921682.shtml> accessed 2 April 2017 (Chinese).

[31] '关于经营者集中简易案件适用标准的暂行规定', available at <http://fldj.mofcom.gov.cn/article/c/201409/20140900743277.shtml> accessed 2 April 2017 (Chinese).

[32] '关于经营者集中简易案件申报的指导意见(试行)', available at <http://fldj.mofcom.gov.cn/article/c/201404/20140400555353.shtml> accessed 2 April 2017 (Chinese).

[33] '关于经营者集中申报的指导意见', available at <http://fldj.mofcom.gov.cn/article/c/201406/20140600614679.shtml> accessed 2 April 2017 (Chinese).

[34] '关于经营者集中附加限制性条件的规定(试行)', available at <http://www.mofcom.gov.cn/article/b/c/201412/20141200835207.shtml> accessed 2 April 2017 (Chinese).

SAIC's AML-related publications include:

- *Regulations on the Procedures for Investigating and Handling Cases Concerning Monopoly Agreements and Abuses of Dominant Market Positions* (26 May 2009);[35]
- *Regulations on the Procedures for Prohibiting Abuses of Administrative Power to Eliminate or Restrict Competition* (26 May 2009);[36]
- *Regulations on Prohibiting Monopoly Agreements* (31 December 2010);[37]
- *Regulations on Prohibiting Abuses of Dominant Market Positions* (31 December 2010);[38]
- *Regulations on Prohibiting Abuses of Administrative Power to Eliminate or Restrict Competition* (31 December 2010);[39] and
- *Regulations on Prohibiting Abuses of Intellectual Property Rights to Eliminate or Restrict Competition* (7 April 2015).[40]

NDRC's AML-related publications include:

- *Regulations Against Price Monopolies* (29 December 2010);[41]
- *Regulations on Administrative Enforcement Procedures Against Price Monopolies* (29 December 2010);[42]

In addition to the departmental rules issued by the three AML enforcement agencies, the Supreme People's Court also published a judicial interpretation in May 2012 on the civil actions initiated by private parties under the AML titled *Several Provisions Regarding the Application of Laws in Civil Suits Caused by Anti-monopoly Conduct* (Judicial Interpretation [2012] No 5).[43]

---

[35] '工商行政管理机关查处垄断协议、滥用市场支配地位案件程序规定', available at <http://www.gov.cn/flfg/2009-06/16/content_1341338.htm> accessed 2 April 2017 (Chinese).
[36] '工商行政管理机关制止滥用行政权利排除、限制竞争行为程序规定', available at <http://www.gov.cn/gongbao/content/2010/content_1511009.htm> accessed 2 April 2017 (Chinese).
[37] '工商行政管理机关禁止垄断协议行为的规定', available at <http://www.gov.cn/flfg/2011-01/07/content_1779945.htm> accessed 2 April 2017 (Chinese).
[38] '工商行政管理机关禁止滥用市场支配地位行为的规定', available at <http://www.gov.cn/flfg/2011-01/07/content_1779980.htm> accessed 2 April 2017 (Chinese).
[39] '工商行政管理机关制止滥用行政权利排除、限制竞争行为的规定', available at <http://www.gov.cn/flfg/2011-01/07/content_1780003.htm> accessed 2 April 2017 (Chinese).
[40] '关于禁止滥用知识产权排除、限制竞争行为的规定'<http://www.saic.gov.cn/zcfg/xzgzjgfxwj/201508/t20150820_160841.html> accessed 2 April 2017 (Chinese).
[41] '反价格垄断规定', available at <http://jjs.ndrc.gov.cn/zcfg/201101/t20110104_389399.html> accessed 2 April 2017 (Chinese).
[42] '反价格垄断行政执法程序规定', available at <http://jjs.ndrc.gov.cn/zcfg/201101/t20110104_389401.html> accessed 2 April 2017 (Chinese).
[43] '最高人民法院关于审理因垄断行为引发的民事纠纷案件应用法律若干问题的规定'(法释[2012] 5 号) , available at <http://www.court.gov.cn/fabu-xiangqing-3989.html> accessed 2 April 2017 (Chinese).

3. Industrial Policy in China

3.1 Defining 'industrial policy' in China

Like competition policy, industrial policy is a tool which governments can use to intervene in the economy.[44] The origin of the concept of 'industrial policy' is often attributed to post-World War II Japan.[45] The goal of industrial policy in Japan from the mid-1950s to 1970s was to achieve rapid economic development and to 'catch up' with the developed economies.[46]

Although the term 'industrial policy' has been frequently used, it has been observed that there is neither an official nor a universally accepted definition of the term, which can be understood at different levels of abstraction.[47] At the broadest level, some commentators see industrial policy as 'all laws and policies concerning industries in a country'.[48] One might even include policies such as environmental and educational policies, which have an indirect effect on the industries, as part of the rubric of 'industrial policy'.[49]

A more useful approach towards defining industrial policy, that would facilitate the comparative analysis with competition policy that this chapter is trying to engage in, is to narrow the goal of industrial policy to the attainment of a specified economic or social goal. For the purpose of this chapter, we adopt Professor Liu Guiqing's definition of industrial policy, which is 'the sum total of intervening measures adopted by a government to guide, promote, protect, support or restrict industries or enterprises within an industry to achieve a specific economic or social goal, such as to realise the adjustment or transition of industrial structures, to achieve economic recovery or "catching up", or to improve the international competitiveness of industries, etc.'.[50] Industrial policies may be implemented in various different forms, examples of which include pricing, taxation, finance, foreign exchange, trade, market entry requirements, and administrative regulations.[51]

---

[44] Liu Guiqing (刘桂清), *The Relation between Competition Policy and Industrial Policy in Antitrust Law* ('反垄断法中的产业政策与竞争政策') (Peking University Press, 2010) 1 (hereafter Liu, *Antitrust Law*) (Chinese).
[45] Liu, *Antitrust Law* (n 44) 11; Bin Xuehua (宾雪花), *A Study on the Coordination between Industrial Policy Law and Competition Policy Law* ('产业政策法与反垄断法之协调制度研究') (China Social Sciences Press, 2013) 2 (Chinese).
[46] Liu, *Antitrust Law* (n 44) 11.
[47] Ibid. 9.
[48] Ibid. 9.
[49] Xu Shiying (徐士英), 'On the Functional Challenges During the Implementation of Anti-monopoly Law—The Coordination Between Competition Policy and Industrial Policy' ('反垄断法实施面临功能性挑战——兼论竞争政策与产业政策的协调') 3 (hereafter Xu, 'Functional Challenges') (Chinese).
[50] Liu, *Antitrust Law* (n 44) 10.
[51] Ibid. 13.

This conception of industrial policy can be further refined into four sub-categories: industrial structure policies, industrial organization policies, industrial technology policies, and industrial layout policies:[52]

- Industrial structure policies: 'Industrial structure' refers to the interrelationship between the various industries in an economy.[53] Industrial structure policies aim to regulate the roles and relative weights of different industries. The goal of industrial structure policies is to promote the optimization and advancement of the industrial structure.[54]
- Industrial organization policies: In contrast to industrial structure policies which regulate the interrelationship between different industries, 'industrial organization policies' are policies which concern the relationship between different enterprises within the same industry. Examples of industrial organization policies include those aimed at promoting competition, promoting formation of large enterprises and promoting the modernization of small and medium enterprises ('SMEs').[55]
- Industrial technology policies: These are policies which promote and support the research and development of technology in industries. The rationale for industrial technology policies is to cure the market failure arising from the reluctance of private investment in research and development of new technologies because of the significant capital required and the uncertainty of outcome.[56]
- Industrial layout policies: Industrial layout policies concern the geographical distribution of industries in a country or regional area.[57]

The rest of this chapter illustrates the interaction between competition law and industrial policy with examples that might fall within the first three sub-categories—that is, situations where China's competition laws have been applied in pursuit of industrial structure, industrial organization, and industrial technology policies.

3.2 The relationship between industrial policy and competition policy

The underlying common ground between competition policy and industrial policy is to spur China's economic development by providing the government with the necessary tools to correct market failures,[58] thereby improving allocation efficiency and facilitating economic growth.[59]

---

[52] Ibid. 12; Xu, 'Functional Challenges' (n 49) 2; *Outline of State Industrial Policies for the 1990s* ('九十年代国家产业政策纲要') passed by the State Council on 25 March 1994, available at <http://cpc.people.com.cn/GB/64184/64186/66685/4494201.html> accessed 2 April 2017 (hereafter *Outline 1990s*) (Chinese).

[53] Liu, *Antitrust Law* (n 44) 13.

[54] Ibid.

[55] Ibid.

[56] Ibid.

[57] Ibid.

[58] Ibid. 19.

[59] Ibid. 20.

Competition policy enables government intervention to prevent undertakings from injuring the market mechanism by engaging in anti-competitive conduct, such as engaging in collusion or abusing their dominant positions, that cannot be corrected by the market itself.

Industrial policy enables government intervention is to correct perceived allocation inefficiencies in the market. Such allocation inefficiency may arise, for example, because of the lack of competitiveness of an infant industry, or because of insufficient support for strategic industries. One of the goals of industrial policy is therefore to allocate resources among industries or among undertakings within an industry in an optimal manner so as to achieve the greatest economic growth for the country as a whole.[60]

Despite the fact that both industrial policy and competition law and policy are essentially modes of government intervention in the market, there are significant differences between them.

First and foremost, industrial policy and competition law give different weight to the role of the government. Competition policy can be seen as serving a ring-fence: it prescribes certain types of anti-competitive conduct which the undertakings are not allowed to engage in, but leaves the 'invisible hand' of the market to work out the optimal allocation of resources within these broadly-defined boundaries. On the other hand, industrial policy seeks to use the 'visible hand' of the government to directly influence the allocation of resources among industries or within an industry, and seeks to use the government to supplant the role of the market in allocating resources.[61]

Secondly, competition policy has a general scope of application, apart from certain exempted industries. Competition laws are therefore supposed to be 'industry-blind' in general.[62] On the other hand, industrial policy is targeted at certain industries or undertakings.[63] As a matter of competition policy, the government should not decide which industries or firms should prosper—that is a matter for market forces to decide. However, from the viewpoint of industrial policy, the government will pick the 'winners' and channel resources to industries or undertakings which the government thinks should develop at a greater speed.[64]

Thirdly, apart from correcting allocative inefficiency, industrial policy in developing economies often has the goal of enabling the country to 'catch up' with developed economies.[65] On the assumption that the development of a country's industrial

---

[60] Ibid. 20.
[61] Ibid. 21.
[62] Ibid. 22.
[63] Ibid. 22.
[64] Ibid. 22.
[65] Ibid. 21; Xu, 'Functional Challenges' (n 49) 2.

structure usually follows the same stages, industrial policy may be deployed to push the industries to follow the same trajectory that the industries in developed economies have already followed, such that the time needed to industrialize the country is significantly reduced.[66] Such considerations go beyond the pursuit of allocation efficiency or the protection of the competition process, which is the domain of competition policy.

From the brief comparison of the differences between industrial policy and competition policy above, it is not hard to see why the two may conflict with each other in their respective application. In the context of monopoly agreements, while competition policy takes a very strict view towards such agreements, industrial policy may sometimes tolerate such agreements when there is too much excess capacity in the industry which results in falling prices and increasing losses suffered by the firms in that industry.[67] With regard to concentration of undertakings, competition policy is cautious towards mergers which will have an adverse effect on market competition. However, industrial policy may sometimes favour mergers which are perceived as being capable of creating economies of scale and 'national champions' to improve competitiveness of that industry or undertaking.[68] One of the industrial organization policy measures in the *Outline 1990s*[69] was to 'encourage enterprises to voluntarily unite and restructure or to form multi-regional, multi-sectoral, multi-ownership or multi-national group corporations through fair competition and merger, takeover, cross-shareholding etc.'

With the above in mind, we examine how the text and implementation of the AML accommodates the goals of industrial policy. However, before looking at the role of industrial policy within China's AML framework, it is helpful to look at the implementation of industrial policy prior to the enactment of the AML in order to understand the mindset of market players and government officials just before the AML came into force.

3.3 The significance of industrial policy in pre- and post-AML China

3.3.1 *The effect of industrial policy on market competition before the AML*

Although China gradually embraced the development of a 'socialist market economy' after the commencement of the 'Reform and Opening Up' state policy in 1978, due to the long period during which it operated as a command economy and the significant amount of state capital in the economy, regulatory mindsets entrenched during the command economy period remained. Given that the

---

[66] Ibid. 21.
[67] Ibid. 22.
[68] Ibid. 22.
[69] *Outline 1990s* (n 52).

development of the market economy was still at its nascent stage, the idea of protecting market competition was still foreign to many undertakings and government officials.[70] Some state policies even went directly against the market mechanism and may be regarded as anti-competitive.

Two types of common industrial policies which had adverse effects on market competitions were 'production control' policies and 'self-disciplined price' policies.[71]

The impetus for implementing 'production control' policies was the presence of excess capacity in certain industries which faced the problem of oversupply of goods.[72] Rather than allowing the market to adjust the level of supply and demand by phasing out inefficient firms and inferior products, the government implemented policies to limit production. For example, the State Council issued the '*Notice on Strictly Controlling Enterprises from Continuing with Production of Oversupplied Goods*'[73] in 1991 to direct all ministries and provincial governments to implement measures to control the oversupply of goods. More recent examples of such production control agreements between undertakings include the aluminum producers, coal producers, penicillin producers, and silk processors.[74] Such production control agreements subvert the competition process because instead of letting the market decide the optimum output and price, the undertakings collude to decide the market output, with the likely effect of raising market prices to the detriment of consumer interests.

The so-called 'self-disciplined' pricing policies involve an even more overt form of price-fixing conduct. Such self-disciplined pricing was often issued by a trade association and applied to all undertakings in a specific industry. The reason was usually excess capacity and oversupply, which caused undertakings to engage in price wars, which in turn led to diminishing revenue and profit.[75] Such price wars were seen as 'disorderly competition' to be avoided. Again, instead of allowing the market to correct itself, trade associations, which were in effect quasi-government bodies, often issued 'self-disciplined' pricing guidelines which all undertakings were required to comply with. The government's endorsement of such 'self-disciplined' pricing practices is apparent from the *Opinion on the Implementation of Sectoral Self-disciplined Pricing for Certain Industrial Products*[76] issued by the former State

---

[70] Liu, *Antitrust Law* (n 44) 180.

[71] Ibid. 180–83.

[72] Ibid. 180.

[73] *Notice on Strictly Controlling Enterprises from Continuing with Production of Oversupplied Goods* ('国务院关于严格控制企业继续生产积压产品的通知') issued by the State Council on 1 July 1991, available at <http://www.gov.cn/zhengce/content/2015-12/01/content_10365.htm> accessed 2 April 2017 (Chinese).

[74] Liu, *Antitrust Law* (n 44) 181.

[75] Ibid. 182.

[76] *Opinion of the State Economic and Trade Commission on the Implementation of Sectoral Self-disciplined Pricing for Certain Industrial Products*

Economic and Trade Commission (dissolved in 2003) on 17 August 1998, which endorsed the practice of 'self-disciplined' pricing among undertakings for certain categories of products and recognized the primary role of trade associations in formulating and supervising the implementation of 'self-disciplined' pricing practices. It can be argued that such 'self-disciplined' pricing guidelines were in effect price-fixing agreements among undertakings. Financial penalties were often imposed on undertakings for breaching the 'self-disciplined' pricing guidelines.[77]

3.3.2. *The accommodation of industrial policy within the AML*

The AML explicitly incorporates industrial policy goals within China's competition law framework in a number of ways. Professor Xu Shiying has observed that this is demonstrated through: (1) multiple legislative aims of the AML, (2) exemptions and exceptions in the AML, (3) standard of review of monopolistic conduct, and (4) jurisdictional allocation between AML and other sectoral regulatory laws and the allocation of enforcement powers.[78]

Certain provisions in the AML give the state a significant role in the interpretation and administration of the Act and have a strong industrial policy bent. In particular, Articles 4, 5, and 7 of the AML provide as follows:

> **Article 4:** The State shall formulate and implement competition rules which are compatible with the socialist market economy, in order to improve macro-economic regulation and build up a sound market network which operates in an integrated, open, competitive and orderly manner.

> **Article 5:** Undertakings may, through fair competition and voluntary association, get themselves concentrated according to law, to expand the scale of their business operations and enhance their competitiveness on the market.

> **Article 7:** With respect to the industries which are under the control of by the State-owned economic sector and have a bearing on the lifeline of the national economy or national security and the industries which exercise monopoly over the production and sale of certain commodities according to law, the State shall protect the lawful business operations of undertakings in these industries, and shall, in accordance with the law, supervise and regulate their business operations and the prices of the commodities and services provided by them, in order to protect the consumers' interests and facilitate technological advance.

> The undertakings mentioned in the preceding paragraph shall do business according to law, be honest, faithful and strictly self-disciplined, and subject themselves to public supervision, and they shall not harm the consumers' interests by taking

---

('国家经济贸易委员会关于部分工业产品实行行业自律价的意见') issued by the former State Economic and Trade Commission on 17 August 1998, available at <http://www.51wf.com/print-law?id=1130857> accessed 2 April 2017 (Chinese); see also Liu, *Antitrust Law* (n 44) 182.

[77] Liu, *Antitrust Law* (n 44) 183.
[78] Xu, 'Functional Challenges' (n 49) 5.

advantage of their position of control or their monopolistic production and sale of certain commodities.

It has been observed that it is somewhat odd that Articles 4 and 5 were included in the AML since the AML is not a piece of legislation on macro-economic regulation or industrial policy.[79] What is clear from the language of these provisions is that the AML is that competition authorities in China have some latitude to interpret the legislative prohibitions found in the AML in a manner that also advances the industrial policy goals of the state.

4. Merger Regulation in China: Industrial Policy and State-owned Enterprises

The impact of industrial policy on China's competition law regime is most visible in the area of merger regulation, particularly where the parties to the merger are both state-owned enterprises ('**SOEs**') in key industrial sectors.

SOEs continue to play a major role in China's economy. Article 6 of the PRC Constitution expressly recognizes the dominance of public ownership, while recognizing the status of 'diverse forms of ownership'.[80] Article 7 of the PRC Constitution goes on to confirm the leading role of SOEs:

> **Article 7:** The State-owned economy, namely, the socialist economy under ownership by the whole people, is the leading force in the national economy. The State ensures the consolidation and growth of the State-owned economy.

The government body which performs the state's role as the investor in SOEs is the State-owned Assets Supervision and Administration Commission of the State Council ('**SASAC**'). SASAC's role includes the supervision of state-owned assets of SOEs (excluding financial enterprises), the employment of top executives at SOEs, overseeing the reform and restructuring of SOEs and formulating relevant policies and regulations.[81] Financial enterprises (such as enterprises which require banking business licences, securities business licences and insurance business licences) are generally not under the purview of the SASAC.[82] There are 102 'centrally administered enterprises' under the direct purview of SASAC, while SOEs incorporated

---

[79] Ge, 'AML draftsman' (n 18).

[80] The Constitution of the People's Republic of China ('中华人民共和国宪法'). English version (full text after the 2004 amendment) available at <http://www.npc.gov.cn/englishnpc/Constitution/node_2825.htm> accessed 2 April 2017.

[81] 'What we do', SASAC available at <http://en.sasac.gov.cn/2018/07/17/c_7.htm> accessed 9 October 2018.

[82] Charles Qin and Tomy Xia, 'Introduction to the Regulatory Framework for the State-owned Assets in Financial Enterprises' (Llinks Law Offices, August 2008), available at <http://www.llinkslaw.com/uploadfile/publication/60_1422438483.pdf> accessed 2 April 2017.

in a provincial-level or municipal-level administrative area are under the purview of the local SASACs. The 102 centrally administered enterprises include some of the biggest enterprises in China, such as Sinopec, China National Petroleum Corporation,[83] State Grid, China Telecom, China Mobile, China Unicom, FAW Group, Angang Iron & Steel, Air China, China Eastern Airlines, COSCO, China Merchants Group, and China Resources.[84]

SOE restructuring has occurred frequently over the years. Such restructuring (including mergers) often took place under the government's direction for policy reasons. Mergers among SOEs were often encouraged because of the perceived economies of scale and the desire to nurture 'national champions' who might compete on the international stage.

However, while mergers among SOEs may potentially produce economies of scale or improve the international competitiveness of the enterprises, such mergers may also restrict or limit domestic market competition. Since mergers among SOEs are often under the direction of the government, it raises the question of whether such mergers are also subject to the notification requirements under the relevant provisions of the AML and the subsidiary legislation. Article 28 of the AML provides the following:

> **Article 28:** If the concentration of undertakings leads, or may lead, to elimination or restriction of competition, the authority for enforcement of the Anti-Monopoly Law under the State Council shall make a decision to prohibit their concentration. However, if the undertaking concerned can prove that the advantages of such concentration to competition obviously outweigh the disadvantages, or that the concentration is in the public interest, the authority for enforcement of the Anti-Monopoly Law under the State Council may decide not to prohibit their concentration.

Article 21 provides that undertakings must notify the authority for anti-monopoly enforcement under the State Council if their intended concentration reaches the threshold level as set by the State Council. Article 3 of the *Regulations of the State Council on the Thresholds for Declaring Concentrations of Undertakings* issued by the State Council on 3 August 2008[85] provides that the following concentrations of undertakings shall be notified to MOFCOM:

(a) where the combined worldwide turnover of all the undertakings concerned in the preceding financial year exceeds RMB 10 billion, and at least 2 of the

---

[83] The better-known PetroChina is the listed arm of China National Petroleum Corporation.

[84] List of centrally administered enterprises as at 20 December 2016 available at <http://www.sasac.gov.cn/n86114/n86137/index.html> accessed 2 April 2017 (Chinese).

[85] '国务院关于经营者集中申报标准的规定', available at <http://www.gov.cn/zwgk/2008-08/04/content_1063769.htm> accessed 2 April 2017 (hereafter '*Threshold Regulations*') (Chinese); unofficial English translation available at <http://www.cpahkltd.com/EN/info.aspx?n=20100716155215657680> accessed 2 April 2017.

undertakings concerned have domestic turnovers within China in the preceding financial year exceeding RMB 400 million each; or

(b) where the combined domestic turnover within China of all the undertakings concerned in the preceding financial year is more than RMB 2 billion, and at least 2 of the undertakings concerned have domestic turnovers within China in the preceding financial year exceeding RMB 400 million each.

Furthermore, MOFCOM can investigate a concentration even if the above thresholds are not reached, where the facts and evidence indicate that the concentration has or is likely to have the effect of eliminating or restricting competition.[86]

Two high-profile mergers between SOEs will be examined below to illustrate the impact of China's industrial policy on the operation of its merger control system.

4.1 The China Unicom-China Netcom merger

2008 was a significant year for the telecommunications industry in China: six state-owned telecommunication enterprises[87] in China were restructured into three new companies. Prior to the restructuring exercise, fixed-line operators were not permitted to offer mobile services, and vice versa.[88] After the exercise, three restructured companies emerged: China Telecom, China Mobile, and China Unicom, each operating its own fixed-line, mobile, and broadband services.

The announcement for the restructuring exercise was jointly issued by the Ministry of Industry and Information Technology, NDRC and the Ministry of Finance of China on 24 May 2008.[89] The impetus for the restructuring was the imminent issuance of 3G telecoms licences. They declared that the telecommunications industry in China had developed from a monopolistic industry to a 'competitive' industry with six telecommunications enterprises at the time of this announcement. However, a market restructuring exercise was still required because the 'competitive structure' in the industry was imbalanced, as the rapid development in the mobile sector and stagnation in the fixed-line sector had led to growing gaps in the development of the market players. Therefore, the purpose of the restructuring was to reallocate the existing network infrastructure between three full-service enterprises,

---

[86] Article 4 of the *Threshold Regulations*.

[87] The six telecommunications enterprises were China Telecom, China Mobile, China Unicom, China Netcom, China Tietong, and China Satcom. For a broad overview of the restructuring exercise, see Sumner Lemon, 'China Announces Telecom Restructuring, Clearing Way for 3G' (PCWorld, 25 May 2008), available at <http://www.pcworld.com/article/146297/article.html> accessed 2 April 2017.

[88] Ibid.

[89] *Announcement on Deepening Reform in the Telecommunications System* ('关于深化电信体制改革的通告') issued on 24 May 2008, available at <http://www.gov.cn/gzdt/2008-05/24/content_991345.htm> accessed 2 April 2017 (Chinese).

each of which was issued a 3G licence after the restructuring exercise. The goal was not just to avoid monopoly, but also to avoid 'excessive competition' and unnecessary infrastructure duplication.[90]

Under the restructuring plan, China United Telecommunications Corporation Ltd ('**China Unicom**')[91] merged with China Network Communications Group Corporation ('**China Netcom**') to form China United Network Communications Group Co Ltd ('**merged China Unicom**'). The two companies eventually merged on 15 October 2008, which was after the AML came into force. However, China Unicom and China Netcom did not appear to have notified MOFCOM of their intended merger under the merger clearance regime under the AML.

In late April 2009, almost a year after the restructuring of these telecommunications firms was jointly announced by the Ministry of Industry and Information Technology, NDRC and the Ministry of Finance, MOFCOM pointed out that the merger was probably in violation of the AML as neither China Unicom nor China Netcom had notified MOFCOM prior to carrying out the merger although their turnovers far exceeded the necessary thresholds for merger notification.[92] This was despite the fact that the lawyers advising the companies on the merger had already highlighted the issue of merger clearance in their legal opinion. However, no penalty seems to have been imposed on the merged China Unicom for failing to notify MOFCOM of the merger.

As one of the earliest high-profile merger cases after the AML came into force, the China Unicom-China Netcom merger highlighted several difficulties with the implementation of merger clearance regime for mergers between SOEs.

Firstly, mergers between SOEs almost invariably involve industrial policy considerations and are often carried out under the orders of the central government. Such mergers often involve more than one ministry. That the merging parties in the China Unicom-China Netcom case were not penalized for their failure to notify the merger highlights this problem. SOEs may face a tricky situation if they are caught in the middle of conflicting signals from the government: on the one hand, these SOEs may have been given mandatory orders to merge, while on the other hand, they may fail the merger clearance process at MOFCOM if the anti-competitive effects of their merger are deemed to outweigh the potential benefits their merger may bring about.

---

[90] Ibid.

[91] The CDMA business of China Unicom was to be acquired by China Telecom. Prior to the restructuring, China Unicom had both CDMA and GSM businesses.

[92] Wang Biqiang, 'Telecom Giants' Merger May Have Breached Antitrust Law' (The Economic Observer, 6 May 2009), available at <http://www.eeo.com.cn/ens/Industry/2009/05/06/136933.shtml> accessed 2 April 2017.

An easy solution may be to carve out such telecom-sector mergers between SOEs by invoking Article 7 of the AML. However, MOFCOM's statements made in relation to the China Unicom-China Netcom merger already made it clear that Article 7 of the AML is not a blanket exemption for SOEs from the merger clearance regime, and that MOFCOM would not simply rubber stamp such mergers.[93] Furthermore, subsequent cases such as the China Eastern Airlines-Shanghai Airlines merger and the COSCO-China Shipping merger also show that mergers between SOEs must go through the same merger clearance process so long as the threshold requirements in the AML are satisfied. The *Operational Rules on Transactions Involving State-owned Property in Enterprises*[94] published by SASAC on 15 June 2009 also stipulated that in cases where a transfer of state-owned property involves an anti-monopoly review, the transacting parties shall submit the property transfer agreement and related documents to the relevant government agencies for approval, and that the property transfer institution should only issue the property transfer certificate after approvals from the relevant government agencies has been granted.[95]

Secondly, a further complication is the application of Article 22 of the AML. Article 22 of the AML, which pertains to the 'single economic entity' doctrine, provides that:

> **Article 22**: In any of the following circumstances, undertakings may dispense with declaration to the authority for enforcement of the Anti-Monopoly Law under the State Council:
>
> (1) one of the undertakings involved in the concentration owns 50 percent or more of the voting shares or assets of each of the other undertakings; or
> (2) one and the same undertaking not involved in the concentration owns 50 percent or more of the voting shares or assets of each of the undertakings involved in the concentration.

It has been argued that Article 22 of the AML applied to the China Unicom-China Netcom merger because both enterprises were majority-owned by the State.[96] However, Article 22(2) of the AML only applies when an 'undertaking' owns at least 50 per cent of both undertakings involved in the merger. 'Undertaking' is defined in Article 12 of the AML as including '*natural persons, legal persons, and other organizations that engage in manufacturing, or selling commodities or providing*

---

[93] Ibid.

[94] *Operational Rules on Transactions Involving State-owned Property in Enterprises* ('企业国有产权交易操作规则') issued on 15 June 2009, available at <http://www.gov.cn/gzdt/2009-06/25/content_1350113.htm> accessed 2 April 2017 (hereafter *SOE Operational Rules*) (Chinese).

[95] Articles 37 and 44, *SOE Operational Rules*.

[96] Sipu (思朴), 'Was the merger between China Unicom and China Netcom in breach of AML?' ('联通网通合并违反"反垄断法"吗?' (Sina, 1 May 2009), available at <http://blog.sina.com.cn/s/blog_45f5343b0100cvz3.html> accessed 2 April 2017 (Chinese).

services', and does not seem to include the state within this definition. Furthermore, MOFCOM's statement in relation to the China Unicom-China Netcom merger clearly expressed its view that SOEs are not exempted from the merger clearance regime under the AML.

Thirdly, this case also exposes the coordination difficulties between different government agencies and SOEs when it comes to the enforcement of the AML. The merger between China Unicom and China Netcom was carried out with the joint approval of the Ministry of Industry and Information Technology, NDRC, and Ministry of Finance, which are all ministry-level bodies under the State Council. MOFCOM is also another ministry-level body under the State Council. Consequently, if MOFCOM had decided that the merger between China Unicom and China Netcom should be prohibited under the AML, it would have become a struggle between the different ministries, each guided by their own policy goals. Because MOFCOM was not a powerful and independent anti-monopoly enforcement agency, it would not have had enough 'teeth' to block the merger between China Unicom and China Netcom. It is also notable that NDRC, one of the three government bodies which jointly issued the announcement for the China Unicom-China Netcom merger, was itself one of China's three anti-monopoly enforcement agencies, although it was not the agency in charge of merger clearance.

4.2 The China Eastern Airlines-Shanghai Airlines merger

A year later, another high-profile merger between Chinese SOEs took place. This time, the merger was between China Eastern Airlines Corporation Limited ('China Eastern Airlines') and Shanghai Airlines Co Ltd ('Shanghai Airlines').[97]

The merger was announced by both companies on 13 July 2009. Prior to the merger, China Eastern Airlines was majority owned by China Eastern Airlines Group Corporation, which was in turn a centrally administered SOE administered by SASAC and was one of the 'big three' national airlines in China, the other two of which were Air China and China Southern Airlines. As for Shanghai Airlines, its ultimate controlling shareholder was the Shanghai SASAC.[98]

---

[97] Wu Xiaofeng (吴晓峰) and Huang Xiwei (黄希韦), 'The China Eastern Airlines-Shanghai Airlines Merger Plan is Released' ('上航东航合并方案出台') (Legal Daily, 16 July 2009), available at <http://www.legaldaily.com.cn/zmbm/content/2009-07/16/content_1123845.htm?node=7570> accessed 2 April 2017 (hereafter Wu and Huang, 'Merger Plan') (Chinese); 'China Eastern to merge with Shanghai Airlines' (China Daily, 13 July 2009), available at <http://www.chinadaily.com.cn/china/2009-07/13/content_8419844.htm> accessed 2 April 2017.

[98] '东方航空凤凰涅槃 详解东方航空吸收合并上海航空' (163.com), available at <http://money.163.com/special/00253H5T/eastair.html> accessed 2 April 2017 (Chinese). The two biggest shareholders of Shanghai Airlines at that time, Shanghai Lianhe Investment Co Ltd and Jinjiang International (Holdings) Co Ltd, were both wholly owned by the Shanghai SASAC.

The merger between China Eastern Airlines and Shanghai Airlines received the backing from both the SASAC and the Shanghai SASAC.[99] The merger also received the approval of the State Council.[100] It was observed that China Eastern Airlines made a net loss of around RMB 13.9 billion in 2008, while Shanghai Airlines made a net loss of around RMB 1.2 billion in the same period.[101] Shanghai Airlines was rumoured to have not been in favour of being absorbed by the equally loss-making China Eastern Airlines, and some commentators were of the view that the merger was the idea of the government instead of the two enterprises involved.[102] One view was that the main impetus for the merger was the Shanghai government's policy goal of further developing Shanghai as an aviation hub.[103]

Both China Eastern Airlines and Shanghai Airlines were airlines headquartered in Shanghai. Prior to the merger, the market shares of China Eastern Airlines and Shanghai Airlines in the Shanghai market were 36–40 per cent and 15 per cent respectively, which means that the combined market share of China Eastern Airlines and Shanghai Airlines in the Shanghai market would exceed 50 per cent.[104] Furthermore, both airlines operated overlapping routes,[105] which would typically raise competition law concerns.

The combined annual turnover of China Eastern Airlines and Shanghai Airlines was more than RMB 50 billion, far exceeding the threshold for merger notification of RMB 10 billion under the AML. Unlike the China Unicom-China Netcom merger, the China Eastern Airlines-Shanghai Airlines merger was duly notified to MOFCOM and had received clearance from MOFCOM in November 2009.[106] Unfortunately, MOFCOM did not release any detailed grounds for approving the merger. Different views have emerged as to whether the merger should have been

---

[99] Dong Jun (董珺) 'China Eastern Airlines and Shanghai Airlines met to discuss reorganization with coordination from SASAC' ('国资委出面协调 东航、上航密会启动重组') (JRJ.com, 9 June 2009), available at <http://hk.jrj.com.cn/2009/06/0908275192421.shtml> accessed 2 April 2017 (Chinese).

[100] Fang Ye (方烨), 'China Eastern Airlines and Shanghai Airlines in "weak-weak merger" in a bid to resist Air China' ('东航上航'弱弱整合'重组 联手抵御国航入侵') (163.com, 10 June 2009) , available at <http://money.163.com/09/0610/11/5BEM5TV400252605.html> accessed 2 April 2017 (hereafter Fang, 'Weak-weak Merger') (Chinese).

[101] Wu and Huang, 'Merger Plan' (n 97).

[102] Wu and Huang, 'Merger Plan' (n 97); 'Who is the loser in the China Eastern Airlines-Shanghai Airlines merger?' ('东航上航纠结重组 谁是失意者?') (Shanhuojiaoyi.com, 17 June 2009), available at <http://money.163.com/09/0613/11/5BMDJI3000253B0H.html> accessed 2 April 2017 (hereafter 'Who is the loser') (Chinese).

[103] Fang, 'Weak-weak Merger' (n 100).

[104] Wu and Huang, 'Merger Plan' (n 97).

[105] 'Who is the loser' (n 102).

[106] Zhang Ruobin (张若斌), 'China Eastern Airlines and Shanghai Airlines have cleared MOFCOM review. Merger expected to complete by end of the year' ('东航上航合并方案通过商务部调查 有望年内完成') (People's Daily, 25 November 2009), available at <http://ccnews.people.com.cn/GB/10449436.html> accessed 2 April 2017 (Chinese).

blocked by MOFCOM.[107] Given that the combined market share of China Eastern Airlines and Shanghai Airlines for flights into and out of Shanghai was more than 50 per cent, it could be argued that MOFCOM should have subjected the merger to more rigorous scrutiny, such as whether the merger would lead to potentially higher fares or particular flight routes from Shanghai or whether there were high barriers to entry. Article 27 of the AML sets out the factors which MOFCOM should have taken into account when assessing mergers under the AML:

Article 27: The following factors shall be taken into consideration in the review of the concentration of undertakings:

(1) the market shares of the undertakings involved in concentration in a relevant market and their power of control over the market;

(2) the degree of concentration in relevant market;

(3) the impact of their concentration on access to the market and technological advance;

(4) the impact of their concentration on consumers and other relevant undertakings concerned;

(5) the impact of their concentration on the development of the national economy; and

(6) other factors which the authority for enforcement of the Anti-Monopoly Law under the State Council deems to need consideration in terms of its impact on market competition.

It is not clear whether MOFCOM conducted a full assessment the impact of the China Eastern Airlines-Shanghai Airlines merger based on the factors above or whether MOFCOM had simply given the green light to the merger since it was already endorsed by both SASAC and Shanghai SASAC.

In fact, a cursory examination of the list of MOFCOM's announcements on its website pertaining to merger clearance cases from 2008 to date[108] shows that almost all cases with published decisions from MOFCOM were cases involving foreign enterprises. On the other hand, high-profile mergers between Chinese SOEs such as the China Eastern Airlines-Shanghai Airlines merger, China CNR Corp-CSR Corp merger[109] and COSCO-China Shipping merger[110] were approved by

---

[107] Liu Liang (刘亮), 'Analysing the anti-trust issues in the China Eastern Airlines-Shanghai Airlines Merger' ('解析东航上航合并案中的反垄断问题') (Civil Aviation Resource Net of China, 10 June 2009), available at <http://news.carnoc.com/list/135/135638.html> accessed 2 April 2017 (Chinese); Suo Peimin (索佩敏) 'The new China Eastern Airlines takes half of the Shanghai market. The merger needs to clear anti-trust review' ('新东航占上海半壁江山 联姻须过反垄断审查') (QQ Finance, 14 July 2009), available at <http://finance.qq.com/a/20090714/000044.htm> accessed 2 April 2017 (Chinese).

[108] Notifications and Announcements, MOFCOM Anti-monopoly Bureau, available at <http://fldj.mofcom.gov.cn/article/ztxx/> accessed 2 April 2017 (Chinese).

[109] 'CSR and CNR issued statements regarding approvals for merger' ('南车、北车先后公告合并事宜获批') (Xinhua News Agency, 7 April 2015), available at <http://news.xinhuanet.com/fortune/2015-04/07/c_127661537.htm> accessed 2 April 2017 (Chinese).

[110] 'COSCO and China Shipping have cleared anti-trust review' ('中远中海合并通过反垄断审查') (Xinhua News Agency, 4 February 2016), available at <http://news.xinhuanet.com/fortune/2016-02/04/c_128700974.htm> accessed 2 April 2017 (Chinese)

MOFCOM without any published details about the grounds on which these mergers were approved, despite the fact that there were concerns that these mergers would lead to reduced competition in the relevant markets.[111] This raises the question of whether MOFCOM had in fact undertaken any rigorous analysis in those cases as it had done in cases not involving mergers between SOEs.

An interesting case in contrast would be the Coca-Cola-Huiyuan merger case, where MOFCOM issued a formal decision in 2009 that blocked a proposed acquisition of Huiyuan by Coca-Cola on conventional competition policy grounds.[112] While brief, this merger decision did articulate MOFCOM's theory of harm about the proposed concentration—that it would put the merged entity in a position to engaged in tying, bundling, and other forms of commercial conduct that would result in market foreclosure, resulting in harms to consumer welfare, while recognizing that the strength of the brands owned by the parties would operate as barriers to market entry for other competitors and impede effective competition from other small and medium-sized juice companies. This decision attracted criticism that the Chinese merger control framework had been applied in a protectionist manner to block a foreign acquisition of one of China's domestically successful local enterprises.[113]

5. Industrial Policy Considerations in the Application of the AML to Intellectual Property Rights

5.1 Regulations and guidelines concerned with abuses of intellectual property rights

Another part of China's competition law landscape whose contours have been clearly shaped by industrial policy lies in the application of the AML to intellectual property rights (IPRs)—specifically patent holders who have secured legal monopolies over key technologies that Chinese mobile device manufacturers need to license in order to produce standard-compliant telecommunications products.

---

[111] Huang Xiaopeng (黄小鹏), 'It is important whether the merger between CSR and CNR promotes competition or monopoly' ('南车北车合并竞争还是垄断, 真的很重要') (Xinhua News Agency, 29 October 2014), available at <http://news.xinhuanet.com/finance/2014-10/29/c_1113016690.htm> accessed 2 April 2017 (Chinese).

[112] *Notification of MOFCOM's Decision Prohibiting Coca-Cola Company's Acquisition of China Huiyuan Company* (MOFCOM Notification [2009] No 22) ('商务部关于禁止可口可乐公司收购中国汇源公司审查决定的公告'(中华人民共和国商务部公告[2009]年第22号)) (18 March 2009), available at <http://fldj.mofcom.gov.cn/article/ztxx/200903/20090306108494.shtml> accessed 2 April 2017 (Chinese); Andrew Batson, 'China' Statement Blocking Coca-Cola Huiyuan Deal' (Wall Street Journal, 18 March 2009), available at <http://blogs.wsj.com/chinarealtime/2009/03/18/china%E2%80%99s-statement-blocking-coca-cola-huiyuan-deal/> accessed 2 April 2017.

[113] 'Coca-Cola's Failed Bid for China Huiyuan Juice: The Return of Protectionism?' (University of Pennsylvania, 1 April 2009), available at <http://knowledge.wharton.upenn.edu/article/coca-colas-failed-bid-for-china-huiyuan-juice-the-return-of-protectionism/> accessed 2 April 2017.

Regulations and guidelines issued, whether in draft or final form, by the Chinese anti-monopoly authorities in this field include:

- SAIC Regulations on Prohibiting Abuses of Intellectual Property Rights to Eliminate or Restrict Competition (published on 7 April 2015; came into force on 1 August 2015);[114]
- SAIC Draft Guidelines on Anti-Monopoly Enforcement for Abuses of Intellectual Property Rights (7th Draft) (published on 4 February 2016);[115]
- NDRC Draft Anti-Monopoly Guidelines for Abuses of Intellectual Property Rights (published on 31 December 2015);[116]

The level of regulatory interest in delimiting the lawful scope of conduct which owners of IPRs may engage in is driven by the dependence of many Chinese market players in high-technology industries on licences granted by foreign intellectual property licensors. Given the commercial significance of IPR licensing to many of China's tertiary industries—from telecommunications to computer devices, consumer electronics to commercial-scale technology solution providers—there is considerable scope for the competition law regime to be moulded by industrial technology policy considerations, particularly when the owner of the IPR enjoys a high degree of market power because there are no substitute technologies for the subject matter protected by the IPRs. In was precisely within this arena—involving Standard Essential Patents ('SEP') and Fair Reasonable And Non-Discriminatory ('FRAND') licensing disputes, where the SEP holder is alleged to have abused his dominant position by not licensing his patent, which covers a technology that is essential towards achieving compliance with a particular industry standard, on FRAND terms—that the Chinese courts have had to apply the provisions of the AML.

5.2 Industrial policy and the AML in patent licensing disputes before the Chinese courts: *Huawei v IDC (2013)*

On 4 February 2013, the Shenzhen Intermediate People's Court delivered its verdict[117] in favour of Huawei against IDC,[118] finding that the latter had contravened the AML by abusing its dominant position as an SEP holder by charging

---

[114] '关于禁止滥用知识产权排除、限制竞争行为的规定', available at <http://www.saic.gov.cn/zcfg/xzgzjgfxwj/201508/t20150820_160841.html> accessed 2 April 2017 (Chinese).

[115] '关于滥用知识产权的反垄断执法指南(国家工商总局第七稿)', available at <http://www.saic.gov.cn/fldyfbzdjz/gzdt/201602/W020160204541775274849.doc> accessed 2 April 2017 (Chinese).

[116] '关于滥用知识产权的反垄断指南'(征求意见稿), available at <http://www.sdpc.gov.cn/gzdt/201512/t20151231_770313.html> accessed 2 April 2017 (Chinese).

[117] The citations for the two first-instance judgments of the Shenzhen Intermediate People's Court are (2011) 深中法知民初字第857号 and (2011) 深中法知民初字第858号.

[118] The parties to the suit were Huawei Technologies Co. Ltd. ('Huawei'), InterDigital Inc. and its subsidiaries InterDigital Technology Corporation, InterDigital Communications Inc., InterDigital Patent Holdings Inc., and IPR Licensing Inc. (collectively, 'IDC').

the former excessive patent royalty rates and engaging in unlawful tying practices. IDC's appeal against the trial court's decision was largely dismissed by the Guangdong High People's Court on 28 October 2013, which released two heavily redacted judgments on 17 April 2014 affirming most of the findings of the trial court.[119] These were landmark decisions for the Chinese courts because it was the first time any national court had scrutinized the commercial royalty rates charged by a patent licensor to determine if the amounts charged crossed the FRAND threshold or not. The decision was a clear victory for Huawei, one of China's biggest mobile technology market players, providing it with a legal precedent it could use to its advantage in future licensing negotiations with other SEP holders. What was striking about this case was way the appellate court (i.e. Guangdong High People's Court) couched its decision, providing a glimpse into what appears to be a line of judicial reasoning that appeared to be shaped by industrial policy considerations.

5.2.1 *An SEP holder's FRAND licensing obligations under Chinese law:* Huawei v IDC *(2013–305)*

The appellate court's decision to uphold the trial court's findings that Chinese law imposed FRAND licensing obligations on SEP holders such as IDC, and its willingness to make a judicial assessment that quantified what exactly amounted to a FRAND royalty rate, reflects a pro-industrial policy stance that will benefit numerous Chinese enterprises dependent on SEP licences to incorporate standard-compliant technologies into their manufactured goods. Recognizing that FRAND principles attempt to strike a balance between ensuring that SEP holders are adequately rewarded for their innovation and preventing SEP holders from engaging anti-competitive conduct, the appellate court essentially constructed an obligation under Chinese law restricting IDC from licensing its SEP above FRAND royalty rates, churning out a FRAND royalty rate in this case that was 0.019 per cent of the SEP implementer's product sales revenue.

---

[119] The citations for the two appellate judgments of the Guangdong High People's Court are (2013) 粤高法民三终字第305号 (dated 16 October 2013), available at <http://www.mlex.com/China/Attachments/2014-04-18_AXRC879FW8P38IO7/guangdonghpc_IDChuawei_SEP_18042014.pdf> accessed 2 April 2017 (Chinese) (which deals with the issue of the SEP holder's FRAND obligation and how the court reached its conclusion that the SEP royalty rate exceeded the FRAND threshold—'2013–305') and (2013) 粤高法民三终字第306号 (dated 21 October 2013), available at <http://www.gdcourts.gov.cn/gdgy/s/cpwsgk/findWsnrByid?wsid=LM430000002014041703090215 8689> accessed 2 April 2017 (Chinese) (which deals with the issue of how the SEP holder abused its dominant position by excessive pricing and tying the licensing of the SEP with other non-essential technologies—'2013-306'). For completeness, Huawei's cross-appeal against the trial court's decision was also dismissed by the appellate court. It was reported in 2015 (PaRR—Policy and Regulatory Report—online news service, 'China's Supreme Court holds second hearing with InterDigital on FRAND retrial request' 16 April 2015, by Joy C Shaw in Washington DC) that the SEP holder was seeking a retrial of the FRAND issues from the Supreme People's Court but the outcome of that request has not been publicly announced.

Given that parties in this case had not been able to reach a mutually agreeable patent royalty rate for IDC to grant Huawei a licence to use the SEP in China, there was no *contractual* obligation owed by IDC to licence its SEP on FRAND terms since no licensing contract had been concluded between them. The appellate court held that Chinese law was the governing law applicable to this dispute because China was the place of Huawei's business operations, the jurisdiction which granted IDC the patents which Huawei had sought to license and the place where patent licensing negotiations had taken place—albeit unsuccessfully—between the parties. Even in the absence of any specific legislation empowering the Chinese courts to intervene in such SEP-related disputes, or any particular written law which provided a legal definition of the FRAND concept, the Guangdong High People's Court invoked general legal principles from PRC General Principles of Civil Law[120] and PRC Contract Law,[121] alongside the compulsory patent licensing provisions of the PRC Patent Law,[122] to formulate a FRAND licensing obligation under Chinese law that constrained an SEP holder's freedom to determine how much to charge implementers who sought SEP licences. While explicitly recognizing that the dispute between Huawei and IDC was *not* a case within the scope of the PRC Patent Law's compulsory licensing provisions, the appellate court held that if the negotiations between the SEP holder and the implementer on the patent royalties payable to the SEP holder failed, then they could request for a ruling from the People's Court to determine the FRAND royalty rate that should be paid for use of the SEP. Intriguingly, it appears that the appellate court regarded the FRAND obligation owed by the SEP holder under Chinese law as spawning directly from the earlier irrevocable FRAND undertaking given by the SEP holder to the foreign standard-setting organization (ETSI in this case) when the patented technology was originally selected for inclusion in the industry standard.

Apart from crafting and imposing a FRAND obligation on the SEP holder under Chinese law, the Guangdong High People's Court also articulated a fairly pro-implementer framework of principles for calculating the FRAND royalty rate at

---

[120] General Principles of the Civil Law of the People's Republic of China ('中华人民共和国民法通则'), adopted at the Fourth Session of the Sixth National People's Congress and promulgated by Order No 37 of the President of the People's Republic of China on 12 April 1986. English version available at <http://www.npc.gov.cn/englishnpc/Law/2007-12/12/content_1383941.htm> accessed on 2 April 2017.
[121] Contract Law of the People's Republic of China ('中华人民共和国合同法'), adopted at the Second Session of the Ninth National People's Congress and promulgated by Order No 15 of the President of the People's Republic of China on 15 March 1999. English version available at <http://www.npc.gov.cn/englishnpc/Law/2007-12/11/content_1383564.htm> accessed on 2 April 2017.
[122] Articles 57 and 58 of the PRC Patent Law ('中华人民共和国专利法'), available at, <http://www.npc.gov.cn/englishnpc/Law/2007-12/13/content_1383992.htm> accessed on 2 April 2017) require those who have been granted compulsory licences of a patent to pay reasonable royalties to the patentee, subject to mutual agreement between the patentee and the licensee, failing which an application may be made to the State Council's patent administration department for a ruling on the royalty rate payable to the patentee, a ruling which can be appealed against before the People's Courts thereafter.

which the SEP holder is entitled to charge. The multi-factorial framework set out in the appellate court's judgment was buttressed by an overarching policy to avoid royalty-stacking—that the patent holder is only entitled to charge a royalty rate that is only a proportion of the profits made by the implementer which is proportionate to the contribution made by the SEP, measured against the other patents used by the implementer, taking into account the actual innovation embodied by the technology protected by the SEP, the number of other SEPs involved, and the need to ensure a reasonable allocation of royalties between different SEP holders such that the total royalties paid for SEPs only constituted a limited portion of the profits made from product sales. Furthermore, the 'non-discriminatory' nature of the FRAND licensing obligation was held to require the SEP holder to charge similar royalty rates to implementers in similar transactions—adopting this comparative approach meant that the appellate court made close reference to the patent licensing fees paid by other mobile phone manufacturers to IDC for use of the SEP to facilitate its calculation of what would amount to a FRAND royalty rate for the SEP. The exact royalty rate quoted by IDC to Huawei, which was redacted from the judgment, was regarded by the court as much higher than the SEP royalty rates derived from earlier licensing transactions for the SEP in IDC's agreements with Apple and Samsung. In the end, the royalty rate charged by IDC to Apple that was derived from a 'completely equal and voluntary' negotiation between the parties, calculated at 0.0187 per cent of product sales revenue, was affirmed as the appropriate basis for a FRAND royalty rate (which was rounded off by the trial court to 0.019 per cent) rather than the higher royalty rate of 0.19 per cent charged by IDC to Samsung (which was apparently agreed upon by the parties while they were in litigation against each other). Putting aside the logical difficulties with making such linear comparisons between past transactions with the benefit of hindsight and the ongoing royalty rate disputes of the SEP holder, where the final numbers were arrived at simply by dividing the published annual sales revenues of each implementer by the SEP licence fees previously paid to IDC, the practical economic impact of the approach taken by the court towards calculating the FRAND limit to what the SEP holder can charge implementers seems clear enough: Huawei was not to be charged more for using the SEP-protected technology in its mobile phone devices than what its foreign competitors—Apple and Samsung—had paid to the SEP holder in earlier transactions, thereby ensuring that Huawei was not at a competitive disadvantage as far as this particular technological input cost was concerned.

5.2.2 *Abuse of dominance by an SEP holder under Chinese law:* Huawei v IDC *(2013–306)*

By reaffirming the trial court's decision that IDC had abused its dominant position as an SEP holder by charging excessive patent licensing fees, the Guangdong High People's Court's judgment reveals a number of different ways in which industrial policy considerations have been woven into the fabric of China's AML framework. Firstly, the court waded into what was essentially a commercial dispute between an SEP holder and an SEP implementer over the quantum of royalties charged by the former as patent licence fees. By holding that the SEP holder had charged the licensee an excessive higher-than-FRAND royalty rate, the court essentially neutralized the SEP holder's market power and strengthened the bargaining position of Huawei substantially in its future negotiations with other SEP holders. The grounds of the judgment also revealed that, in reaching its conclusion, the court took notice of the economic significance of Huawei to China's economic landscape, including its global revenues in excess of CNY185 billion in 2010, the size of its research and development operations in China and abroad and that it had applied for and obtained tens of thousands of patents for the technologies it has developed.

Secondly, the court awarded Huawei CNY20 million in damages against IDC for the latter's abuse of dominance, based on the excessive patent royalty rates charged by IDC and its package licensing practices which tied the licensing of SEPs to non-essential technologies, even though Huawei was unable to prove the losses it had suffered, or the gains made by IDC, as a result of IDC's abusive conduct. It is not exactly clear why such a large fine was justified, but reference was made by the court to IDC's commencement of patent infringement proceedings in the United States as an aggravating factor intended to place pressure on its licensee through the additional legal fees that Huawei would have to bear while their dispute remained unsettled.

Finally, it is worth noting that the outcome of this case also led the NDRC to open a formal antitrust investigation into IDC in December 2013 as well, placing additional pressure on IDC after it had lost its appeal to the Guangdong High People's Court while it contemplated a petition to the Supreme People's Court for a retrial. The timing of the NDRC's investigations may suggest that the competition authority had taken the view that a stronger message of deterrence ought to be sent to the SEP holder over and above the adverse findings of the Guangdong High People's Court. Furthermore, the presiding judge from the Guangdong High People's Court was reported to have issued a statement about the case which encouraged other firms to follow Huawei's example of using antitrust lawsuits as a 'weapon' to break into 'technological fortresses'.[123] Eventually, the NDRC announced a suspension of its investigations against IDC in May 2014 based on

---

[123] The exact statement made was '本案中, 华为提起反垄断诉讼的成功意义重大。审判长邱永清认为, 华为公司善于运用反垄断法律武器进行反制, 值得其他中国企业学习。邱永清建议国内企业, 在突破技术壁垒为自己赢得发展空间上, 要大胆运用反垄断诉讼的手段'—see 'Guangdong High People's Court closes the Huawei v IDC abuse of dominance case' ('广东高院审结华为公司与美国IDC公司滥用市场地位垄断纠纷案') (Guangdong Courts, 1 November 2013), available at <http://www.gdcourts.gov.cn/ecdomain/framework/gdcourt/mafkmclllipfbboflbbdindpekeendbh/nlokbojmlipfbboflbbdindpekeendbh.do?isfloat=1&disp_template=pchlilmiaebdbboeljehjhkjkkgjbjie&fileid=20131101104516982014&moduleIDPage=nlokbojmlipfbboflbbdindpekeendbh&siteIDPage=gdcourt&infoChecked=0&keyword=&dateFrom=&dateTo> accessed 2 April 2017 (Chinese).

commitments given by IDC that IDC would not charge Chinese enterprises discriminatory and excessive patent licensing fees, bundle SEPs with non-SEPs in patent licences, require Chinese manufacturers to grant IDC royalty-free reciprocal cross-licences, or force Chinese enterprises to accept unreasonable licence conditions through direct legal action.[124]

6. Conclusion

The discussion above has sought to analyse and explain the various interactions between competition law and industrial policy within the Chinese context, with specific illustrations drawn from the experience of its competition authorities (in the context of merger regulation) and judicial organs (in the context of standard essential patent disputes). China's experience with competition law and industrial policy reveals a deeply intertwined set of common economic policy imperatives that have played a significant role in the way the AML has been interpreted and applied. This interconnection between competition and industrial policies is one of the distinctive attributes of the 'socialist' character of China's market economy reforms that is, unsurprisingly, fuelled by its desire to promote rapid economic development across multiple sectors of its economy. It is likely that China's competition law regime will continue along this industrial-policy-influenced trajectory in the near future, at least until its domestic economic development agenda and attitudes towards intellectual property evolve further in response to these economic reforms. In the meantime, we should continue to expect noteworthy developments from the Middle Kingdom on this front.

---

[124] He Jing and Dong Xue, 'China Patents: Excessive Pricing and Standard-Essential Patents' (Managing Intellectual Property, 16 July 2014), available at <http://www.managingip.com/Article/3362388/China-patents-Excessive-pricing-and-standard-essential-patents.html> accessed 2 April 2017.

12

MERGER CONTROL AND ITS IMPACT ON INNOVATION IN CHINA[*]

François Renard and Charles Pommiès

1. Introduction

Recent years have witnessed a growing emphasis by competition authorities on the concept of innovation in merger control policy as well as actual decisions. Regulators traditionally focus their review on a transaction's effects on actual competition (determining the impact of the elimination of a rival in the market place), potential competition (measuring the risk of a likely entrant being eliminated), and even future competition (assessing whether a specific new product could be prevented from emerging). Despite the stochastic character of research and development (R&D) efforts and, more broadly, the serendipitous nature of invention, regulators are now willing to move beyond the confines of this conventional framework and engage in a more uncertain analysis, in a long-term perspective, of the ability and incentives of merging players to reduce innovation in general and ultimately restrict competition.

Officials in the US and in the EU have on several occasions been prompt to express their concerns on the potential impact that transactions may have on innovation. For instance, the US Federal Trade Commission Chairwoman Edith Ramirez declared: 'Innovation drives economic growth and expands consumer welfare. Innovation also plays a central role in the competitive dynamics of high-tech markets. Firms in this sector are more likely to compete on the basis of new products and business models rather than on price. So the risk of harm to competition and consumers through a lessening of incentives to innovate is more acute.'[1] European Commissioner for competition Margrethe Vestager described the need for scrutiny of transactions through an innovation lens in even bolder terms: 'one of the simplest defenses against innovation is to buy up rivals that create innovative products.

---

[1] This chapter reflects the law and practice of merger control in China as at 1 August 2018.

That's why, when we look at high-tech mergers, we just don't look at whether they may raise prices. We also assess whether they could be bad for innovation.'[2]

New policy instruments have been adopted to prioritize the protection of innovation as an inherent value of the competitive process. The European Commission issued a policy brief in April 2016 where it summarized its views on how EU merger control can contribute to safeguarding innovation in clear terms:

> Innovation is essential to increasing productivity in the EU, and thus contributes to boosting growth and jobs. The EU framework for merger control allows the Commission to assess the impact of mergers and acquisitions on innovation. The framework puts the competitive harm caused by reduction of innovation on an equal footing with increased prices and reduced output.[3]

China is also focused on innovation, not only for the development of its own industry but also for the protection of competition. Innovation has arguably become an important, if not central, concept in merger control in China. While the Anti-Monopoly Bureau of China's Ministry of Commerce (MOFCOM), the previous merger control authority in China, now replaced by the State Administration for Market Regulation (SAMR), had rarely explicitly brought it to the forefront of its analyses when reviewing notified transactions, it appears from a careful reading of its decisions that innovation has actually been a significant underlying factor in its decision-making process, possibly from the beginning of the enforcement of the People's Republic of China's Anti-Monopoly Law (the AML) in 2008.

It is difficult to evaluate at first sight how determinative concerns about potential harm to innovation have actually been in informing MOFCOM's clearance and prohibition decisions. Because only conditional clearance decisions and prohibition decisions are published, there is actually little transparency in the substantive analysis conducted by the authority in respect of all the transactions that have been reviewed. Even in those decisions that are published, the Chinese regulator is known for the brevity of the reasoning and for the absence of detailed discussions of the facts and the theories of harm debated during its decision-making process.

Nevertheless, there are mentions of a transaction's impact on innovation in a few of MOFCOM's decisions, and in particular since 2017. In the Chinese context, one should also expand the notion of 'innovation' broadly to encompass key features of the domestic high-tech sectors, including access to intellectual property rights (IPRs).[4] If one does so, more than half of MOFCOM's clearance and prohibition

---

[2] 'Competition: the mother of innovation', speech at the European Competition and Consumer Day in Amsterdam, 18 April 2016.

[3] Competition Directorate-general of the European Commission, *EU Merger Control and Innovation*, Competition Policy Brief 2016-01 (April 2016).

[4] It is noted that innovation is a broad concept which cannot be limited to technologies and IPRs—as MOFCOM's own practice has illustrated in some of the cases that will be discussed in the

decisions[5] discuss—directly or indirectly—'innovation' as a relevant factor in the outcome of these cases.

In order to set the scene, this chapter first briefly discusses the importance of innovation for China's industrial policy generally (Section 2) as well as the legislative framework in which merger cases are generally decided and the role it plays in supporting innovation (Section 3). The main purpose of this chapter, however, is to uncover any underlying discussion on innovation and what role this may have played in the outcome of the relevant published merger control decisions. Section 4 discusses interventions in notified transactions on the basis of innovation-related grounds.

2. Innovation at the Core of the Chinese Government's Industrial Policy

Industrial policy is a fundamental component of China's economic structure. The country's economy is evolving rapidly under the direction of the government. In particular, the 'supply-side reform' agenda adopted by the Chinese government calls for a comprehensive upgrading of China's industrial capabilities, an increase in the overall quality and volume of production in China, and an accrued responsibility of market forces in the allocation of resources. IPRs play a central role in that agenda.

One of the main objectives pursued by the Chinese government's 'supply-side reform' is to propel innovation in China with the aim of making the Chinese industry more competitive and less dependent on foreign technologies. This objective was outlined in a speech delivered in June 2014, in which President Xi Jinping remarked that 'China's foundation for science and technology innovation is still not firm. China's capacity for indigenous innovation, and especially original innovation, is still weak. Fundamentally, the fact that we are controlled by others in critical fields and key technologies has not changed.'[6]

It is in that political context that China launched in May 2015 the strategic 'Made in China 2025' initiative. This plan constitutes a comprehensive ten-year roadmap for China's ambition to build a world-class manufacturing industry. Ten industries

---

present chapter. Technologies and IPRs, however, are useful (even if imperfect) tools for identifying and measuring innovation efforts.

[5] Twenty-one out of thirty-nine conditional or prohibition decisions issued by MOFCOM as at 1 August 2018.

[6] Xi Jinping, Speech at the 17th conference of the Chinese Academy of Sciences and 12th Conference of the Chinese Academy of Engineering, Chinese Communist Party News, 9 June 2014 (http://cpc.people.com.cn/2014/0610/c64094-25125594.html).

were picked by central planners to lead—with extensive public support in the form of policies and subsidies—the efforts required for China's manufacturing and operational capabilities to become more efficient, sustainable, and competitive. Many of these ten sectors are connected one way or another with new technologies or high-tech products, including: new information technologies; high-performance automated tools and robotics; aerospace equipment; ocean engineering equipment and high-end shipping; advanced rail transportation equipment; energy-saving cars and new energy vehicles; power equipment; agricultural machinery; new materials, such as polymers; and bio-medicine and high-end medical equipment.

For each of these sectors, a number of specific priority actions are being devised by private and state-owned enterprises alike to achieve the goals pursued by the Chinese government. These include restructuring the industrial base and integrating advanced technologies in manufacturing processes, establishing research centres and fostering R&D efforts, developing environmentally friendly solutions, promoting Chinese brands, and generally improving the capacity to nurture a talent-based culture of innovation. Once again, many of these priority actions converge into one principle: enhancing innovation and new technologies in China.

The objectives underlying the 'Made in China 2025' plan are part of a broader policy framework aimed at modernizing and upgrading China's economic standing. Innovation is perceived as a transformative tool. The protection and the pursuit of innovation constitutes more than a slogan or a buzzword but actually radiates through actions and regulations at all levels of the Chinese administration.

China's competition policy and enforcement actions in the merger control context reflect the same drive towards furthering domestic innovation capabilities.

3. Innovation and Chinese Competition Law

3.1 Innovation in the AML and other policy instruments

Article 1 of the AML enumerates the goals ascribed to Chinese competition law enforcement agencies[7] by the legislator. Although none explicitly refers to innovation,[8]

---

[7] Three agencies were previously tasked with enforcing the AML: MOFCOM, in charge of merger control; the National Development and Reform Commission (NDRC) for infringements of the AML which related primarily to prices; and the State Administration of Industry and Commerce (SAIC) with respect to anti-competitive non-price conduct. The antitrust divisions of these agencies have been consolidated into the State Administration for Market Regulation (SAMR) created in 2018.

[8] Article 1 of the AML provides that: 'This law is enacted for the purposes of preventing and curbing monopoly acts, protecting fair market competition, raising economic efficiency, safeguarding the interests of consumers and the public interest, and promoting the steady development of the socialist market economy'.

one of the factors that must be taken into consideration when reviewing concentrations[9] refers at least indirectly to innovation. The AML indeed provides that the authority must assess 'the impact of [any concentration under review] on market access *and technological progress*' (emphasis added). If 'innovation' and 'technological progress' are not synonymous, they are at least closely related.

In addition, one of the goals of the AML is to promote the 'steady development of the socialist market economy'. This covers various industrial policy considerations, including pursuing the governments's innovation agenda.

There can be no doubt that this has been the intention since 2011 at least. In its 2011 Rules on the Assessment of the Competitive Effect of a Concentration of Business Operators, MOFCOM indeed detailed the way concentrations can affect, positively and negatively, 'technological progress' and referred to Article 27(3) of the AML in the following terms:

> It is also possible for a concentration to have negative effects on technological advancement in the following ways: by reducing the competitive pressures faced by the business operators involved in the concentration, *reducing their incentive for technical innovation and reducing their investment in technical innovation*; the operators to a concentration might also increase their ability to control the market as a result of the concentration, *preventing investment in, research into and development and use of relevant technologies by other business operators*.[10]

The importance of R&D in the assessment of concentrations had been recognized as early as 2009, in MOFCOM's *Guidelines on Documents to be Submitted for Notification of a Concentration of Business Operators*, which required that parties to a concentration include in their filing an analysis of possible barriers to entry, including restrictions arising from the existence of IPRs,[11] and an analysis of the impact on the structure of the market, including the prospects for development of the industry, and technological improvements.[12]

3.2 Innovation in the Draft AMC IPR Guidelines

Despite these references to innovation and technological development in the AML and other implementing rules, SAMR is expected to further clarify its position on its analysis of innovation when formal guidelines on the application of the AML in the context of the interplay between IPRs and competition law will be adopted.

---

[9] Article 27 of the AML.
[10] Article 8, para. 2 of these Rules; emphasis added.
[11] Article 6 of the *Guidelines on Documents to be Submitted for Notification of a Concentration of Business Operators*.
[12] Article 8 of the *Guidelines on Documents to Be Submitted for Notification of a Concentration of Business Operators*.

In 2015, the Anti-Monopoly Commission (the AMC) of China's State Council authorized four agencies, i.e. the NDRC, the SAIC, MOFCOM, together with the State Intellectual Property Office (SIPO), to propose separate draft guidelines on the circumstances in which the exercise of IPRs might constitute a violation of the AML. Several drafts were prepared by the four agencies, discussed in closed-door meetings with other public bodies, domestic and multinational enterprises, trade associations and chambers of commerce, law firms, and scholars, and, in some instances, made available for public comments.

The AMC eventually collected a draft from each of the four agencies in late 2016 and established a special working group to consolidate them into one, which was eventually released for public comments on 23 March 2017 (the Draft AMC IPR Guidelines). At the time of writing, the final version had not yet been adopted, but the SAMR's position on the subject ought to be relatively clear already since the previously published draft captures the essential principles that the Chinese government has announced it would rely on.

3.2.1 *General principles in the Draft AMC IPR Guidelines*

The Draft AMC IPR Guidelines purport to have a very broad scope of application. They are not limited to considerations relevant for the analysis of merger filings. They cover multiple other aspects of the interplay between competition law and IPRs, including all possible forms of anti-competitive agreements and abuses of dominance. They nonetheless define general principles that unequivocally put the emphasis on innovation as a central part of the assessment of the existence and exercise of IPRs under the AML.

The preamble of the Draft AMC IPR Guidelines states what the AML itself did not recognize:

> The Anti-Monopoly Law and the protection afforded to intellectual property rights share a common objective, which is to promote innovation and competition, improve economic efficiency, and safeguard consumer and public interests.

The first section of the Draft AMC IPR Guidelines defining a general framework for the analysis of the interplay between IPRs and competition policy also contains multiple references to innovation, making this concept the cornerstone of any investigation into whether specific conduct, including mergers and acquisitions, could be detrimental to competition or, on the contrary, have an overall positive impact.

For instance, the Draft AMC IPR Guidelines make a distinction between relevant product or service markets and relevant technology markets. In some cases, the Draft AMC IPR guidelines recognize that the assessment of the impact of a conduct (including a concentration) by merely defining the relevant product or service markets may be insufficient or unsatisfactory, and proposes that the assessment of the relevant technology markets is necessary to measure the impact of that conduct on innovation and R&D. The Draft AMC IPR Guidelines define a relevant technology market not by reference to the products that can be invented from a particular technology but as a market consisting of 'technologies that are considered substitutable by those business operators that implement them'. Similarly the factors taken into consideration when defining a relevant technology market do not refer to the products made out of the technologies, but instead include the characteristics, usage, licensing fees, degree of compatibility, duration of the IPRs concerned, possibility and costs of switching to other substitutable technologies. Generally, if different technologies can be used to supply substitutable products, such technologies would be substitutable. Moreover, when considering whether a technology is substitutable with another technology, it is not only necessary to consider the technology's current fields of application, but also the potential ones.[13] The focus on technology gives the necessary tools to competition officials in China to assess the impact of any monopolistic conduct, including a concentration, on the technological progress or 'innovation'.

Although the Draft AMC IPR Guidelines, at least under the current form, fall short of proposing to define relevant innovation markets, as it had been the case in earlier drafts,[14] this omission does not mean that 'innovation markets' could not be defined, when relevant, by reference to competition *in the R&D field*, for instance in the case of merger filings involving business operators holding significant R&D resources. The recent *Dow/Dupont* decision confirms that this is exactly what the authority's intention is.

3.2.2 Merger control in the Draft AMC IPR Guidelines

A whole section of the Draft AMC IPR Guidelines is devoted to concentrations. It highlights that the specific nature of IPRs must be taken into consideration when reviewing merger filings, in particular if IPRs represent a 'substantial part' of the transaction under review, or are of 'vital importance' for the achievement of the purpose of that transaction.[15]

---

[13] See Article 3 of the Draft AMC IPR Guidelines.

[14] For instance, the 7th draft issued by the SAIC on 5 February 2016 defined a relevant innovation market as the 'market formed as a result of the competition amongst business operators in R&D for future technologies or goods'. A relevant innovation market shall be defined by taking into consideration the input factors required for R&D and the IPRs concerned, including relevant assets, key R&D facilities, R&D costs, as well as the number of entities which have the ability and incentives to conduct R&D in the relevant fields and their respective R&D resources.

[15] See Article 20 of the Draft AMC IPR Guidelines. It also confirms, in line with the position long adopted in other jurisdictions, that the transfer or licensing of a revenue-generating IPR can constitute a notifiable concentration—see, for instance, paragraph 24, in particular footnote 31, of the European Commission Consolidated Jurisdictional Notice under Council Regulation (EC) No

However, the Draft AMC IPR guidelines offer little guidance regarding the actual assessment of these transactions. Rather the main focus of the section on concentrations is on IPR-based remedies that can be proposed by merging parties to resolve identified competitive concerns.

Structural remedies are generally the most clear-cut solution to issues that a transaction may raise. To address competition concerns, a business operator may propose 'remedies', which can take the form, in transactions involving IPRs, of exclusive, long-term, and non-revocable licences, or divestitures, of IPRs or business activities involving IPRs. In such cases, the authority would verify that the IPR licensee or buyer has adequate resources, capacity, and willingness to engage in market competition through the use of the licensed or divested IPRs or the conduct of the relevant business.[16] These are classic remedies comparable to those typically offered to foreign competition authorities, e.g. in the US or EU.

Somewhat more typical of the practice in China is Article 23 of the Draft AMC IPR Guidelines, which provides a typology (which is not intended to be limitative) of four possible behavioural remedies involving IPRs. MOFCOM has long had a higher degree of acceptance—if not a real preference—for behavioural remedies. Such behavioural remedies, in particular when they relate to IPRs, indeed facilitate the dissemination of technologies on a non-exclusive basis, without altering the transaction as envisaged by the parties, and create the conditions for a level-playing field between competitors (Chinese as well as foreign) that is considered to be more extensive than what a mere divestiture would allow, while enabling the regulator to closely monitor the 'behaviour' of the licensor.

The four behavioural remedies involving IPRs listed by the Draft AMC IPR Guidelines are the following: (i) IPR licences; (ii) hold-separate obligations; (iii) obligations to deal (i.e. obligation to license) on fair, reasonable, and non-discriminatory terms; and (iv) obligations to charge reasonable licensing fees. Whilst some of these remedies may appear inadequate or, at least, unusual to foreign observers, they do not come as a surprise to practitioners in China because they belong to the classic 'tool-box' of commitments that can be proposed to resolve issues in complex cases and have long been deemed generally acceptable in Chinese merger control proceedings.

139/2004 on the control of concentrations between undertakings (OJ C 95, 16.4.2008, p. 1). See also Article 19 of the Draft AMC IPR Guidelines.

[16] See Article 22 of the Draft AMC IPR Guidelines.

4. Innovation-related Issues as Grounds for Interventions

MOFCOM has generally maintained a non-interventionist stance since the entry into force of the AML in 2008. Contrary perhaps to popular belief, conditional decisions are extremely rare in China and blocked deals remain the exception. At the time of drafting this chapter, only thirty-seven cases where conditionally approved out of close to 2,300 notified transactions and only two were ever blocked. This means that since its entry into force in August 2008, less than 3% of cases have been 'frustrated' by MOFCOM/SAMR's intervention, or on average, only four cases per year.

Innovation-related issues, however, undoubtedly played a role in a significant proportion of those decisions. More than half of the merger clearance and prohibition decisions discuss—directly or indirectly—innovation as a relevant factor in the outcome of these cases.[17] Innovation in general, including the dissemination of IPRs, competition on R&D capacity, and access to technological development, is indeed recognized as one dimension of the competitive process along with prices, quality, services, or reputation for instance.

Based on an analysis of MOFCOM's precedents,[18] it is possible to regroup the concerns related to innovation in three main categories:

(i) The impact of concentrations on innovation;
(ii) Concentrations leading to new barriers to entry; and
(iii) Concentrations reducing access to technologies.

4.1 Concentration as a threat to innovation

As it may not always be apparent, MOFCOM has prohibited one decision and imposed remedies in at least six remedy cases, in part because of concerns that transactions may have a negative impact on innovation.

4.1.1 *The 2009 Coca-Cola/Huiyuan case*

There have been only two prohibition decisions since the entry into force of the AML. The concept of 'innovation' was relevant in the first of these two prohibition decisions, which was issued less than a year after the entry into force of the AML: the 2009 *Coca-Cola/Huiyuan* decision.[19]

---

[17] Twenty-one out of thirty-nine conditional or prohibition decisions issued by MOFCOM as at 1 August 2018.

[18] In China, judicial review has not to date played any meaningful role.

[19] *Coca-Cola/Huiyuan*, [2009] MOFCOM Public Announcement No 22, 18 March 2009. The only other prohibition decision ever issued by MOFCOM related to the P3 shipping alliance (*Maersk/MSC/CMA CGM*, [2014] MOFCOM Public Announcement No 46, 17 June 2014), by

On 18 March 2009, MOFCOM blocked the acquisition of the historic Chinese fruit juice producer Huiyuan by US beverage giant Coca-Cola. MOFCOM's decision in *Coca-Cola/Huiyuan* was apparently motivated by the fact that the transaction would have had a negative impact on effective competition on the market for fruit juices in China and hindered the development of that industry.

Although the decision is short on details, it appears that MOFCOM was concerned about the risk of Coca-Cola dominating the juice market—in the same way as it allegedly dominated the carbonated soft drink market—through the control of two major brands, Meizhiyuan (the Chinese name for Minute Maid, which Coca-Cola already owned), and the iconic Chinese brand Huiyuan. MOFCOM noted that the transaction would have raised the barriers to entry for potential competitors and threatened the survival of smaller rivals.

In particular, MOFCOM ruled that the capacity of rivals to contribute to the healthy development of the juice market through innovation would have been reduced. There is, however, no discussion in the decision on what form 'innovation' would take in this market or how the transaction would have impacted on this. Coca-Cola offered remedies, the nature of which is not discussed in the decision, to alleviate the concerns raised during the investigation, but MOFCOM considered these to be insufficient to preserve competitive conditions on the market for fruit juice in China and consequently decided to prohibit the concentration.

It should be noted that the precedential value of that decision is unclear. The main theory of harm was based on conglomerate effects and it is not certain that the outcome of the case would be the same after ten years of implementation of the merger control provisions.[20]

4.1.2 *The 2011 Seagate/Samsung HDD and 2012 Western Digital/Hitachi GST cases: The hard-disk drive saga*

The assessment of innovation capabilities was a central theme in MOFCOM's decisions in the 'HDD saga'. In 2011, MOFCOM received notifications of two parallel transactions taking place between different parties in the market for hard disk drive (HDD): *Seagate/Samsung HDD*[21] and *Western Digital/Hitachi GST*.[22]

---

which three European carriers had decided to join forces and coordinate resources. That decision, however, contains no reference to innovation.

[20] It is, however, very possible that the acquisition of a household domestic brand by a large multinational company could still nowadays raise concerns on the basis of the impact on the 'healthy development of the socialist market economy', or on public interest considerations.

[21] *Seagate/Samsung's HDD Business*, [2011] MOFCOM Public Announcement No 90, 12 December 2011.

[22] *Western Digital/Hitachi Global Storage Technologies*, [2012] MOFCOM Public Announcement No 9, 2 March 2012.

Western Digital's acquisition of Viviti (the HDD business of Hitachi) was filed with MOFCOM on 2 April 2011 and eventually received conditional clearance eleven months later. Seagate's acquisition of the HDD business of Samsung was filed later, on 19 May 2011, but received conditional clearance earlier on 12 December 2011.

It appears from the text of the two decisions that MOFCOM considered the same issues in both cases. Interestingly, MOFCOM ordered—as part of the remedies imposed on Seagate—that the Samsung HDD business continue to be operated only partially independently in China after the transaction closes, while a complete hold-separate remedy was imposed on Western Digital, which was required to let Viviti be run fully independently in China.

MOFCOM's analysis focused on a number of factors, including the structure of supply, the countervailing buying power of customers and what MOFCOM described as the essential nature of their multi-sourcing strategies, and the production capacity constraints. Two other factors, namely innovation and barriers to entry,[23] were critical in the outcome of the cases.

In particular, MOFCOM highlighted the fact that 'innovation plays an important role in the HDD industry'. Newly-launched innovative products typically gain high market shares, hence generate healthy profits, but the profit margin dips sharply and rapidly once competitors are able to replicate these new products. HDD manufacturers are therefore encouraged to develop and market innovative products in a relentless manner. MOFCOM also observed in that respect that competition is a key driver to foster innovation in the market, so that a reduction of competition would have a negative impact on the incentives to innovate and the speed of innovation.

As a result, several innovation-specific remedies were imposed:

- Seagate was required to set up an independent R&D centre for Samsung products, while allowing Seagate to provide technical supports and to implement Seagate's standard process in Samsung HDDs with the aim to ensure a higher efficiency and competitiveness of Samsung products. On the other hand, WD and Viviti were required to maintain separate R&D activities and to prevent any exchange of sensitive information that would jeopardize the autonomy of the two companies, while they were allowed to only 'cooperate on R&D to improve their production efficiency and competitiveness',[24] and
- MOFCOM also imposed on Seagate and WD to keep investing 'in new areas to bring more innovative products and solutions to customers at a rate consistent with their recent history'.[25]

---

[23] Discussed in Section 4.4 below.
[24] Remedy A.6 and A.3 respectively in the *Seagate* and *WD* decisions, cited above.
[25] Remedy E and D respectively in the *Seagate* and *WD* decisions, cited above.

These two decisions arguably constitute the first tangible illustration of MOFCOM's willingness to protect innovation and future competition in China.

4.1.3 *The 2013 MediaTek/MStar case*

MOFCOM's review of the acquisition of MStar Semiconductor by MediaTek[26] led to an interesting discussion on the dynamic nature of the chip industry and its possible implications on the competitive assessment.

Both MediaTek and MStar are active in the market for the design and sale of master control chips for LCD TVs. These chips are part of a larger category of chips for multimedia displays, which are mainly used to receive and convert audio and video signals. Master control chips specifically designed for LCD TVs, however, constitute a distinct relevant market because there is no or little demand and supply-side substitutability with master control chips for other products. MOFCOM noted in particular that successfully shifting to LCD TV master control chips would require designers of LCD monitor chips and set-top box chips to accumulate technology and experience as well as another customer base. MOFCOM also highlighted the high barriers to entry owing to the initial investment and long period of time required for R&D and design. With a combined market share of 80% post transaction, MOFCOM concluded that the combined entity would face limited competition in the short term.

MOFCOM nonetheless carefully considered, with the help of third-party consultants hired to assist the officials on their review of the case, whether the competitive landscape could evolve. Two series of factors in particular were examined:

- First, the authority observed that the market was relatively unstable because of the products' short life cycle and fast replacement pace. It referred to an increasing convergence between the various types of chips for TVs, computers, and mobile phones, leading MOFCOM to consider that chip design companies with sufficient R&D capabilities should be able to enter the market in the future despite high barriers to entry.
- Second, the dual-sourcing strategy of customers should favour competitors. Because the largest Chinese customers usually purchase chips from at least two suppliers, the concentration between the largest two existing suppliers would have created strong growth opportunities for alternative suppliers, even if their current share of the market is very limited.

These positive elements were nonetheless insufficient for MOFCOM to unconditionally approve the proposed transaction, as it was concerned that the concentration could lead, inter alia, to a reduction of R&D investments, and delays

---

[26] *MediaTek/MStar*, [2013] MOFCOM Public Announcement No 61, 26 August 2013.

of introduction of new products in the market. To alleviate these concerns (and others) raised by their transaction, the parties offered to hold their two LCD TV master control chips businesses separate. Although MOFCOM did not impose innovation-specific commitments, that would have been similar to those imposed in *Seagate/Samsung HDD* and *Western Digital/Hitachi GST*, the hold-separate remedy meant that each LCD TV master control chips business had to pursue their respective R&D and innovative activities, independently from one another.

4.1.4 The 2015 Freescale/NXP case

MOFCOM specifically assessed the impact of the transaction on R&D and innovation in the case of the acquisition of Freescale Semiconductor by NXP Semiconductors.[27]

The parties were the two leading and close competitors on the market for radio-frequency (RF) power transistors, with a combined market share over 50%—and close to 85–90% for those RF power transistors using mainstream technologies. Competition between NXP and Freescale was fierce as they used the same technologies and targeted the same customer base. Major customers actually developed a dual-sourcing strategy playing one against the other to increase their bargaining power. The authority, therefore, concluded that the transaction would have a considerable impact on customers' choice and on competitive constraints on the market.

MOFCOM expressly emphasized that the transaction would affect 'technological R&D and innovation' in the market, and considered that the parties' incentives to pursue R&D efforts would decrease after closing their transaction because of the combination of their respective unrivalled technological capabilities.

MOFCOM consequently refused to clear the transaction without conditions and ordered that NXP divest its entire RF power transistor business on a global basis to a third party. Interestingly, in a rare (and, at the time, the first) instance of fix-it-first remedy, that business was sold to the investment arm (specialized in the technology industry) of a large Chinese SOE.

4.1.5 The 2017 Dow/Dupont case

It is quite clear from the foregoing examples that MOFCOM has been concerned for years about the impact of concentrations on the parties' incentive to continue to innovate and supply new products in the market. However, the *Dow/Dupont* transaction offered MOFCOM the best opportunity to spell out its concerns in this area.[28]

---

[27] *NXP Semiconductors/Freescale Semiconductor*, [2015] MOFCOM Public Announcement No 64, 25 November 2015.
[28] *Dow/Dupont*, [2017] MOFCOM Public Announcement No 25, 3 May 2017.

In this transaction where the parties were active at various levels of the production and supply of agro-chemical products, MOFCOM concluded that the transaction would have adverse impact on 'technological progress in the market'. In several markets, MOFCOM observed that the parties were 'major innovation forces, [...] competed in the R& field, made large contribution in R&D, and had relatively strong innovation ability and rich product reserves.' The authority concluded that the transaction would likely 'reduce their incentive in the technological R&D, decrease their respective inputs in the R&D field and delay the launch of new products, [leading] to an adverse effect on technological progress', referring to Article 27(3) of the AML.

As a result, Dow was required to divest its entire R&D products and departments with respect to various herbicide and active ingredient products.

This is probably the first time that the authority is so explicit on its concerns related to 'technological progress', but as shown above, it is surely not the first time that MOFCOM was concerned by the impact of concentrations on innovation.

4.1.6 *The 2017 Silicon Precision Industries/Advanced Semiconductor Engineering case*

In the *Silicon Precision Industries/Advanced Semiconductor Engineering* decision, MOFCOM was once again concerned by the impact of the transaction on innovation, which it considered to distinctly drive technology in the relevant markets for semiconductors and related services and products.[29] It also observed that the main competitive driving force in the market was reflected in 'the [suppliers'] capabilities in the field for technical R&D and product upgrades'. Given the competitive advantages enjoyed by the parties in this field, MOFCOM concluded that their concentration would allow the combined entity to 'widen the difference with its competitors in terms of R&D, promotion, and market exploration for new technology and products'. These concerns led MOFCOM to force the parties to keep their businesses separate although their plans to integrate their R&D capacity were allowed.

4.2 Concentrations leading to new barriers to entry

In at least seven cases, MOFCOM suggested that transactions raised concerns because competitors could not match the merging parties' capability to invest, including in R&D and innovative efforts. The detention of large portfolios of IPRs as well as the high costs of R&D played a particularly important role in these cases. While these concentrations were not threats to innovation as such, the remedies

---

[29] *Silicon Precision Industries/Advanced Semiconductor Engineering*, [2017] MOFCOM Public Announcement No 81, 26 November 2015.

imposed aimed to maintain a sufficient level of innovation in the market and avoid a too wide gap in R&D capabilities between the parties and their competitors.

4.2.1 The 2009 Pfizer/Wyeth case

MOFCOM's first conditional clearance decision in the pharmaceutical industry discussed the impact of the transaction on innovation. On 29 September 2009, MOFCOM authorized the acquisition of a US company, Wyeth, by another US company, Pfizer, on the condition that Pfizer would divest one of its businesses in Mainland China.

In relation to innovation or technological progress, MOFCOM noted that the transaction would increase the difficulties faced by rivals to enter the market because of the high costs and long-time cycles associated with R&D in the pharmaceutical industry. The concentration would also have raised barriers for competing pharmaceutical companies because of the large scale that the combined entity would be able to achieve and benefit from. And MOFCOM concluded, without explicitly referring to innovation capabilities, that the 'development' of rivals in the market for swine mycoplasma pneumonia vaccines would be restricted as a result of the transaction. MOFCOM therefore required the parties to divest this business in its entirety, including all related IPRs.

4.2.2 The 2011 Alpha V/Savio case

MOFCOM assessed the role of IPRs and technology on barriers to entry in the review of the acquisition of Savio Macchine Tessili (Savio) by an entity controlled by Alpha Private Equity Fund V (Alpha V).[30] Savio, through its wholly-owned subsidiary Loepfe, was active in the market for electronic yarn clearers for automatic winders,[31] and Alpha V was the largest shareholder (with a 29.7% equity stake) of Uster Technologies,[32] the only other producer of electronic yarn clearers for automatic winders in the world. The transaction would, according to MOFCOM, have effectively created a monopoly because of the likely coordination between Uster and Loepfe that Alpha V could have orchestrated.

MOFCOM investigated whether entry on the market was possible. Its investigation, however, found that 'patents, know-how and trade secrets [were] essential to

---

[30] *Alpha V-Penelope/Savio Macchine Tessili*, [2011] MOFCOM Public Announcement No 73, 31 October 2011.

[31] An electronic yarn clearer is a monitoring and control device installed on an automatic winder to detect and automatically repair any defect in the yarns. It has the unique function of expeditiously treating yarn defects within an extremely short time frame, and other devices are unable to conduct the same function.

[32] MOFCOM assessed the shareholding structure, governance mechanisms, and records of attendance of Ulster's shareholders' meetings and concluded that there was a possibility that Alpha V could control, through its participation or influence, Ulster's operations.

R&D and production' of the relevant products, and that the relevant technologies are protected by patents and other intellectual property rights. MOFCOM concluded for various reasons, including the one mentioned above and previous failed attempts by others to innovate in the market, that the transaction would restrict competition. MOFCOM eventually approved the transaction only on the condition that Alpha V divests its stake in Uster to a third party.

4.2.3 *The 2011 Seagate/Samsung HDD and 2012 Western Digital/Hitachi GST cases*

The fact that no new competitor entered the HDD market in the previous ten years prompted MOFCOM to discuss the barriers to entry in the HDD market. MOFCOM noted that intellectual property was of particular significance in the industry. This encompasses all kinds of proprietary knowledge, including non-patented technology and production processes, as well as technical teams and R&D resources. The authority concluded that the importance of intellectual property, coupled with the massive investments in production, business development, and R&D required to achieve a sufficient scale to become a credible competitive force, made any entry very unlikely in the future. This further prompted MOFCOM to approve the combination of two of the HDD suppliers only conditionally, i.e. after the two parties committed to continue to compete including on the R&D front.

4.2.4 *The 2012 UTC/Goodrich case*

The role of R&D costs as a possible barrier to entry was also examined by MOFCOM in its review of the acquisition of Goodrich Corporation by United Technologies Corporation (UTC).[33] Both parties are active in the market for aircraft alternating current generation systems. MOFCOM's investigation showed that UTC's dominance (with 72% of the market) would have been enhanced through the acquisition of Goodrich, one of the few suppliers that won bids organized by aircraft manufacturers between 2007 and 2011. UTC and Goodrich's combined share post-transaction would have amounted to 84% on a global basis.

MOFCOM observed that once selected for a particular aircraft, an alternating current power generation system benefits from a large installed base and does not need to be replaced for decades. However, MOFCOM also observed that, at an initial stage, the parties and their competitors have to bear high costs and endure lengthy processes of R&D in order to compete on the market for new aircraft platforms. The authority concluded that large upfront costs and limited opportunities created high barriers to entry due to the technologies involved. Given the concentration of R&D power in the hand of the newly integrated entity, MOFCOM eventually approved the transaction but only subject to the divestiture of Goodrich's power

---

[33] *United Technologies/Goodrich*, [2012] MOFCOM Public Announcement No 35, 15 June 2012.

system business and its 60% interest in a joint venture with Thales, including R&D teams and related IPRs.

4.2.5 The 2013 Baxter/Gambro case

MOFCOM made a passing reference to the costs of R&D when reviewing the acquisition of Gambro by Baxter.[34] Baxter and Gambro are both manufacturers of continuous renal replacement therapy (CCRT) products (including monitors, dialyzers, and bloodlines). Their combined market shares on a global basis would have been around 60% (depending on the products concerned), and up to 84% for CCRT bloodlines, and 79% for CCRT dialyzers in China. The parties were also both active in the supply of hemodialysis dialyzers with lower combined market shares (22% in China), but Baxter's hemodialysis dialyzers were manufactured under an OEM agreement by a third party, Nipro, which was the largest supplier with 26% of the Chinese market.

MOFCOM inquired about the existence of barriers to entry on the markets for the CCRT products and hemodialysis dialyzers. It found that entry is difficult amongst other reasons because of the investments in time and expenses required for proper R&D and because the ownership of relevant IPRs is critical to enter and remain active on these markets. Once again, these market features, including the barriers to entry related to the R&D available in the market, led MOFCOM to approve the transaction but only after the parties agreed to divest Baxter's global CCRT business and to terminate its OEM agreement in relation to hemodialysis dialyzers with Nipro.

4.2.6 The 2015 Freescale/NXP case

While the main concern in the *Freescale/NXP* transaction arguably related to the parties' high combined market shares and the risk on innovation in the relevant market, MOFCOM once again took into consideration the fact that the transaction would further increase the barriers to entry in the market after the parties would combined their already unrivalled patent portfolio in the market for RF power transistors.[35] To alleviate these concerns (combined with other competitive advantages that they had in that market), the parties agreed to divest the acquirer's RF power transistors business.

4.2.7 The 2017 Bayer/Monsanto case

In *Bayer/Monsanto*, MOFCOM specifically discussed the combination of the parties' wide portfolio of patents. Because of increasing regulatory obligations,

---

[34] *Baxter/Gambro*, [2013] MOFCOM Public Announcement No 58, 8 August 2013.
[35] *NXP Semiconductors/Freescale Semiconductor*, [2015] MOFCOM Public Announcement No 64, 25 November 2015.

increasing costs for developing new products and the low success rate of innovation, MOFCOM was concerned that this new combination would create additional barriers to entry for competitors, therefore leading to a potential reduction of innovation in the markets, including in the market for non-selective herbicides.[36] As a result, MOFCOM approved the transaction only after the parties offered to divest the acquirer's entire business, including related patents.

4.3 Concentrations reducing access to technologies

Another important dimension explored by MOFCOM on a number of occasions is the impact that a particular concentration could have on the market for the licensing of technologies. Potential obstacles to the dissemination of technologies through licensing arrangements proved to be of particular concern to MOFCOM in relation to the telecommunications industry (in particular standard-essential patents (SEPs)) but to other industries as well. This type of concern is further evidence of the authority's focus on the need for innovative products to remain available in the market.

4.3.1 *The 2011 General Electric/CSCLC case*

MOFCOM considered whether a transaction could reduce competition in licensing markets when it conditionally cleared the creation of a joint venture between General Electric and China Shenhua Coal to Liquid and Chemical (CSCLC).[37]

The purpose of the joint venture was to provide technology licensing and engineering services for coal-water slurry gasification to industrial and electrical power projects, relying on GE's coal-water slurry gasification technology[38] and raw coal provided by CSCLC. According to MOFCOM, the market for the licensing of similar technologies was highly concentrated: GE was the largest licensor and only two other major competitors were active in China. As far as the raw coal suitable for coal-water slurry gasification[39] was concerned, CSCLC was the largest supplier of such coal.

MOFCOM was concerned that the combination of GE and CSCLC through the joint venture would foreclose competitors on both the market for the licensing of coal-water slurry gasification technology and the market for suitable coal.

---

[36] *Bayer/Monsanto*, [2018] MOFCOM Public Announcement No 31, 15 March 2018.
[37] *GE China/China Shenhua Coal to Liquid and Chemical (CSCLC)*, [2011] MOFCOM Public Announcement No 74, 10 November 2011.
[38] The coal-water slurry gasification technology is a coal gasification technology to transform coal from its solid form into coal-water slurry, which can be further processed to produce different gases, such as carbon monoxide and hydrogen.
[39] Coal-water slurry gasification technology has specific requirements regarding the ash content, ash fusion point, and water content of the raw coal, and a newly built coal-water slurry gasification project by a technology demander must have a reliable supply of raw coal.

MOFCOM noted with respect to the technology concerned that it is a mixture of many sophisticated technologies protected by a large number of patents. Being able to market and implement it successfully requires a long period for the R&D process to be completed and for the technology to mature. This entails significant commercial risks because the technology should be sufficiently tested and initial licensees should be willing to share part of the costs of development and testing. MOFCOM was therefore, concerned that the combination of GE and CSCLC through the joint venture would foreclose competitors on both the market for the licensing of coal-water slurry gasification technology and the market for suitable coal.

Eventually, it approved the joint venture only after the parties offered that their joint venture would not force customers to use the joint venture's technology or use other techniques, including bundling practices, to increase the costs for customers willing to opt for competing technologies.

4.3.2 The 2012 Google/Motorola case

MOFCOM conducted an unusually detailed analysis of competitive conditions on the market for mobile devices in *Google/Motorola*. A feature of Android, the operating system developed by Google, is its free and open-source nature, which has played a critical role in securing a large market share for the company. MOFCOM commented on the eco-system developed around Android, which has formed a complete industry chain of mobile devices manufactures, software and app developers, and consumers all relying, and dependent, on the Android operating system. Switching to another operating system would be extremely difficult because of technical difficulties, commercial risks, and the investment sunk in the development of Android-compatibles devices and programs.

MOFCOM recognised in its assessment of the Android eco-system the vital importance of Android remaining free and open-source in order to avoid material harm to the Android eco-system and, ultimately, to competition. Moreover, MOFCOM considered that it would not be acceptable to let Google favour the Motorola mobile devices business compared to other device manufacturers, including at the stage of testing updated versions of the Android operating system. Finally, MOFCOM was concerned by the risk that Google could impose unfair or unreasonable contractual conditions for the licensing of Motorola's mobile telephony patent portfolio, in particular SEPs.

To remove these concerns, Google committed to maintain its commercial strategy and license the Android platform on a free and open-source basis, as well as to treat all device manufacturers in a non-discriminatory manner, irrespective of whether they create or implement forked versions of Android. Google also committed to continue to comply with Motorola's obligations to license its patent on a FRAND basis.

4.3.3 *The 2012 ARM/G&D/Gemalto case*

MOFCOM reviewed the creation of a joint venture between ARM, G&D, and Gemalto in the trusted execution environment (**TEE**) business[40] which raised concerns in relation to the availability of technologies post transaction.[41] The purpose of the joint venture was to be active in the TEE R&D and marketing business, relying on ARM's intellectual property rights on application processors' technology.

Because of ARM's strong position in the market for licensing of such technology, MOFCOM concluded that the vertical link with the joint venture could have foreclosed competitors, for instance by discriminating against them by refusing to license its technology or doing so on anti-competitive terms, or by seeking to degrade the performance of competitors' solutions.

In order to approve the deal, MOFCOM imposed remedies on ARM securing the access by third parties to ARM's technology. Specifically, ARM committed to publish security control codes and other information necessary for R&D work on its TEE technology in a non-discriminatory manner, and not to create any special design that could compromise the performance of rivals.

4.3.4 *The 2013 MediaTek/MStar case*

MOFCOM required in *MediaTek/MStar* that in addition to their hold-separate commitments, the parties continue their practice of 'the openness of source codes of programs'.[42] This was arguably to ensure that the parties' main customers (LCD TV manufacturers) could continue to manufacture TV sets compatible with the LCD TV main control chip manufactured by the parties.

4.3.5 *The 2014 Microsoft/Nokia case*

The acquisition by Microsoft of Nokia's devices and services businesses led to an extensive discussion by MOFCOM on the competitive conditions on the market for the licensing of patents used in mobile devices.[43]

MOFCOM examined whether Microsoft would have the ability and incentive to exclude or restrict competition on the Chinese smartphone market by abusing its position on the upstream patent licensing market. MOFCOM focused in particular on patents held by Microsoft in the Android licensing project. While Android is a smart device operating system developed by Google, Android does rely on a number

---

[40] TEE is a security solution that can secure an area of a processor, thereby guaranteeing that the confidentiality and integrity of codes and data loaded onto that area are protected.

[41] *ARM/G&D/Gemalto/JV*, [2012] MOFCOM Public Announcement No 87, 6 December 2012.

[42] *MediaTek/MStar*, [2013] MOFCOM Public Announcement No 61, 26 August 2013; see Restrictive Condition (3).

[43] *Microsoft/Nokia Devices and Services Business*, [2014] MOFCOM Public Announcement No 24, 8 April 2014.

of patents held by Microsoft. These patents fall into two categories. Some are SEPs and running on these patents is therefore required to implement telecommunications standards. Others are not SEPs and are thus not necessary. MOFCOM noted that there can be fierce competition for those technologies that are not standard-essential, and, thus, that the prospects of getting a competitive edge on the basis of these technologies would have constituted a powerful driver for innovation. The added value they bring to products incorporating them may be considerable. In some circumstances, there are cases where technologies actually become technically or commercially essential (although not standard-essential) because the absence of certain features would make products unattractive and there are no effective substitutes for these technologies. Like SEPs, non-SEPs can therefore give rise to dominance and allow their holders to block entry onto the downstream market.

This was precisely the conclusion reached by MOFCOM with respect to the patents (both SEPs and non-SEPs) under Microsoft's Android licensing project. They were considered necessary technical components for achieving important functions of the Android operating system and indispensable for the production and manufacturing of Android devices. Chinese manufacturers of Android devices, in particular, would struggle to develop or find commercially viable alternatives. MOFCOM also determined that Microsoft would have an incentive to raise its rivals' costs by increasing the royalties on the Android licensing project's patents because its acquisition of the Nokia business would make it less dependent on competing smartphone manufacturers to promote its own operating system. Chinese manufacturers would not be able to counteract a royalty increase in cross-licensing negotiations because they don't have a sufficient patent portfolio.

In addition, any rise in royalty rates by Microsoft would seriously affect the R&D investments and the sustainable development of Chinese competitors. The mobile device industry is a capital-intensive one, where adapting to consumer demands and coping with technological improvements is critical but costly. As a result, the margins of Chinese competitors would be too low according to MOFCOM to support an increase in royalties. MOFCOM therefore concluded that the transaction was problematic because it would allow Microsoft to take advantage of patents relating to smartphones in order to exclude or restrain competition.

Perhaps more surprisingly, MOFCOM also carefully considered the position of Nokia, the seller, post-transaction. After closing, Nokia will exit the mobile device manufacturing business but will retain a very strong portfolio of relevant patents (made of thousands of SEPs according to MOFCOM, ahead of other IPR holders both in terms of quantity and quality of the patents). This would allow Nokia to act as a gatekeeper to the smartphone market without being constrained by the requirement to hold cross-licensing negotiations with competitors. In order to generate profits, Nokia would have an incentive to raise licensing fees above their current rate. Changes in Nokia's strategy could have a negative effect on smartphone manufacturers and eventually harm end consumers.

This risk related to the licensing ability of Nokia was identified by MOFCOM as a reason to impose conditions not only on the buyer, Microsoft, but also on the seller: Nokia.

The heaviest remedies were imposed on Microsoft. A distinction was made between SEPs and non-SEPs:

(A) As far as SEPs are concerned, Microsoft committed: (i) to keep its FRAND promise to Standard Setting Organizations (**SSOs**) at all times; (ii) not to seek injunctions or exclusion orders against smartphones manufactured in China;[44] (iii) not to force the cross-licensing of non-SEPs from its counterparts when negotiating the licensing of its own SEPs; (iv) to transfer its SEPs to a third party only if the new owner agrees to the above three principles.

(B) As far as non-SEPs are concerned, no FRAND promise to SSOs is applicable to Microsoft, but the remedies create a framework that requires Microsoft to comply with stringent rules for the licensing of patents relevant for the Android project (an indicative list of which is attached to MOFCOM's decision). Microsoft committed: (i) to continue to grant non-exclusive licenses to Chinese manufacturers; (ii) to charge licensing fees that should not be higher than those charged before the transaction and to keep other terms and conditions of the licensing agreement consistent with past practice; (iii) not to transfer non-SEPs to a third party for a period of five years and, thereafter, to carry out the transfer only on the condition that the acquirer agrees to abide by the same commitments made by Microsoft in relation to the transferred patents; (iv) to seek injunctions only in cases where a potential licensee has failed to engage in good faith licensing negotiations.

Nokia's remedies were limited to SEPs. In addition to continuing to keep its FRAND promise to SSOs, Nokia committed in particular: (i) to limit its rights to seek injunctions against alleged SEP infringers that do not act in good faith;[45] (ii) to transfer its patents to a third party only if the acquirer abides by the SSOs' FRAND obligations; (iii) to generally follow the same principles as before the transaction in

---

[44] The commitment not to seek injunctions is not qualified in any way; it is open to debate whether it would also apply in case of obvious infringements of Microsoft's SEPs by a company unwilling to enter into negotiations with Microsoft.

[45] Interestingly, the text of the remedies indicates that one of the relevant factors to determine whether a party in SEP licensing negotiations is acting in good faith is the fact that it does accept to submit any dispute to an arbitration body. This way of defining a bona fide licensor or licensee will later be formally endorsed by MOFCOM in the *Nokia/Alcatel Lucent* decision.

determining the relevant fee rate for each SEP;[46] and (iv) not to bundle SEPs with non-SEPs in licensing negotiations.

4.3.6 The 2014 Merck/AZ Electronic Materials case

The strength of Merck's patent portfolio played a role in the review of Merck's acquisition of AZ Electronic Materials.[47]

Merck and AZ Electronic Materials were not competitors, but MOFCOM concluded that both had strong market positions in different inputs for flat panel displays. Merck supplied liquid crystals, with a market share over 60% on a global basis and 70% in China. AZ Electronic Materials supplied photoresists, with a market share of approximately 35% on a global basis and over 50% in China. Liquid crystals and photoresists belong to different product markets and there is no vertical link between them. MOFCOM was nonetheless concerned that the combined entity would be able to implement tie-in practices, impairing effective market competition and disadvantaging competitors, because the combined entity would have a much stronger position than its competitors, whose market shares are lower and only supply either liquid crystals or photoresists but not both.

In assessing the strength of the combined entity, MOFCOM highlighted the fact that Merck's patent portfolio was unmatched by competitors. Some of these patents constituted, according to MOFCOM, material barriers to entry on the market, making entry in the short term very difficult. A long qualification process (two to three years) for new suppliers, in particular for photoresists, also made switching more difficult for customers and limited the prospects of market entry.

As a result of its findings and presumably to compensate for additional concentration of IPRs, albeit in different markets, MOFCOM approved the transaction under the condition that when Merck licenses its IPRS, it would need to do so based on non-exclusive, non-sub-licensable, commercially reasonable, and non-discriminatory terms.

4.3.7 The 2014 Corun/Toyota/PEVE/Sinogy case

MOFCOM highlighted the importance of R&D costs in its clearance of the creation of a joint venture between Corun, Toyota China, PEVE, Sinogy, and Toyota

---

[46] These principles are, however, defined rather loosely as Nokia undertook to take into account, inter alia, the following factors: the patents and portfolios to be included in different licensing scenarios, the licensing period, the licensed products, the business models for sales or distribution of the licensed products, the standards covered, the degree to which the standardized functions are adopted by the market, the architecture of protocols, the value of any grant-back licence or other types of compensation, the fields of use, the payment conditions, etc.

[47] *Merck/AZ Electronic Materials*, [2014] MOFCOM Public Announcement No 30, 30 April 2014.

Tsusho.[48] The purpose of the joint venture was to manufacture automobile nickel-metal battery modules and packs for hybrid vehicles. This market was already highly concentrated, with PEVE (a joint venture between Panasonic and Toyota) alone holding 66% of the global market, and the four largest players (PEVE, Panasonic, Corun, and Johnson Controls) holding together 97% of that market. MOFCOM concluded that the transaction would allow Toyota (the supplier of 80% of hybrid vehicles in China) to control the market for nickel-metal batteries, and, in particular, to direct the joint venture's sales to the exclusive benefit of Toyota.

The risk of foreclosure by Toyota of competing hybrid vehicle manufacturers could not be alleviated by the prospect of market entry. MOFCOM found that the barriers to entry were high, in particular because of the central role of technology and the necessity to spend large amounts on R&D efforts. And as a result, the parties were required to ensure that their future joint venture would supply automobile nickel-metal battery modules based on fair, reasonable, and non-discriminatory principles.

4.3.8 The 2015 Nokia/Alcatel Lucent case

MOFCOM examined the market for the licensing of telecommunications SEPs again in reviewing the acquisition of Alcatel Lucent by Nokia.[49] Nokia's share of 2G and 3G telecommunications SEPs would increase from [25–35]% to [35–45]% following the transaction. SEPs are major barriers to entry into the downstream market. MOFCOM was concerned that any unreasonable change to Nokia's patent licensing policy would harm the mobile terminal and radio telecommunication network equipment market in China. According to the authority, the patent portfolios of Chinese players are weaker than Nokia's, both in terms of number and quality of the patents, putting these players at a disadvantage in cross-licensing negotiations with Nokia.

MOFCOM concluded that the transaction in the licensing market for SEPs for telecommunication technologies would impact competition not only because of the high number of SEPs controlled by the parties, but also because of the dependency of licensees on these patents and the unlikelihood of new entries in the market given the capital and technology-intensive feature of the industry, and the commercial difficulty for licensees to switch to other technologies.[50]

The risk raised by the combination of the parties' technological strength, and the likely impact on availability of innovative products, led the authority to impose

---

[48] *Corun/Toyota China/PEVE/Sinogy/Toyota Tsusho/JV*, [2014] MOFCOM Public Announcement No 49, 2 July 2014.

[49] *Nokia/Alcatel Lucent*, [2015] MOFCOM Public Announcement No 44, 19 October 2015.

[50] *Nokia/Alcatel Lucent*, [2015] MOFCOM Public Announcement No 44, 19 October 2015.

remedies on Nokia to ensure that the competitive conditions for Chinese licensees on the licensing market would not be negatively impacted by the transaction. These remedies, which effectively amount to giving MOFCOM the possibility of direct oversight of the implementation of Nokia's FRAND commitment to SSOs, are the following:

- First, Nokia agreed to reiterate its FRAND commitment and acknowledged that it would not refuse FRAND licenses or otherwise prevent the implementation of the standards concerned by willing licensees acting in good faith and who have not breached the licence agreement. MOFCOM went one step further by providing guidelines on what good faith negotiations mean in the context of SEP licensing negotiations. Specifically, a bona fide licensee or licensor should be willing to submit without unreasonable delay any dispute on the proposed licensing conditions to an independent arbitration body reasonably acceptable to both parties, and both parties should agree to be bound by the arbitration award, enter into a license on terms consistent with the award, and pay the damages and royalties that may result from the award and the licence agreement.
- Second, Nokia agreed, in the case of the transfer of its patents to a third party, to notify Chinese licensees or Chinese players with whom Nokia was in negotiations at the time of the transfer in a timely manner, and provide them with all relevant information on the acquirer of the patents. Nokia was also required to ensure that the acquirer agrees to be subject to the FRAND obligations that Nokia had committed to. Moreover, Nokia agreed that if such a transfer were to have an impact on the value of Nokia's remaining SEP portfolio, Chinese licensees would be entitled to reopen negotiations with Nokia on the terms of their existing licensing agreements.
- Third, Nokia agreed to report to MOFCOM on an annual basis on the implementation of the remedies for a period of five years. A monitoring trustee could also be appointed to ensure that Nokia complied fully with the remedies.

4.4 The promotion of innovation as an efficiency defence

Whilst concentrations can have a negative impact on innovation, as demonstrated by MOFCOM in the decisions discussed above, they can also have pro-competitive effects. The combination of R&D resources, for instance, can lead to the elimination of duplicative research programmes, the reallocation of resources to alternative programmes, and generally to economies of scale in the conduct of R&D. Merging parties should therefore have the possibility to argue that a proposed transaction would lead to efficiencies with respect to their capacity to innovate.

Efficiencies are generally not discussed extensively by the parties in Chinese merger filings—possibly because of the fear that they would be perceived as a competitive advantage that either could increase market power and/or could not be matched by Chinese rivals. This is also true for claims in relation to enhanced innovation capabilities, which are rarely, if ever, made in filings.

This line of argumentation has, in any event, never been discussed in published decisions to date. As considerations on innovation take increased visibility in merger control proceedings in China as well as in other jurisdictions, it is possible that this may change in the future. Merging parties may find some encouragement in that respect in the Draft AMC IPR Guidelines, which generally define the conditions under which the Chinese competition agency may find that a specific conduct has positive effects on innovation and efficiency.[51] This provision does not expressly mention concentrations and SAMR reviews, but it is included in the introductory chapter of the Draft AMC IPR Guidelines and should be applicable to all of the matters covered by the AML, including merger control reviews.

The provision on innovation and efficiencies is, however, rather strict because it stipulates that all of the following conditions should be met to arrive at a finding of a positive impact:

(i)   There is a causal link between the conduct and the promotion of innovation and the raising of efficiency;
(ii) Compared to other conducts that promote innovation and raise efficiency, the conduct produces a lower negative impact on competition;
(iii) The conduct does not seriously restrict competition on the relevant markets;
(iv) The conduct does not seriously hinder innovation by other undertakings; and
(v)   Consumers are able to share the benefits generated by the conduct.

Condition (ii) in particular may make an efficiency defence difficult to articulate in practice. In the case of a concentration, it would be necessary to prove not only that the efficiencies are merger-specific, but also to effectively compare it to other possible combinations and prove that it is the least harmful option.

5. Conclusion

Over the last ten years, Chinese merger control officials have followed a steady path to protect and nurture innovation capabilities in China. Numerous precedents illustrate the approach taken to date. Concentrations have indeed been systematically scrutinized in China when they threatened to reduce innovation or the ability or incentive to innovate in the market, or to combine wide portfolios of innovative products or technologies that increase barriers to entry, or to limit access to existing or future technologies.

---

[51] See Article 5 of the Draft AMC IPR Guidelines.

This will not change in the foreseeable future. Parties to notifiable concentrations should take note of the necessity to carefully consider possible concerns in relation to innovation capabilities before filing in China. China has made no secret of its eagerness to develop indigenous technology and to benefit from technologies developed off-shore. The AML is one of the tools to achieve this twofold goal. The advent of SAMR, which replaced the Ministry of Commerce as the country's merger regulator, will not affect this policy feature.

INDEX

Please note that 'IP' stands for 'intellectual property' and 'IPRs' for 'intellectual property rights'